AF262982

THE ART ISLES

THE ART ISLES

A 15,000-year story of art in Britain and Ireland

CHARLOTTE MULLINS

YALE UNIVERSITY PRESS
NEW HAVEN AND LONDON

*This book is dedicated to the thousands of volunteers who keep
our cultural heritage alive*

All reasonable efforts have been made to provide accurate sources for all images
that appear in this book. Any discrepancies or omissions will be rectified in future
editions.

For information about this and other Yale University Press publications, please
contact:
U.S. Office: sales.press@yale.edu yalebooks.com
Europe Office: sales@yaleup.co.uk yalebooks.co.uk

Set in Sabon and Trajan Pro by IDSUK (DataConnection) Ltd

Project Editor: Daphne Fordham-Smith
Senior Production Controller: Leonie Kellman
Maps: Martin Brown

Printed in China

Library of Congress Control Number: 2025939438
A catalogue record for this book is available from the British Library.
Authorized Representative in the EU: Easy Access System Europe, Mustamäe tee 50,
10621 Tallinn, Estonia, gpsr.requests@easproject.com

ISBN 978-0-300-27213-0

10 9 8 7 6 5 4 3 2 1

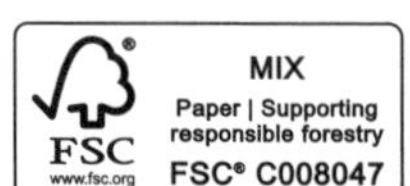

Contents

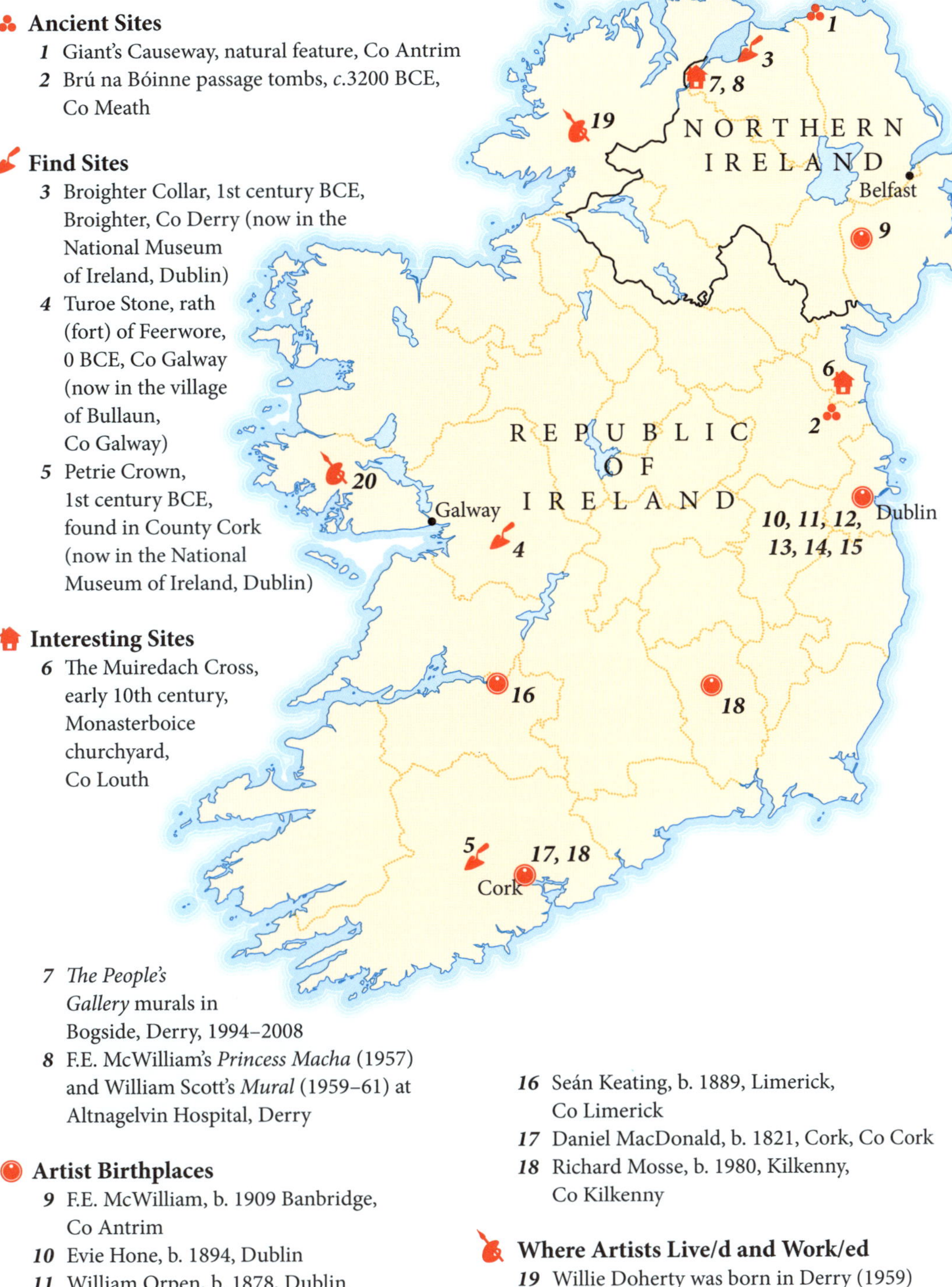

♣ Ancient Sites

1 Giant's Causeway, natural feature, Co Antrim

2 Brú na Bóinne passage tombs, *c.*3200 BCE, Co Meath

Find Sites

3 Broighter Collar, 1st century BCE, Broighter, Co Derry (now in the National Museum of Ireland, Dublin)

4 Turoe Stone, rath (fort) of Feerwore, 0 BCE, Co Galway (now in the village of Bullaun, Co Galway)

5 Petrie Crown, 1st century BCE, found in County Cork (now in the National Museum of Ireland, Dublin)

Interesting Sites

6 The Muiredach Cross, early 10th century, Monasterboice churchyard, Co Louth

7 *The People's Gallery* murals in Bogside, Derry, 1994–2008

8 F.E. McWilliam's *Princess Macha* (1957) and William Scott's *Mural* (1959–61) at Altnagelvin Hospital, Derry

Artist Birthplaces

9 F.E. McWilliam, b. 1909 Banbridge, Co Antrim

10 Evie Hone, b. 1894, Dublin

11 William Orpen, b. 1878, Dublin

12 Phoebe Anna Traquair, b. 1852, Dublin

13 Michael Craig-Martin, b. 1941, Dublin

14 Stanhope Forbes 1857, Dublin

15 Francis Bacon, b. 1909, Dublin

16 Seán Keating, b. 1889, Limerick, Co Limerick

17 Daniel MacDonald, b. 1821, Cork, Co Cork

18 Richard Mosse, b. 1980, Kilkenny, Co Kilkenny

Where Artists Live/d and Work/ed

19 Willie Doherty was born in Derry (1959) but nowlives and works in Co Donegal

20 Dorothy Cross was born in Cork (1956) but now lives and works on Connemara, Co Galway

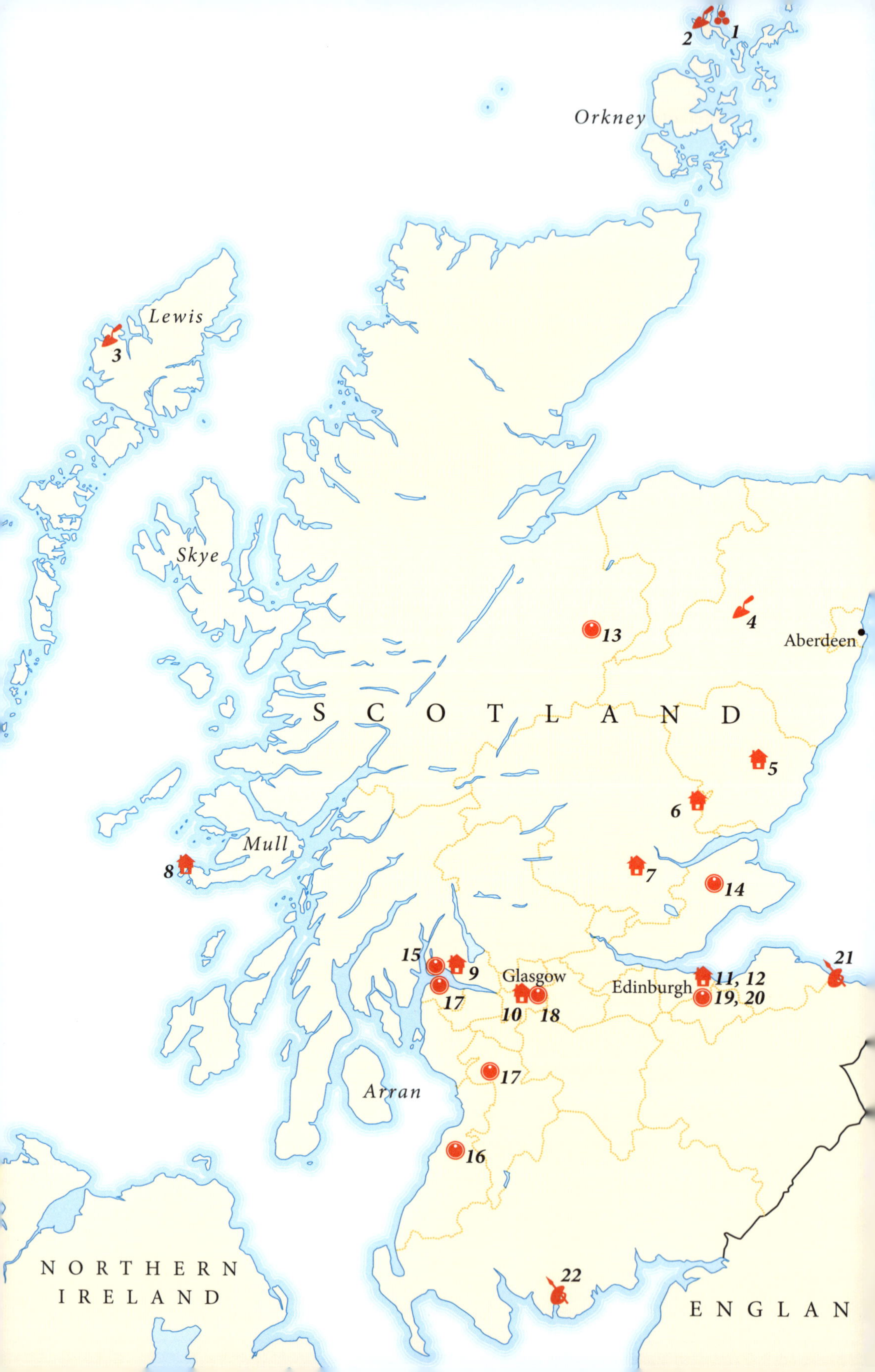

Orkney
Lewis
Skye
Mull
Arran
Aberdeen
Glasgow
Edinburgh
SCOTLAND
NORTHERN
IRELAND
ENGLAN
1
2
3
4
5
6
7
8
9
10
11, 12
13
14
15
16
17
17
18
19, 20
21
22

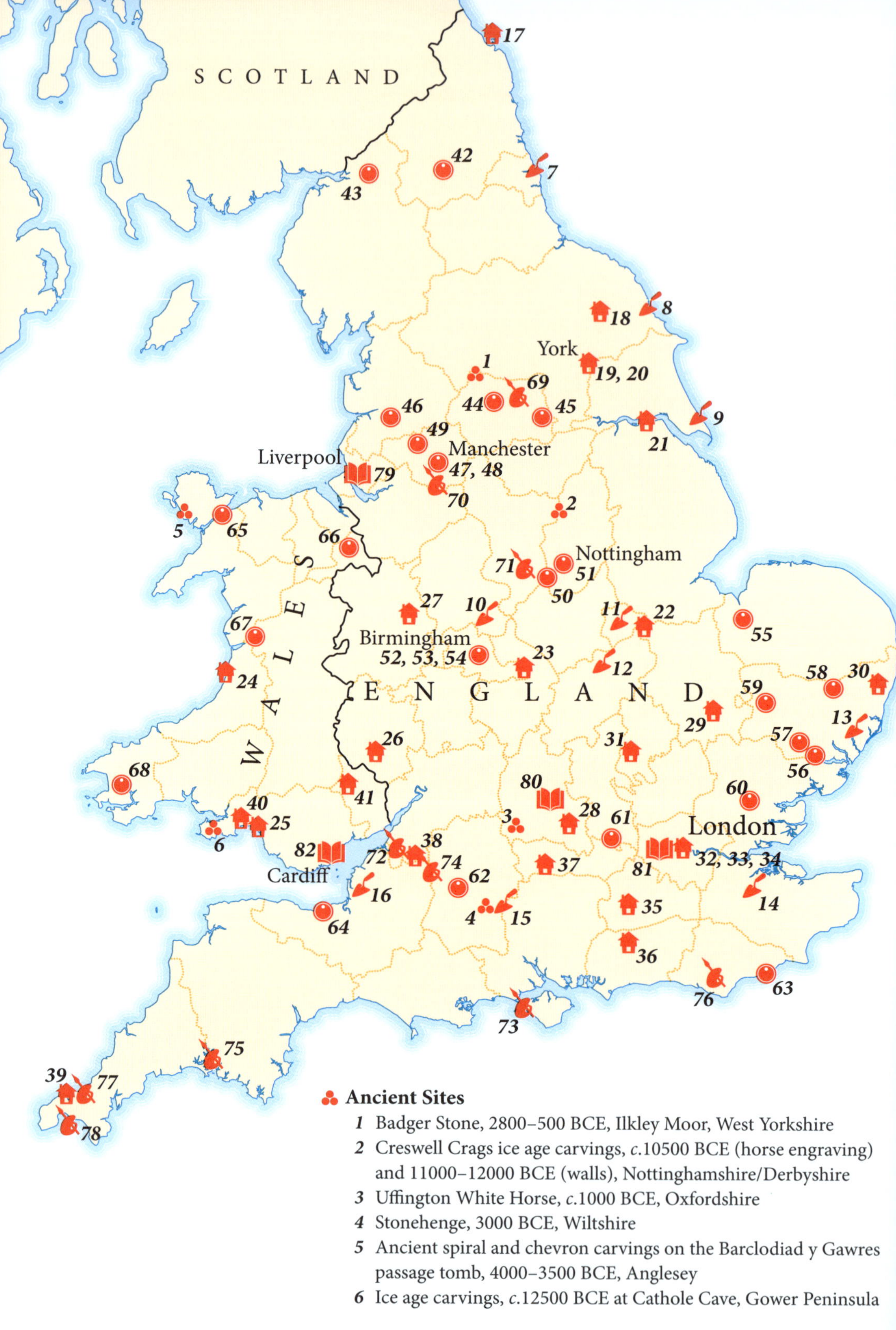

Ancient Sites

1 Badger Stone, 2800–500 BCE, Ilkley Moor, West Yorkshire
2 Creswell Crags ice age carvings, *c.*10500 BCE (horse engraving) and 11000–12000 BCE (walls), Nottinghamshire/Derbyshire
3 Uffington White Horse, *c.*1000 BCE, Oxfordshire
4 Stonehenge, 3000 BCE, Wiltshire
5 Ancient spiral and chevron carvings on the Barclodiad y Gawres passage tomb, 4000–3500 BCE, Anglesey
6 Ice age carvings, *c.*12500 BCE at Cathole Cave, Gower Peninsula

Artist Birthplaces

Where Artists Live/d and Work/ed

Collections

1

WHAT'S IN A NAME?
AN INTRODUCTION

IN THE BASEMENT of the National Museum of Scotland in Edinburgh is a black-and-white photograph of five workmen in a quarry in Ayrshire (see overleaf). The image is old – the men all wear waistcoats and cloth caps, with shirt sleeves rolled up, as they hold still for the photographer. They are dwarfed by the sheer rockface behind them. We cannot see the top or sides – it is too vast for the camera to capture in its entirety. What we see instead is the organic nature of the rock, the way it sweeps up from the quarry floor like a giant wave, a darker seam pressing down from above. This is because the rock was once part of vast sand dunes that time and pressure transformed into stone. But what would sand dunes be doing in Scotland?

The land that now forms the British Isles is well travelled. It has moved from the Antarctic to the equator, then back south before crossing the equator again 380 million years ago and reaching its present position around 60 million years ago. The fossilised sand dunes in the photograph are the legacy of this movement: they date from 260 million years ago, when they were at a similar latitude to the Sahara today.

It seems fitting to encounter this photograph in Scotland, because it is here that the study of the geological age of the earth took a giant leap forwards. In 1788, near the small coastal village of Cockburnspath in Berwickshire, the naturalist James Hutton, accompanied by chemist James Hall and mathematician John Playfair, took a boat to Siccar Point. Hutton was searching for evidence of deep time. He contemplated the jagged Greywacke 'teeth' he saw before him, thrusting up out of the

1

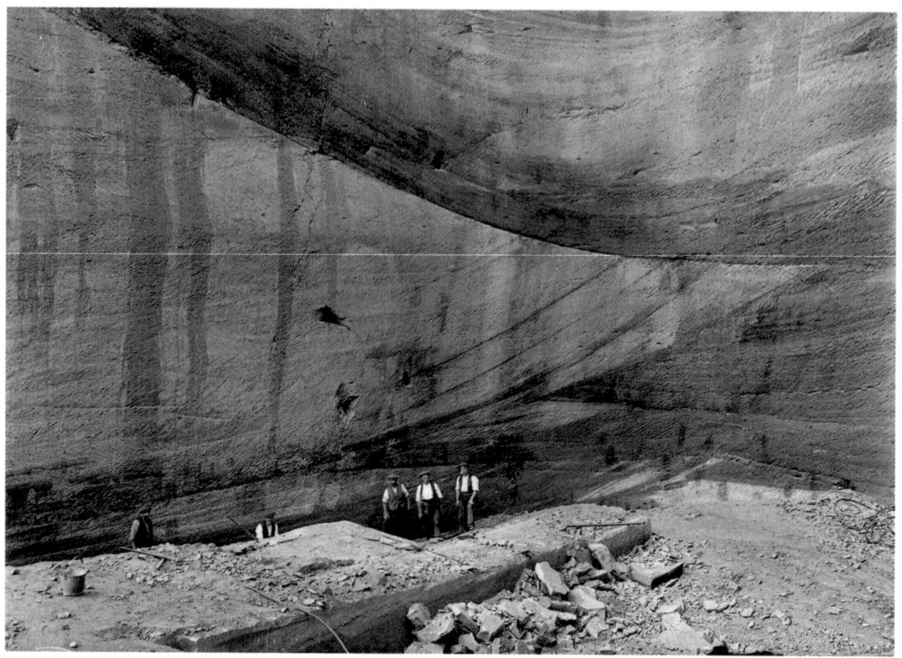

Fossilised sand dunes in Ballochmyle Quarry, 260 million years old, Ayrshire

sea, and realised that these rocks must have once been sediment. It had solidified over millions of years, when momentous tectonic event caused this layer of rock to be rotated and upended. Later beds of sediment then formed a horizontal pink band threaded between the grey rock teeth. Hutton saw this unconformity of Old Red Sandstone in between the near-vertical bands of Greywacke and realised that if the earth existed as different sedimentary layers turned to rock then it couldn't possibly be only 6,000 years old, as the Bible suggested, but must be far, far older.

Today Siccar Point is a site of pilgrimage for geologists and anyone interested in deep time. Based on Hutton's early theories we now know that the earth is a staggering 4.6 billion years old. Hutton's companion John Playfair summed up their experience: 'The mind seemed to grow giddy by looking so far into the abyss of time.'[1] The British Isles comprises rocks made hundreds of millions of years ago. Humans, by comparison, are in their infancy. Let's try to comprehend our insignificance as a species when confronted with the age of the earth. The Natural History Museum in London uses the twenty-four-hour clock to represent the age of the earth – humans don't appear until two minutes to midnight. And we don't live in the British Isles with any constancy until the chimes begin to strike.

For much of this time the British Isles was not a discrete set of islands but simply the northwestern corner of the European landmass, attached to the mainland when seas were up to 125 metres lower. This was one of the most northerly points humans visited, and people repeatedly left these lands for extended periods during ice ages as migrating herds headed south. The last Ice Age was the Devensian, peaking around 21,000 years ago. An ice sheet up to 1.5 kilometres thick ground its way over western Scotland and North Wales, petering out around the Midlands. But 16,000 years ago the climate of Europe began to warm and migrating hunters followed the herds back to the British Isles. With one brief exception, these lands would never be without migrants again.

'THE MAP TERMINATES AT ALL POINTS WITH OCEAN'

This book charts the visual history of the British Isles from the last Ice Age to the present day (and beyond). The British Isles is a collective geographical term that includes the British mainland, Ireland and 6,000 smaller islands that cluster around the coastline. Given the historical breadth of this book it is essential that Ireland be included alongside the British mainland and associated islands, but the idea of the 'British' Isles, the collective term for these countries, remains contentious for some. The Romans first grouped England, Wales and Scotland together when they conquered 'Britannia' 2,000 years ago. Since then the concept of 'Britain' has been used to bind individual countries into a diverse whole that at times has been so strained that it descended into civil war. The geopolitical complexity of this set of islands today is why each of its names – the British Isles, Great Britain, the United Kingdom – represents a different set of territories.[2]

In the National Library of Wales in Aberystwyth is a fifteenth-century copy of the oldest known map of the British Isles (see overleaf), based on coordinates assembled in ancient times by the astronomer and geographer Claudius Ptolemaeus, known today as Ptolemy (c.100–170 CE). The print is believed to be a copy of a lost map from his eight-volume

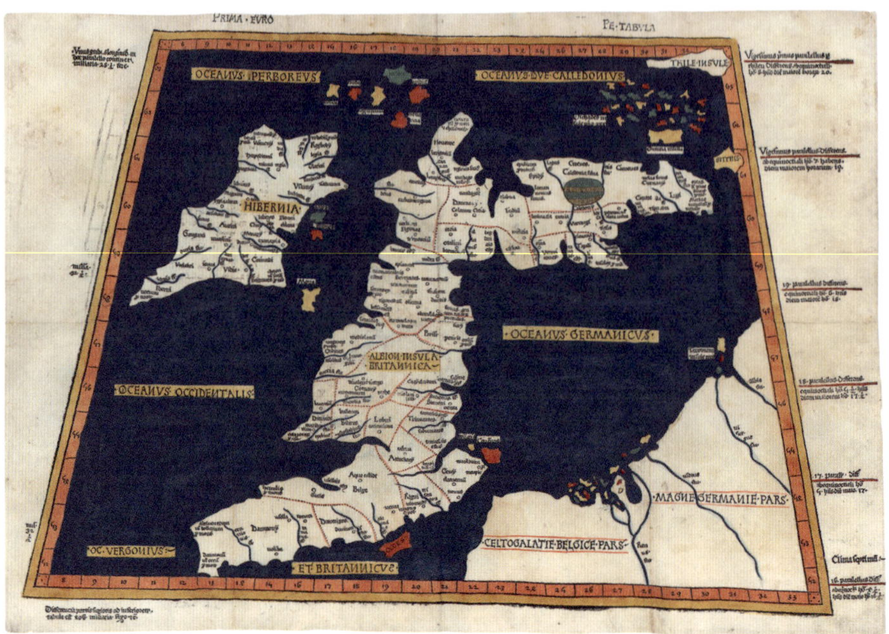

Printed map of the British Isles based on Ptolemy's *Geography*, 2nd century CE, 1486

Guide to Geography, compiled in the great library of Alexandria in Egypt in the second century. This version is derived from copies made by Arabic scholars who were responsible for translating and preserving many Greek and Roman texts.

Ptolemy brought together 1,000 years of Greek and Roman thinking in his *Geography* and included 170 sets of coordinates for the British Isles. On the map we see many Roman towns, including Aquae Calidae (Bath), Londinium (London) and Cataractonium (Catterick). The British mainland is carefully labelled 'Albion Insula Britannica', with both the ancient name for Britain (Albion) and the new Roman name, Britannica, along with the word for island. Ireland is labelled separately as 'Hibernia'. Smaller islands are coloured like autumn leaves in red, yellow and green, blowing around the coastline in clusters. While we can make out the rough outline of Ireland, the swell of Wales and the southwestern thrust of Cornwall, Scotland appears to have been partially severed from England. It lurches to the east, a decapitated head filled with dense forests and snaking firths.

What is clear from the map is that the British Isles in its entirety was very much a part of the Roman world view. The printed Latin inscription on the back of the map describes the British Isles as: *terminatur autem tabula ab omni pte oceano* – 'the map terminates at all points with ocean'.[3] It was distinct due to its entirely coastal boundaries and yet simultaneously part of something larger, a network of diverse peoples and places that Ptolemy corralled into a singular whole – the known world – for his *Geography*. This dual perspective, as something discrete and yet also connected, is key to the story of visual art in the British Isles. It is crucial to understanding why Hans Holbein the Younger and Artemisia Gentileschi sought work in Britain, and why the Scottish Colourists and early Irish abstract artists were inspired by their French neighbours. It helps us understand the importance of the ancient Nebra Sky Disc – made with Cornish gold and copper from the Austrian Alps – and the Norwegian chessmen found in Lewis in the Outer Hebrides. It is our connectivity, and not our remoteness, that makes the story of art in the British Isles so dynamic and exciting.

THE UNITED KINGDOM?

The Aberystwyth version of Ptolemy's map was the first woodcut map of the British Isles to be printed. In China printed woodcuts had been in existence since the eighth century, but the mechanics of printing only arrived in Europe in the fifteenth century. William Caxton introduced the printing press to England in the 1470s and this map was printed less than ten years later. By modern standards it is woefully inaccurate, but it was based on the best empirical knowledge of Ptolemy's time (some 1,200 years earlier). It offered landmasses that approximated geographic reality (despite Scotland's reorientation) and included named rivers and towns. By contrast, Hereford Cathedral's *Mappa Mundi* (*c*.1300) relegated the British Isles to the far edge of a circular design, as far away from the spiritual and physical centre of the map – Jerusalem – as possible. It is a religious map in the guise of a world view. Its primary concern was to communicate not geographical reality but a larger spiritual connection, a network that extended from Hereford and the British Isles to Jerusalem and the wider Christian world.

Artists reconfigure maps today to help us understand the complexities they contain. This allows us to consider our sense of place and belonging from new, unexpected perspectives. In 1999 Layla Curtis (born 1975) severed Scotland from the rest of the British mainland and floated it where Ireland should be. *United Kingdom*, a collage of maps, is human-sized, making the decapitation seem somehow personal. Beyond this rearrangement of landmasses, Curtis meticulously removed and rewove the towns and roads of Scotland so they became the arteries and nodes of England. Aberdeen and Dundee combined forces to replace London as England's capital, while St Andrews and Inverness relocated to Kent. Welsh and Irish cities also became part of the fabric of England, with Morfa Nefyn replacing St Ives. English towns, meanwhile, repopulated the Scottish highlands and lowlands, with London supplanting Edinburgh. Scotland itself masqueraded as the island of Ireland. This work is uncanny because it tricks you into believing its topographic accuracy when viewed from a distance, and yet is completely alien to our understanding of place and identity when studied up close.

Curtis completed her degree in painting at Edinburgh School of Art. She had been born near Bath and raised in Yorkshire by parents from the northeast of England. Her time in Edinburgh coincided with Scottish devolution, which dominated the media and her student conversations. 'It absolutely came out of being an English person living in Scotland at the time of devolution,' she says.

> It was first displayed in Scotland in my degree show and the response to making mainland Britain two separate islands was really strong. Some people were offended because I had moved English places into Scotland; others were delighted because it was like a divorce. So there was a very strong political response. But then it was displayed in the *New Contemporaries* exhibition in Liverpool. There it had an English [and international] audience and the feedback I received was different. There was less anger or delight in the politics of what I was doing and it was much more about the poetry and playfulness of the work, about opening up new possibilities. What happens when you break these systems that you've learnt to trust and make new juxtapositions? What does that mean? And how do you orient yourself in this new presented world? These conversations delighted me too because of course that's what the work is about as well.[4]

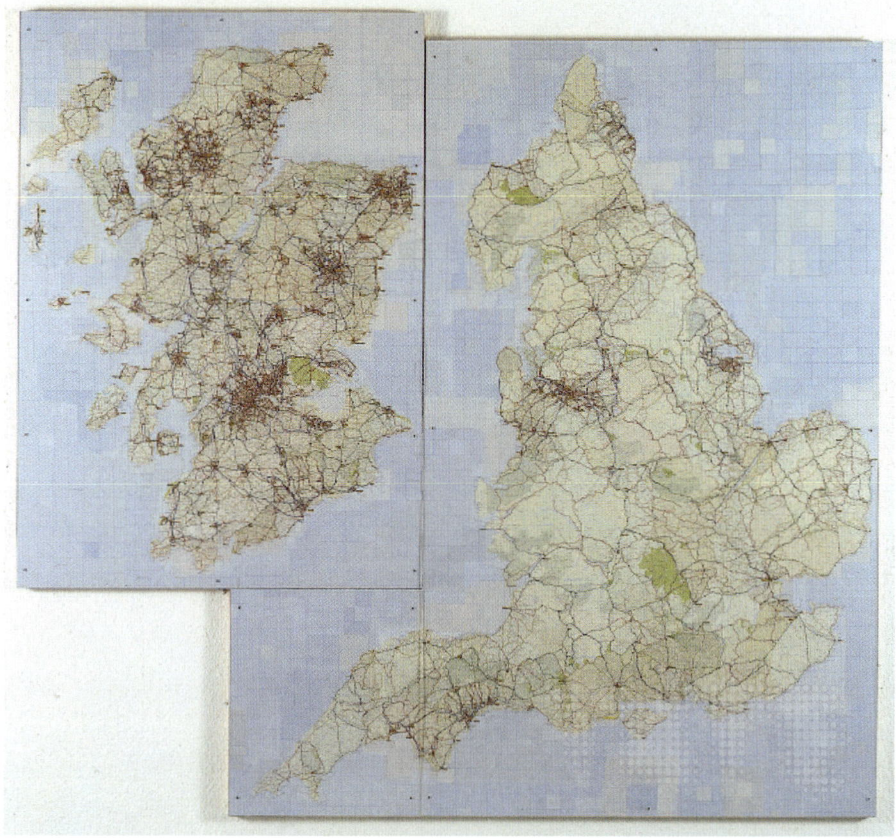

Layla Curtis, *United Kingdom*, collage, 1999

Maps allow us to think about what the British Isles is as a geographical place, but artists' responses to them help us begin to question what such maps have been used for, how they control and shape us, how they can be exclusive while appearing inclusive. Who made them and for whom? What do they purport to show, and what is being suppressed? And what do they tell us about nationhood and identity?

'NO MAN [*SIC*] IS AN ISLAND'

When people put down roots in the British Isles, where does their sense of being British or Irish come from? Do those who are British prefer to be seen as Scottish, Welsh, English or Northern Irish? The charismatic Grayson Perry (born 1960), who refers to himself as a transvestite potter turned national treasure, believes that identity these days is built on regional foundations, rather than anything inherently British. He was born in Essex and now lives and works in London. In 2023 he toured England trying to get to grips with national identity. 'Administratively people would say they were British,' he says, 'but if you want an emotional response they would say, "I'm a scouser," "I'm from Yorkshire," "I'm a northerner".'[5]

Identity is complex. Perry's own way of working serves as a useful framework for us to consider how it is constructed. First is our inner world, the one inside our head, what his therapist called his 'internal landscape'.[6] As a boy growing up with an abusive stepfather he created an imaginary set of islands that he retreated to, playing games there with his teddy bear, Alan Measles, in charge. 'It was about having a place where I was in control, a safe space, a sanctuary.' As an artist he used this experience to create his first large-scale etching, *Map of an Englishman* (2004), the year after he won the prestigious Turner Prize. It depicts a fictitious archipelago of human emotions. The island of dreams flanks the bay of delusions and the river of psychosis, beyond which are the forested mountains of fear.

This unique internal landscape is the first tier of identity. It is the landscape that we carry around with us every day, wherever we travel. Few of us exteriorise it as Perry has done, as actual maps of our psyche, but it is an integral part of all of us. However, Perry is quick to note that identity in its wider sense is 'an experience, a process, not a box you tick'. It stems from the world you inhabit on a local level – where you go to school or university, where you work, where your family live. It isn't something that is attached to you at birth or something you choose. 'It's how you feel from your embodied experience over your lifetime, how it accretes onto you.'[7] This is our second layer of identity, the one we live with on a day-to-day basis. This is being a Brummie, a Glaswegian, an *Eastender* or a *Derry Girl*.

Beyond this is our sense of self in the world at large. This is our networked self, where our connections allow us to span continents through letter-writing and travel and more recently through the internet and metaverse. Perry created another large-scale print, the *Map of Nowhere*, in 2008. Inspired by *Mappae Mundi* like the one in Hereford Cathedral, it shows Perry as a Christ-like figure, his body spanning the world, stretching back through history, through space-time. 'No man

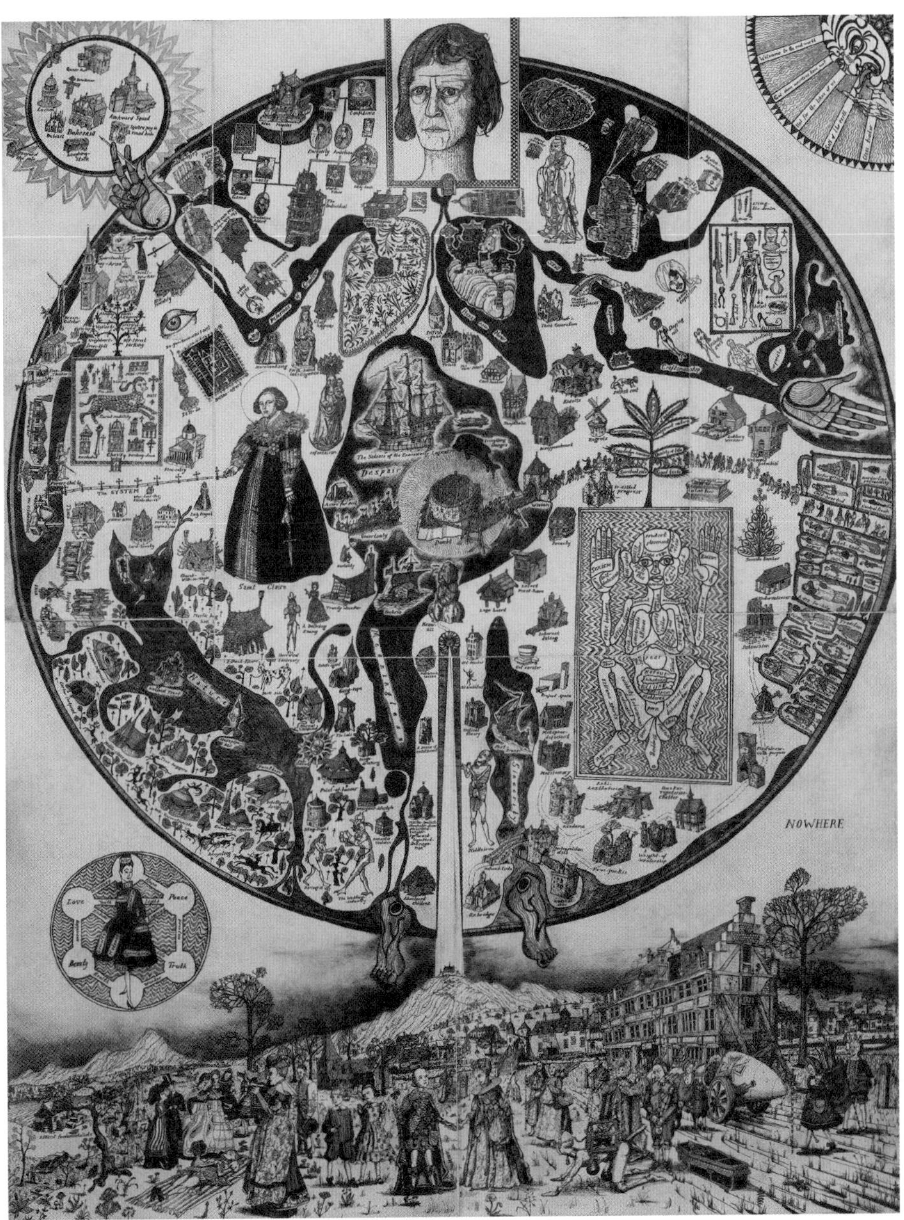

Grayson Perry, *Map of Nowhere*, etching, 2008

[*sic*] is an island,' wrote the poet John Donne in 1624: 'Every man is a piece of the continent, a part of the main.' We are all connected through time and space. These three versions of identity – internal, local, networked – combine to create our unique sense of place in the world.

This book explores all three tiers of British and Irish identity. It does not hold with the anachronistic exploration of art as somehow inherently 'British' or 'Irish'. It does not dwell on the limitations (or otherwise) of an imagined 'British School' or present the British Isles as remote and insular, as many previous volumes have done. Instead it shows that these islands have consistently attracted migratory inhabitants, and artists – the most peripatetic of species – have travelled to and fro. They have moved into and out of these islands, bringing with them new ideas and new materials, as well as responding in kind to the art they found being produced and exploring new connections.

'WE ARE HERE BECAUSE YOU WERE THERE'

As with many other countries on the planet, the history of the British Isles is one of continual migration. As Robert Winder acknowledged in *Bloody Foreigners*, 'Britain has absorbed migrants at a thousand points and times. Its history is the sum of countless muddled and contradictory experiences.'[8] At times this migration has been aggressive, with Romans, Anglo-Saxons, Vikings and Normans targeting these islands, keen to capitalise on their resources. At other times the British Isles have been a place of refuge, where Huguenots, Jews, Ugandans and Syrians could rebuild lives after conflict in their homelands. At times Britain has invited people from across its empire to supplement the workforce and help rebuild the country. At other times Britons have shamefully persecuted those who previously lived there peacefully, mistakenly believing they did not belong.

Britain's own empire had its roots in Tudor times, and by the 1920s it covered a quarter of the world's landmass. The Jamaican British cultural theorist Stuart Hall wrote of 'an umbilical connection' stretching between Britain and its empire. But when the empire collapsed after the Second World War, it was as if 500 years of British history was erased. As Catherine Hall and Sonya Rose noted in *At Home with the Empire*, 'The West Indians and South Asians who were arriving [in the British Isles] were thought of as postwar migrants rather than imperial subjects with a long history connecting them to Britain.'[9] Black and Asian authors including Afua Hirsch, Akala and Sathnam Sanghera include accounts of racism in their personal narratives that frequently revolve around being told to 'go home', despite the fact they were born in Britain. In *Empireland* Sanghera sums up the reason for the ethnic

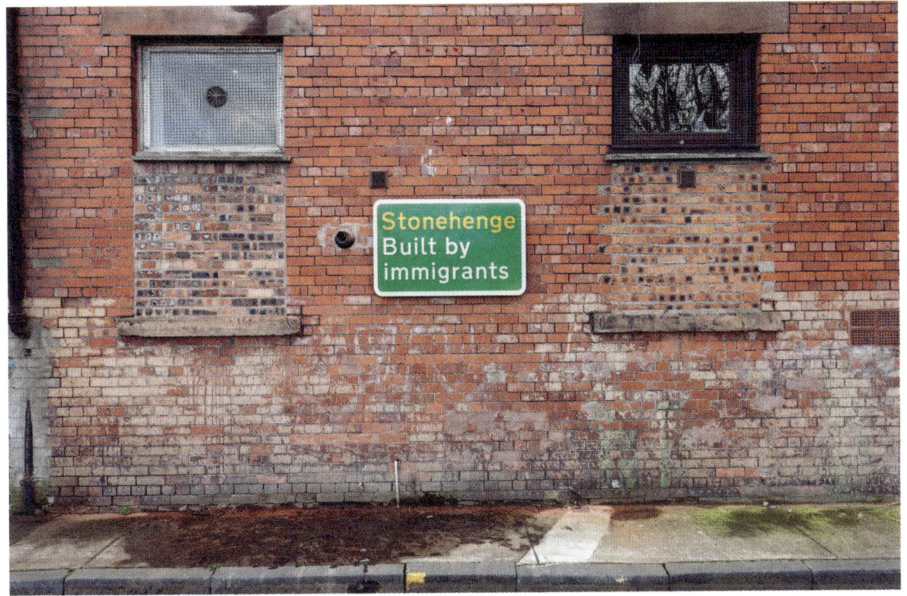

Jeremy Deller, *Stonehenge: Built by Immigrants*, sign, 2019

diversity in contemporary Britain. 'It is a multicultural, racially diverse society because it once had a multicultural, racially diverse empire. Or as the Sri Lankan writer Ambalavaner Sivanandan once famously put it: "we are here because you were there".'[10] And as the historian David Olusoga echoed after enduring racist abuse: 'If you don't want Nigerians in the UK all you need to do is go back to the nineteenth century and persuade the Victorians not to invade Nigeria.'[11]

THE STORY OF THE BRITISH ISLES

The British Isles is constantly in the process of becoming. It is always shifting and mutating, and this can be disorienting. If we crave order and certainty, thinking like this can feel profoundly unsettling, and many seek solace in the past. But instead of seeing the past as something known, unchanging, a place where life was simpler and more straightforward, let's consider for a moment that it was in fact much like our own time. There would have been new faces at the market, technological advances, disease and death, births and brave deeds. New materials were traded across the Channel and the North Sea.

One thousand years ago artists in the British Isles used lapis lazuli from Afghanistan, walrus ivory from Greenland and elephant ivory from Africa. New ideas moved with materials, allowing for improved kiln designs and more complex knotwork patterns and the introduction of one-point perspective. European artists were attracted to the British Isles by the wealth of royal courts and the opportunities these facilitated. British and Irish artists relocated to colonial territories to paint both the colonisers and the indigenous leaders as those from the colonies travelled to Britain and Ireland. The past was not simpler – it was just as messy and exciting and dangerous and changeable and interconnected as today. This book hopes to give you a flavour of this, from the monks fleeing 'the stinging hornets', clutching the Lindisfarne Gospels, to the protest murals of Northern Ireland. We will see the destruction of history as Henry VIII burns religious icons, and the inhumanity of the Middle Passage, but we will also witness the growing understanding of how bodies work, how we can unlock the subconscious and how we can work in partnership with artificial intelligence. This is the 15,000-year story of art made in the British Isles, a chronological feet-first journey through the islands' past, present and future. Strap in – it's an exhilarating ride.

2

LIFE BEFORE HISTORY
15,000–3,000 YEARS AGO

O**N A MISTY** autumnal morning at the end of September, I stand in a waterproof and walking boots in the middle of a Welsh woodland that smells of pine needles and wet dogs. I am waiting for Pippa Hardman from Natural Resources Wales to arrive. This visit has taken months to arrange and has involved archaeologists, academics, land-management officers and much paperwork. Pippa is bringing the key to unlock a protective grille so I can enter Cathole Cave in the Gower Peninsula, home to the earliest known Ice Age engravings in the British Isles.

The engravings were discovered by Dr George Nash and his team in 2010 and made the national news. One set of markings, no more than 15 centimetres long and identified as a reindeer, was scientifically proven to be at least 14,500 years old. The team attempted to keep the exact location of the engravings private, but news footage enabled some to piece together the clues. Within three months the site had been vandalised by a man who carved his girlfriend's name beneath the reindeer. Since then a heavy metal grille has blocked off the entrance to the cave and it has taken some negotiation to unlock it.

In a niche off the main chamber, 11 metres from the opening, lies the reindeer. A couple of horseshoe bats, their bodies like furry plums, circle above and cave spiders crawl between crevices. I know what I am looking for, as I have studied Nash's papers on the discovery: a tapering cylindrical body with four lines for legs and three others streaming backwards, indicating antlers.[1] But I can't see anything. I run my eyes over the surface, looking for human-made marks. Slowly I make out

13

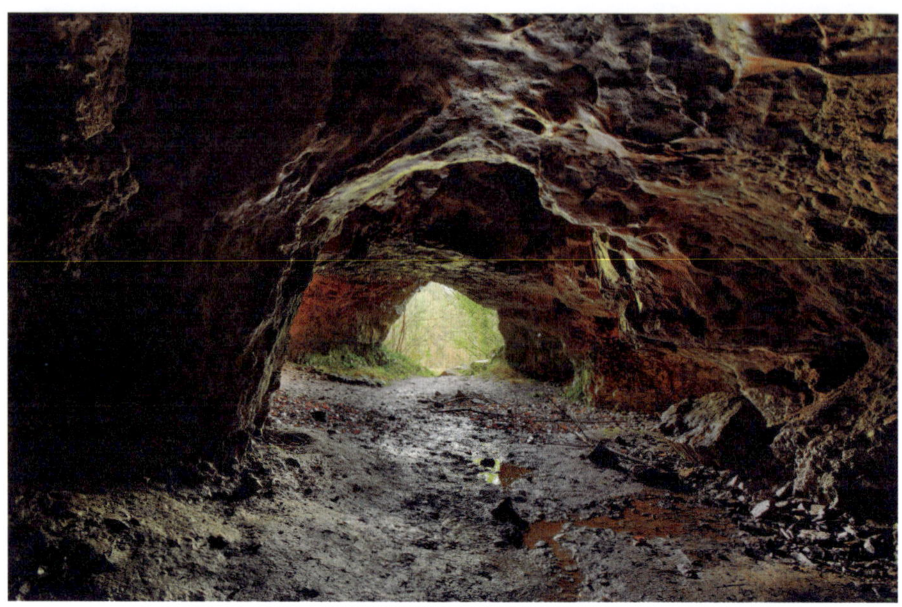

Cathole Cave, the Gower Peninsula, home to Britain's oldest Ice Age carvings

two near-horizontal lines, perhaps the antlers, but nothing else. And then I remember Dr Nash's caveat when we spoke on the phone several days earlier. He said that, following the vandalism, the reindeer had been covered up to protect it and that I may be best served looking for the other, less publicised carvings in the cave that survived intact.

It is there, on an adjacent cave wall, next to a slow trickle of water and a resting herald moth, that I see my first definitive Ice Age carving. A ladder of lines climbs the rockface from beneath calcified deposits, a purposeful series of marks made before the last Ice Age fully ended. Time concertinas. Imagine the effort to take a hard stone, probably a flint, and hit it with another to chip away at the limestone wall to make this pattern. Now imagine that it is still visible nearly 15,000 years later, next to the moth, bats and spiders who live in this small cave today. Why did they do it? Why did someone feel a need to mark the world in this way, to leave a trace of themselves? And why do such marks still have the power to move us, to connect with us, to make us consider our own place in the world? Why does such mark-making – what we have come to refer to as art – matter? And how can it help us understand our place in the world, understand the nation we live in, understand ourselves?

THE ICE RETREATS

Prior to the last Ice Age the art of our ancestors connected animals and humans in a spiritual, collective way. Drawings of animals prowling along European cave walls tell of hunts and being hunted and may have illustrated the stories of shamans (spiritual leaders). Handprints on the walls speak of rites of passage; art in hard-to-reach places was secretive, personal, possibly life-changing. Even just 10,000 years ago, twenty-two reindeer headdresses found at Star Carr in Yorkshire suggest a group performance. Two holes have been drilled through each skull below the antlers – they are the width of human eye sockets. Were these strapped to people's heads while they were hunting deer or used around the campfire to invoke spirits? They may not have been considered art when they were made, but to our eyes they connect to performance and theatre. Sadly we know very little about how these would have been used, as they were abandoned thousands of years before the written record began in the British Isles.

Artistic carvings on cave walls and bones seem easier to interpret today because the language of visual art is unbroken. These represent the oldest works of art remaining in the British Isles. But my time at Cathole Cave taught me that unless you are a trained Palaeolithic archaeologist, it is not always easy to spot early examples. At Creswell Crags, on the border of Nottinghamshire and Derbyshire, you can also see Ice Age carvings dating to 13,000–14,000 years ago. They have been interpreted as a horned bovid, flying birds and a reindeer as well as marks that appear abstract to us today. The caves have been a visitor attraction for over 150 years but it wasn't until 2003 that the ninety wall engravings were found. The fact that they had been overlooked for all that time illustrates the difficulty in identifying this ancient art form.

Books on Scottish, Welsh and Irish art typically do not start with the Ice Age. They begin with the rock carvings of Brú na Bóinne and Kintyre, with Beaker pottery and Celtic metalwork. Volumes on English art often bypass the ancient past altogether. They skip all the above plus Stonehenge and the Roman occupation in favour of launching straight into medieval piety or Tudor iconoclasm. Yet Ice Age art forms part of a shift in prehistoric thinking that signalled the development of the modern human brain. While hand axes can be dated to over one and a half million years ago, there is no evidence of our ancestors expressing themselves through painting or sculpture even 100,000 years ago. It has been argued that evolutionary changes to our brains, and the development of higher-order consciousness, were responsible for the introduction of the artistic impulse. Humans stopped living solely in the moment and started thinking about the hereafter, about our collective past and our possible futures. Memories no longer stored only the things needed to keep us alive but also hopes and fears, plans and beliefs. Art in all its guises became a means of expressing these increasingly complex thoughts, of reaching beyond words and into unknown territories.

Perhaps because of the damp climate or the repeated scourings of glaciers, no art older than 14,500 years old has yet been found anywhere in the British Isles. A small engraving of a horse on a rib bone from around 12,500 years ago represents the earliest example of portable Ice Age art – what we would today call relief carving – ever found in England. The outline of a horse's outstretched head, mane bristling, nostril flared, can still be seen despite someone having scratched angry lines over much of the body before snapping the rib in two. We can see the technical ability of the artist who conjured the horse and feel the anger of the person – perhaps the artist themselves – who attempted to deface it.[2] It was found in July 1876 at Creswell Crags. Nothing like it had ever been seen before in Britain and consequently some questioned its authenticity, but in 1924 a further three engraved bone fragments were found depicting a reindeer and a bison.

Creswell Crags and Cathole Cave allow us to glimpse the world of our Ice Age ancestors, but only for a moment. The temperature plummeted again around 13,000 years ago and communities in the British Isles abandoned their cave dwellings, places that had been significant enough for them to have spent time carving into the walls. Humans left the British Isles once more for a thousand years, with permanent residency only taking hold as the last Ice Age finally waned.

HERE COMES THE SUN

As the ice retreated, the seas rose. No one can agree when Ireland became an island but it seems to have happened around the end of the

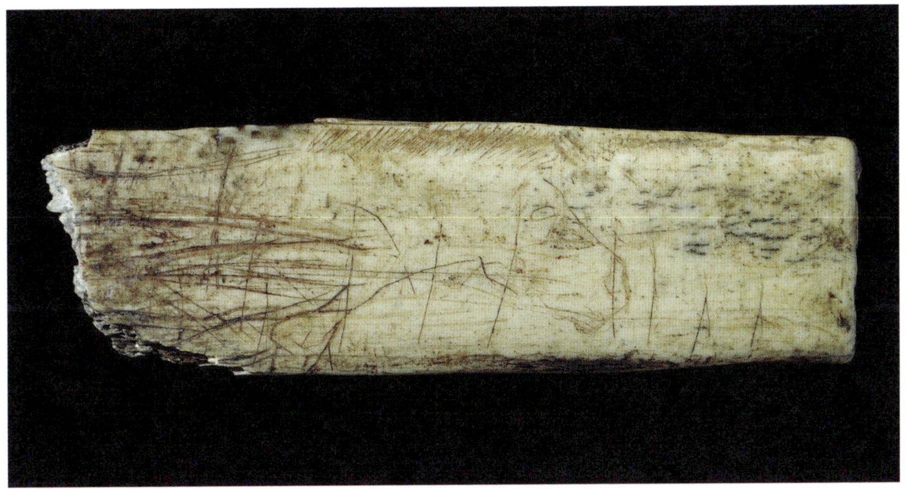

Horse engraved on a rib bone 12,500 years ago, found in Robin Hood Cave,
Creswell Crags

last Ice Age. In 6100 BCE a giant tsunami was triggered by an underwater landslip of colossal proportions near Norway and washed away the remaining land bridge between modern-day France and mainland Britain. It was only after this that another momentous change took place – people in the British Isles began to settle down.

The concept of farming had spread from the Fertile Crescent (in today's Middle East) to the cooler climes of western Europe by around 5000 BCE, slowly displacing the hunter-gatherer way of life for a more settled and static existence and introducing the period we now call the Neolithic. As people turned untamed land into managed fields, the population continued to move northwest, looking for individual plots until the coast was reached. Stories must have been passed down the generations of a land further north, beyond the sea, that used to be connected to the European mainland. Perhaps this is why farmers living in France used boats to reach Ireland, where there's evidence of complex field systems in place by 3500 BCE. Hunter-gatherers had returned to Ireland after the last Ice Age but this new way of farming the land was imported from the south and brought with it an increased sense of connection to specific tracts of land. Perhaps this is why we see a change in the way the dead were buried. Instead of shallow graves, tombs were constructed and used to bury the remains of multiple people. Some of the earliest and most spectacular of these are in County Meath in Ireland at Brú na Bóinne, a 5,200-year-old UNESCO World Heritage site and the largest and most important location for prehistoric megalithic art in Europe.

Brú na Bóinne comprises three major tomb structures and thirty-five smaller mounds. The first tomb to be rediscovered was Newgrange. In 1699 Edward Lhwyd, the keeper of Oxford's Ashmolean Museum, found it while he was conducting fieldwork in Ireland. However, its central passage tomb wasn't explored until 1968, when the Irish archaeologist Michael J. O'Kelly climbed inside. Knowth, the largest tomb, has been systematically excavated since 1962.

Passage tombs feature a central burial chamber reached by a stone-lined tunnel. At Knowth two central passage tombs are back to back within a vast circular earthwork 67 metres in diameter. There were originally 127 large rocks called kerbstones that circled the base and nearly all of them remain. They are carved with spirals, serpentine lines, crescents, arcs and circles. One kerbstone has been interpreted as a solar calendar, with lines radiating out from a central point and a giant spiral that seems to pulse like a radiating sun.

The solar calendar theory is just that: a theory. No one can agree what these stones mean, or what they represent. Academics have variously argued that they were designed after the artists took psychotropic drugs or that they are linked to a shared ancestral language still visible in the rock and sand art of indigenous Australians. The most persuasive theories link the motifs to a Neolithic understanding of the sun, moon and stars, because the people who built these complex tombs understood the cyclical movement of the sun with the seasons. The two tombs at Knowth are oriented east–west, their entrances marking the position of the sun during the spring and autumn equinoxes. The tomb at Newgrange is lit throughout its 19-metre passage by the rising sun for a few mornings at the winter solstice, with sunlight striking a complex triple-headed spiral called a triskele on the far wall of the chamber.

Walking around the tombs at Brú na Bóinne is like trying to understand a lost language. For a population who did not write, visual culture was the prime source of expression beyond speech. So while some historians believe the markings on the kerbstones and tomb walls to be abstract, I'm not convinced. The solar calendar theory gives us a clue – the stones seem to be an expression of a world view: of the stars above, of the rising and setting sun, of the lunar cycle. For

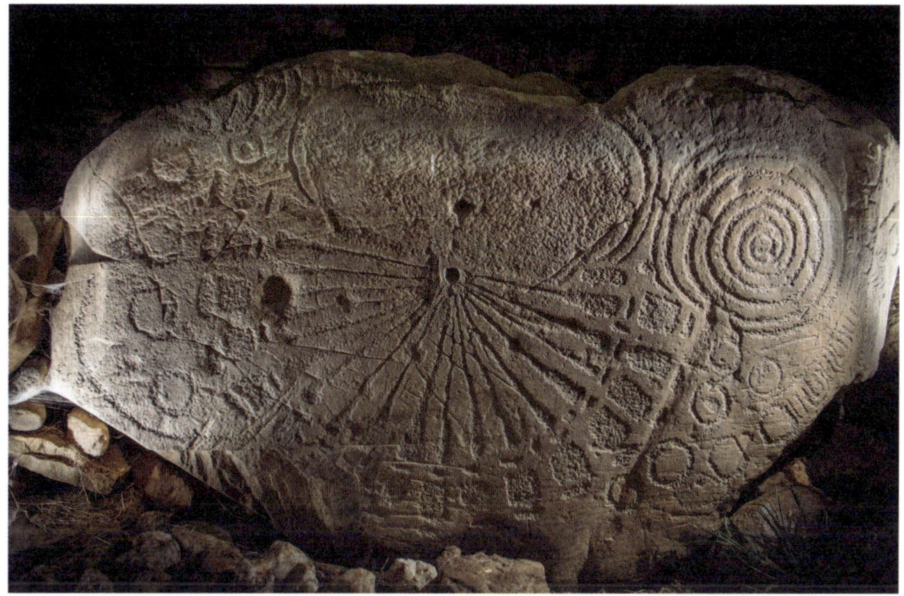

Kerbstone 15, Knowth passage tomb, Brú na Bóinne, County Meath, *c.*3200 BCE

example, the lines radiating from a fixed point on one (kerbstone 15) suggest a sundial. Another (kerbstone 52) features a cycle of crescent arcs and circles that could be interpreted as the waxing and waning of the moon.

There are nine recurring motifs across the kerbstones, from circles and arcs to zigzags and chevrons. In the middle of kerbstone 52, surrounded by crescent markings, is a long serpentine line. Two rivers flank this burial site, allowing access to the sea beyond. This is how the first farmers reached Ireland, coming over water not land, and it is where the raw materials to build these complex tombs came from. Navigable water was crucial; this central motif could well be an expression of its importance. There are hundreds of spirals across the site, too. These could be interpreted as the continuation of life through its annual cycle of decay and rebirth, of wintering and new growth. Cremated remains have been discovered near the triskele inside the Newgrange tomb, and perhaps these motifs were a way of people connecting to an afterlife, or the idea that life didn't end but seeped into the earth to be reborn.

Ultimately, frustratingly, we have no way of knowing if we are close to the mark with any of these interpretations. Despite 850 pages of in-depth study of Knowth's megalithic art, Elizabeth Shee Twohig concludes: 'The 5,000-year-old art remains essentially unknowable to us at present.'[3] But what we can do is place ourselves there. Imagine taking part in a ceremony at Knowth, walking slowly around the circumference of the grass-covered tomb and 'reading' or absorbing the message of the kerbstones, much as the ancient Greeks would do with the frieze along the top of the Parthenon as they processed towards the great goddess Athena inside 2,500 years later. We may no longer have the visual acuity to understand these kerbstones, but they still retain their power through their mapping of ancient ancestral thoughts and beliefs.

We can also appreciate the effort it took to carve these stones. Some straight lines were incised by using a sharp piece of flint or quartz and repeatedly dragging it across the stone's surface. But 'picking' was the most widely used process, where a stone tool with a rounded point would be hammered into the rock to pick away at it, piece by piece. Try it yourself and you will see it takes many attempts to create anything resembling a line, even if you have the accuracy to hit the rock in the same place time and time again. Now imagine holding a complex arrangement of shapes in your mind's eye, an arrangement that you probably planned in advance (because quite often the designs follow the contours of the rock). And then think of what patience you would need to chip away at it. It would have taken hundreds of hours, hours in which you wouldn't be able to farm or cook or sleep. It would require a community that was happy to support you in your endeavour, that believed your efforts were more important than your help bringing in the harvest or sharpening stone tools. And it would require more than just you – many hands can be detected at work on the stones, showing different levels of competence. This level of community support for artists is most often associated with the ancient civilisations of Egypt and Assyria, but the Brú na Bóinne kerbstones were carved before these empires were even founded.

The tombs, in use from 3200 BCE, were created, expanded and remade in several stages, with earlier carvings being repurposed and sometimes reworked. The Greywacke kerbstones, each around 2.5 metres wide, were quarried 30 kilometres away and transported to the site using the sea and river network. The patterns on the kerbstones have affinities with those found in Brittany, southern Spain and Portugal. The spiral and chevron motifs can also be found in North Wales and

Anglesey, Argyll & Bute and Orkney, and there are similar concentric circles and 'cup marks' (small cup-like indentations carved into the rock) on the Badger Stone on Ilkley Moor in Yorkshire. This suggests not only that the Brú na Bóinne artists drew on collective memories of more southerly tombs but also that their work in turn influenced those working further north, all connected via the sea and river network. Despite having left behind their nomadic life as hunter-gatherers, it would seem that these Neolithic artists still maintained connections far beyond their own shores.

A highly decorated mace head from 3300–2800 BCE was found on the chamber floor of the east tomb at Knowth, under cremated remains. Maces were a form of battle hammer but this one was probably ceremonial. It is decorated on all six faces with elegant curving spirals, and the artist who carved it used the natural colouration of the flint to suggest a face. Two spirals turn into eyes, while the hole designed to take the mace handle looks like an open mouth. The flint is cream and brown, and the brown areas form a crown of unruly hair and a goatee beard. The spirals stand proud of the surface: the artist who carved them had to remove stone from around each and every line, a far more laborious process than carving the spiral directly into the rock.

This mace head is similar in style to those found in Wales, but the flint may have originated as far away as Orkney. If you look at a map of Europe and visualise the spread of decorated passage tombs from Portugal and Spain up to France and Ireland and then Wales, Anglesey and Orkney, the sea reveals itself as the conduit at the heart of the network. Relatively small and intricately carved pieces like the mace head could be transported long distances and traded or gifted to other communities to strengthen ties. In Scotland more than 400 carved stone balls have been unearthed. The Towie Ball is of a similar date and size to the mace head. It is carved from a fine-grained black stone and features four protruding domes, three of which are covered with raised spirals. The carvings must have taken hundreds of hours to complete and are very precise. No one can agree why such balls were made – were they mathematical exercises, engineering tools or carving practice for trainee artists? Or were they objects that conveyed power on their owner?

When we talk about such early works, we have to be careful not to retrofit our language and assumptions onto them. Often these spiral designs are referred to as abstract. Abstraction goes beyond figuration and concerns itself with colour and pure form. But there may well have been specific meanings attributed to the spirals at Brú na Bóinne and on the Towie Ball that would have meant they did not appear abstract when first carved. Some experts, however, caution against figurative readings, suggesting that it may have been the commitment to carving that was the primary driving force.

THE STARS ALIGN

There are approximately 1,600 passage tombs known in Ireland today. In Galicia, in northwestern Spain, there are around 10,000, despite the region being three times smaller. Britain and Ireland were further north, colder, less hospitable and bounded by sea. But with the introduction of farming, lives became rooted to one area and the disappearance of migrating herds from the south (once the land bridge disappeared) was compensated for by the domestication of animals. The existence of large tombs and complex artworks points to a population who committed time and energy to create them. Communities used their tombs and communal structures to explore the meaning of the known universe: the giant stone circle we call Stonehenge was the Neolithic equivalent of Westminster Abbey, a place for gatherings, rituals and worship.

The movement of materials and the proliferation of similar designs across the British Isles and beyond helps us to understand that even though Neolithic communities began to put down roots, they remained connected to their continental counterparts through maritime trade and the exchange of ideas. Prized objects travelled long distances – hand axes of jadeite stone from Monte Viso in the Italian Alps have been found in Kent, Somerset and Berwickshire. And it wasn't all one way. The Nebra Sky Disc, from around 1600 BCE and found in Germany in 1999, was made using Cornish gold.

The gold used for the stars and moons came from the Carnon River in Cornwall, where gold and tin were extracted at the time the disc was made. The celestial bodies appear on a circular bronze disc, just over 30 centimetres wide, that would have originally been black like the night sky (it now has a green patina). It shows a full and crescent moon and the constellation of the Pleiades, used by Europeans as a guide to the farming season as it rises above the horizon in March and sets in October.

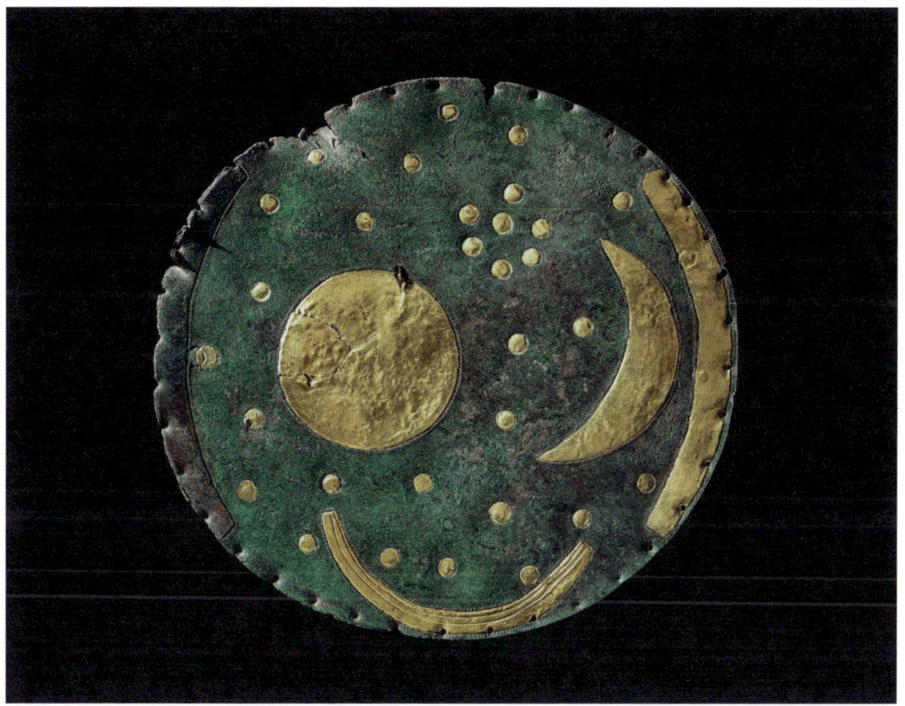

Nebra Sky Disc, bronze and gold, 1600 BCE

It is a startling thing to stand in front of. It seems to encapsulate a world that was connected by materials, ideas, science and belief. It also offers concrete evidence that trade in such materials existed between the British Isles and the continent. We know the bluestones of Stonehenge were moved a staggering 290 kilometres from the Welsh Preseli Mountains to Salisbury Plain in Wiltshire around 3000 BCE, and that much of their journey was by river and sea. The kerbstones at Brú na Bóinne were similarly transported along the east coast of Ireland. But the Nebra Sky Disc provides early evidence of materials being transported across open water, and of artists and makers obtaining the best materials from an extensive network of sources. The geological specificity of these stones and metals may have been a considerable draw, as they would indicate the lengths artists, makers and patrons would go to in order to acquire the best materials.

People were also on the move. Those who were well established in the British Isles created grooved ware pots, first seen in Orkney around 3200 BCE, with examples found across the British Isles. But from around 2450 BCE the Beaker people appeared. Named after their distinctive pottery 'beakers' that were decorated with geometric patterns and accompanied their dead into large graves, they migrated to the British Isles from the Eurasian Steppe. The Beaker man dubbed the Amesbury Archer was buried on the banks of the river Avon, close to Stonehenge, in 2335 BCE, but he had been born near the Alps. The Beaker culture introduced the smelting of metal, transforming the production of art, tools, weapons and body adornment.

When looking at the earliest examples of visual culture, we must be mindful of the resilience of raw materials and how this can skew our reading of what was created. A tiny stone figurine, discovered at Links of Noltland in Westray in Orkney, is only 4 centimetres high but has survived for 5,000 years, its pinhole eyes, scratched-in nose and raised 'eyebrow' giving it a worried air. If this had been made of wood, a soft organic material prone to decay, it wouldn't have survived – or, at least, not in this location. For, against all the odds, a few wooden sculptures from the Neolithic do still exist. A lumpen figure, not 10 centimetres tall, with both breasts and a penis, survived for 4,500 years in the wetlands of the Somerset Levels. It is known today as a 'god dolly' and may have been purposefully dropped from an elevated walkway as an offering to the gods. Figures such as this could be carved in soft wood with far greater ease than any stone equivalent. They were probably the most common form of portable sculpture from this period, but with so few remaining it is impossible to know for sure.

A rare set of wooden sculptures created over 2,500 years ago was found at Roos Carr in East Yorkshire by workmen clearing out a ditch in 1836. Buried 2 metres down in blue clay they found a cache of figures carved from yew with quartzite eyes. These figures would once have stood upright in the small boat they were found alongside, their white eyes staring out across time. Each body has sockets carved into the torso to attach arms and penises. They were found with shields so may represent a group of warriors.

By this time warfare was common across northwest Europe, fuelled by land ownership and the control of trade in raw materials such as copper and tin. Despite this, one community chose to come together and create what is still one of the largest and most enigmatic pieces of land art in the British Isles.

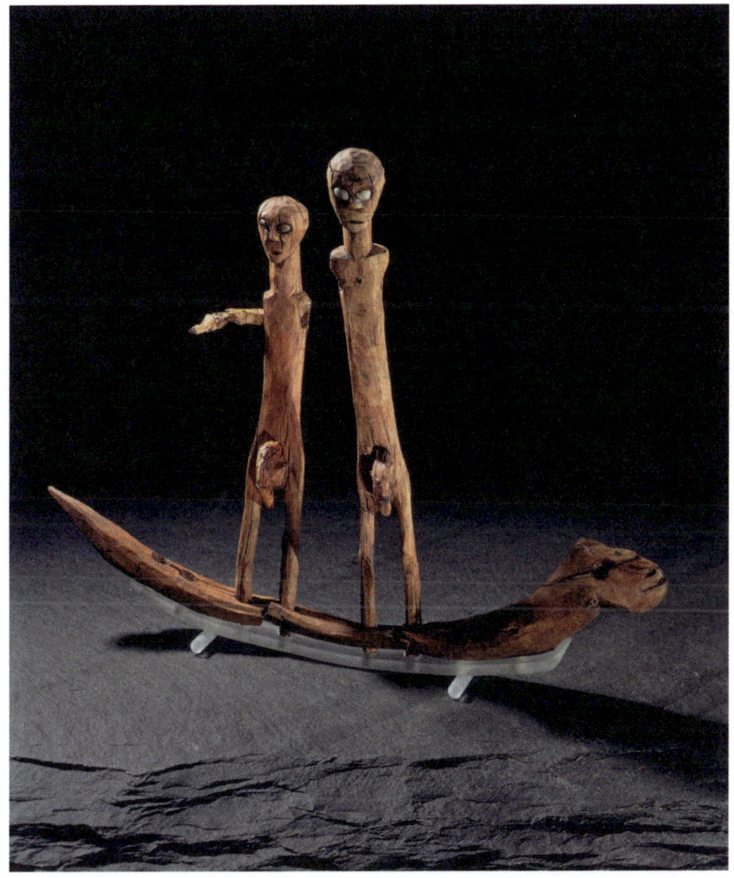

Roos Carr Figures, yew wood and quartzite, *c.*600–500 BCE

TO RIDE A WHITE HORSE

Stretched across an Oxfordshire hillside, 20 kilometres east of Swindon, the Uffington White Horse has been galloping across England for 3,000 years. Now looked after jointly by the National Trust and English Heritage, it is the oldest example of collaborative art in the British Isles. If the 110-metre-long chalk horse isn't maintained every few years it will simply disappear, subsumed by the grass that edges its elegant curved neck, its long streaming tail, its circular eye and beak-like mouth.

If you visit on the last weekend in August you can hear the deep thud-thud of lump hammers pounding the earth like hoofbeats. This is equine land, an area now renowned for breeding racehorses. It is as if the Uffington White Horse is the area's talisman. Across the August Bank Holiday weekend the local population pays its respects – when I visit there are young families with dogs, octogenarians in camping chairs, a teenager in a TikTok hoodie. There's also a man taking drone footage and a camera crew from *BBC Breakfast*. Dotted around the horse's body are giant bags of lumpy white chalk, 15 tons of it, destined to be scooped up by volunteers and laid over the horse's slender limbs before being smashed into white dust.

Kneeling by the horse's neck on a windy summer's day, the chatter of volunteers in your ears, it's not hard to imagine what it would have been like to work on this 3,000 years ago. Initially the horse was formed by digging metre-deep trenches and filling them with freshly crushed chalk to ensure maximum brightness. New blocks of chalk would have been cut periodically and carried to the horse's flanks, where they could be chipped before being hammered into place. Chalk is a soft stone – you can rub it into pieces between your fingers – so everyone would have been able to get involved. And because the horse is the length of a football pitch, it would have required the whole community.

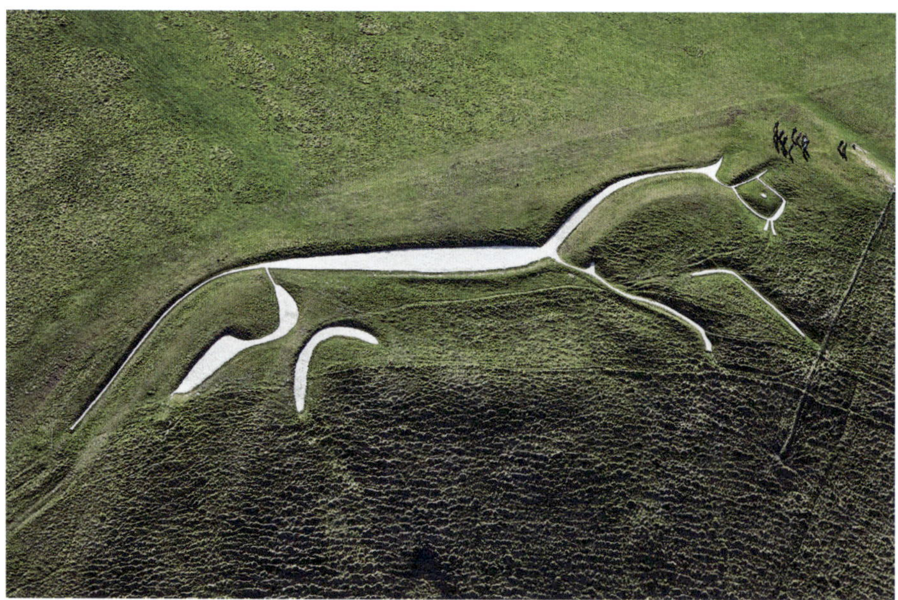

Uffington White Horse, Oxfordshire, *c.*1000 BCE

Why was this horse originally made? It sits on a chalk ridge close to an Iron Age hillfort, but it may pre-date it. Was it a marker of territory or connected to belief systems? Was it a fertility symbol or representative of the importance of the horse to the community? No one can be sure. Its meaning has changed over the years just as its outline has done; using aerial photographs, archaeologists can see the outline of a more conventional horse beneath this stylised example. Was the horse connected to a lost early religion? Similar horses appear in Scandinavian rock carvings dating to the same period, and across Europe and Asia horses were believed to pull the sun god's chariot on its daily arc across the sky. Was the horse worshipped as bringing life, the sun, on a daily basis?

It has been estimated that 150 generations have looked after this site – not one has failed to maintain it, and something continues to draw people to it. They feel connected to their ancestors who kept it alive through wars and famines and plagues. There's been a notable revival of folklore traditions across the British Isles in recent years, documented by the artist Ben Edge (born 1985) in his film *Frontline Folklore*. It was Edge who first told me about chalking the White Horse. His film captures the growing desire to tap back into this sense of collective belonging, of being rooted to the land, connected to your neighbours, while welcoming others to celebrate alongside you. But what of the people who originally made the horse? What do we know of the Celts?

3

IMMIGRATION OR ATTACK?
1000 BCE–700 CE

LOOKING FOR CELTIC art can be like looking for dark matter. It exists, but we must reconfigure our expectations to see it. Today we would not expect to find art on the rim of a bucket, the back of a mirror or the partial remains of battle armour. But this is where some of the best examples of Celtic art can be found. In the British Museum in London, a bronze shield boss found in the river Thames at Wandsworth from 350–150 BCE features a sinuous circular design of leafy tendrils and seed pods that turn into birds' faces as you look at them. A bucket from 75–25 BCE that was found in Aylesford in Kent and once held cremated remains has been reconstructed from the bronze bands that encircled it. Around the rim stylised horses prance, their heads ending in beaks like the Uffington White Horse. All these intricate designs feature flowing lines, an abundance of circular and crescent forms that bring to mind the skies above, and a joy in turning an oval into an eye, an arc into a wing, a line into a coiled body.

Ironically, given the name of the UK's oldest national public museum, the British Museum's collection is largely non-British, and the museum only (reluctantly) appointed a curator of British archaeological finds in 1851. Augustus Franks joined the staff and it is him we have to thank for Celtic finds from La Tène in Switzerland entering the British Museum collection in 1867. He was the first to date these to the Iron Age and they matter to us today because they have become the bench-mark for identifying pan-European Celtic art, both on the continent and within the British Isles.

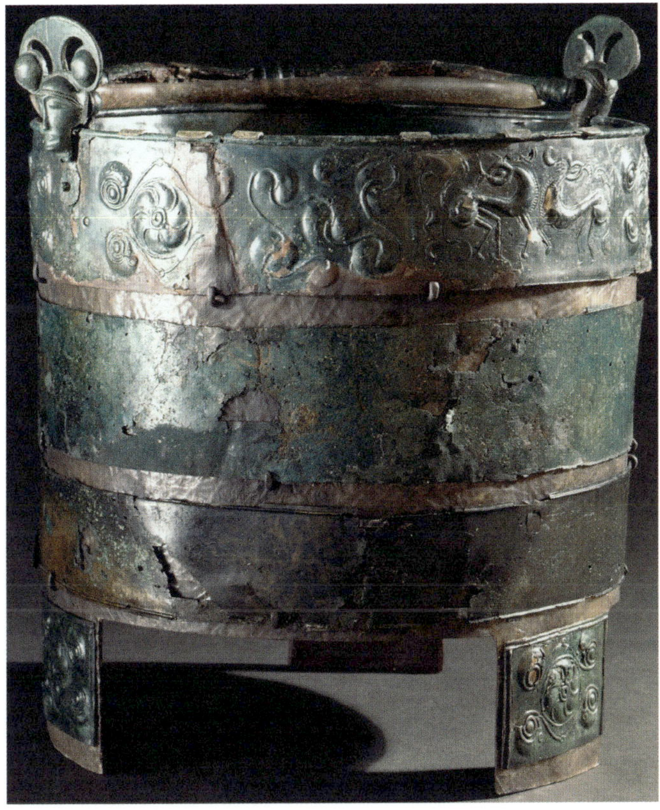

Funereal bucket, copper, iron and wood, *c*.75–25 BCE

The term Celtic art is still in use and is a style we feel we know instinctively. Its loops and arabesques, invoking spreading wings and slithering snakes, have reappeared throughout history, from medieval manuscripts and Pre-Raphaelite paintings to Margaret Macdonald Mackintosh's *fin de siècle* Art Nouveau and the props in *Game of Thrones* and *The Lord of the Rings*. But who were the original Celts? Did they really exist, and why do artists circle back to their way of seeing the world time and time again?

MIRROR IMAGE

There is scant Celtic writing and none has been discovered so far in Britain or Ireland. We only know of the 'Celts' because Julius Caesar wrote about them in *The Gallic Wars* and the Greek geographer Strabo referred to the Celtae tribe in southern France as 'Celti', suggesting multiple linked tribes.[1] There is huge disagreement as to where these 'Celti' came from, but a shared language seems to have made its way along the ports on the Atlantic coast from Portugal and Spain to Britain and Ireland by around 1300 BCE. There was already a buoyant trade in metals and salt and a common language would no doubt have greased the wheels. In Ireland and Britain the natural resources of copper and tin meant bronze could be made, and those skilled in metalwork probably travelled using this Atlantic network. In central Europe, away from the coast, archaeological finds point to another migratory route north for artists and ideas from the Mediterranean. Etruscans from south of the Alps may have had a hand in the Celtic use of animals to decorate swords, shields and jewellery. But where Etruscan artists aimed for naturalism, those north of the Alps turned the animals into fantastical writhing shapes, often barely recognisable under a sea of constantly moving lines.

Two large discoveries at Hallstatt in Austria and La Tène in Switzerland now lend their name to two periods in Celtic art, with Hallstatt spanning 1200 BCE to around 450 BCE, and La Tène covering the next 500 years. These two periods roughly coincide with the decline of bronze as an elite metal of choice and the rise of iron. Bronze was a metal alloy that was liquid when heated and could be cast using complex moulds. Not content with unadorned blades and weaponry, artists took the time to embellish such equipment with organic curves and animal forms. They also produced neck torcs (prestige necklaces) from beaten panels and woven strands of gold, some patterned with vegetal designs that curled around them.

The attachment to bronze faded as the climate worsened. Wetter, darker summers brought about by natural climate change meant stores of wheat became the most valued possession. Imagine, hundreds of years of just trying to survive without enough sun to yield strong harvests. There would be little spare capacity to make elaborate art if you all had to work simply to stay alive. By 450 BCE the climate was improving and the sun shone more readily. However, the love affair with bronze weaponry was over. Bronze had been replaced by a new metal, iron, and a new way of working it. Iron required brute strength, patience, teamwork, and was primarily used for industry. It did not reflect the sun (no longer such a reliable ally) but came from the earth; it was not shiny and ceremonial but strong and pragmatic.

For artists, iron was a difficult substance to work with. It was purified from iron ore, which was far more widely available than copper or tin, but it had a higher melting point. Even with bellows it was a challenge to reach this, so it tended to be heated until it was pliable and then hammered into shape. Consequently, when we look around our museums, we see that many of the objects from the Iron Age (*c.*800 BCE–43 CE) that we would consider to be artistic are not made in iron but continued to be made in bronze. Bronze, when first cast and polished, has the bright sheen of gold. Gold was the material of choice for body adornment and jewellery but it was too soft to create large items. Bronze was a halfway house – gleaming like the sun but strong enough to be used for shields and funereal buckets. While it could still be melted and cast into intricate moulds it was now increasingly used in sheet form, with designs hammered into the surface from behind, causing the metal to bulge in a technique called repoussé.

Large bronze shields have been found in the Thames dating from the Iron Age. While wood and iron may have created strong shields for battle, these bronze shields would have been for ceremonial use. They survived because they were thrown into the river, perhaps as an offering to ancient gods. The Battersea Shield (*c.*350–50 BCE) is a striking example of Celtic La Tène art. Three circular repoussé designs cover the long bronze panel that would have originally been attached to a wooden shield. Tendrils loop and curl around smaller circles that have red enamel centres (other shields feature red coral, imported from the Mediterranean). Imagine wielding this in a procession. It would cover your entire body and reflect the sun, dazzling onlookers, while the symmetrical designs are astounding in their precision and artistry.

The Celtic 'Mirror Style' was intrinsic to the British Isles and something of a speciality. Using a pair of compasses, an artist would design increasingly complicated patterns formed from sections of circles that were then engraved onto the backs of polished bronze mirrors. These lines, cut into the metal freehand, were sometimes further embellished, as with the Desborough Mirror, found in Northamptonshire (1–60 CE; see overleaf). An alternating cross-hatching pattern called basketry has been used to texture many of the irregular segments, while all the crescent moons are striped. The free-flowing lines and curves give

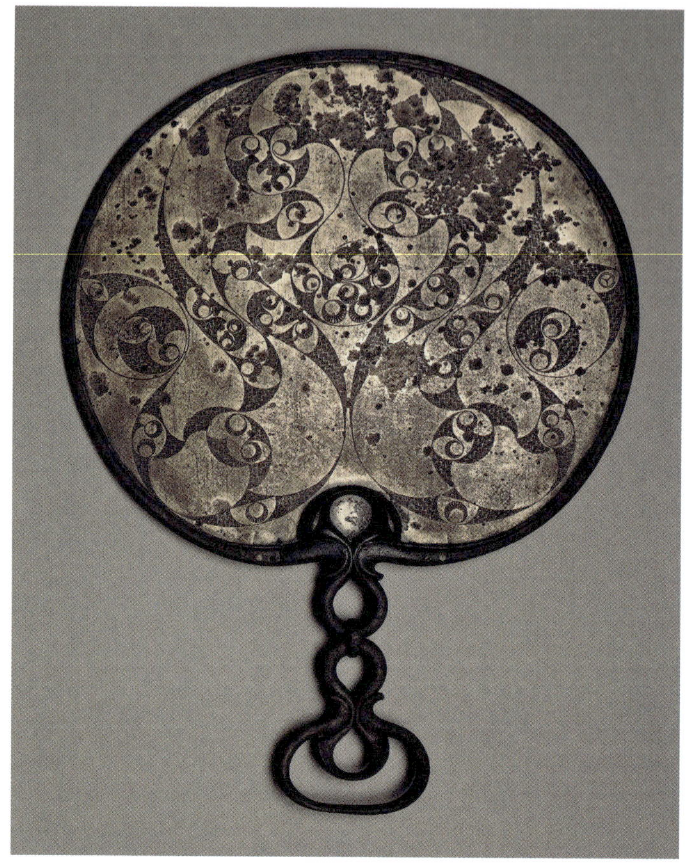

Desborough Mirror, bronze 1–60 CE

the appearance of organic fluidity but often the designs are rigorously symmetrical or follow a pre-ordained order.

The Turoe Stone, found in 1902 at the rath (ring fort) of Feerwore in County Galway, perhaps gives us a clue to interpreting these abstract forms. It is around 2,000 years old and stands as tall as an adult, its dome covered with wave-like tendrils that stand proud of the surface. These have been interpreted as symbolising the stars above and the sun's daily sweep across the sky and are reminiscent of the markings carved on the kerbstones at Newgrange. The Celts, like their ancestors before them, placed the sun at the centre of their world, constructing roads along solstice lines and venerating the horse as the sun's guide across the heavens.

Other examples of Celtic art have animal faces and human heads camouflaged within seemingly abstract patterns. In among the circular leaves on the Wandsworth bronze shield boss (now in the British Museum) two bird-like heads peek out. With a little imagination these morph into a pair of dragons that pursue each other around the central boss. Celtic myths were passed down orally for centuries before being recorded in Wales and Ireland during the medieval period, and feature many creatures who could shape-shift and metamorphose. These would have been brought to life by Druid storytellers who were entrusted with learning all the Celtic myths to ensure their survival (in *The Gallic Wars* Julius Caesar noted this could take up to twenty years).[2]

Celtic art does show signs of regional difference, but it is like different dialects rather than distinct languages. This is why much British and Irish Celtic art is referred to as La Tène today, despite the fact it was made in the British Isles rather than in Switzerland. For example, the sun-like design on the legs of the Kent bucket are similar to those that light up the Broighter Collar, a torc found in County Derry. Similarly, there are visual connections between the birds on the Wandsworth shield boss and the Petrie Crown, found in County Cork.

THE GROUND BENEATH OUR FEET

The British Iron Age is seen as coming to a close with the invasion of Britain by Emperor Claudius in 43 CE. (The Romans never made it to Ireland, and consequently the fluid organic lines of Celtic art continued uninterrupted well into the second century CE.) The Romans knew the British Isles existed long before setting foot there themselves. Around 325 BCE a Greek man called Pytheas left his home town of Massalia (Marseille) to embark on a journey that saw him sail around the entire coastline of mainland Britain. In his subsequent travel memoir *On the Ocean* he wrote of his encounters with Prettanikai (Britain). He began his circumnavigation in Cornwall, the source of tin, and sailed north to the Orkney islands, before heading south along the east coast towards Kent.

Initially Greek historians were sceptical that there even was a land beyond the sea at the far edge of mainland Europe. In the fifth century BCE Herodotus had heard talk of the islands called the Cassiterides ('tin islands') but couldn't find anyone to corroborate the rumour. Pytheas changed all this, and subsequent Greek accounts relayed that Britons lived in regional tribes led by male and female rulers.

The Romans steamed up through Europe, conquering Greece and Turkey before entering Gaul (France) in 121 BCE. The Gauls – also known as Celts – put up quite a fight, not succumbing to the Roman military machine for nearly seventy years. This was three years after Julius Caesar made the first Roman foray into Britain. He met with more resistance than expected, and when storms destroyed many of his ships, he retreated. Caesar returned the following year, in 54 BCE, and despite the Celts mobilising under Cassivellaunus and conducting a form of guerrilla warfare, they were defeated. Caesar took hostages and demanded Britain pay tribute to Rome but the country was largely left alone for nearly ninety years. However, in 43 CE, Claudius decided that the time was ripe for a full-scale invasion.

To convey a sense of the Britain the Romans knew, I want you to travel with me to a ploughed field in Rutland. Jim Irvine, an engineer who has spent the last thirty summers working this land with his father, is crouched down next to us, his hand closing in on a small lump of pale stone. Jim's father has farmed the land since 1960, and until the first Covid lockdown of 2020, neither of them had given a moment's thought to the proliferation of stones that peppered the soil in one particular field.

Jim stands up and balances the piece of stone on his open palm. It's no more than 3 centimetres across, a cube of pale rock with sharp edges like a die. 'That's a bit of tesserae,' he says. And there, in that muddy field, with the sound of the Stamford to Birmingham express train thundering by and birds wheeling overhead, time folds in on itself. We are back in the third century and this field that slopes towards a narrow river is a building site. There's an engineer (like Jim) with dividers checking measurements as workers install vertical flue bricks to ensure the new villa will be warm throughout. There are farm buildings and vineyards, a corn dryer and forge, all supporting the household's needs. Later a team of workers will arrive to lay thousands upon thousands of pre-cut tesserae like the one Jim now holds in his hand. They will create the villa's mosaic centrepiece, which will tell the story of an epic battle and the heavy price of defeat.

When finished the mosaic pavement stretched across the floor of the triclinium (dining room) and measured 11 × 7 metres. The small cube of pale stone in Jim's hand would have been laid at the edge of the room, part of a plain border, like floorboards peeking out from under an ornate rug. The narrative mosaic occupied the centre of the room and was made of smaller pieces, each less than a centimetre across.

Stone and tile tesserae in red, blue, white and yellow were combined to form a complex knotwork border around three detailed narrative panels that quite literally seem to pop out of the floor, thanks to the ingenuity of the artist who designed them.

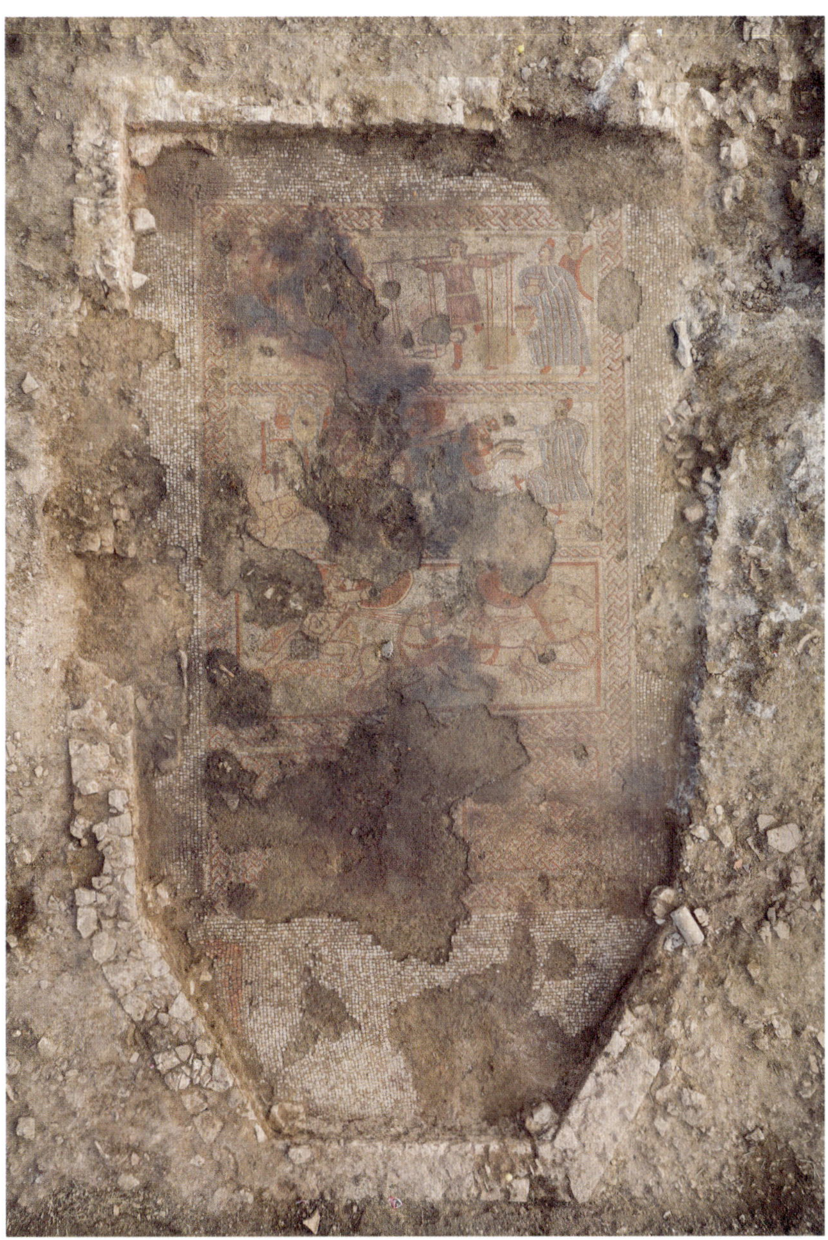

Mosaic pavement, Rutland, 3rd century CE

We can't see any of this when standing in the field today; there is only ploughed earth under our feet. The mosaic that was excavated between 2021 and 2023 has been covered in white silica sand and buried again under the original earth. But with Jim's help, we can relive his find and begin to understand its significance. For he had discovered the first Roman mosaic depicting scenes from the Trojan Wars in Britain – by any reckoning, the find of a lifetime.

The mosaic tells the story of the battle between the Greek hero Achilles and Hector, prince of Troy. Hector has killed Achilles' close friend Patroclus and Achilles shows up in the first panel hellbent on revenge. Their chariots speed towards each other and the men are braced for battle, wielding spears. This panel is at the bottom of the mosaic but is the beginning of the story. The story was designed to be seen from couches in the dining area, in the apse-like north end of the room, and so the action began closest to the dinner guest.

The second panel has Achilles victorious. Hector is stripped and lashed to the back of Achilles' chariot and his dead body is pulled through the mud. Hector's father King Priam runs into the scene with no time to put his shoes on, his striped blue robe billowing around him. He begs Achilles to release Hector's body and let him grieve. Those who know this story from Homer's *Iliad* will remember that Achilles told the dying Hector that he wouldn't give his body back to his parents, even if King Priam offered him his weight in gold. But what we see in the final panel of the mosaic contradicts this. Priam re-enters, fully dressed in red boots this time, holding two large gold pots. Next to him a man struggles to balance a giant weighing scale. On one side we see Hector's dead body, blood dripping down his chest; on the other the beginnings of Priam literally paying his weight in gold.

What are we to make of this divergence from the *Iliad*? Homer recounts Priam piling up gifts in a wagon to deliver to Achilles, but there is no mention of gold. The story of the Trojan Wars was in fact relayed by many narrators and in Roman Britain it seems that the account in the tragic play *Phrygians* by Aeschylus, a fifth-century BCE Greek playwright, was as prevalent as Homer's. Aeschylus added the weighing scene for dramatic effect – imagine it on stage! – and the artist behind this design has followed his lead. In the first century BCE the Roman poet Virgil also wrote of Troy and the exchange of Hector's body for gold in the *Aeneid*. The owner of this Rutland villa seems to have been well versed in this ancient tale and was keen to have such knowledge on display.

The Roman empire extended south to Greece (and beyond), and early Romano-British mosaics are thought to have been made by Greek artists because there are no examples that pre-date the Roman invasion. But by the third century these early Greek artists may well have recruited British assistants who developed the necessary techniques to become highly skilled. Corinium (Cirencester) was a known centre – more than ninety mosaics have been found there to date – but so too was Durobrivae, just 20 kilometres from Jim's Rutland villa. Perhaps you pre-ordered your mosaic from a central studio and it arrived in numbered bags (like Lego); more likely a team of artists would bring coloured tesserae with them and create your design in situ, reserving special pieces of imported quartz for eyes. The tesserae, carefully cut from local stone and coloured tile, would have been pushed into a wet cement layer to lock them in place, then rolled flat and polished. It was a skilled job: according to the Roman emperor Diocletian's Edict of 301, a maximum fee of 60 denarii a day was appropriate for a mosaicist; a stonemason could only earn 50 denarii and an unskilled labourer 25.[3]

The owner of the villa who commissioned the mosaic must have felt a deep connection to Greek stories, and the mosaic's creator shows an awareness of artistic styles from the Mediterranean. But while artists working in Britain at this time were part of the Roman empire, they also put their own stamp on things. Could this be the reason for Achilles and Hector fighting in chariots, despite Greek accounts suggesting the battle was on foot? Julius Caesar begrudgingly admired the British warriors he encountered – they used chariots both to position themselves on the battlefield and as a means of escape. Perhaps these ancient heroes were depicted in chariots because that is how warriors fought in Britain?

While British traditions may have made an impact on this mosaic's design, Roman culture was like a blanket of Pompeiian ash following the invasion. The Romans brought with them their imperial cult – where the emperor was worshipped as a god – and an obsessive desire for portraiture in all its forms. This led to a proliferation of figurative sculptures, mosaics and paintings, but on the whole these lack the imaginative beauty of art produced in Britain prior to the occupation. The sinuous complexity of the Desborough Mirror or the Battersea Shield, with their enigmatic designs, makes the Roman busts and tombstones seem rather prosaic, literal translations of life into stone rather than reflections of deeper spiritual concerns. Yet Roman art, in terms of social record, supplies much of what we know today about the Roman way of life. A second-century tombstone offers us a good example of this.

Regina sits up straight in a curved wicker chair in an architectural niche. Her dress hangs in soft folds to her ankles, the sleeves short enough for us to see bracelets on each wrist. Her right hand is opening an armoured box, used for keeping jewellery and money safe, indicative of her wealth. Beneath her feet runs an inscription in Latin, which translates as: 'To the spirits of the departed, Regina, his freedwoman and wife, a Catuvellaunian by tribe, aged 30, Barates of Palmyra [erected this]'. Below there is a shorter inscription in Palmyran, a form of Aramaic: 'Regina, freedwoman of Barate, alas!'

Regina was the wife of a Roman soldier. She was thirty when she died near the fort of Arbeia, now South Shields, 400 kilometres from

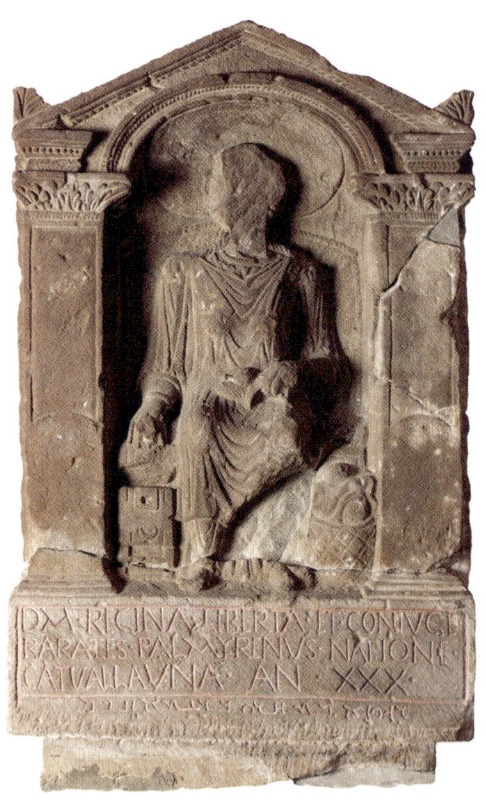

Tombstone of Regina from the Fort of Arbeia,
South Shields, 2nd century CE

where she was born, in the second half of the second century. She was a member of the Catuvellaunian tribe, the people who raised armies against Julius Caesar and Claudius. Regina had been a slave, perhaps as the result of Claudius enslaving her ancestors over a century earlier, but Barates freed her and married her, only to lose her to death.

As a soldier of Rome Barates would have been expected to converse in Latin, the language of the empire, but the line of text in Aramaic suggests he originated 5,000 kilometres away in Palmyra, Syria. He was a man born in Asia, wedded to the Roman empire and serving in northeast England, in a fort that guarded the main sea route to Hadrian's Wall. Was he originally part of the First Hamian Cohort of Syrian archers known to have been stationed nearby at Magnis (Carvoran) during the second century?

His was a time of mass consumption of figurative images. Coins printed with the emperor's portrait were in use across the empire and soldiers wore glass medallions of the emperor's family on their uniforms to showcase their fidelity. The emperor's own likeness accompanied the Roman legions into battle – a silver portrait bust was held aloft at the head of the regiment by the imaginifer, a standard-bearer who was paid double the wages of a regular soldier due to the importance of the task. You have to wonder what the Celts who had weathered the Roman invasion made of it all. They refused to write down their own myths and stories, preferring the rigour of memorised narration. Their art was sinuous and suggestive, geometrically complex, related to the cycles of the earth rather than the human figure. It interwove animal characteristics with natural forms, suggesting a deep understanding of the interconnectivity of life. The Romans, like Narcissus, preferred to look at themselves.

In fact Celtic artists continued to produce their own style of art despite this Roman obsession with physiognomy. A copper-alloy geometric flask that would once have been filled with imported perfume was found at Walbrook in London, its surface covered with Celtic spirals, suggesting Celtic artistry was adapted to the needs of this lucrative Roman market. 'Dragonesque' brooches also date to the Roman occupation, their symmetrical Celtic designs fusing animal forms with intricate patterns picked out in enamel. These traditions would come to the fore once again as the Roman empire lost its grip on Britain.

DANCING WITH WOLVES

Emperor Diocletian had found the Roman empire too unwieldy when he took power in 284 CE. He divided it in two, appointed another emperor to help him run the western portion, then appointed two further deputies to help him keep it all under control. Constantius I Chlorus was put in charge of Spain, Gaul and Britain. In Britain he fought with his young son Constantine, who was crowned emperor in Eboracum (York) when his father died there in 306. Constantine went on to revitalise the empire, moving its capital to Byzantium and renaming it Constantinople (now Istanbul). He turned his gaze to the east and his back on Britain, and within a century the Romans were gone.

As the Romans retreated, their buildings fell into disrepair and the import of wine and olive oil from the Mediterranean stopped. The Picts assailed Hadrian's Wall and the Scoti from Ireland launched attacks on resource-rich west Britain. Jutes, Saxons and Angles sent raiding parties across the sea from Germany. By the fifth century many Saxons had crossed the Channel from north Germany and settled in the south and east of England. By the late sixth century they had moved as far west as Bath and Gloucester, right up to the borders of modern-day Wales and Cornwall. Irish raiders had settled in these areas and held their ground and so the Saxons went north, as far as the Antonine Wall in Scotland, the former Roman border that marked the edge of their most northerly territory. (The Picts held the land beyond this; we will visit them in the next chapter.)

Looking at the seventh-century Staffordshire Hoard, you could be forgiven for thinking that the Roman conquest had been nothing more than a bad dream. There are more than 3,500 fragments of gold and silver in the hoard, largely taken from swords and the machinery of war. It was discovered in 2009 by metal-detectorist Terry Herbert but it had been buried around 660 on a ridge overlooking a former Roman road (now known by its ninth-century name of Watling Street) in the Anglo-Saxon kingdom of Mercia (roughly the Midlands today). While the straight road that ran beneath the hoard is clearly of Roman origin, the hoard itself suggests a continuation of Celtic design fused with the impact of centuries of migration to England's lowlands by Germanic and Scandinavian Saxons, Angles and Jutes.

You may be thinking, how can a pile of battered sword hilts and pommels be art? But what is quite extraordinary about this group of objects is the extent of design across their surfaces. Many feature intricate arrangements of gold filigree (twisted wire) or cloisonné (flat wire) frames into which ruby-red garnets have been slotted. These interwoven patterns of animals, their bodies streamlined to ribbons, snake across gold fittings once pinned to swords. There are boars' heads and bearded faces, zoomorphs with duck-like beaks and muscular hind legs. There are seahorses and fishes and contortionist quadrupeds.

Saxon migrants brought with them a style of art that fused animal and human hybridity with geometric complexity. The arrival in Britain of Jutes and Angles also contributed dense patterning and animals transformed into woven ribbons. Anglo-Saxon artists used gold from Merovingian (French) coins and the Byzantine empire, as well as garnets that had been mined in India and Sri Lanka. Their art combined with Celtic forms to give the British Isles a unique style known as Insular art (from the Roman word for island).

Did these hybrid figures and zoomorphs connect to the ancestor stories and myths of those who commissioned and made them? The Anglo-Saxons had brought with them their belief in the connectivity of the world, of unspoken ties between animals and people and plants, as expressed through their art. In this respect they had much in common with the Celts who preceded them. Anglo-Saxons lived in farmsteads rather than urban communities, worshipped multiple gods and believed in supernatural creatures such as dragons and elves. This belief system created a richly imaginative art that went far beyond the stoic naturalism of the Romans, and deep into the psyche of a northern European population whose days dramatically changed length throughout the year and who would spend the dark months embellishing stories that inspired such art.

We cannot know who particular items in the Staffordshire Hoard were originally made for, or why they were collected together in this way. They were bent out of shape and removed from their original contexts – while the hoard features hundreds of fittings from swords, for example, the iron blades are missing, despite also being valuable. Warriors who may once have wielded such weapons appear only on silver-gilt panels in the hoard. In one, handlebar moustaches flow from face to face; in another a trio of barefoot soldiers hold small shields and large spears while marching in step wearing helmets with predatory beaks. Some pieces were over 100 years old when they were buried and had been well used. Could they have been kept to honour those who had fallen? Or did the hoard belong to a metalworker who would use the pieces as raw materials, recycling the gold and garnets, or as inspiration? The spread of material, spanning 110 years, suggests it was not just kept as bullion, like gold bars in a safe. Was it in fact a prized collection that was stolen and buried for later retrieval? Infuriatingly, we just don't know.

Some of the most highly finished and complex pieces, such as the gold cloisonné hilt fitting with red ribbon-like creatures, are thought to have been made in the same workshop as an intricate gold and garnet purse lid found at a site in Suffolk. This was one of the greatest burials ever unearthed in the British Isles: Sutton Hoo.

While the Staffordshire Hoard is invaluable for art historians and archaeologists, it can be hard to give it social context. It was hidden in a location far from any farmstead or burial ground. There is no clue as to who left it there or why. The opposite is true of the Sutton Hoo burial. In 1939 the imprint of a seventh-century ship 27 metres long was found under an earth mound on the outskirts of Woodbridge. The timbers had dissolved into the acidic soil (as had the corpse) but the non-organic contents of the burial remained. Thought to be the grave of Raedwald, the powerful ruler of East Anglia, the site included drinking horns, a purse of coins, swords, shields and decorated battle armour. These indicate that Raedwald was once a powerful individual with international connections. There were Celtic bowls and Saxon jewellery, silverware from the Byzantine empire, Frankish coins and goods from Scandinavia and Germany.

How many people must have collaborated to haul his ship uphill from the river Deben, to dig a pit to slide it into, to cover it in a vast earth mound? Who could command such a burial? The quality of goods buried inside is exemplary and the purse lid is a fine example. It was made from gold inlaid with garnets and millefiori (patterned) glass and would have originally opened onto a leather pouch (since perished). The intricate design features men being attacked by wolves, beaked creatures and ribbon-like beasts that bring to mind the Staffordshire Hoard hilt fittings.

There are other intriguing parallels between objects in the tomb itself. The artist who made the Sutton Hoo Purse Lid must have been familiar with Scandinavian art. Bronze stamps (known as dies) were used to produce figurative panels for ceremonial helmets in pre-Viking

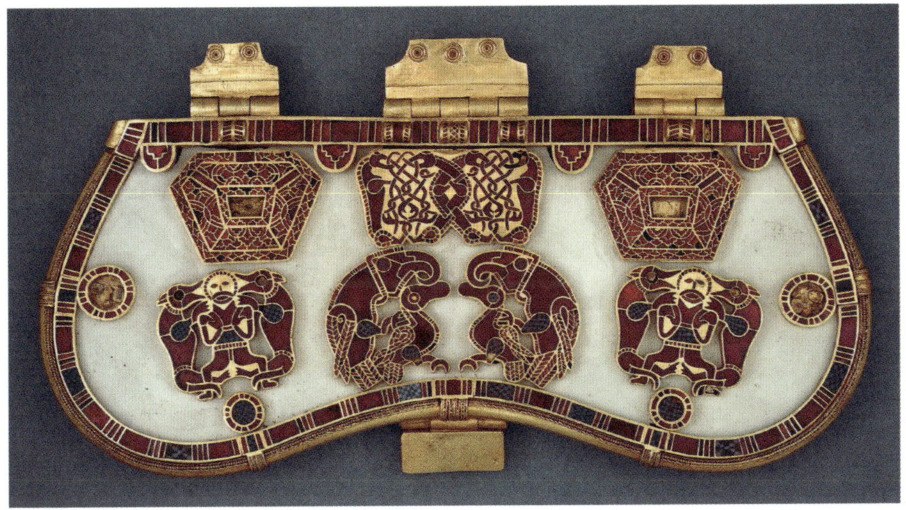

Sutton Hoo Purse Lid, gold, garnet and millefiori, 7th century

Scandinavia. They were produced on the island of Öland in Sweden and show warriors doing battle with fantastical beasts. One shows a man fighting two bears simultaneously. They rear on their hind legs so they are his height; their paws hold his arms as they bite his hair and they use their legs to pin him down. On the purse lid the beasts appear more like barrel-chested wolves, but they similarly restrict the warrior's arms and legs while opening their jaws to bite his head. The artist has even copied the man's hairstyle, the textured nubs of the stamp replicated as a skullcap of garnets. If we think the distance between the two artists who made these items is too great for this influence to exist in seventh-century Britain, we would be wrong – one of the ceremonial helmets from Öland was buried alongside the Anglo-Saxon purse at Sutton Hoo.

LET THERE BE LIGHT

All the sites we have looked at so far – the Brú na Bóinne tombs, the buried Rutland villa, the Sutton Hoo burial mound – gave me goosebumps when I visited them. Not only do they whisk you back in time but they also highlight the serendipity of history. If people hadn't been curious about what lay behind that decorated stone or under that mound of earth, we would be none the wiser and these treasures would still lie undiscovered. What else survives buried in the British Isles? Finds like these can cause entire tracts of history to be rewritten. Sutton Hoo revealed that Anglo-Saxon leaders did not live in isolation but were connected to the world through the exchange of goods, and that they used such goods to shape their image. There are dishes and military ware that connect this leader to imperial Roman power as well as the highest-quality Anglo-Saxon artistry with its pagan iconography. There may also have been Christian elements to the leader's burial, although the evidence remains inconclusive.

If this is the grave of Raedwald, the most powerful leader of the time following the death of the Kentish king Aethelberht, the appearance of Christianity should not surprise us. The eighth-century monk Bede, who wrote the earliest surviving account of Christianity in Britain, recounted how Raedwald had been initiated into the Christian faith but couldn't let go of his traditional beliefs, so built dual altars in one temple to honour both Anglo-Saxon gods and Christ.[4] Christianity was spreading, evidence of which can also be seen in the Staffordshire Hoard.

As research progressed into the Staffordshire Hoard, a tangled knot of gold strips was digitally 'unfolded' to reveal a large cross. It is one of three in the hoard and originally stood 30 centimetres tall. Its thin metal arms, 1 millimetre thick, were probably mounted on wood and it would have originally stood on a solid base. It was a jewelled cross known as a *crux gemmata*, and was found with six fittings for gemstones. All four arms are engraved with zoomorphic forms. Beaks close over writhing bodies on the vertical shaft of the cross, a design also seen on the Sutton Hoo Purse Lid.

It is this adaptation of Anglo-Saxon art to serve a new master that interests us. A work of art is made when many ideas and influences are circulating. Art is always in a period of transition as artists challenge themselves to come up with more spectacular pieces or adapt to new expectations. But in the British Isles in the sixth and seventh centuries, a huge new opportunity presented itself. This was the nascent patronage of the Christian Church, with its deep coffers and desire to proselytise through all artistic media.

4

CHRISTIANITY AS CREATIVE IMPULSE
700–1100

THE BOOK OF Kells is rightly hailed as one of the masterpieces of the medieval era. Created around the year 800, probably at the monastery on the small island of Iona off the west coast of Scotland, it has been in the care of Trinity College Library in Dublin since 1661. It's a 340-page account of the Christian gospels of Matthew, Mark, Luke and John and includes whole-page images of the saints, holy crosses and intricate title pages.

Manuscripts like these were created by monks and nuns working in scriptoria (dedicated writing rooms) over a thousand years ago. Occasionally they left tiny clues for us: an unnamed nun from St Mary's Abbey in Winchester transcribed Smaragdus's ninth-century *The Crown of Monks*, leaving a plea to God on the colophon (final page): 'Save the scribe, may she remain unharmed forever'.[1] Others occasionally left self-portraits hidden inside illuminated letters. But on the whole they worked anonymously and we have to imagine how many hands came together to produce manuscripts such as the Book of Kells.

I remember my first visit to see the Book of Kells, more than twenty years ago. I left Dublin in awe of its beauty, its age, its survival against the odds and its place in our shared history. The twelfth-century historian Gerald of Wales described the experience of seeing a similar volume as looking at 'the work, not of men, but of angels'.[2] That first time there were other comparative manuscripts on display, illustrating the huge importance of libraries such as Trinity in protecting these works for future generations to contemplate.

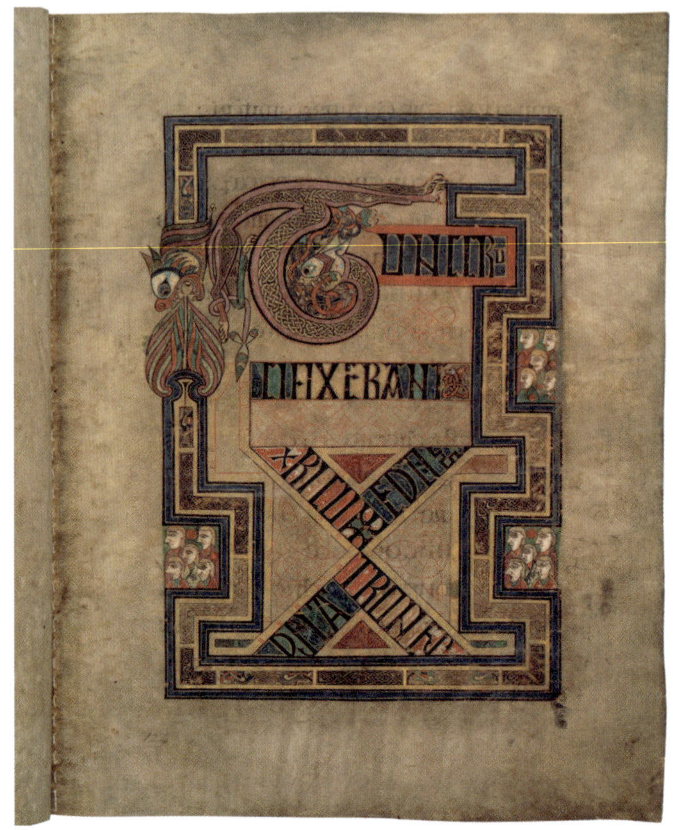

Manuscript Page from Matthew's gospel, Book of Kells, fol. 124r, *c.*800

Today the Book of Kells resides in isolated splendour inside a bespoke glass case. Only one page is on view each day, and on my most recent visit it was Matthew 27:38 (fol. 124r). This was fortunate – the ornate full-page design centres on an initial capital 'T' that is transformed into a two-headed dragon, its tongues of feathered fire and snaking necks taking up nearly a quarter of the page, while a crowd of onlookers throngs the borders.

The three major artists associated with this manuscript are known today by evocative names: the 'goldsmith', the 'illustrator' and the 'portrait painter'. We can sense their love of intricacy, colour and connectivity just from looking at this single page. They would not have been called artists at the time, but limners, from the Latin *luminer* (illuminator). These monks, working in their scriptorium, were part of a network that stretched across the Middle East, North Africa and

Europe. We have seen similar dragons in the zoomorphic art that was introduced by the Anglo-Saxons. Recognise that twisting, looping, sinuous interlace that weaves through the borders that flank the central text? It resembles Celtic knotwork, as well as Roman patterns like those surrounding the Homer mosaic seen in the last chapter. The red dots that arc between the bars of the cross bring to mind another star of the last chapter – the Desborough Mirror with its free-flowing geometry. Even the tiny heads suggest a knowledge of portrait conventions beyond Europe – they are all in profile while their eyes look directly at us, as they do in ancient Egyptian hieroglyphics.

The perennial problem of displaying medieval manuscripts is that you can only reveal one page at a time. It is impossible to comprehend the importance of the Book of Kells as a work of art, ecclesiastical object and vital witness of medieval history based on a single page. Digitisation has revolutionised the study of such works and you can access a digital version of the Book of Kells for free online, but we still need access to multiple originals when we see them in real life to enable us to make comparisons for ourselves. Individual scribes looped their letters differently and specific artists excelled at fantastical beasts or charismatic Christs. Only by coming face to face with these do we begin to glimpse what it must have been like to hunch over the paper, quill or brush in hand, pricking holes in the vellum to create guidelines, working through bad light and fasting days and monastic attacks, creating exceptional works of art dedicated to your one God.

THE CARPET PAGES OF CHRISTIANITY

Christianity had infiltrated all parts of the British Isles by the time the Book of Kells was made. The faith was originally introduced by the Romans and there's a fourth-century mosaic pavement of Christ found in Hinton St Mary in Dorset that suggests it had taken root. Following Emperor Constantine's Edict of Milan in 313, the persecution of Christians in the Roman empire came to an end. Christianity became the official religion of the empire later that century and was imported to Britannia along with amphorae of wine and olive oil. But as the Romans withdrew and Anglo-Saxon settlers arrived, Christianity seems to have gone underground once more, and there was a wholesale return to polytheism (a belief in multiple gods). Ireland was never a Roman territory and Christianity didn't appear there until the fifth century. It took until 597 to gain momentum once more in England, when Pope Gregory the Great sent a mission to Kent from Rome. Headed by St Augustine and welcomed by King Aethelberht, the mission saw the establishment of a church in Canterbury and the steady spread of Christianity across England and Wales.

I imagine Christianity's progress like two tongues of fire licking through parchment. It burnt across Ireland and from there leapt over the Irish Sea to the west coast of Scotland, where the first monastery on the island of Iona was built in 563 by St Columba. Columba sent missionaries across Dál Riada, the lands in the west of Scotland, and into Pictland in the east, and he established the Columban Church. The year he died, 597, was when Christianity began to burn brightly in Kent. This fanned Christianity to the west, east and north, through the kingdoms of Wessex and East Anglia, Mercia and Northumbria until, by 686, England and Wales were also ablaze.

In 664 the Synod of Whitby was hosted by Abbess Hild, founder of Whitby Abbey in North Yorkshire. It was held to iron out some wrinkles that had developed between Columba's Celtic variant of Christian practice and its Roman equivalent. Most notable was the dating of Easter. King Oswiu of Northumbria, ruler of a vast swathe of the north from Elmet to Edinburgh, ultimately ruled in favour of the Roman Church; the Columban community took it hard. Those who refused to change retreated to Dál Riada and Iona. Lindisfarne, a monastery on a tidal island off the northeast coast, had been established as a dependency of Iona in 635. But now it rallied around a monk called Cuthbert (who would later be canonised) who moved north from Ripon monastery in Yorkshire to oversee the change to Roman practices.

It is the combined (and competing) forces of the Columban and Roman Churches that we have to thank for some of the most exceptional medieval manuscripts. Christianity was centred on the word of God with the Bible at its heart, and all would be trained in promulgating its message. Bishop Biscop, seventh-century founder of the Wearmouth–Jarrow monastery in Northumbria, would regularly visit Rome and come home laden with books that could be copied. Books would move with monks and nuns as they journeyed from one scriptorium to another, often crossing modern-day national boundaries but remaining within the singular Christian network, unified by their faith and the shared language of Latin. They were literate at a time when the vast majority of the population was not, and these books existed within a closed loop of Christian service.

Iona's scriptorium produced such masterpieces as the Book of Kells and the Book of Durrow. Before European printing presses became established in the fifteenth century, the only way to reproduce a book was to have someone copy it, and monasteries and nunneries were the publishing houses of their day. Scribes would copy texts in Latin as dictated by the book's overall design and then hand the pages back to the artists, who completed elaborate miniature paintings in the Insular style, which dominated artistic production from the sixth to the ninth century.

In most manuscripts several hands can be seen, but one book seems to be an exception to this. Thanks to a later inscription on the colophon by a tenth-century monk, Aldred, we learn that Bishop Eadfrith (died 721) was responsible for creating the entire Lindisfarne Gospels (715–21) on his own. He became Bishop of Lindisfarne in 698, the same year St Cuthbert was enshrined there. Eadfrith fanned the flames of the cult that grew around St Cuthbert and commissioned the monk Bede to write his history. Eadfrith's own illuminated book may also have been to honour him. He would have received support in the early stages, for the pricking of the guides across 259 pages of vellum (animal skin) for example, but experts believe Aldred is correct and the entire text and the phenomenally intricate images are all by one hand. Eadfrith was bishop of a region that stretched into Scotland and covered the north of England, and his time would have been pressured. He may have therefore worked on this when he went on month-long retreats for Lent and Advent, shaping the text as he fasted and prayed until his death in 721, when the volume was left incomplete.

Like the Book of Kells it brings together the four accounts of Christ's life by the evangelists Matthew, Mark, Luke and John. They are all represented by full-page 'portraits' showing them hard at work, writing with quills on parchment or books, or reading back their texts. I am using inverted commas for 'portrait' because these are symbolic rather than representational likenesses. They are based on Greco-Roman examples – the saints sit in toga-like robes and open-toed sandals with generic almond eyes and heads full of bouncy curls. Their Christian symbols (a lion for St Mark, for example) float above them as they also hover on the page, untethered by any adherence to naturalism.

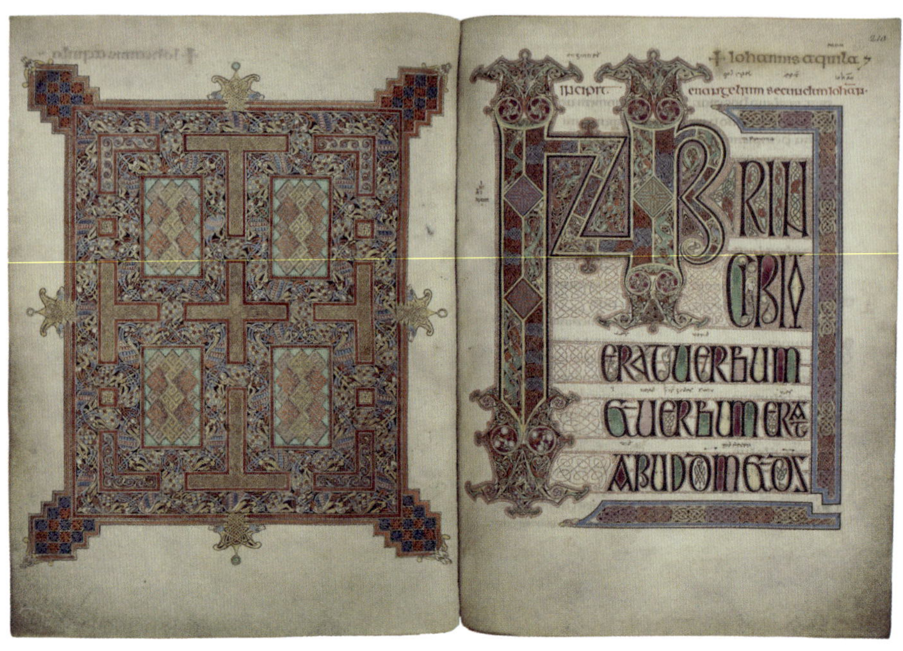

Carpet and incipit pages, St John's gospel, Lindisfarne Gospels,
f. 210v–211r, 715–21

Each gospel begins with a giant illuminated letter, and the entire
text on the opening page (known as an incipit page) is written in
large decorated capitals. These pages are magnificent. Each capital is
carefully surrounded by a border of tiny red dots and coloured yellow,
blue, red or green. The opening letter is even more elaborate, its body
filled with interlace, its finials ending in triskeles and spirals. As your
eye adjusts to such staggering complexity you start to see other eyes
looking out at you – the serpentine forms of snakes and birds that
twine around the 'Q' on the opening page of St Luke's gospel or the
dragons and dogs that bite their way through St John's.

Between the gospel portraits and the start of each text are the most
famous pages in the Lindisfarne Gospels. It is through these carpet
pages that we plunge feet-first into the teeming brilliance of Eadfrith's
spiritual world. These pages of dizzying intensity remind us today of
Islamic carpet pages found in the Qur'an. Both may have shared a
common root in Coptic (Christian Egyptian) art, although no examples have so far come to light that pre-date the Insular carpet pages
from the British Isles. Different crosses form the base of each design,

where the tessellation makes you feel as if you are looking down at a patterned floor (making the term 'carpet page' seem rather apposite). They are designed to look like a *crux gemmata* and are the most complex pages of interlace and zoomorphic ribbonwork ever made in the British Isles. Pale pink spirals turn into the elongated bodies of flamingo-like creatures who bite the necks of blue-feathered birds; verdigris arabesques end in skewbald dog heads. These pages seem effervescent, full of latent energy, and yet follow rigorous designs that reveal an immense amount of planning.

What did monks and nuns think when they looked at this book in the eighth century? Originally it would have had a heavy jewelled cover and would have remained on the altar for use in important liturgical services. The complex symmetries that underpin the carpet pages would have been seen to relate to what Bede and others called divine geometry, the basis of God's Creation. For a society that held scribes and artists in the highest regard and believed they provided a channel between God and his flock, this book must have been seen as the ultimate conduit.

So few books from this period have survived to the present day that we should be grateful these volumes exist at all. They were created during the early years of Christian practice in the British Isles at monasteries such as Lindisfarne and Iona that were remote and surrounded by water. It seems monks and nuns could better concentrate on the spiritual world if they retreated to the watery edges of the physical land. That is, until the end of the eighth century, when the Vikings attacked from the sea.

THE STINGING HORNETS

In 793 the monks at Lindisfarne worshipped in churches made of oak. St Cuthbert's shrine was by the high altar, close to the burial site of Lindisfarne's founder St Aidan. On the altar sat the illuminated gospel, now nearly seventy-five years old. The cult of Cuthbert made Lindisfarne an important site of pilgrimage, the final few kilometres completed by walking across rippling sands that flooded at high tide. Lindisfarne is a flat, exposed island, shaped like a ray. The medieval church and monastery occupied the ray's body while the tail stretched westwards, a run of shallow sandy bays facing the sea. Cattle would have filled the fields around the monastery, reared to provide the calfskins needed for the best manuscripts. For any would-be assailant it offered easy pickings. There were no cliffs to scale, no spiked ditches or stone walls to navigate. The occupants were armed only with prayers.

Viking raiders sailed from the west coast of Norway and in June 793 they chose Lindisfarne as the first site to attack in the British Isles. No doubt they didn't target wealthy Lindisfarne by chance. Trade links between the countries that fringed the North Sea would have ensured they knew where the highest quantities of gold and silver were to be found.

Bede's monastery of Wearmouth–Jarrow was targeted the year after Lindisfarne, then in 795 the Vikings attacked Iona on the west coast. Stone sculptures were smashed and monks who resisted were killed. Young Viking warriors, both men and women, took part in these raids to prove themselves in battle and raise funds, repurposing loot such as book mounts and sword fittings as brooches and pendants. Ireland was next in their sights and over forty years the Vikings systematically raided the entire Irish coast.

'Never before has such terror appeared in Britain', wrote the English cleric Alcuin.[3] He heard of the raid on Lindisfarne while working in Charlemagne's Frankish court: 'Behold, the church of St Cuthbert spattered with the blood of the priests of God, despoiled of all its ornaments.'[4] In *A History of the Kings of England* the twelfth-century monk Simeon of Durham recounted the ferocity of the Viking onslaught. They attacked 'like stinging hornets, and overran the country in all directions, like fierce wolves, plundering, tearing, and killing not only sheep and oxen, but priests and choirs of monks and nuns'. At Lindisfarne they 'laid all waste with dreadful havoc, trod with unhallowed feet the holy places, dug up the altars, and carried off all the treasures of the holy church'.[5] English poets called the Vikings 'slaughter-wolves'.[6]

Not surprisingly, the marauding Vikings disrupted book production in the British Isles. Many gospels were left incomplete and the golden age of manuscript-making was over. We should be thankful that manuscripts are portable and that some were protected from the raids. The Book of Kells was moved to its new home, a monastery at Kells in County Meath built in the hope that its inland location would protect it from Viking raids.

The art the Vikings were used to was not dissimilar to that of Anglo-Saxon Britain. It shared a common root in the art of the Germanic tribes of Scandinavia, as seen in the ribbon-like animal decorations on Viking metalwork. Similarly the Vikings, like the Anglo-Saxons, would add intricate designs to everything from the clothes and jewellery they wore to the swords they carried and the harnesses of the horses they rode. The twentieth-century Irish poet Seamus Heaney described Viking art as having 'interlacings elaborate / as the netted routes / of ancestry and trade', and the close relationship between the British Isles and Scandinavia prior to the Viking incursions meant there were many synergies between their art forms.[7] But where the complex interlace of the Lindisfarne Gospels has birds resting open beaks on each other's necks, the Vikings' animal figureheads approached British and Irish shores with fanged mouths ready to bite. And the Vikings, when they invaded, were pagan, not Christian.

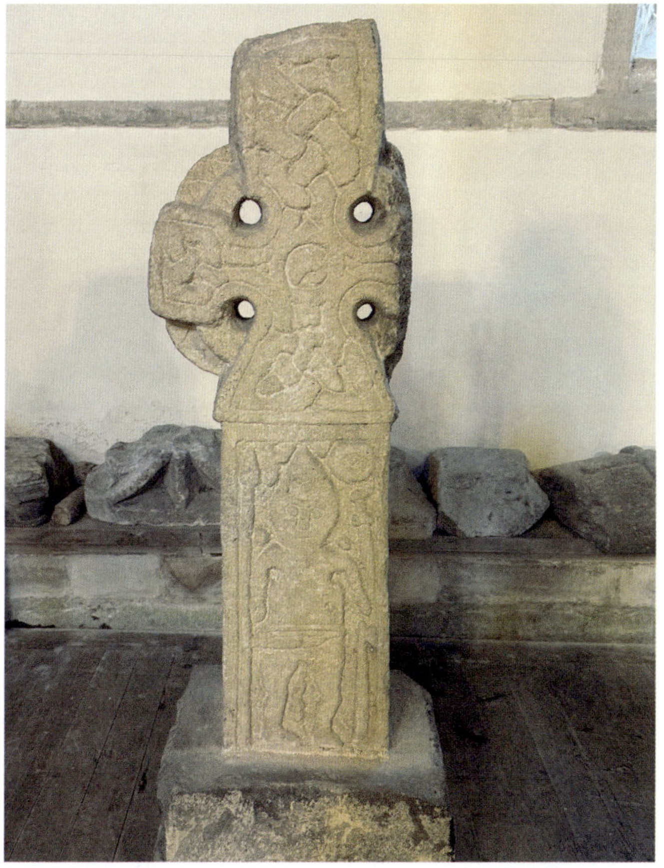

Viking cross (Cross B), St Andrew's church, Middleton, Yorkshire, 10th century

In the early raids there may have been one or two longships, but soon there were dozens working together as attack flotillas. By 834 Vikings were travelling in fleets with hundreds of ships, thousands of warriors and whole migratory communities in tow. They built winter camps in Nottingham and York and fought their way across kingdoms until they seized control. York, which they called Jórvík, became their northern stronghold in England in 866. Ultimately many Anglo-Saxon kingdoms were subsumed into the Danelaw and the Vikings controlled an area of eastern England that stretched from East Anglia to Yorkshire and Northumbria. In Ireland the Vikings established large camps at Wexford, Waterford, Dublin and Cork with good access to water, each camp within a day's sail of the next. The Vikings went from being smash-and-grab raiders to colonialists.

The Viking presence in Britain and Ireland lingers in the art they left behind, in the tenth-century crosses at Middleton in North Yorkshire (see previous page) and in the twelfth-century carved chess pieces found on the island of Lewis in the Outer Hebrides. Both these works feature armed warriors. A Viking lord displays an impressive array of weaponry on one of the Middleton Crosses, with a sword, axe, spear and scramasax (small dagger), while the chess pieces include three warders (or rooks) who may be 'berserkers'. These fearless warriors are known from Norse sagas and allegedly fought unclothed and unarmoured after biting the edges of their shields in a haka-like display of bravado prior to battle that must have been very intimidating.

There are seventy-eight chess pieces in total. These tiny figures with their intense stares are no more than 10 centimetres high and are intricately carved from walrus ivory and sperm whale tooth. They were found buried on the island of Lewis in the early nineteenth century (possibly as early as the 1780s). Believed to have been made in Trondheim in Norway, they help us understand the extent of the Viking network – the Outer Hebrides were considered part of Norway until 1266, when the islands were ceded to Scotland.

Both the Lewis Chess Pieces and the Middleton Crosses also reveal another major aspect of Viking culture in the British Isles – the wholesale conversion to Christianity. There are sixteen bishops in the chess hoard. They wear mitres and are clean-shaven, unlike the bearded knights, warders and kings. Dressed in liturgical garments, they carry tall croziers (staffs) that curl into spirals at nose height. Sometimes they raise their hands in blessing or hold a prayer book. In earlier chess

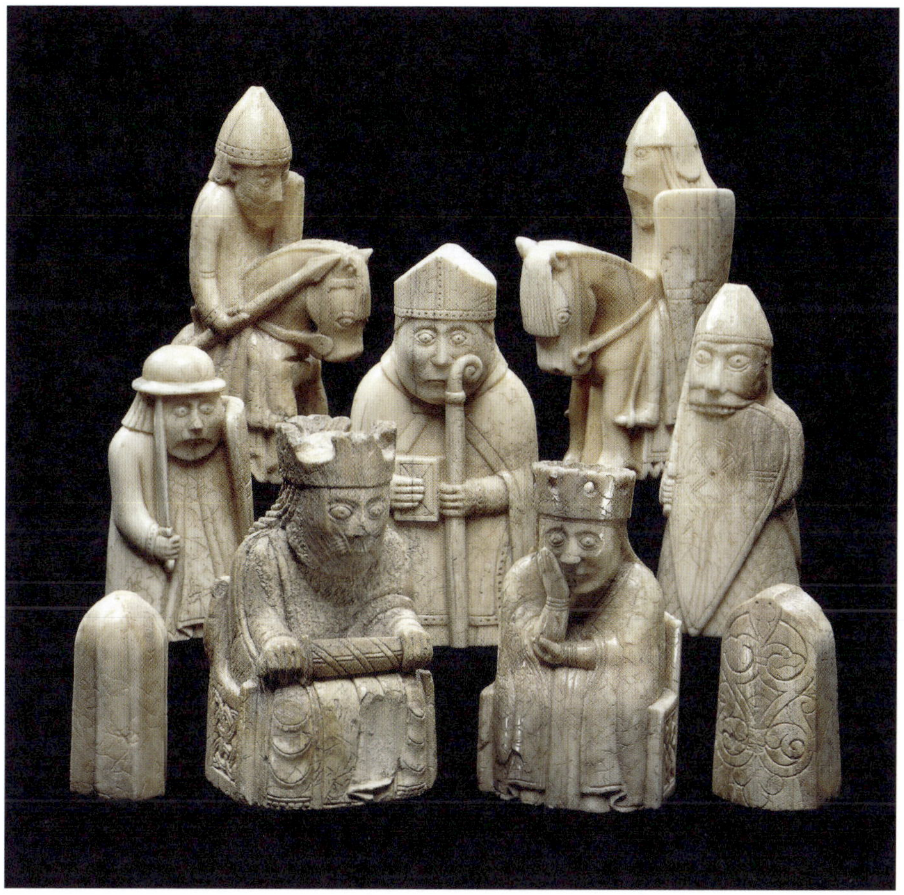

Lewis Chess Pieces, carved walrus ivory and sperm whale tooth, *c.*1150–1200

sets you would have found war elephants instead of bishops and their presence among the pieces indicates the growing reach and power of the Christian Church.

Two centuries before these elaborate pieces were carved, sculptors in and around York were using local stone for Viking tombstones that already showed the impact of Christianity on the Viking way of life. In St Andrew's church in Middleton are three Viking crosses (known as Crosses A, B and C). They are modest in height, roughly a metre tall, and set on stone plinths. Fragments of two other crosses lean against a window recess and another remains built into the eleventh-century church tower. When the tower was repaired following the Second World War the crosses that now stand in the church were liberated – they had all been used as building material just a century or so after they had first been carved.

Because of the ring-head shape of the Middleton Crosses, their colonial patrons are thought to have been Scandinavian by way of Ireland, for the ring-head cross – which looks like a halo encircling the cross – originated there. When we look at Cross B we come face to face with one of these Viking colonists. Admittedly it isn't a good likeness. (Traces of paint on Cross C suggest that all these crosses would have been painted and this warrior lord may have originally seemed more lifelike.) When we look at him today we notice the crudely carved face, the shortened arms and both feet facing in one direction. He is sitting on a throne-like chair – we can just see the curved back above his shoulders – and he is surrounded by an arsenal of weapons. This level of figuration hadn't been seen since the Romans, but the carving on Cross B is not detailed or naturalistic. It is as if the stonemason didn't have much experience in this kind of carving. If there had been little demand for figurative work and much demand for crosses and tombs covered with intricate interlace, it should come as no surprise that the sculptors were less adept in these areas.

Five hundred pieces of Viking sculpture have been found in Yorkshire, almost all ecclesiastical. Most date to the tenth century, indicating they were made when Vikings settled in the region. There is no evidence of this type of stone carving in Scandinavia at the time, so these crosses were probably made by Anglo-Saxon artists who adapted to the needs of a new clientele.

A LOST LANGUAGE

The Vikings didn't always have things their own way. An early attack at Wearmouth–Jarrow saw many of their boats founder, their leader killed in battle and the stranded crews massacred. They conquered many of the islands that fringe Scotland in the eighth and ninth centuries, including Shetland and Orkney, but when they tried to push into the Scottish mainland they met with fierce resistance. It may have been the Viking threat that united the warring communities of east-coast Picts and west-coast Gaels for the first time.

The Gaels occupied territories centred around the island of Iona in the land known as Dál Riada. The Picts occupied most of modern Scotland, from Perth to John O'Groats. For many years it was thought that the Picts were illiterate, as they did not use the written Celtic language of

Ogham, or Scandinavian runes. But more recently it has become clear that the complex symbol stones that still dot the Scottish landscape were a significant method of communication for the Picts. Around 200 remain, spanning a 700-year period from the fourth to the tenth century. Frustratingly we still cannot decipher these northern hieroglyphs, but nevertheless the stones can tell us much about Pictish culture.

The earliest Pictish stones were incised with symbols from a lexicon of close to forty artistic designs. These range from serpents and eagles to personal items (hammers, mirrors) and shapes that seem abstract to us today, based on circles, crescents and straight lines. Geometric shapes appear with regularity, often overlaid one over the other. One shape is known today as the Z-rod because it takes a Z-shaped path across the rock. Another is a crescent that lies prone, resembling a headdress or coronet; it is often coupled with a V-rod, a pair of lines that look like dividers. These symbols are thought to denote the names of leaders, while the repetition of particular pairs may suggest their importance and their right to rule.

Experts believe these symbols developed from an understanding of the Roman alphabet, but Egyptian hieroglyphics seem a closer match. We have seen that Syrian soldiers served at Hadrian's Wall so it is not unreasonable to think that the Egyptian language system may have travelled this far north, either as an idea in stories or inscribed on objects that were gifted or sold. For the Pictish language is also a visual one, with symbols used in different combinations to express names or statements. It does not appear to have the same word range as Latin but its level of sophistication should not be underestimated. It is frustrating not to be able to read these proclamations from 1,400 years ago: we need a Pictish Rosetta Stone with a Latin or Ogham translation to offer us a foothold into this forgotten language.

Three Pictish stones stand along the roadside in Aberlemno in Angus, with a further stone in the graveyard of Aberlemno kirk (church). They have survived the Scottish climate and still appear legible today under a veneer of yellow lichen. These stones offer us insights into the first half of the Picts' story. On the Serpent Stone (Aberlemno 1) a snake writhes above a Z-rod and double disc with a single mirror shape below, showcasing Pictish symbology. By comparison, the tallest stone (Aberlemno 3) allows us to see how Pictish carving evolved. This stone is not a natural shape but has been dressed: cut to size, smoothed flat then carved on both sides. It towered above me on its original plinth

when I visited on a blowy day in August. In the top third of the side that
faces away from the road are elaborate symbols. I could make out the
same pairing as on the Serpent Stone up the road: a Z-rod and double
disc. But now, instead of carved lines outlining the symbols we have
an explosion of details, with flaming suns and triskele flares filling the
discs. The difference is so notable it is like comparing a Roman letter
from Regina's tombstone with an illuminated capital from the Book of
Kells. The level of complexity in how they are carved is notable too:
instead of incised lines the sculptor has carved away the background
so the symbols sit proud on the surface of the stone.

Aberlemno 3 was probably completed 200 years after the Serpent
Stone. The complexity of the symbols announces that there had been a
big jump in artistic ability. We don't just see a name or proclamation

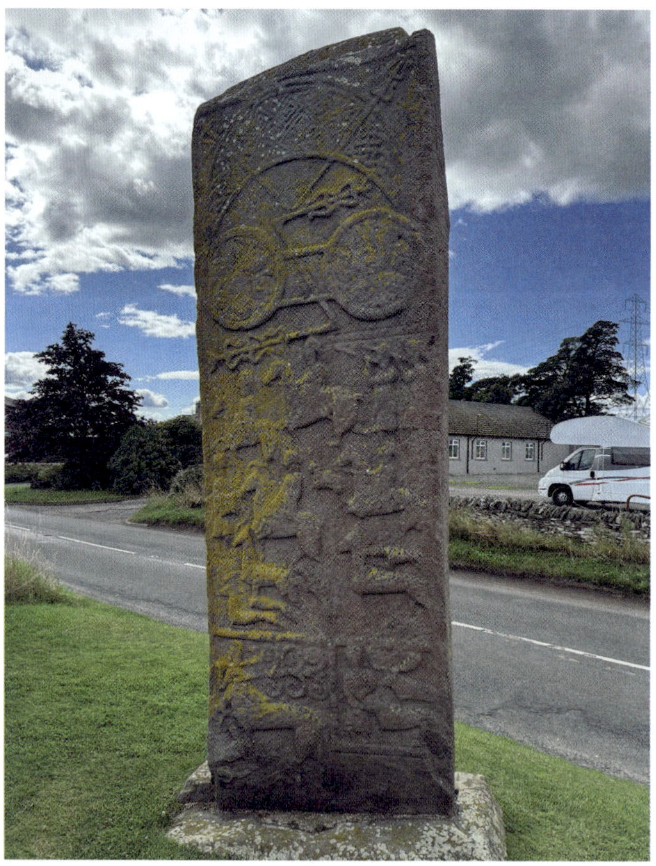

Pictish carved stone (Aberlemno 3), Aberlemno, Angus, 9th century

written out in symbols: the stones also now include several narrative scenes. A hunting scene asserts the leader's power, for hunting was associated with the ruling elite. Below this a man can be seen saving his flock from a lion attack, also symbolic of leadership.

This additional scene may give you a clue as to what caused such a pronounced artistic change. By the time Aberlemno 3 was carved, the world of the Picts had visually expanded to include a biblical scene of David protecting his sheep. If I had first described the side of the stone that faces the road you would have known this from the outset, because it features a 3-metre ring-head cross complete with singing angels. Christianity had arrived in Pictland.

Following St Columba's establishment of the monastic settlement on Iona in 563, his followers attempted to spread the word of God. Initially they were restricted to the Christian lands of the Gaels in Dál Riada, but by the seventh century they had established small monasteries in Pictland. This cross suggests Irish influence because of the ring-head design, but Northumbrian sculptors also influenced Pictish crosses. This is the complexity of Insular art: it is recognisable as art made in the British Isles yet it is often unclear as to which way influences moved within Britain and Ireland.

However, we must consider other stones if we are to understand the second half of the Pictish story. In the Sculptured Stones Museum in Meigle, Perthshire, the stone called Meigle 2 occupies a central position. There's an ornate ring-head cross on the front and a complex scene on the back that fuses a hunt with a biblical scene showing Daniel unharmed in the lion's den. The rider at the top is accompanied by collared dogs and his body is directly above that of Daniel, suggesting a comparison. But what is particularly interesting about this stone is that it no longer features Pictish hieroglyphs. The inscriptions have gone. Why?

In St Serf's church in the village of Dunning in Perthshire, a unique red sandstone cross corroborates this new development (see overleaf). This is the only free-standing cross to have survived in Pictland, although they were once common in Ireland, Dál Riada and Northumbria. This elaborate example represents the grand finale of Pictish stones. Carved around 820, it features an inscription in Latin on the back that dates it to the time of Constantín, son of Vurguist. Narrative panels depict King Constantín on his horse with an army of young clean-shaven soldiers and older bearded warriors. There are hunting dogs to symbolise his nobility and biblical scenes to show him as a brave, protective leader. There are ribbon animals and interlaced horses as decoration. It is twice my height and every facet teems with life.

The cross was only moved to St Serf's church in 2002; previously it stood on a sloping field where it once overlooked the palace of Forteviot, on a route that linked Dál Riada and Pictland and marked a crossing point for the river below. Forteviot was Constantín's palace. He may have been the first ruler to unite both Picts and Dál Riadans, or it may have been his son Domnall. The Gael Kenneth MacAlpin

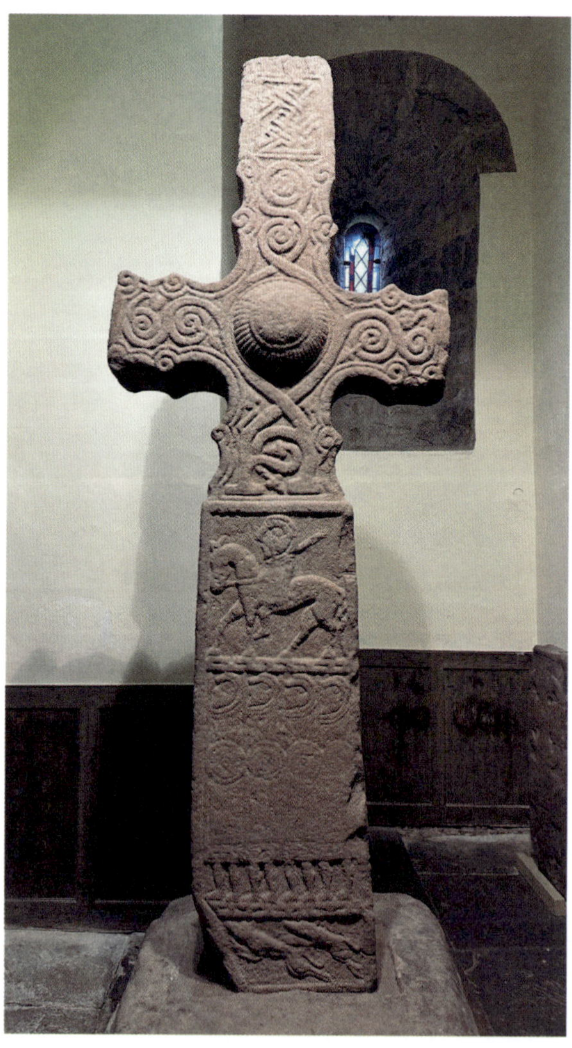

Red sandstone cross, St Serf's church, Dunning, Perthshire, c.820

is also credited with the union. Driven together by a common Viking enemy, the Picts may have been the first leaders of Scotland but along the way their unique visual language was lost and Gaelic, the language of the Gaels, became the language of Scotland. The Dupplin Cross features no Pictish symbols and instead uses Latin, the international language of the Church, to tell its story.

THE SENSE OF AN ENDING

Monumental free-standing crosses appeared across the British Isles from the rise of Christianity to the tenth and eleventh centuries, when they ebbed away. They do not exist anywhere else in Europe, suggesting they developed from a homegrown root (possibly the Pictish stones). In Glamorgan in Wales there is the great wheel cross of Conbelin, its ring-head filled with interlace and a hunting scene that runs along the base. In Monasterboice churchyard in County Louth the Muiredach Cross looms large, standing over 5 metres high and featuring a proliferation of biblical narrative scenes as well as an impressive ring-head cross topped with what looks like a tiny shrine or reliquary. Earlier examples of crosses like this one are thought to have influenced the Dupplin Cross. English crosses are largely fragments today, often with only the decorated shafts remaining. Henry VIII's Reformation was largely responsible, a devastating annihilation of England's ecclesiastical past meted out in the mid-sixteenth century (as we will see in Chapter 6).

The British Isles were part of an international artistic network that saw the movement of ideas, materials and artists across the known world. Egyptian hieroglyphs and Middle Eastern vine scrolls fed into Insular art, along with Germanic and Scandinavian zoomorphism. But why did this unique method of offering praise to God – while simultaneously showing off your wealth and power as a leader – die out in the eleventh century? We have to look beyond the English Channel for our answer, and the machinations of the Norman commander William, son of Duke Robert I of Normandy, France, now remembered in the British Isles as William the Conqueror.

5

TO BE A PILGRIM
1066–1400

A BARE-LEGGED MAN with a moustache like Errol Flynn wades into the shallows of the English Channel, fresh from the hunt and with a hawk on his outstretched arm. He will soon be bound for France; ships full of armed men await his arrival. This is Harold, the future king of England, who is travelling to meet William, duke of Normandy, fourteen years before they fight each other for the right to wear the English crown. It is the backstory to the Battle of Hastings, to 1066, the year that changed England forever, and it was sewn into history as the Bayeux Tapestry.

The first thing to note about the Bayeux Tapestry is that it is not a tapestry at all, but rather an intricate embroidery on linen that is half a metre tall and an eye-watering 68 metres long. It was created in the years following the battle, probably in Kent, and most probably for Odo, half-brother of William the Conqueror and bishop of Bayeux in Normandy. The cathedral was consecrated in 1077 and in all likelihood the tapestry was commissioned by Odo for that occasion. It is now housed in a dedicated museum in Bayeux where you can see first-hand the political machinations of the French and English leaders and the heavy body count of the battle itself, as corpses spill over the edges into the decorative borders below. The battle scenes are a whirr of action, with spears lowered to the diagonal to inject movement. In certain places care has been taken to include telling details, such as the pair of peacocks with crested heads like crowns that occupy the border directly above William and Harold when they meet for the first (and only) time.

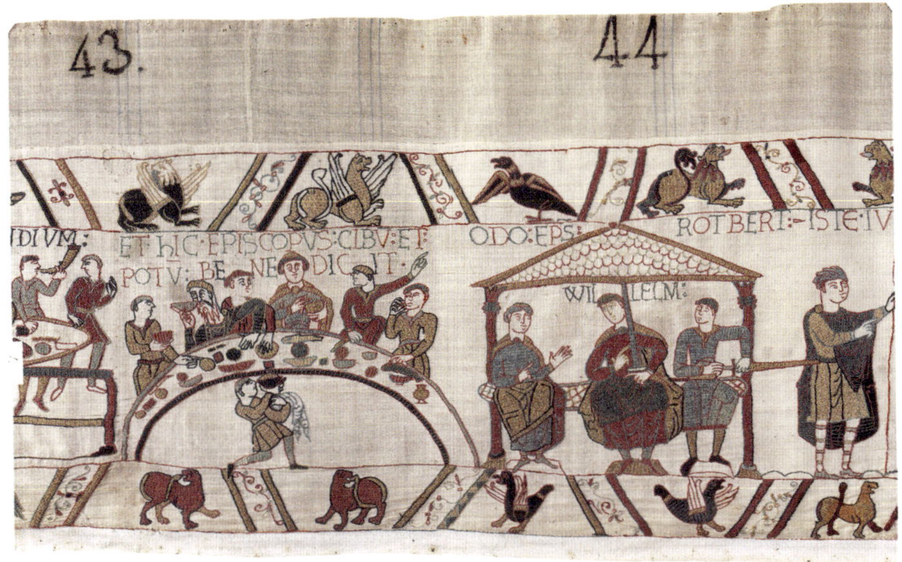

Bayeux Tapestry (detail), embroidery on linen, 11th century

The tapestry (for everyone calls it this, even though it is an embroidery) is nothing less than incredible, not only for its survival but also for the wealth of detail preserved in its coloured wool scenes. There are more than 600 figures accompanied by 200 horses, fifty-five dogs and forty ships. It was stored in the cathedral's crypt, where the dark preserved the plant dyes that give the wool its colour – we can still see claret-and-gold tunics, pale grey spears and axes, black-and-dun horses. It is so intricate we can make out stripes on stockings, the contrasting manes and hooves on horses and each circle of chainmail.

It documents contemporary events before the battle, so we see Westminster Abbey newly built and Halley's comet streaking overhead. There are scenes set in Rouen and Bayeux as well as Hastings and London. It was clearly designed as a whole but it would have been worked on in sections by skilled embroiderers, who used stem stitch for the outlines before infilling them with what is known today as Bayeux stitch.

QUEEN EMMA'S FAMILY TREE

To understand the Battle of Hastings we must first understand the complex international relations of the rival families vying to rule parts of the British Isles at this time. Queen Emma, William the Conqueror's great-aunt, was daughter of Richard I, duke of Normandy. She married two successive kings of England: one an Anglo-Saxon and one a Viking.

England had only been ruled by a single king for less than a century and rival royal families from France and Scandinavia sensed an opening when Emma's first husband, Aethelred, died in 1016. The Danish prince Cnut swiftly claimed the throne (and Emma) for his own. She had a son with Cnut who later became king, followed by her son from her first marriage. This son, Edward the Confessor, ruled England for twenty-four years, until his death in January 1066. This makes Queen Emma wife to two kings, mother to two kings and great-aunt to the victorious William, duke of Normandy and king of England. Confused? Her life illustrates the complex international nature of English rule and frames the power struggle that was to develop between Harold and William. Harold was brother-in-law to Edward the Confessor and the choice of the English nobility to become the next king. However, William, duke of Normandy, believed King Edward had promised him the English crown. To further complicate matters, Harold's exiled brother, Tostig Godwinson, supported King Harald of Norway, who also made a bid for the throne.

Consequently the Bayeux Tapestry unfolds like a saga, covering various moments in the build-up to the final battle at Hastings that decided England's fate when Harold died on the battlefield and William emerged victorious. Although it is believed to have been made in England, the order and inclusion of events suggests it was a Norman commission. For example, there's no account of Harold facing down his brother and the king of Norway in the Battle of Stamford Bridge in Yorkshire in September 1066, just one month before he had to fight William at the other end of the country. But we are presented with the meeting of Harold and William on French soil some years before Edward's death, and we witness Harold riding to battle with William in Brittany and swearing his allegiance. While a French version of history is presented, elements of the narrative clearly favour the English – for example, near Mont Saint-Michel Harold is shown in the guise of St Christopher, rescuing two Normans from a fast-flowing river – suggesting a French commission but probably an English artist in charge.

The multiple appearances of William's half-brother Odo point to him as the French patron. He fought alongside William in the Battle of Hastings and was gifted the lucrative county of Kent for his labours.

On the tapestry we see Odo seated on a joint throne with William as he learns the news that Harold has taken the English crown. He also holds court at a Norman camp in England as if he were Christ surrounded by his disciples, and he even joins the council of war, held on the eve of battle. William is depicted as uncertain, leaning towards Odo for advice. Odo calms the situation with his raised flat hand and gestures onwards with the other. He carries no sword, as if he is the ideas man, the brains behind the outfit. The tapestry is an assured work of self-promotion by Odo, made for the cathedral he was building in Bayeux while he managed England as William's proxy as the new king of England dealt with matters at home following his victory in battle.

A SLICE OF HISTORY

Home, for William, was Normandy. It is the reason we know this invading force as the Normans, and William was swift to reward fellow countrymen who contributed to his victory. The Normans only ever made up a small percentage of England's population but they were awarded almost all the positions of power, controlling the territory using a network of new castles. An early northern rebellion against Norman rule was quashed with unimaginable brutality and Norman kings and queens subsequently ruled for 300 years.

Today the Norman legacy is ever-present – Norman churches were built at Winchester, Durham and Ely in the continental Romanesque style, and half of the words in modern English are of Anglo-Norman origin. You will use them if you paint on canvas or panel, if you read romances or journals, if you eat salmon, oysters, beef or pork, if you are called William. Ten thousand new words were added to English after the Norman invasion, while French became the language at court.

While the Normans were nominally in charge, it was the Church that was growing ever more powerful. Manuscripts were commissioned, sculptures installed, crosses and caskets decorated with jewels and windows filled with stained glass. Expressive stone carvings of Christ raising Lazarus from the dead were installed in Chichester Cathedral early in the twelfth century, each panel intricately painted with jewels for eyes. The archbishop of Canterbury, Thomas Becket, gifted an ivory carving of the Virgin Mary to Westminster Abbey. For a largely illiterate congregation the carvings and stained glass brought to life the stories they heard in church; for those in holy orders these visualisations provided a focus for prayer and reflection.

It wasn't just art that became a conduit for prayer – body parts were also hugely popular. By the twelfth century relics of saints were a big business and artists were quick to capitalise on this new market. Arms, heads and bones were venerated, but so too were tiny squares of cloth said to be soaked in a saint's blood, body fluids or even brains. All these sacred fragments needed suitably elaborate homes and many were housed in enamelled caskets. The reliquaries were often placed on the altar, decorated with scenes of Christ's Passion or the life of a particular saint, and topped with a band of gilded metal decorated with a keyhole pattern and cabochons of crystal and glass.

The feverish obsession with saints came to a head when Thomas Becket was murdered in 1170. Becket's parents were prosperous Normans who lived in London and their son Thomas quickly rose through the official ranks to become chancellor of England at just thirty-seven years old. As chancellor he was the king's secretary – it was the highest-paid position in the king's household and he had the power to issue documents in the king's name. He was also a close friend of King Henry II, who gifted him the archbishopric of Canterbury. The king hadn't factored in Becket's strong religious beliefs and was angry when Becket chose to dedicate himself to the Church, resigning as chancellor and taking issue with many of the king's policies. Even a stint in exile didn't dent his resolve and the frustrated king railed to his courtiers that he needed to be rid of this thorn in his side. Four knights took the initiative and on 29 December 1170 Becket was murdered inside Canterbury Cathedral. His death was brutal. An account by his clerk William FitzStephen recorded that he was struck four times on the head, the blows slicing through his crown and spilling his brains onto the stone floor. His spilled blood and body parts were scooped into a basin by resourceful monks and the cult of Becket had begun.

The martyred archbishop was canonised within three years. (The only other man to be immortalised as a saint in the second half of the twelfth century was Edward the Confessor, ninety-five years after his death.) Churches across England began collecting parts of Becket – Glastonbury Abbey claimed to have his shoes and hair shirt while Westminster Abbey had his cloak and comb. The chronicle of St Augustine's Abbey in

Canterbury relayed that it owned 'a great part of the blood that he shed' and 'not a little' brain.[1] The French also embraced the cult of Becket and workshops in Limoges were quick to create enamelled reliquary caskets featuring the new saint to sell to English bishops and abbesses.

Around fifty such caskets still exist. The figures that adorn the caskets are reminiscent of those seen in illuminated manuscripts. In examples from the Burrell Collection in Glasgow and the British Museum, two lean knights attack Becket as he stands at the altar. Their swords are raised as they aim for his head. An example in the Victoria and Albert Museum in London (V&A), believed to be one of the first made, is larger and more complex. Three knights armed with swords approach Becket, while two monks look helplessly on, their arms in the air. In a separate panel above, Becket is laid to rest before ascending to heaven, a halo encircling his restored head.

While the V&A casket is the most ornate of the three Limoges caskets, they have much in common. It was thought that before 1190

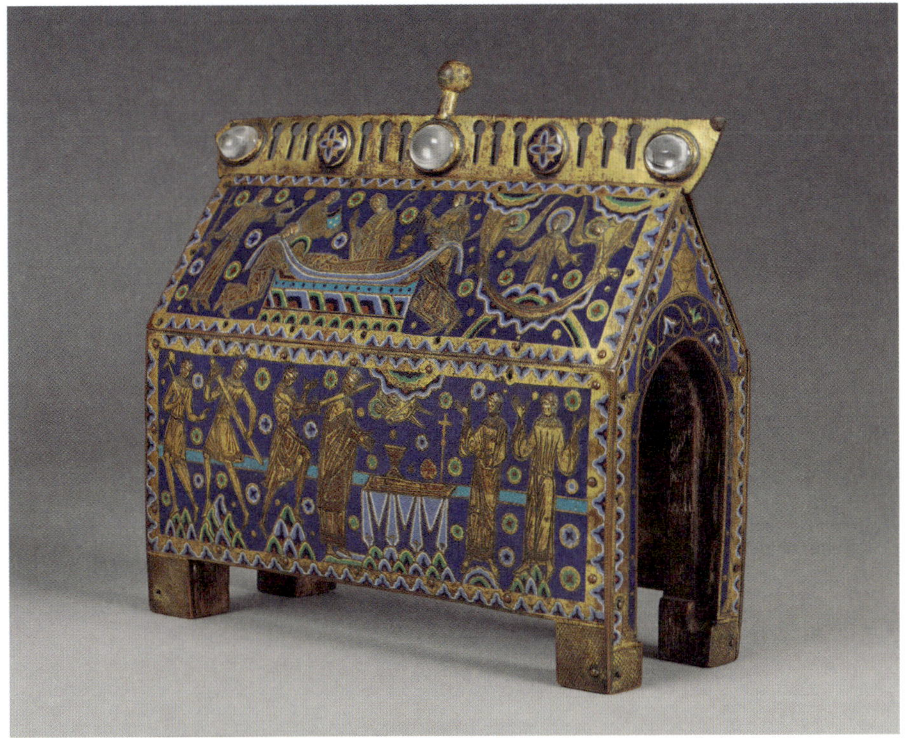

Becket casket from Limoges, destined for Peterborough Abbey, *c.*1180–90

such caskets (or chasses) featured enamelled figures against engraved gilded backgrounds. But all three of these examples have the opposite – rich blue enamelled backgrounds with engraved figures and modelled copper heads. Using sheets of copper, recessed cells would be hammered around the engraved figures. These would be filled with ground glass using a sharpened quill for pinpoint accuracy. This powdered glass was heated slowly to fuse the enamel, a process that had to be repeated several times to fill the cell before polishing. The copper heads would finally be gilded using a mixture of mercury and gold. It would require a team of skilled artists to accomplish such high-quality work and this was the reason that Limoges enamels were highly valued across Europe.

The Becket casket now in the V&A was originally made for Peterborough Abbey and was probably taken there by Abbot Benedict in 1177. Becket had visited this abbey in his capacity as chancellor with King Henry II in 1154; twenty years later the monks built a chapel in his memory and this reliquary would have been a fitting addition to the chapel's altar. The combined popularity of Limoges enamels and the cult of Becket mean caskets depicting his murder have been found across Europe, suggesting monks and nuns were highly successful in spreading the cult of Becket beyond English shores. While the caskets were imported, the cult itself was exported, creating an international market for Becket relics and Limoges reliquaries and adding a new destination to the international pilgrimage trail, a network that stretched from Jerusalem to Santiago de Compostela.

TALES FROM CANTERBURY

While the reliquary caskets were marketed to bishops, abbots and abbesses for their cathedrals and churches, other visualisations of the cult of Becket were destined for personal use. Pilgrimages – journeys to a sacred place motivated by religious belief – were embarked upon by a wide range of men and women from all social classes. They had been undertaken since the sixth century – Bede wrote of English kings travelling to Rome to spend time 'as a pilgrim in the neighbourhood of the holy places'. He also noted: 'At this time many Englishmen, nobles and commons, layfolk and clergy, men and women, were eager to do the same thing.'[2] Christianity united all classes and genders in the desire to make a pilgrimage to the epicentre of the Church in

Rome. But by the twelfth century this had expanded into a connected web of holy places thanks to the canonisation of saints and reports of miracles. Some pilgrims visited these sites to further their faith and others to atone for past sins; some believed their journey would end in a cure. Becket's violent death and rapid canonisation ensured that Canterbury became one of the most important pilgrimage sites in Europe. His bodily fluids were believed to infuse a vat of water that was sold in tiny amounts in lead vials and tin ampullae imprinted with a portrait of St Thomas, a source of income that never seemed to run dry.

Many souvenirs for pilgrims were designed to be worn, either around the neck or pinned to clothes. The twelfth-century priest and historian Gerald of Wales recounted that the bishop of Winchester had spotted that he had visited Canterbury by the seal hanging around his neck. Others bought badges at religious sites that could be attached to their hats, illustrating where they had been. William Langland's fourteenth-century poem *The Vision of Piers Plowman* satirises an avid pilgrim: 'On his hat were perched a hundred tiny phials, as well as tokens of shells from Galicia, cross-ornaments on his cloak, a model of the keys of Rome and on his breast a vernicle.'[3]

The most famous medieval pilgrim story is Chaucer's *Canterbury Tales*, left unfinished when he died in 1400. It features a band of thirty travellers bound together by their shared purpose of visiting Becket's shrine in Canterbury Cathedral. Chaucer's Wife of Bath was what Neil MacGregor called 'one of the great frequent flyers of medieval pilgrimage'.[4] She visited Rome and Cologne, Santiago de Compostela and Jerusalem – three times. You can imagine her buying metal pilgrim badges from market stalls close to shrines to pin on her wide-brimmed hat – a scallop shell from Santiago de Compostela, the crossed keys of St Peter from Rome, Becket riding a horse and holding a large cross from Canterbury.

Trade in religious souvenirs had existed for centuries in the Byzantine empire; the rise in northern pilgrims led European artists and makers to produce work in a similar way, and souvenirs were widely available in England by the beginning of the fourteenth century. The pilgrim badges sold at Canterbury ranged widely in style and quality. Figurines of Becket show the saint in full regalia for Mass, holding a cross and raising his right hand in a blessing. His hand is oversized, drawing your eye to it, allowing you to take comfort from it.

Others preferred to buy badges telling the story of Becket – we can see him variously returning from exile on a square-rigged ship, proselytising on the road and succumbing to the four blades in Canterbury Cathedral. Some of the murder scenes are poorly conceived, the knights squashed together like a chorus line, the church setting barely articulated. But some are rich in detail: one badge includes all four knights attacking a kneeling Becket, who is praying at the altar while his clerk watches on. Their bodies are in proportion and we can make out the hauberks (chainmail surcoats), shields and helmets of the murderous knights. There's even room to show the architecture of the church within a decorative roundel that frames the scene.

Like buying merchandise at a pop concert today, wearing a Becket badge after worshipping at his shrine would make you feel closer

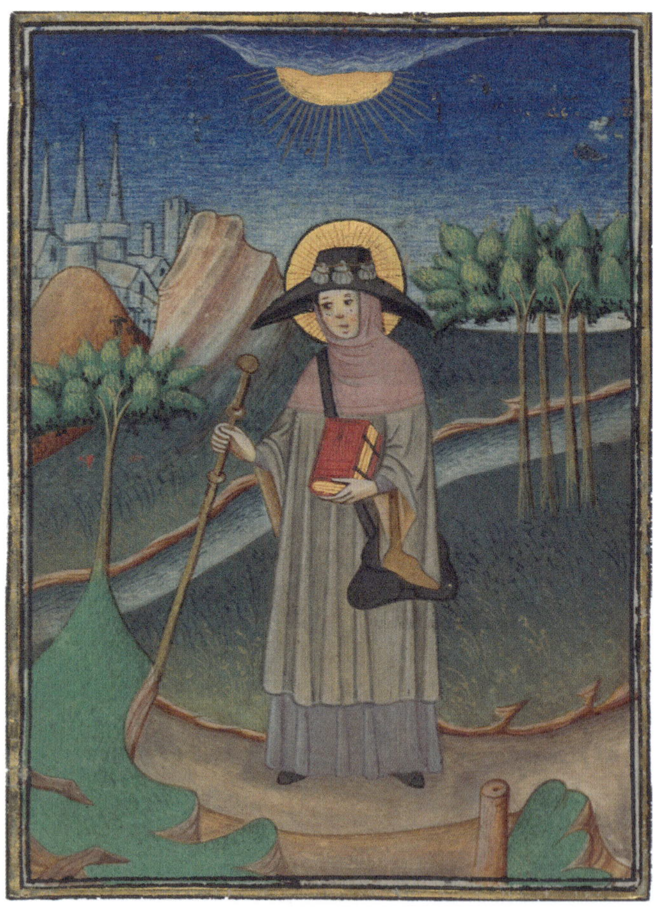

Pilgrim wearing badges on her hat in a
Flemish Book of Hours, *c.*1440

to him, even protected by him. The London Museum holds a large collection of pilgrim badges as many have been found along the silty foreshore of the Thames, thrown there to thank God for a successful pilgrimage or dropped while crossing the river. Canterbury badges have also been found in Scotland and Ireland, France and Germany, Norway and the Netherlands, showing the extent of the saint's allure.

Pilgrim badges are an early example of the mass production of art. Kings would buy handfuls of badges for their entourage, some cast in gold and silver for favourites and some in pewter (a mix of tin and lead) for lower-ranking members. Millions of badges were made and distributed all over Europe, and the English badges made at Canterbury were part of this international network of religious exchange. They are easy to overlook in museum display cases, being not much bigger than coins, but each one represents an individual's pilgrimage and as such they are potent portals to the past.

THE ALABLASTERERS OF ENGLAND

The cult of Becket existed from his death in 1170 to the 1530s, when Henry VIII's Reformation attempted to erase all trace of him from history. Up to this date there was a vast trade in visual material relating to Becket, from pilgrim badges to reliquary caskets, stained-glass windows, ivory sculptures and alabaster panels.

Ivory and alabaster were the most popular materials used for religious sculpture in England at this time, but they couldn't have been more different. Elephant tusks had to be imported from Mozambique and Zimbabwe via the markets of Cairo and the Mediterranean ports, but the highest-quality alabaster could be quarried in Derbyshire and Staffordshire and transported by cart to nearby Nottingham for carving. Ivory sculptures were necessarily limited in size; alabaster could be quarried in large blocks. However, the hard creamy dentine material could be carved into the most intricate details whereas soft alabaster stone, with its translucent quality, was prone to fracturing. But both could be polished to form a lustrous surface that suggested warmth, as if it were somehow alive. Artists adapted their practice to bring out the best of both materials: ivory was used for portable, highly detailed devotional works whereas alabaster was carved into life-size tomb effigies and multi-panelled altarpieces encased in wooden frames to protect the fragile stone.

Medieval ivories are highly prized today, despite their contentious materiality. Many originated in France and Germany and were imported to England but there are fine English examples too, such as the Grandisson Triptych, carved in Exeter in 1330–40. It was commissioned by John de Grandisson, bishop of Exeter, and his coat of arms appears on the wings above St Stephen and St Thomas (Becket again). The central panel features two scenes showing the coronation of the Virgin in heaven above the Crucifixion in intricate detail. These are carved more deeply than the wings, but even when the two outer wings are folded over, the whole piece has a depth of less than 3 centimetres. It is a small object for private devotion, completely without ornament when closed, making it perfect for travelling. It could easily be carried on a bishop's person or slipped in between boxed vestments, like packing a book in your suitcase today.

Alabaster, like ivory, was carved throughout Europe, but England was a major source of both raw material and finished panels. The designs were drawn onto thin parchment, then perforated along the lines so that the drawing could be transferred to the raw alabaster by shaking powder through the tiny holes. Artists would bequeath their rolls of designs to their heirs or partners, so they were clearly highly valued. Carving the same subjects time and again would have led to a certain standardisation and a reuse of designs to speed up production.

Once the design had been transferred, the 'alablasterers' – also referred to as 'imagemakers' or 'alabastermen' – set to work. The best alabaster was quarried in southern Derbyshire and Staffordshire from the mid-fourteenth to the mid-sixteenth century. Cartloads rolled down the Roman road network to London, ordered by royalty for grandiose tombs, while others travelled the far shorter distance to Nottingham, the epicentre of alabaster production in England (York and Burton-on-Trent were also important alabaster-carving centres). There it would be worked up into panels: popular narrative cycles included the Passion of Christ – his arrest, trial and Crucifixion – and the Joys of the Virgin Mary, starting with the Annunciation and Nativity and ending with her coronation in heaven. Today we only see stone figures but when these panels were first made they would have looked quite different, with highly polished bodies, clothing painted in bright colours and gilded backgrounds.

In a late fourteenth-century Deposition, Christ is being taken off the cross by the wealthy Joseph of Arimathea while a young man in doublet and hose moves to remove the nail that skewers his feet together.

This scene was a popular one, part of the Passion of Christ, and many examples exist, but this version, now in the V&A, conveys a real sense of pathos. Where others show Joseph's hand resting flat on Christ's belly, a frozen movement, this Deposition shows Joseph leaning in to take Christ's weight, his arms stretched around his waist as if embracing him. The connected hands of the five linked figures convey so much emotion they bring a lump to your throat, irrespective of your beliefs. Mary Magdalene's supportive touch rests on the Virgin Mary's

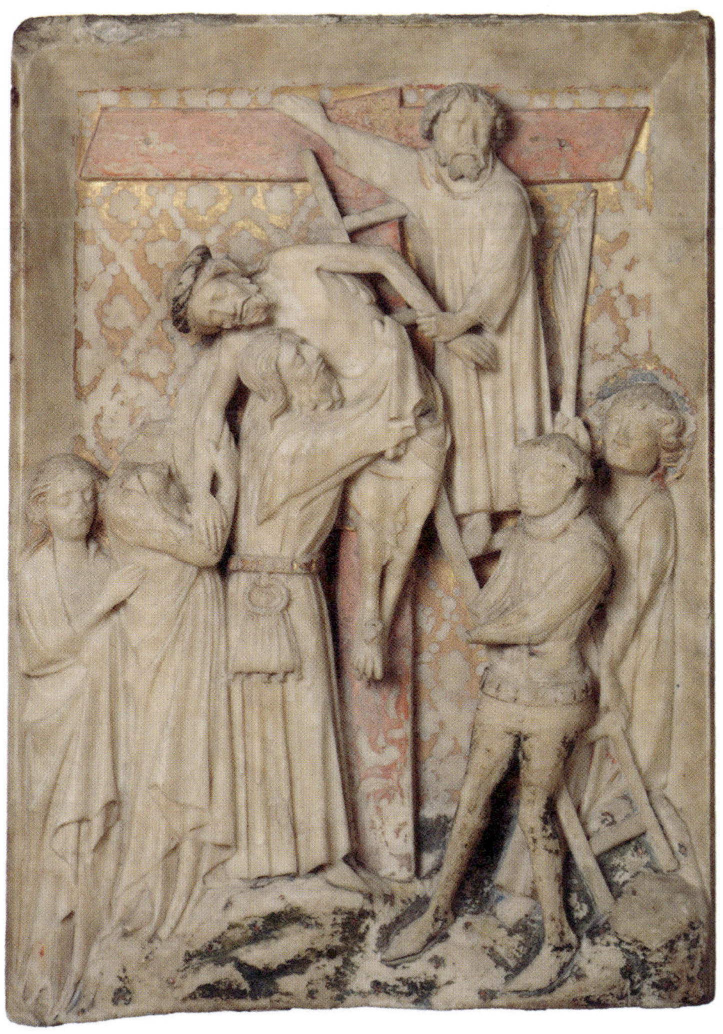

Deposition, alabaster relief, 1380–1400

back while her soft connection with Christ's forearm is mirrored by his own lifeless hand, which grazes her elbow. There is also great attention to detail – the purse hanging from a ring on Joseph's belt sags with the weight of its contents. We can still see flecks of paint on this panel – the cross is red-brown and the ground dark green, while the background has gilding like flocked wallpaper. Painting such detailed carvings would have made them seem more lifelike. The stone would have glowed in sunlight, further intensifying the experience of looking at something 'real'.

There are thirty recorded English alabaster panels showing the Deposition. Many of them, like this one, would have originally been part of larger altarpieces. Altarpieces had become an increasingly important part of the church service from around 1000, when the celebrant of Mass began to turn his back to the congregation in order to face the altar. The altarpiece provided a visual counterpoint that could be studied during this time. The Swansea Altarpiece dates to the second half of the fifteenth century and narrates the Joys of the Virgin Mary. It is striking because it remains intact and in its original oak frame. (Most were destroyed during the Reformation, or hastily exported.) The frame is painted crimson, blue and green, and an alabaster canopy, carved to look like Gothic tracery, projects beyond the seven panels. Alablasterers would probably have employed painters to colour panels such as these after their carvings were complete. This was common practice on the continent, and given the scale of production there is no reason to think it was not the case in England as well. However, while stone and wood sculptures were often coloured all over, alabaster was often only partially polychromed, allowing the natural luminescence of the stone to shine through.

TOMB BOOM

While many English alabaster sculptures and carvings were exported to the continent, the traffic was not all one-way. Artists such as Jean de Liège (*c.*1330–1381) from Flanders travelled to England to work on important alabaster commissions. His life is well documented and we can track his artistic career in a way we cannot do for most of the now anonymous English alablasterers. De Liège worked on the tomb of Queen Philippa, who had previously ordered six cartloads of alabaster from the Tutbury quarry to be delivered to London.

Queen Philippa came from the territorial county of Hainault, an area spanning the border of France and Belgium today, and was married to King Edward III at York Minster when she was seventeen. She was a popular queen – when Edward was fighting in France in the Hundred Years' War she successfully rallied English troops to see off a Scottish invasion, addressing the men from horseback before the Battle of Neville's Cross. She died in 1369 and her alabaster tomb effigy remains in its original location close to the shrine of Edward the Confessor in Westminster Abbey. Today it is partially obscured by the later installation of Henry V's Chantry Chapel. We can still see her slightly pursed

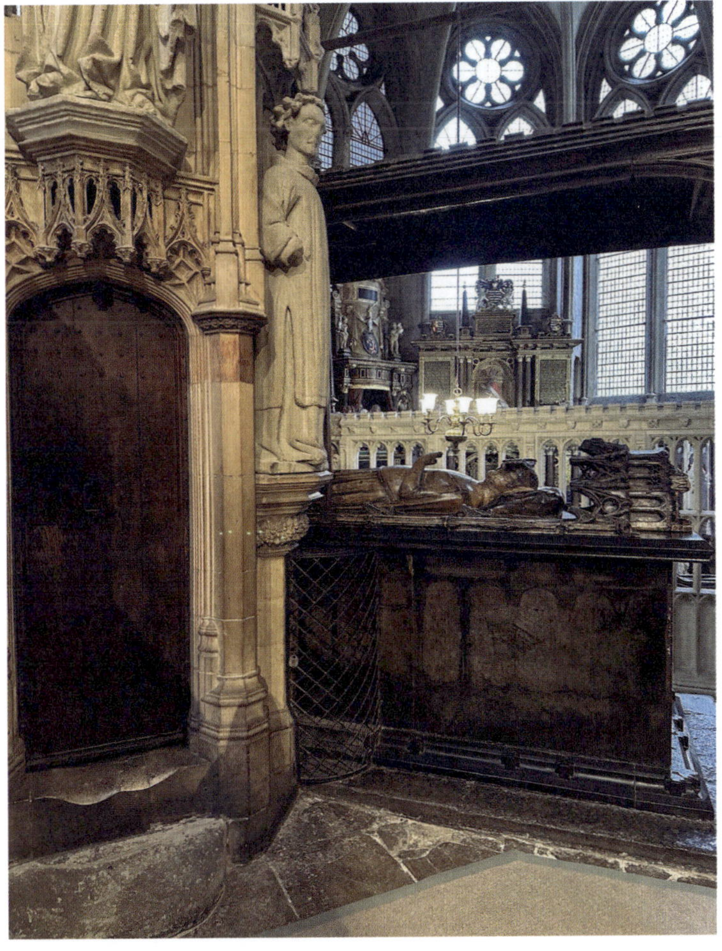

Queen Philippa of Hainault's tomb at Westminster Abbey, London, alabaster, *c.*1370

lips, her heavyset neck and her well-filled dress, but it is as if history is swallowing her up, with only her torso and face remaining visible.

King Edward III paid De Liège £133 (about £66,000 today) to carve Philippa's tomb. It would have taken a skilled tradesman twenty-two years to earn that amount in the fourteenth century.[5] De Liège wouldn't have worked alone on such a major commission. His contemporary André Beauneveu (*c*.1335–*c*.1400) may have been in London at this time and he is thought to have made some of the tomb's weepers (small statuettes that represented mourning family members), while John Orchard supplied the angels. Little remains of these figures today but they would have once adorned the architectural niches around the base in much the same way as those that surround the tomb of her husband, King Edward III, located next to hers in the Confessor's Chapel.

By the fourteenth century tomb production was an industry, and Queen Philippa's tomb offers us an insight into how medieval sculptors collaborated on prestigious projects. While some artists were specialists, others would have worked across a range of genres and styles. Alabaster was favoured by royalty for their tombs, and because of this, high-ranking clergy, knights and nobility often selected it too. A tomb made of alabaster or stone was seen as a permanent structure. It was a way of immortalising the recipient and channelling the prayers of the living. Such monuments added prestige to the nation's churches and monasteries, confirming patronage from the county's leading families, and in most of the churches I visited there was at least one alabaster tomb. The difference between the tombs of rich and poor was quality of carving, and this was reflected in the cost. The alabaster tomb effigies commissioned for Queen Philippa's fourth son John of Gaunt and his wife in old St Paul's in London cost £486 (about £240,000 today); fifty years later a double tomb in Berkshire cost only £22 (about £14,500 today).

Much of England's alabaster history has been lost to iconoclasm and fire. As a stone it is less robust than marble. It is soluble in water and turns to dust when burnt. But it continued to be the material of choice for sculptors until the seventeenth century, when marble took precedence and all eyes turned to Rome and its ancient and Renaissance marble masterpieces. For now the alabaster tomb sculptures that remained in the British Isles point us in another direction: to the ever-growing importance of the preservation and memorialisation of family dynasties, and the rise of portraiture as likeness once more.

6

APOCALYPSE NOW: THE ANNIHILATION OF HISTORY

1395–1570

BENDING DOWN TO look closely at the Wilton Diptych (*c.*1395–9; see overleaf) is like falling into an exquisite jewel box. It is a masterpiece of the refined French court style now known as International Gothic, which spread across Europe in the early decades of the fifteenth century. Folded and closed, this two-panel (diptych) painting is the size of a large book and is decorated with the arms of the king of England and his emblem, a white hart (a male deer). Opened, it reveals a highly detailed golden interior. On the left panel is Richard II. He is on his knees, his elegant hands coming together in prayer, attended by John the Baptist and two former kings, both patron saints of medieval England. Ninth-century Edmund wears red shoes and holds an arrow as a symbol of his martyrdom (he refused to renounce Christ when captured by the Vikings). Edward the Confessor holds out an oversized ring, recollecting his generosity when a poor man asked for alms. John extends his bare arm towards the king, who is dressed in an ornate red-and-gold cloak bearing the white hart. He faces a vision of the Virgin Mary and Christ on the right panel. They stand in a perfumed garden thronged with female angels all dressed in robes of ultramarine (the most expensive pigment available). The flag of England ripples on a tall pole, a tiny reflection of the British Isles just visible in the end finial. This level of detail suggests the artist was skilled in book illumination. But this is not from a manuscript.

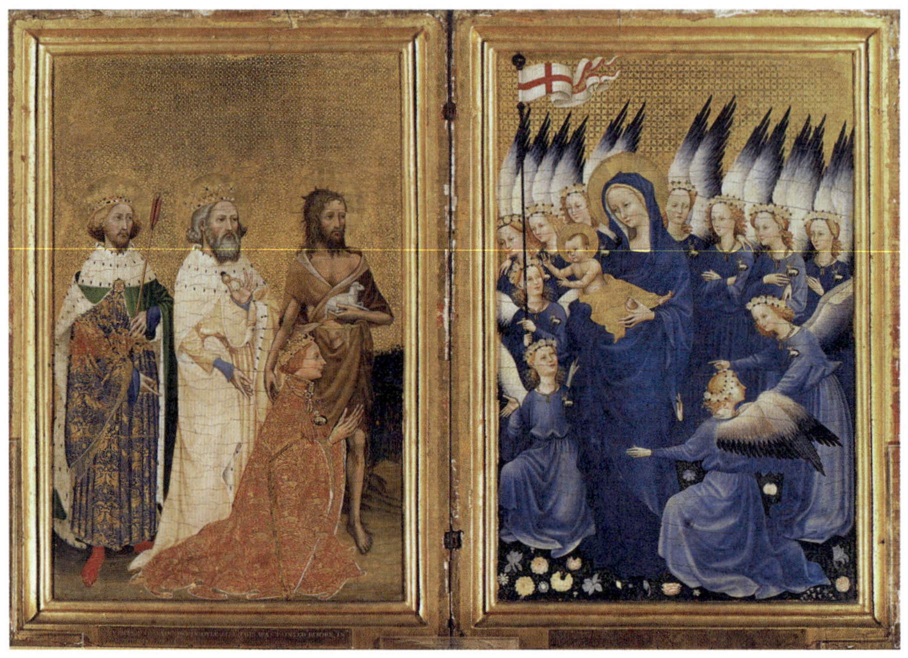

Wilton Diptych, egg tempera on wood, *c*.1395–9

It is a portrait of a king at prayer, a donor portrait but also a credible likeness. It marks the reappearance in British art of the identifiable individual – last seen 1,000 years earlier during the Roman occupation.

It is displayed at the National Gallery in a glass case, upright and open like a giant greetings card, much as it would have stood on a private altar when it was first made. Who could paint something so skilful? The artist who painted it is unknown today. In all likelihood it would have been commissioned in England from an artist working at Richard's court. Were they French? Although the king was born in France, he grew up in England and only ventured back once as an adult, to wed the six-year-old Isabella in Calais. The specific order of the saints behind the king mirrors the order of their chapels at Westminster Abbey, and the alignment of Richard with Edward the Confessor, centred in a white ermine cloak, is carefully considered. The nationality of the artist is lost but they were highly skilled, like the Limbourg brothers who created the sumptuous Book of Hours for the duc de Berry a decade or so later.

Edward was canonised for his religious dedication and Richard chose to align himself with the eleventh-century king to underline his own piety. Edward was held in high regard for employing diplomacy over warmongering and for his pious outlook – Richard used this portable altarpiece to suggest he was similarly dedicated to the Church and to peace. Marrying Isabella cemented a new peace treaty with France and Richard and the angels wear white harts under necklaces of broomcods, seeds of the broom plant, the emblem of French royalty.

IMMORTALISING DEATH

Richard II appears again, life-size with a forked goatee and luscious curls, on the vast stone screen that separates the quire from the nave in York Minster. On this fifteenth-century *pulpitum* he is surrounded by his ancestors, but not his hero Edward the Confessor. For the screen begins with William the Conqueror, Edward's Norman successor. All the subsequent kings of England up to Henry VI are represented, fifteen generations of men who supported the church through its Norman and Gothic incarnations. Traces of red paint around the neck of Richard II's robe, and on his hair and beard suggest the kings were once as brightly coloured as the scarlet niches in which they stand. It is a spectacular display of royal genealogy, designed to articulate a long and stable history for both church and state, one that filled me with awe as I walked towards it down the fourteenth-century Gothic nave (the widest and highest in England).

The screen originally had seven kings on either side. Henry VI was added later and stands a little shorter, his oversized crown dropping over his forehead as he looks down to read a book rather than looking out and wielding a sword like his forebears. He was seen as a shy and timid leader who disliked conflict. There is some irony therefore that his ineffectual rule led to civil war, what we now know as the War of the Roses (1455–87). This battle for royal supremacy between two rival houses from the Plantagenet line saw power switch hands between the House of Lancaster and the House of York several times before the final Tudor ascendancy.

During his reign Henry VI, the third king from the House of Lancaster, leaned heavily on advisers such as William de la Pole, first duke of Suffolk, who were subsequently blamed for the king's failures abroad and at home. Suffolk was a military commander and a prominent figure in the government but this didn't stop him being beheaded in 1450 when he was sailing to exile. His wife, Alice de la Pole, buried him at the Carthusian priory in Hull, where he had financed a hospital for the poor, but her own tomb is in her family church at Ewelme in Oxfordshire.

Alice de la Pole was Chaucer's granddaughter and the second cousin of Henry VI's father. She was a well-connected patron of the arts who supported the poet John Lydgate, maintained a well-stocked library and commissioned a series of tapestries on the life of St Anne. She had Lancastrian family connections but supported the House of York during the civil war, only reasserting her Lancastrian ties on her alabaster tomb. It is adorned with the arms of the Chaucer family and favours a new design used by other supporters of the House of Lancaster, including the seventh earl of Arundel. This novel design, known as a cadaver tomb, was first seen in continental Europe in the late fourteenth century, and in England after 1425. De la Pole's is the only one of its kind in England to feature a woman.

Nothing quite prepares you for seeing a desiccated corpse lying prone by a church altar. Initially the tomb looks fairly regular – a life-size effigy lying on top of an alabaster chest, dressed in a cloak, wimple and coronet. The rosary hanging from her belt and her praying hands emphasise Alice de la Pole's piety, while her powerful position at court is marked by the Order of the Garter (the highest chivalric honour in the land) worn on her left forearm. The tomb chest is covered with gilded angels standing in flowering meadows holding her family's coat of arms. It would have originally been brightly painted – traces of red, blue, green and white paint still cling to recessed niches. It is as you are looking at this that you first notice the open tracery windows that rim the base. Intrigued, you crouch down to take a look through and catch sight of something wholly unexpected: an emaciated alabaster cadaver.

Beneath the painted and gilded tomb lies a second carved figure of Alice de la Pole. It is her decaying body. Collarbones and ribs protrude, her brow is wrinkled and her long hair flows freely around her shoulders. You can see the sinews in her arms and her legs are bare and wizened. Why on earth would she have wanted to be immortalised in this way? It turns out the earth has a lot to do with it. Read this tomb from the ground up and the cadaver represents earthly reality, an indicator of our brief lifespan before we are reclaimed by the soil. The tomb effigy of the pious De la Pole above was for her family so they could say prayers for her soul while she lay there immobile, as

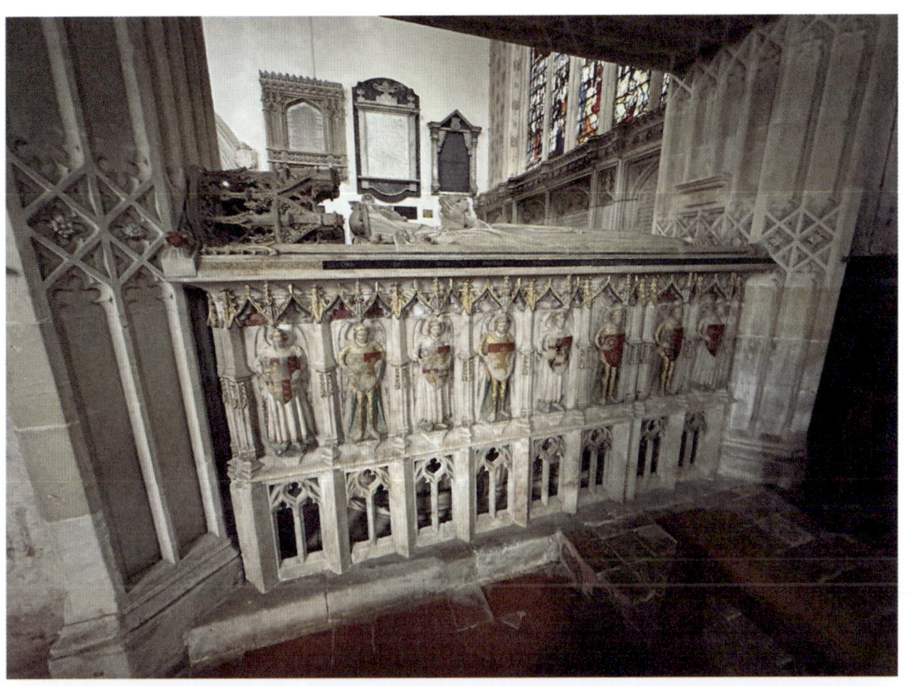

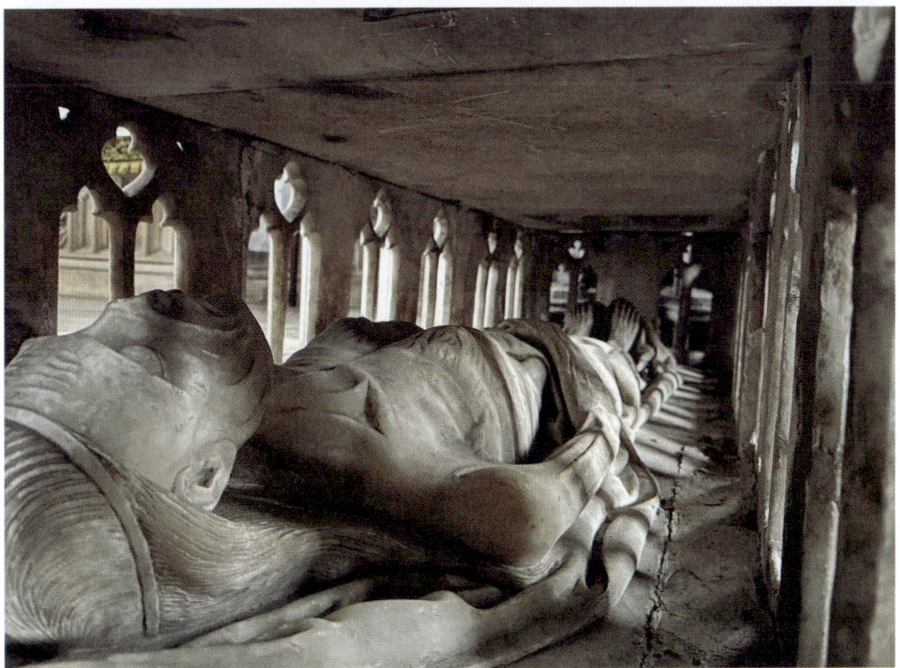

Alice de la Pole's alabaster cadaver tomb, Ewelme church, Oxfordshire, *c.*1475

if sleeping. But the unknown sculptor of her tomb indicates she will ascend to heaven imminently – four angels hold the pillow under her head, as if about to carry her towards her maker.

THE END OF THE WORLD AS WE KNOW IT

If royalty and nobility were keen to show their genealogical family trees inside churches and cathedrals, this may have been because there was a Christian precedent. In the Bible, Isaiah 11:1 says: 'And there shall come forth a rod out of the stem of Jesse and a Branch shall grow out of his roots.' From the twelfth century artists working across Europe visualised the prophecy of Isaiah and created ornate family trees showing Christ's ancestral line from Jesse and King David to the Virgin Mary. They sprouted in illuminated manuscripts, stained-glass windows and sculptures. This 'rod' would variously look like a tree trunk, a curling vine or the stem of a flowering plant. At times it sprouted from Jesse's genitals and at others from his heart or under his ribs.

In St Mary's Priory church in Abergavenny is a carved reclining fifteenth-century figure of Jesse. He is huge, double life-size, resting on his right elbow while an angel positions a cushion under his head. He wears a heavy robe cinched with a belt and a thick hat, but we still get a sense of his form shaping the cloth that drapes across his shoulders and is pulled to a peak by his knee. Today we can walk behind him and see he was carved from a single trunk of oak, hollowed out to make it lighter, but for its original audience it would have seemed solid and immutable. From his side once sprouted a multi-branched trunk that is thought to have reached up to 9 metres into the air to form a reredos (a screen positioned behind the altar). It was destroyed by Oliver Cromwell's troops in the seventeenth-century civil war (it was not alone, as we will see in Chapter 7) and a new stained-glass window behind Jesse now recreates the branching tree.

This Jesse is just one of many examples across the British Isles that would have enlivened church buildings. The oldest remaining stained-glass fragment in England, from around 1150, is at York Minster, and features a Tree of Jesse. A complete Tree of Jesse window from around 1310 still remains (although heavily restored), the red of Jesse's robes complementing the emerald green of the tree's two central stems. These repeatedly loop across each other to create oval mandorlas in the central windows for the main characters – King David with his harp, the Virgin, Christ – and end in spirals in the two outer windows, where other ancestors are represented.

Stained glass is often left out of histories such as this one, discounted as a 'minor art' or as a craft. But the artists who created these complex scenes must have studied, if not painted, illuminated manuscripts, and for many medieval people the interiors of churches would have been their main experience of figurative art. These windows represent the missing link between medieval manuscripts, with their heavily symbolic figures, and a growing sense of realism seen in the donor portraits that were now included in stained glass, such as in the *Pricke of Conscience* Window (*c.*1410) at All Saints North Street church in York.

If the Tree of Jesse reflects the long lineage of the Virgin Mary's family – forty-three generations from King David to Christ – then the *Pricke of Conscience* Window is at the other end of the spectrum. Gone is the security of a family tree, any sense of continuity and balance. This window is nothing less than a cataclysmic depiction of the end of the world. It is based on *The Pricke of Conscience*, a poem from around 1340 by an unknown poet from the north of England. The window features the section of the poem in which the world ends. There are floods and droughts, earthquakes and fires. Graves burst open and stars fall from the sky. The world ends all aflame – no wonder the

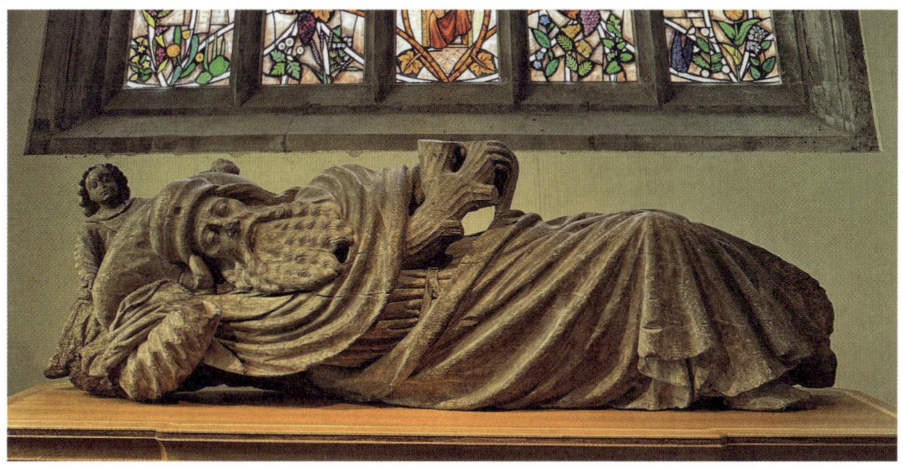

Carved oak sculpture of Jesse, St Mary's Priory church,
Abergavenny, late 15th century

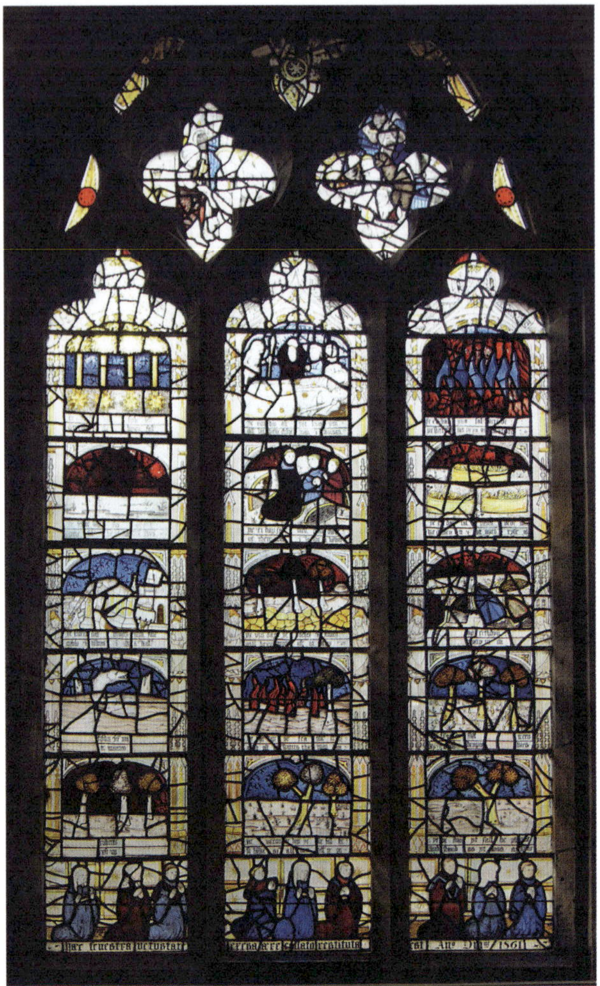

Pricke of Conscience
Window, All Saints
North Street church,
York, stained glass
*c.*1410

donors represented at the bottom of the window look so serious in
their prayers.

This window is highly unusual because when you stand in front
of it, you can read it visually and as a text. It is the only known
medieval window in Europe to incorporate the words of a poem and
belies the idea that stained glass was only for illiterate observers. It is
also unusual in that it is believed to be attributable to a single artist,
John Thornton of Coventry (*c.*1360s–1433). Thornton also made the
Great East Window in York Minster (1405–8) that recounts the entire
biblical story from the Creation to the Apocalypse. This window is

so huge that there are two stone walkways criss-crossing its tracery frame. It has more than 100 main lights (panels) and rises nearly 24 metres in height. Angels, prophets and saints throng the upper lights between the tracery. A contract still exists for the window, stipulating that Thornton had to work to a schedule and provide his own workforce and materials. It also lays out the money he would receive if he completed the commission. He would have used illuminated manuscripts for design ideas as he composed his cartoons (working drawings), and his style is reminiscent of the International Gothic of the Wilton Diptych. Mindful to include a portrait of the man paying for the window, Bishop Skirlaw of Durham, he includes him in a panel at the foot of the stained glass. Sitting in front of this vast wall of glowing glass today, reading individual scenes as a crescendo of organ music builds around you, still feels rather overwhelming.

PORTRAITS AS PROPAGANDA

If stained-glass windows implied the end of the world would be on a biblical scale, the reality was more terrifying. Between 1348 and 1351 a third of the population had been killed, not by the Four Horsemen of the Apocalypse but by bubonic plague. Three further bouts in the 1360s and 1370s decimated the remaining workforce. By the time Thornton completed his apocalyptic windows the population of the British Isles had shrunk from around eight million to just two or three million. Following this came the War of the Roses, which only ended when the grandson of Welsh adventurer Owain Tudur (a Lancaster veteran) defeated Richard III in the Battle of Bosworth in 1485 to become King Henry VII.

The Tudors were strategic. Henry VII combined the red rose of Lancaster with the white rose of Yorkshire to create the Tudor double rose that became emblematic of his union of the two rival houses when he married Elizabeth of York in 1486. You can still see evidence of them today. At York Minster, the thirteenth-century Rose Window was reglazed with alternating red and double roses, and Tudor roses were carved on the choir stalls in St Mary's Priory church in Abergavenny. These celebrated the marriage of Henry VII's eldest son and heir Arthur, aged fifteen, to Catherine of Aragon, as they set up court at nearby Ludlow Castle in Shropshire. But within a year Arthur was dead and Catherine was betrothed to his younger brother, Henry.

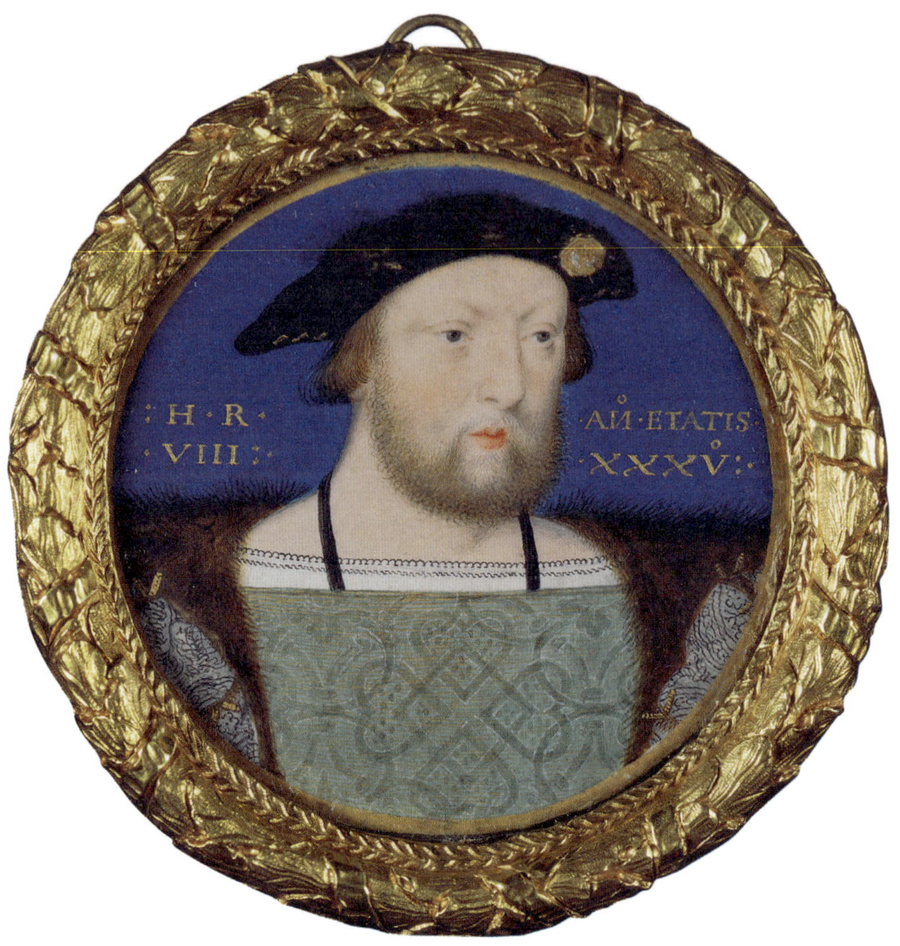

Susannah Horenbout, miniature of Henry VIII, watercolour on vellum laid
on playing card, 1526–7

When Henry VIII came to the throne in 1509 he was not shy of
the battlefield, but he also understood the benefit of soft power. He
assembled around him the very best artists, musicians and scientists from
across Europe while holding showy jousts in the tiltyard at Greenwich
Palace to demonstrate his sporting ability for an international audience
of ambassadors and diplomats. At this time in London we see the Italian
sculptor Pietro Torrigiano (1472–1528), the Flemish miniaturists Lucas
(1490–1544) and Susannah Horenbout (1503–1554) and the German-
Swiss painter Hans Holbein the Younger (1497/98–1543). Their art
was used by Henry to impress, flatter and seduce international guests,

from the greatest spectacles at court to the smallest miniatures that could be slipped into an ambassador's pocket and transported across the Channel. The Venetian envoy witnessed a theatrical exchange of gifts in 1527 to mark the 'Eternal Peace' with France, whereby the king's astronomer Nicolaus Kratzer (from Germany) worked with Holbein to create a dramatic cosmological ceiling in a specially constructed banqueting house in Greenwich, causing the envoy to write of 'never having witnessed the like anywhere [else]'.[1]

The cosmological ceiling was Holbein's first royal commission. He had been in London six months, having left Basel in Switzerland as the Protestant Reformation gathered pace and religious commissions dried up. He carried a letter of introduction from the Dutch humanist Erasmus to Sir Thomas More, the king's chancellor. These men were part of an intellectual circle that stretched across Europe. Erasmus had published More's radical satire *Utopia* a decade earlier; Holbein and his older brother Ambrosius had furnished it with woodcut illustrations. Holbein painted More's portrait in 1528 but he left London later that year, returning to Basel to capitalise on the void left by the death of the Renaissance master Albrecht Dürer (1471–1528). But by 1532 he had been lured back to London and was employed as the 'king's painter' on a salary of £30 a year (£13,000 today).

What was London like for a foreigner who lived there, rather than one who was passing through? When Holbein returned to London for the second time he began with commissions to paint Hanseatic League members of the Steelyard, a community of wealthy European merchants who enjoyed privileged trading rights in the city. Holbein may have felt comfortable working for German merchants such as twenty-three-year-old Derich Born, as they spoke the same language. Holbein's Born is mesmeric. He appears in front of a vine, his black clothes finely painted so we notice the shine of his satin sleeves and the texture of his fur collar. He looks out at us with calm solemnity, one arm resting on a parapet. His cheekbones are chiselled, his lips pressed together. Under the lip of the parapet Latin words appear to be carved in stone. Translated, these read: 'If you added a voice, this would be Derich his very self. You would be in doubt whether the painter or his father made him.' This mirrors the text on a Dürer portrait and suggests Holbein still saw himself as competing to be Dürer's successor.

These artists from continental Europe brought with them the latest Renaissance thinking. While the Flemish Horenbouts continued the tradition of illuminated manuscript painting they had been taught by their father, they reworked it to capitalise on the new fashion for portrait miniatures. Susannah Horenbout had sold her work to Dürer and such artists would have been acutely aware of his breathtaking naturalism. Henry VIII purposefully stocked his court with Europeans well versed in Italian humanism and Renaissance fidelity to nature, and they learned from one another – Holbein asked Susannah's brother Lucas to teach him how to paint in miniature. Susannah was officially recorded as a gentlewoman in the service of the queen, but she may have been responsible for reshaping her brother's image of Henry from doughy-faced jouster to bearded and imposing king of England. In the case of many women artists from this period, despite being feted during their lifetimes their paintings have subsequently been reattributed to their male contemporaries, making it very difficult to identify their hand with any certainty. Scholars are now trying to redress this, and there's strong reason to believe that it was Susannah's brush that broadened Henry's shoulders and gave him gravitas in miniature, a likeness that Holbein later used as the basis for his larger-than-life wall paintings of the king in the newly fashioned Whitehall Palace.

Holbein painted and sketched many men and women of the court, including a pair of travelling diplomats in *The Ambassadors* (1533). The fur trim on Jean de Dinteville and Bishop Georges de Selve's robes makes you want to reach out and stroke them even though the distorted skull in the foreground suggests we should not be so easily seduced by material things. Portraiture was increasingly popular in the British Isles, growing out of an interest in genealogy and lineage and seen as a way of recording existence, of cheating death. Portraits were commissioned to mark promotions – Thomas Cromwell had Holbein paint him when he was appointed master of the Jewel House in 1532 – and were also commissioned to mark marriages and births, or to celebrate friendship. But few had the impact of Holbein's portrait of Henry VIII and his third wife Jane Seymour, painted on the wall of the Privy Chamber of Henry's new palace at Whitehall in 1537, in the room where Henry greeted his most important guests.

The Whitehall Mural was lost in a palace fire in 1698, but part of the original cartoon (scale drawing) survives, as do numerous painted copies. There were four full-length figures, with Henry's parents, Henry VII and Elizabeth of York, on the steps behind the reigning couple. They stand on a lavish rug that has been arranged around a central sarcophagus, which is engraved with Latin verses celebrating the Tudor lineage. Henry VIII

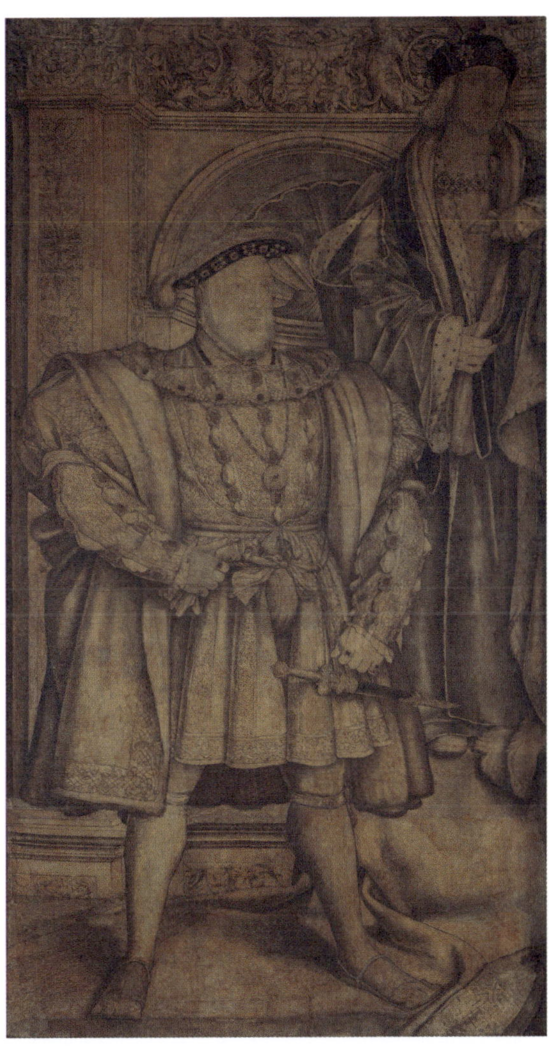

Hans Holbein the Younger,
ink and watercolour
cartoon for his Whitehall
Mural of Henry VIII and
family, *c*.1536–7

is forty-six, ten years older than he is in the Horenbout miniatures, and his expanding girth is balanced by his exaggerated shoulder span. Legs spread wide, codpiece poking through his golden robes, his shoulders swathed in red velvet and fur, he looks directly out at us, his subjects. While he is life-size he is also positioned on a step, so if you were standing on the ground next to him he would tower over you. His wife and mother have been painted as quiet and passive players in the scene, and despite the elevation of his father behind him, all eyes would have been on his expansive, macho son.

There is only one complete copy of the Whitehall Mural, painted by Flemish artist Remigius van Leemput (1607–1675) over 100 years later in 1667, and it measures less than a metre square. But the original wall painting inspired a myriad portraits of Henry VIII, some by Holbein and others by artists cashing in on this iconic image of the Tudor king. A copy at Petworth has Henry clad in a black cloak with white ermine trim, standing in a flattened Renaissance interior. If we compare it to Holbein's Whitehall cartoon we see how masterful Holbein was at creating credible space while simultaneously restricting depth, so the people he painted were as close as they could be to our own world. The Petworth copy may have originated in his studio but it lacks the skill and touch of his own brush.

IDOLS AND ICONOCLASM

Henry's court was one of the richest in Europe and it teemed with artists and musicians. But there was another, darker side to Henry, a destructive and avaricious side, that would stop at nothing to get his own way. The pope says divorce and remarriage are not allowed? Let's turn our back on the Catholic Church, then, the one that has had a monopoly on faith in the British Isles for 1,000 years. Coffers running low? Let's shut down the monasteries and nunneries, pension off the remaining servants of God and take their lands, properties and wealth for our own. For all the beautiful palaces he built and the books, tapestries and paintings he commissioned, Henry's true legacy was the destruction of the vast majority of medieval art in his kingdom and with it a considerable chunk of British history.

This destruction is evident everywhere you go. I could see it in the empty niches of York Minster's main entrance and on the ornate tracery screen behind the high altar in St Illtud's church in Llantwit Major, Glamorgan, where not one sculpture remains. It is visible in the ruins of Margam Abbey in Glamorgan, of Easby Abbey in North Yorkshire, in Glastonbury and Lewes, Whitby and Walsingham. On the island of Lindisfarne only traces of the once great priory remain – a few chevroned pillars, the odd open fireplace, a worn spiral staircase that once led to the monks' dormitories. Twelfth-century Lindisfarne Priory was one of the first monasteries to be targeted by Henry VIII in 1537 as he systematically stripped the Church of its assets. Between

1536 and 1540 he closed down around 800 religious houses, evicted 9,000 nuns and monks and seized £120,000 of land (£50 million today).

Henry VIII's iconoclasm was twofold. By seizing land he could enrich his own purse and settle debts. But he cloaked this in a rigorous desire to rid the country of bloated religious houses as he rejected the pope's version of Christianity for his own. The new Church of England experienced much reform: candles could no longer be burnt in front of images of saints, and relics were soon banned too. Saints' feast days were abolished; pilgrimages were forbidden. Henry had a particular dislike for the cult of St Thomas Becket, and his gold jewelled shrine – one of the richest in Europe – was completely destroyed. Incidents of iconoclasm became frequent, with Henry's right-hand man Cromwell storing up treasures taken from priories and abbeys before burning them.

Henry had set himself up as the head of the newly formed Church of England but it was during the brief reign of his teenage son, Edward VI (r. 1547–53), that the worst of the iconoclasm occurred, when the Crown doubled down on its desire to remove all 'idolatrous' images of Christ, the Virgin and the saints, including roods (Crucifixion sculptures) and wall paintings. Scotland followed suit in the 1560s, with similar rigour. This broadly reflected the goals of the Reformation that swept across Europe, aided by the printing press and the relative ease with which the religious pamphlets of the Protestant Martin Luther could now be disseminated to propel change.

When we look back at Britain's religious heritage, there is a gaping void where works from this period and earlier should be. When we visit churches, we can see holes in beams where roods were once displayed. Many portable works of art were sold into continental Europe and gold and silver church plate was melted down. Other works of art were hidden: religious sculptures were bricked into narrow stairwells and wall paintings were whitewashed in situ. Many were not discovered again until the nineteenth or twentieth centuries, such as the Wenhaston Doom in St Peter's church in Wenhaston, Suffolk (see overleaf).

The church had begun raising money to replace its rood beam in the 1480s. Below this was a rood screen; above was to be a Doom. The Wenhaston Doom, painted on Baltic oak panels, was an evocation of the Day of Judgement (or Doomsday), and was completed around 1520. Nailed to its surface was a wooden crucifix and figures of the Virgin Mary and St John the Evangelist. You can still see the bare wood and

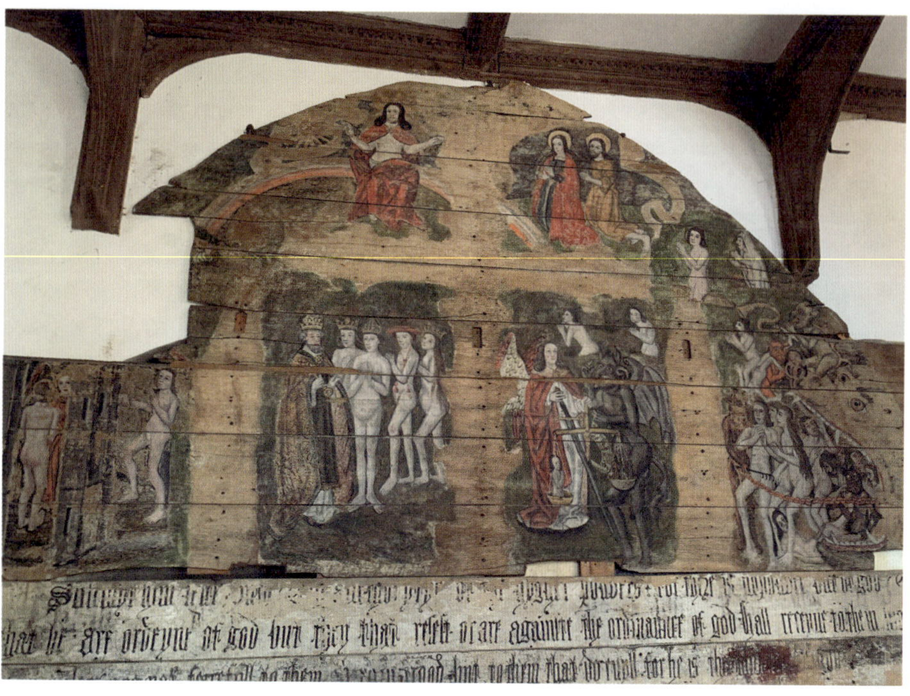

Wenhaston Doom, St Peter's church, Suffolk, tempera on oak boards, 1500–20

nail holes where these sculptures were hammered into place, ghostly reminders of past violence. The Doom artist used the original sculptures as punctuation marks for the painted scene. Christ sits in majesty in the arched upper portion, along with the Virgin Mary and John the Baptist, their golden haloes gleaming. Today the painting occupies a low wall facing you as you enter, adjacent to the nave. But originally it was up high and the artist positioned the heavenly figures as if we are looking up at them, the red underside of the painted tracery arch on which Christ sits clearly visible. In the lower sections we see naked virtuous men and women on the left, those who have been condemned to imprisonment in hell on the right, and the archangel Michael weighing souls in front of an impatient Devil in the centre.

This Doom was most likely painted by journeymen (hired hands) who moved around East Anglia, as the painting is not of a high quality. Bodies are not in proportion and the colours are rudimentary, but it communicates the story simply and effectively. Probably in response to King Edward VI's edict of 1547 that demanded the destruction of roods and the whitewashing of church walls, this Doom was painted over less than thirty years after it was installed. It was only in 1892, when St Peter's was being renovated, that the painting was rediscovered. Timbers from the nave had been placed in the churchyard to be burnt but there was heavy rain overnight and the whitewash that had covered them started to dissolve. The Doom saw daylight after nearly 450 years.

There would once have been hundreds of Doom paintings across the British Isles. Many would have been positioned like the one at Wenhaston so the congregation, facing the altar, would always be aware of the impending Judgement Day. This was the day when (hopefully) their good deeds would take them to Christ's side rather than see them chained up by the Devil. If Henry VIII were to face similar judgement, he would surely be heading straight to the winged beast to be tortured for eternity for crimes against culture. Would his daughter Elizabeth fare any better?

FOLK ICONS FROM DEEP TIME

Before we move on to Elizabeth's reign, I want to share with you a church that was not mutilated, decapitated, burnt or whitewashed during the Reformation. This was probably because it featured sculptures that were not inspired by the Bible but drew on ancient folklore and an altogether different sense of belonging. The twelfth-century carvings on St Mary's church in Kilpeck, Herefordshire are ranged around the exterior of the red sandstone church and include dozens of small corbels (supporting trusses) carved into animal and human heads. One man peeps out from inside a dragon's mouth; another hangs limp in the jaws of a bear. The carvings are no longer detailed but still communicate through their bulging eyes and expressive mouths. There are pigs' heads and moustachioed men, rams and fishes. And, the most unexpected of all, a naked woman holding open her enlarged vagina (see overleaf).

This woman is not a one-off. She is known as a Sheela-na-Gig, a character found on medieval churches across the British Isles from Tipperary to Anglesey, Orkney to Essex, as well as in France and Spain. Was she an ancient Celtic goddess, a remnant of a religion that once spanned much of Atlantic Europe? But why then would she be

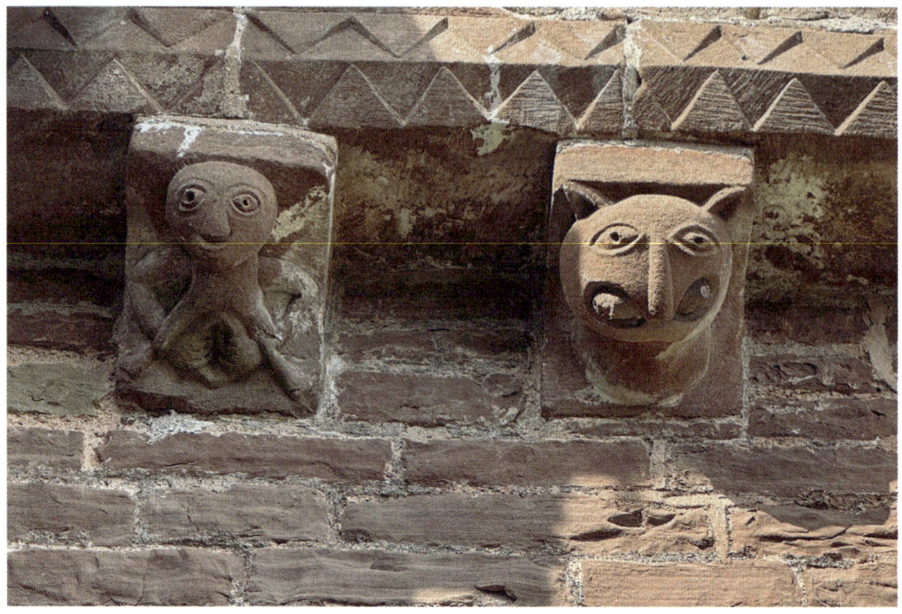

Sheela-na-Gig (left), St Mary's church, Kilpeck, Herefordshire, red sandstone corbel,
12th century

carved afresh on a twelfth-century church? Was she rather seen as a warning for pious Christians to stay away from the temptations of the body? Given the emphasis on the birth canal, it is more likely that the Sheela-na-Gig was linked to fertility, perhaps the embodiment of a folkloric tale or someone to pray to for a swift and trouble-free birth. (Childbirth killed Edward VI's mother, Jane Seymour, and during the Tudor period, one in forty births resulted in a mother's death.)

Also at Kilpeck is a Green Man sculpture. He flanks the church door, as if holding up the central tympanum (the arched space above the lintel). Visually he links to the tree of life on the tympanum above, a Christian motif from the Garden of Eden that also symbolised Christ's position as the vine from which we all sprout and grow. Two vines bearing grapes also curve across this sculpture, but these ones grow out of the Green Man's mouth.

The Green Man is a modern name for sculptures across Europe that share the symbolism of a man with leaves growing across his face or out of his mouth or beard. Max Porter, in his experimental novel *Lanny*, envisioned him as having arms made of larch and cuckoo spit on his chin.[2] He is as old as time, moving across generations as easily as we cross the road. He represents the land, the earth, the cyclical patterns of nature. He may have originally been a forest god, worshipped to bring good harvests and hearty yields from the land, but here we cannot help but see the parallels between Christ's vine (and Jesse's vine) and the Green Man's vine. The Christian Church adopted many pagan festivals as their own, including Christmas and Easter. Could these festivals once have been the preserve of the Green Man and the Sheela-na-Gig? Was the Green Man worshipped on the winter solstice to bring good harvests the following year? Was Easter a time of rebirth and fertility, when the Sheela-na-Gig would seem most significant? This could explain the unusual fusion at Kilpeck that marries a Christian place of worship with folk figures sprouting from an ancient European root.

$$7$$

FOR QUEEN (AND KING) AND COUNTRY

1558–1700

AT BURGHLEY HOUSE in Lincolnshire Sir William Cecil, later Lord Burghley, looks out at us today from a wall of portraits. He is wearing plush red velvet garter robes and holds a slender staff indicating his position as lord high treasurer. The portrait is attributed to Marcus Gheeraerts the Younger (1561–1636), a Flemish artist who moved to London with his family as a young boy. The Gheeraerts family had fled the persecution of Protestants by the Spanish in Flanders, three years into what became the Eighty Years' War.

On the same wall is Gheeraerts the Younger's portrait of Queen Elizabeth I, the daughter of Henry VIII and Anne Boleyn, who ascended the throne after her brother Edward and elder sister Mary died. Edward was a child king, faithful to his father's new Church of England, who succumbed to tuberculosis in 1553. Mary, the daughter of Henry VIII's first wife, Catherine of Aragon, was fiercely Catholic and restored many aspects of the faith during her five-year reign. She died of stomach cancer in 1558, and Elizabeth, aged twenty-five, became queen. She was a Protestant and quickly reversed Mary's religious policies, building a court of Protestant allies around her. Lord Burghley was there from the beginning, a trusted officer who was a knight of the Garter and, from 1571, controlled England's purse-strings.

What was the country like in 1571, when Burghley became lord treasurer? England and Scotland were teeming with Protestant refugees from France and the Low Countries who sought refuge from persecution. They brought with them sought-after skills – Gheeraerts's father had been an etcher in Bruges and Antwerp and set himself up in business in London, offering both prints and portraits. Lord Burghley was halfway through building his vast house in the middle of England, a three-day ride from London, although given his duties at court it is unlikely that he would have had the opportunity to spend much time there. London increasingly welcomed ships from further afield and in this year the Royal Exchange opened, London's first purpose-built international trading market. Elizabeth had been on the throne for thirteen years and was thirty-eight years old. She remained unmarried and controlled her image through restricting those who painted her from life, forcing artists to work from pre-approved patterns.

THE VIRGIN QUEEN

Now scroll forwards twenty years and we find Gheeraerts the Younger working on a full-length painting of Elizabeth I. He was one of the first artists in Britain to use canvas rather than panels for such portraits, allowing him to work on a large scale like this. Completed the year before she turned sixty, the picture features the queen as if she is an allegory of Fortune. She wears an ornate white dress studded with pearls, symbolising her virginity. She is literally festooned with pearls – they drip from her hair and hang in long strings around her neck. Lightning crackles to her left but the sun burns through cloud on her right. She stands immobile, holding her fan and gloves, poised on a giant map of England. She meets our gaze calmly, unsmiling and unemotional. Her satin toes point to Ditchley Park in Oxfordshire, where this painting once hung. It was commissioned by Sir Henry Lee, a former master of the armouries and queen's champion who had fallen out of favour but who hoped to win back her support with an elaborate pageant of which this was to be the *pièce de résistance.*

Portraits of Elizabeth exist from when she was a young girl to the year of her death. Early portraits show her wearing a court headdress over neatly parted auburn hair or white and red roses in a furze of sandy curls. At times she looks modestly away, but more often than not she meets our eye. She wears a crown, a ruff or pearls in her hair; she is framed against pricey aquamarine in miniature or standing full height straddling the globe. As she became queen she tried to control the quality of images of her in circulation – Walter Raleigh said she ordered second-rate likenesses to be burnt – and many artists had to work from sanctioned portraits rather than from life, borrowing suitable props and clothing. Her motto was *Semper Eadem*, Latin for 'always the same', adopted to suggest her steadfastness and the stability of the country. It also reflects her desire to control how she was portrayed – to show herself as an ageless queen, ruling Britain with undiminishing power.

Many portraits of the queen were in miniature. Susannah Horenbout briefly overlapped at court with Levina Teerlinc (1510s–1576), a fellow limner (miniaturist) who was paid more per year than Holbein and worked at the royal court for thirty years until her death in 1576, when she was in her sixties. Frustratingly, it is hard to pinpoint any

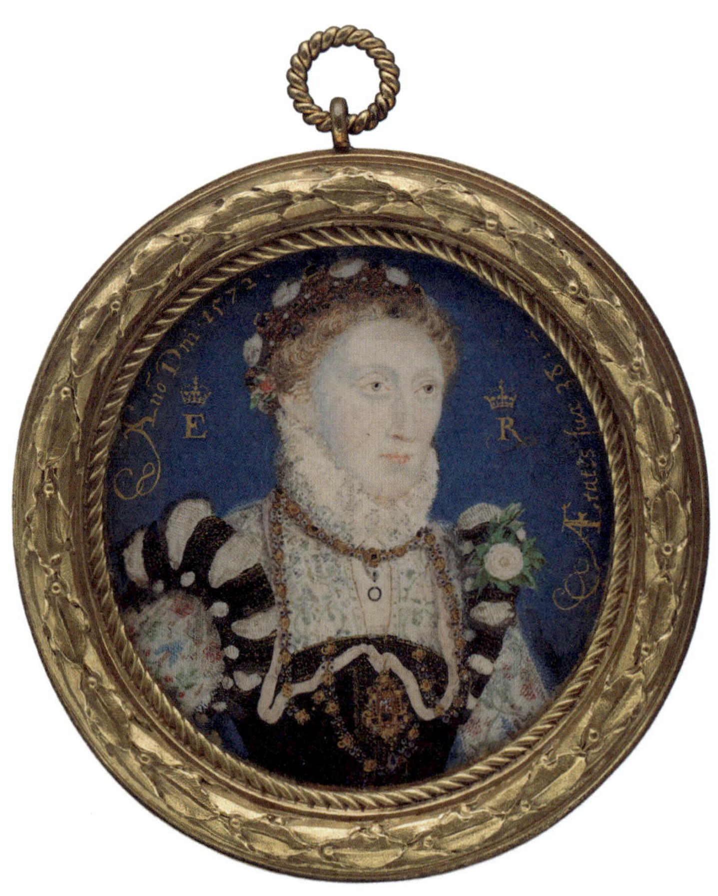

Nicholas Hilliard, miniature of Elizabeth I, watercolour on vellum, 1572

of her miniatures with accuracy today because they were misattributed to Nicholas Hilliard (1547–1619) and other male painters after her death. Teerlinc, like the Horenbouts, was from Flanders but Hilliard was born in England, probably in Exeter where his father worked as a goldsmith. He completed his first miniatures aged thirteen and had secured himself a position at court by the age of twenty-five, when he first painted Elizabeth I.

Hilliard had an unusual amount of access to the queen and was her official limner. In an oval watercolour just 5 centimetres tall we see the queen looking young and not sporting the heavy trappings of office. There are fresh flowers on her left shoulder and she wears a floral undershirt with a modest ruff. No shadows darken her face – it is as if Hilliard has shone a flashlight on her features, leaving only the lips, nostrils, pupils and a hint of eyebrow visible. He achieved this by having her pose in her garden in bright sunlight. This pale ageless approach chimed with the queen's motto of *Semper Eadem*, for she was already nearly forty.

Portrait miniatures were designed to be handled at close range, but even so it is hard to see the layers of hatching that Hilliard applied to puff up sleeves and curl hair. He used powdered gold in later miniatures to convey the warmth of her crown and applied coloured resin over silver to suggest luminescent rubies and emeralds. In his *Treatise on the Arte of Limning*, written around 1600, he explained that he had learned his skills from copying engravings by Dürer, the European master of Renaissance naturalism. His miniatures were used by royalty as international negotiation tools for betrothals and political unions, as well as for gifts and as jewellery, where they could be worn hanging from a ribbon. The scale meant they could be most discreet, perfect for secret lovers, and their size made them easy to carry abroad.

THE BEGINNINGS OF EMPIRE

Perhaps Gheeraerts used a Hilliard miniature for his Ditchley Portrait – the queen's pale face lacks detail in contrast to her ornate gown. Or perhaps he had seen one of the Armada portraits, completed by artists unknown to us today, that celebrate Elizabeth I's defeat of the Spanish Armada off the English coast in 1588. Three examples of this painting survive from three separate workshops. Elizabeth's right hand rests lightly on a small globe, as if she is commanding the seas visible in the paintings behind her. British fireships attack the Spanish to her right, but it is the storm seen over her left shoulder that will ultimately destroy the fleet. Like the symbolic views, her clothing appears representative of power rather than a worn reality. The sheer number of ropes of pearls would surely topple any leader and it would be highly restrictive to wear a ruff at such an angle or sleeves of that magnitude. The artists commissioned to celebrate Elizabeth's great victory against the Spanish did not turn to realism to convey her power. Like the globe under her hand, this portrait values the symbolic over the real, in defiance of the Renaissance naturalism that had been wowing mainland Europe for over 100 years. It was painted to assert Elizabeth's supremacy and tell a story of a thwarted Catholic takeover of Protestant England. In a country that no longer supported religious imagery and icons, the Virgin Queen took the

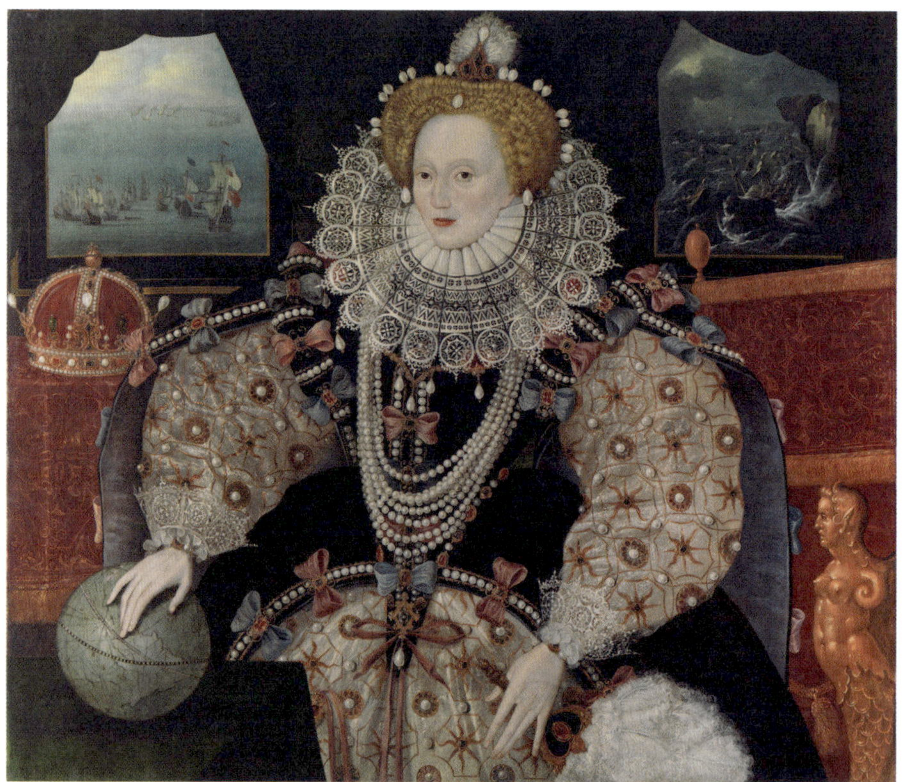

Armada portrait (Drake version) of Elizabeth I, oil on oak panel, *c.*1588

place of the Virgin Mary as head of the Church, the state and Britain's destiny.

Let's look again at the globe Elizabeth is touching in the Drake version (possibly commissioned by Sir Francis Drake, and owned by his descendants for many years). Elizabeth's hand is not resting on England but on the Americas. This is a portrait of a monarch who has not just successfully defended her own territory, but who also has an eye on the expansion of it. Surrounding Elizabeth's court in London was a city teeming with diversity. We have already met the merchants of the Hanseatic League with whom Holbein did business, and the Huguenot and Flemish artists fleeing the long reach of Spain. In 1585 the Barbary Company was established to trade exclusively with the large coastal states of North Africa. Ambassadors such as 'Abd al-Wahid bin Mas'ud from Morocco visited London for long enough to have their portraits painted. In his portrait from 1600 he appears in white robes and turban, sword hanging from a cross-body strap, aged forty-two. He was not unique in visiting London from another continent. Ottoman Turks and North Africans were present in Elizabethan London, so much so that Shakespeare could confidently centre his 1601 play *Othello* around a Moorish (North African) general in the Venetian army. In 1600 the East India Company was founded to extend trade links to India and Southeast Asia (we will witness the impact of this in Chapter 9).

Elizabeth did not grant Mas'ud's request for aid to support a Moorish attack on Catholic Spain. She had sent her own fleet there after the failed Spanish Armada and later captured Cádiz with Robert Devereux, second earl of Essex and court favourite, in command. (We can see him bloom at court as the handsome young man in Hilliard's *Young Man among Roses* from around 1587.) She was also fighting the Nine Years' War in Ireland. Since Norman times Ireland had experienced repeated colonisation by Britain and in 1542 Henry VIII had declared himself king of Ireland. Irish chieftains in Ulster rebelled against English rule and the Nine Years' War engulfed the whole country. The Irish were supported by the Spanish, clearly keen to weaken their Protestant rival that they had failed to conquer.

With the war in Ireland and ongoing battles in Spain, as well as increasing international trade that turned London into the 'choicest storehouse in the world',[1] you would think Elizabeth would have had her hands full. But an acute awareness of Spain and Portugal's success in monetising exploration and harvesting resources in South America, Africa and India caused Elizabeth to look northwest to try and find a safe and speedy passage to the rich spice islands of Southeast Asia. While a path through the ice remained elusive, rich fishing grounds were discovered, as was the coastline of North America.

In 1585 an English expedition set sail for Roanoke in the newly named Virginia. The land was named by Raleigh in honour of England's Virgin Queen. On this particular voyage was John White (*c.*1539–*c.*1593), a gentleman painter in his forties. White was the eyes of the voyage and was tasked with mapping the ground, documenting the landscape and its flora and fauna, and sketching the people he met. As a result England received its first images of America, painted in watercolour and circulated at court on White's return.

Over the course of five voyages White traversed the coast from Frobisher Bay in modern-day Canada to Puerto Rico in the Caribbean. More than fifty paintings survive showing scorpions and shark-suckers,

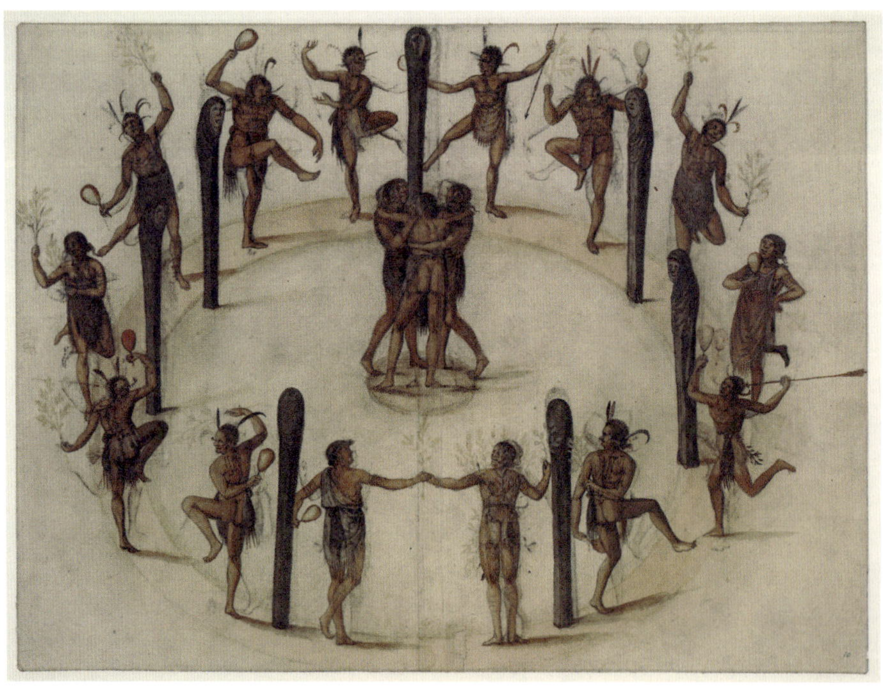

John White, *A festive dance*, watercolour over graphite on paper, *c.*1585–90

frigate birds and fireflies. In the British Museum's print room I came face to face with men with Mohicans and tattooed women, hunters, fishermen and dancers. The dead were laid out in a charnel house while the living formed circles alongside ancestral statues, offering prayers to unknown gods. White painted the houses and settlements of the Algonquian Indians with their bark-covered roofs and circular enclosures, as well as the hastily erected English camps with their moats and fortified walls. The land he paints looks well tended and fertile and the seas literally jump with fish. The Algonquians appear to pose for him, well fed and smiling. But we should treat these images with caution. White did not paint the atrocities the English carried out when they set fire to the town and crops of Aquascogoc over a missing silver cup or when they beheaded Wingina, the chieftain of Roanoke. White also didn't show the indigenous Algonquians dying of European diseases.

White was the only British artist to venture to the New World in these early years of European colonisation and in 1590 thirty of his watercolours were turned into engravings in Thomas Harriot's *A Briefe and True Report of the New Found Land of Virginia*, published by Theodor de Bry. While White's Algonquian Indians appear with brown skin, black hair, tattoos and oversized ear ornaments, their fringed clothes made from natural fibres and skins, in the hand-coloured engravings the same figures become exotic dancers in yellow skirts who sport red feathers in their hair like court jesters. In *A Festive Dance* the totems of hooded ancestors become classical sculptures and the three indigenous figures in the centre of the print morph into a pale-skinned, plump-bottomed incarnation of the Three Graces. White's original paintings were later gathered together in two albums, but it was the prints that were reproduced across Europe and shaped continental views of America's indigenous population.

GREAT BRITAIN?

Despite ruling for an impressive forty-five years, Elizabeth I could not halt time and remain *Semper Eadem*. She died on 24 March 1603 aged sixty-nine and without an heir. Within three days her personal ring was delivered to King James VI of Scotland, indicating his accession to the English throne. He was her first cousin twice removed and her closest living relative; within a fortnight he was on the road to London to claim his new crown as King James I of England. He promised to return to Scotland every three years, but over the course of his twenty-two-year reign over both countries he only returned once.

James VI of Scotland was the only son of Elizabeth's cousin and nemesis, the Catholic Mary, Queen of Scots. Mary had been brought up in the French court as the future wife of the dauphin, who had ascended to the French Crown in 1559 only to die seventeen months later. As a childless widow she had to negotiate with the newly powerful Protestant lords to ensure her return to Scotland was not a risk to her life. She married her half-cousin Henry Stewart, Lord Darnley, and had a baby boy, James, before her increasingly malevolent husband was blown up and suspicion fell on Mary. Elizabeth used this as an excuse to keep her under house arrest until she was executed for treason in 1587. James, meanwhile, was raised away from his mother with a Protestant tutor, and became king of Scotland when he was thirteen months old when she was forced to abdicate. When she was killed a few months shy of his twenty-first birthday he was quick to ease tensions with Elizabeth, writing to her and expressing his hope that they could work together 'to strengthen and unite this isle'.[2]

James VI hated sitting for portraits and consequently few were done from life, but we can still track him from boy to man through those that remain. The Scottish court, like Elizabeth's, was attractive to Protestant artists from northern Europe, and a portrait of James aged eight was completed by Arnold Bronckhorst (*fl.*1565–1583), a Flemish painter who became James's first official artist. James is dressed in black with a small white ruff tight to his chin. His black hat sits far back on his head and we see his fair cropped hair and pale eyebrows. On his gloved left hand he holds a sparrowhawk with a bright golden eye. This is the only indication he is the king of Scotland, because falconry was a pursuit reserved for royalty and the aristocracy.

Ten years later James appointed Adrian Vanson (also from Flanders) as his court painter, who served him until 1603, when James moved to London and replaced him with John de Critz (1551/2–1642), another Flemish artist. There's also a miniature by Hilliard of James from this time, a tiny likeness in watercolour on vellum mounted on a playing card and framed with the inscription 'James, by the grace of God King of Great Britain, France and Scotland'. James's love of jewellery comes to the fore in the portraits of him as king. Many of the pieces he designed himself; they have names such as the 'Great George', a jewelled incarnation of England's patron saint that would hang from his gold Garter collar. When he wasn't sketching designs for the Union flag, splicing together the red cross of St George with the Scottish saltire, he was commissioning jewellery. He ordered a huge jewel to be made to celebrate his double kingship and called it the 'Mirror of Great Britain'. We can see it in a half-length portrait of him from 1604, painted by De Critz. Mounted on his wide-brimmed hat, it features a cabochon ruby, two large pearls, three table-cut diamonds and – dangling down – a 55-carat pale yellow diamond known as the Sancy. While the four stones that make up the central diamond shape represent Scotland, England, Wales and Ireland, you can't help but wonder if the Sancy represented France, a country where his mother was once queen, and one over which he too claimed sovereignty.

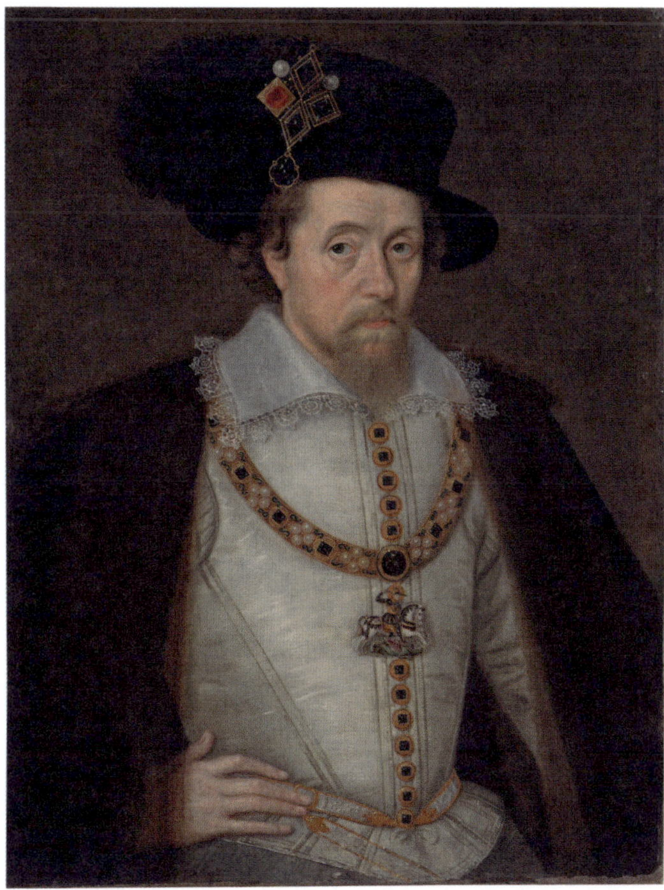

John de Critz, portrait of James VI and I, oil on canvas, 1604

What does this portrait tell us about the new king? He looks uneasy and wary, as if he is someone who prefers solitude to show. His fine lace collar and black plumed hat do not detract from the real subject of the painting, the large jewels sparkling on his head and breast. But this portrait also offers us a glimpse of James's dream of a united country, where England and Scotland were equal partners. Great Britain would be a partnership cemented by Protestantism. The only problem was that the English saw themselves as being from a strong, assertive country that didn't need a bedfellow, and the Scottish resolutely didn't want to give up their long-fought-for independence. There were also religious interventions. James survived a Catholic attempt to blow up Parliament in 1605. He displaced Catholics in Ulster by installing 'Plantations' of Protestant aristocrats across the county and tried to install Protestant settlers in Lewis, causing the Gaelic chieftains of the Hebrides to rise against him. Perhaps this explains the woeful look on his face in many of his portraits, his mouth downturned and eyes guarded despite his array of jewels.

NO GLASS CEILINGS

With his death in 1625, James VI and I's attempt to create a viable Great Britain came to an end when his son, Charles I, took the throne. Charles wanted to honour his father and commissioned the *Apotheosis of James I* from Peter Paul Rubens (1577–1640) for the ceiling of Banqueting House in London, where it was installed in 1636. This neoclassical building was designed by Inigo Jones based on the principles of the Italian Renaissance architect Andrea Palladio. It was the first of its kind in the British Isles and was part of the sprawling Whitehall Palace. The ceiling is 37 metres long and 17 metres wide and was designed to house nine vast canvases in ornate frames.

Look up at the central oval panel: it is like being sucked into a vortex. (Binoculars intensify the experience today – it's a high ceiling.) Figures soar above you as they convey James from earth to heaven. The *Apotheosis of James I* is a religious painting reworked for a Protestant sensibility – instead of the Virgin, Christ and angels we have the aged king being lifted up by an eagle, escorted by personifications of wisdom, peace and justice, a clever negotiation of a changing religious climate. We stand beneath their bare feet, feeling the breeze from their swirling drapery, while trying to make out their heads in the clouds 17 metres above our own. It is a masterclass in foreshortening, the technique that makes us believe these figures are vertically ascending even though they are painted on flat canvas. I used to find such Baroque scenes rather overblown, packed full of fleshy putti (cherubs) and vast swathes of superfluous fabric, but I have come to appreciate the consummate skill in conjuring such movement and three-dimensionality. Sometimes more is more.

European artists often travelled to Rome as part of their training, sketching ancient Greek and Roman statues as well as the latest masterpieces. They could gaze up at Michelangelo's Sistine Chapel ceiling at the Vatican and marvel at the painted trompe l'oeil architecture and impeccable musculature, then cross the Tiber to study the foreshortening of Caravaggio's spotlit scenes in the newly opened Cerasi Chapel. Rubens spent eight years touring Italy and Spain, learning from such masters, and by the time his canvases were shipped to Britain he was running one of the most successful studios in Europe.

The project was first mooted in 1621, during the reign of James VI and I, while the latest wing of Whitehall Palace was being built. The Banqueting Hall had been designed to be the most dramatic place in the palace, a beautifully proportioned high-ceilinged room painted to look like it was built of white marble and decorated with gold. While meetings had been held in Rubens's studio in Antwerp, there was no movement on the design at this time. But when Rubens appeared in London eight years later as an emissary for the king of Spain to broker a peace treaty between the two countries, Charles was quick to renew the agreement. Rubens painted oil sketches and a large canvas *modello*, a painting he sent to Charles I to show him the design and which the king rated so highly he mounted it on the ceiling of the Cabinet Room in Whitehall Palace. His studio then painted the individual canvases, with Rubens adding the finishing touches before they were sent to England. (A confusion between the measurement of an English and Antwerp foot meant the assistant who had accompanied the rolled canvases to London to oversee installation had to quickly trim some paintings to fit the frames and extend others.)

Unlike his father, Charles loved being around artists and was amassing what would become one of the best art collections in Europe. He had spent time with the king of Spain in 1623 when he unsuccessfully sought the hand of the infanta, Maria Anna, and had enjoyed studying King Philip IV's magnificent art collection. He commissioned his portrait from Philip IV's court painter Diego Velázquez and was given two Titians, buying himself another before he left. The same year, Charles commissioned a self-portrait from Rubens, so it was clever politicking by Philip IV to send Rubens as his chief negotiator in 1629.

It wasn't just the king commissioning art at this phenomenal level – his friends and associates followed suit. George Villiers, duke of Buckingham, commissioned a giant portrait of himself on horseback from Rubens and acquired Giambologna's sculptural tour de force *Samson Slaying a Philistine* (1560–2). When Rubens was in London he was surprised by the standard of such collections, writing to the French astronomer Peiresc: 'When it comes to fine pictures by the hands of first-class masters, I have never seen such a large number in one place as in the royal palace and in the gallery of the late duke of Buckingham.'[3]

By the time Rubens's finished canvases were installed in the Banqueting Hall in 1636 the Flemish artist Anthony van Dyck (1599–1641), Rubens's former assistant, was Charles I's court painter. He painted Charles with such élan that Gian Lorenzo Bernini in Rome was able to carve his likeness without ever having met him. Van Dyck was one of the most gifted portrait artists ever to have worked in the British Isles and was to have a huge influence over the next generation of British artists.

Dürer had advocated the use of self-portraiture to showcase an artist's ability to paint from nature. You could compare the painting to the life model (the artist themself) when you visited the studio. Other artists, including Rembrandt van Rijn and Van Dyck, followed suit. In 1633 Van Dyck painted himself in a slashed crimson silk doublet, his body turned towards a large sunflower. This could symbolise his devotion to King Charles I, but in Flemish literature the sunflower was also associated with painting itself, indicating his commitment to painting from nature. His head looks over his shoulder and his eye meets our own. There's a sense of optimism in the forward thrust of his chin and the upward curl of his moustache. His left hand toys with a heavy gold chain that he wears cross-body, gifted to him by the king in this year.

Just seven years later and a different Van Dyck looks out from another self-portrait. He is thirty-nine years old and looks deeply unhappy. The aspiration and joy of the sunflower portrait has gone. His dark curly hair is brushed back; his moustache is downturned. His pink-rimmed eyes seem to water and there's a flush spreading across

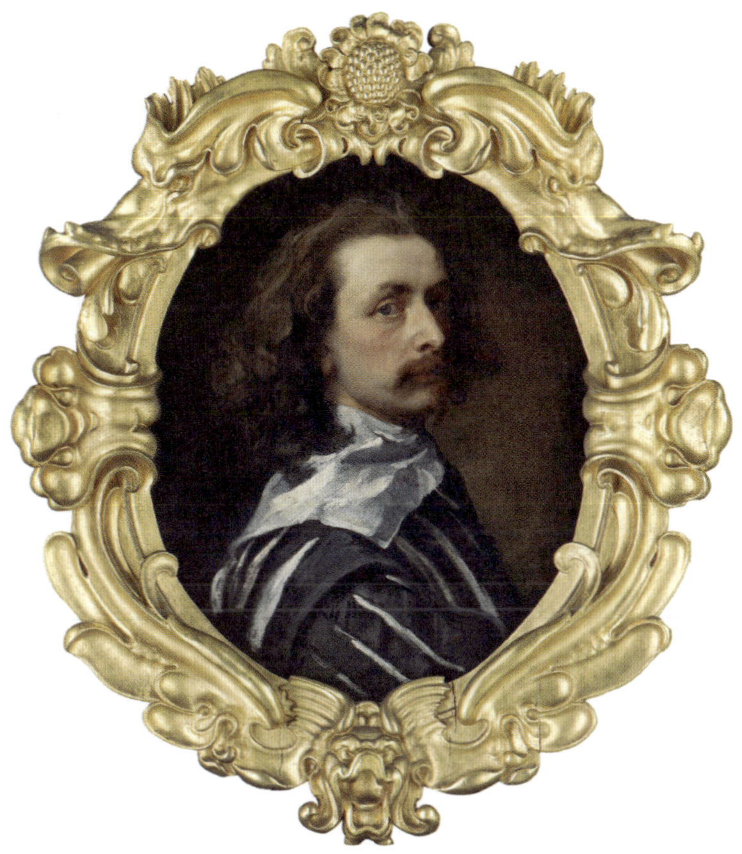

Anthony van Dyck, self-portrait, oil on canvas, *c*.1640

his cheeks. Even the light that catches the side of his nose and his right temple seems to sap him of life. There's bravura energy in his painting of his slashed black doublet and white collar, dashed in to the point of abstraction, a manic counterpoint to his achingly melancholic face. He would be dead within the year.

Charles's wife Henrietta Maria also commissioned artists, specifically for her new home built close to Greenwich Palace in London. Now known as the Queen's House, it was also designed by Inigo Jones and is all that remains of this important royal complex. The light-filled central hall with a gallery extending around all four sides was the perfect location for a ceiling by the Italian Orazio Gentileschi (1563–1639) and his supremely talented daughter, Artemisia (1593–*c*.1656). Peace reigns supreme on a central cloud, the sun forming a blazing halo behind her, while twelve women representing disciplines and concepts such as astronomy, music, wisdom and fortune encircle her. Orazio had been invited to England by Charles I and Henrietta Maria, and began the ceiling in 1635. Charles I already owned paintings by his daughter and she was repeatedly invited to court. She finally arrived in 1638 and began helping her ageing father complete the Queen's House ceiling. Orazio was seventy-four years old and she may have finished the ceiling on her own. There is no surviving documentation about the level of her involvement and we can only use differences in style to identify the figures on which she worked.

As a young artist in Rome Orazio had been a follower of Caravaggio and adopted his use of dramatic lighting, but his later work appears more evenly lit and classically polished and his women are tempered beauties. By contrast Artemisia's women are strong and powerful. We feel their heft, their weight, as they saw off heads and pledge oaths. Despite the ceiling having been moved to Marlborough House in the eighteenth century, and substantially cut down, we can still recognise Artemisia's touch. The entrance hall of Marlborough House is significantly darker than the glorious light-filled Queen's House, but her women assert themselves nevertheless. Most of the women are pale and interchangeable, but look at the two with their feet on column bases, Wisdom and Astronomy. Their cheeks are ruddy and their hair dishevelled. There's a dynamism to the drapery that clothes their solid bodies. Wisdom (the Roman goddess Minerva) sits in her gleaming breastplate, red ribbons from her helmet catching our eye, Medusa screaming from her shield. Her face has all the vivacity of a portrait, her eyes raised momentarily as she demurs to Victory, who brandishes a palm frond.

Artemisia worked on several other paintings during her stay in England, including a self-portrait as Pittura, the female personification of painting, which was owned by Charles I. We see her at work with a brown smock over her green silk dress, a palette in her left hand and a fine brush lifted to a blank canvas in her right. She is not so much depicting herself as an artist but as Painting itself. Traditionally, in popular books such as Cesare Ripa's *Iconologia*, Pittura was female. Artemisia could employ this allegory in a way no male painter could – she is not only an artist in her own right but in this work she embodies the entire concept of painting, a mask hanging from a gold chain around her neck symbolising that all painting is imitation.

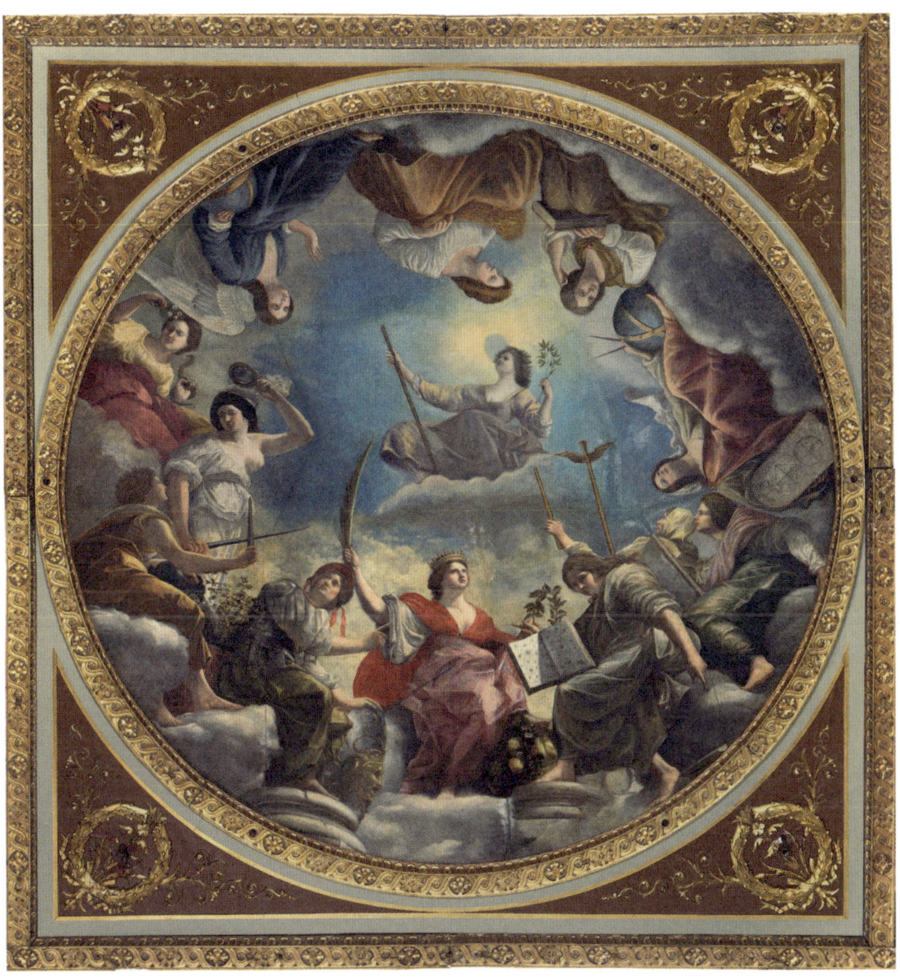

Orazio and Artemisia Gentileschi, *An Allegory of Peace and the Arts*, ceiling of the
Queen's House, Greenwich (now in Marlborough House), oil on canvas mounted on
board, *c.*1635–8

THE KING IS DEAD – LONG LIVE THE KING!

Charles I had dismissed Parliament in 1629 and refused to recall it,
claiming he ruled by divine right. For the next thirteen years, a period
known as the Personal Rule of Charles I, he persecuted Catholics (despite
being married to one), imposed a new Book of Common Prayer on
Scotland and raised controversial new taxes. The Scottish Covenanters
rose against Charles I and war ensued, weakening the king and forcing him to recall Parliament. Tensions rose, radical Protestants began

destroying images in churches again, Irish Catholics rose up against Protestant colonists and in England battle lines were drawn between Royalists and Parliamentarians. Civil war began in 1642 against a backdrop of violent unrest in Scotland, Ireland and Wales.

The English Civil War was a second iconoclastic lightning strike for art. Many churches were commandeered as army barracks, their works of art burnt as firewood, decapitated or covered in graffiti. The tomb of Sir Richard Pembridge (died 1375; Hereford Cathedral) lost a leg during the Civil War; the Fitzalan Chapel at Arundel Castle in West Sussex was used as a stable by Parliamentarians, who left their names carved into the tomb sculptures, and badly damaged the building. Charles I set up his wartime court in Oxford, taking William Dobson (1611–1646) with him as official painter. Van Dyck had encouraged and supported the British-born Dobson and his style was a rich fusion of Van Dyck's form and Titian's colour. During his time in Oxford with the king he painted Endymion Porter (1642–5), the king's groom of the bedchamber and his overseas art agent. Porter had been instrumental in bringing Van Dyck to England. Dobson paints him surrounded by classical sculpture, reflecting his importance as an art connoisseur and agent, and he is dressed in the finest lace. He is tanned and alert, painted with a grandeur that reflects his position as a loyal Royalist. But the dark clouds massing over the sunset behind him suggest Dobson and Porter knew the king's days were numbered.

By 1649 the Parliamentarians were the victors and Charles I was sentenced to death. His fine art collection, including Gentileschi's *Self-Portrait as the Allegory of Painting (La Pittura)*, was sold off. Oliver Cromwell, one of the Parliamentarian generals, became lord protector of the British Isles. He was a Puritan, a powerful subset of the Protestant faith who lived by a very strict religious code, and he reformed the law and improved education, ruling until his death in 1658. Two portraits by John Michael Wright (1617–1694) sum up the change in temperament from Cromwell to his successor. In the year of Cromwell's death Wright painted his daughter Elizabeth, the wife of John Claypole. She died in August 1658, and her father died a month later, his death (from malaria) speeded by heartbreak. Elizabeth wears Minerva's breastplate over her satin gown and occupies the foreground, drawing parallels with the goddess of wisdom (and war), for this is as much a painting of her father as it is of her. She holds a cameo of his likeness to her heart. An olive tree grows behind her, a play on his name, and the block of stone on which she rests her arm is decorated with a carving of Jupiter, Minerva's father. But the shipwrecks in the distant sea and the sun shrouded by dark cloud signal the changing political landscape as well as marking the great storm that preceded his death.

A decade or so later we see Wright commissioned to paint a portrait of Charles II following the restoration of the monarchy in 1660. Painting the family of the lord protector and then the new king of England seems like an incredible stretch, but artists were often able to cross barriers that were not so permeable for others. Wright, born in London, served his apprenticeship with George Jamesone (1587–1644) in Scotland, and spent the Civil War working successfully in Rome. He only returned to London in 1656, and with the restoration of the monarchy he eventually became an official court painter alongside Peter Lely (1618–1680). Now in the Palace of Holyroodhouse in Edinburgh, this giant painting, nearly 3 metres tall, shows Charles II in full regalia, the large crown of state on his head and a newly fashioned orb and sceptre in his hands. Each ribbon of his Order of the Garter costume has been painstakingly painted, as have his parliamentary robes. It is a painting that fiercely asserts his right to rule and is a magnificent piece of propaganda. However, rather like the Ditchley Portrait, this wasn't an official commission. It was probably begun a few years after Charles II's coronation, commissioned by wealthy banker and goldsmith Robert Vyner. He had supplied the new orb and sceptre for the coronation – the old set had been melted down when Charles I was executed – and had one eye on his future prospects. His investment paid off and he became lord mayor of London in 1674, around the time this was completed.

If Cromwell was all Puritanical reservation, Charles II was flamboyant, lustful and with an eye for spectacle. During his reign artists from across Europe worked in England once more, creating theatrical rooms and ceilings, following the lead of Rubens and his dizzying trompe l'oeil. Grinling Gibbons (1648–1721), a woodcarver from Rotterdam, created intricate schemes for many of England's stately homes, including the Carved Room at Petworth in Surrey. Working in limewood, he turned decorative wood carving into an art form. The Petworth Carved Room from 1692 was commissioned by Charles Seymour and Elizabeth Percy, sixth duke and duchess of Somerset, to showcase Gibbons's ability and features flowers, violins and recorders, classical urns and cherubic putti in dynamic limewood swags that defy gravity.

The Italian painter Antonio Verrio (*c*.1636–1707) was commissioned by Charles II to decorate fifteen ceilings in the royal apartments at Windsor in a bid to rival French King Louis XIV's flamboyant opulence. However, one of Verrio's most spectacular ceilings dates to the end of the seventeenth century and is at Burghley House in Lincolnshire (1697–9). The Heaven Room is reached after ascending the Hell Staircase. It is pure theatre. As I entered the room I was transported to a classical nirvana where elegant gods and goddesses weave between classical columns. Clouds of onlookers throng the sky while a winged Mercury seems to float in front of you. I caught my breath as a white horse leapt over the lofty cornice straight at me – Verrio's ability to conjure such movement and three-dimensionality has you wanting to step between the columns and enter this mythical world for yourself.

Art such as the Heaven Room was for the one per cent, the owners of the country's grandest houses with the deepest pockets. Verrio's commissions were a far cry from those experienced by most artists. Portraiture was the most lucrative business in town, and was how the majority of artists made their money in the seventeenth century.

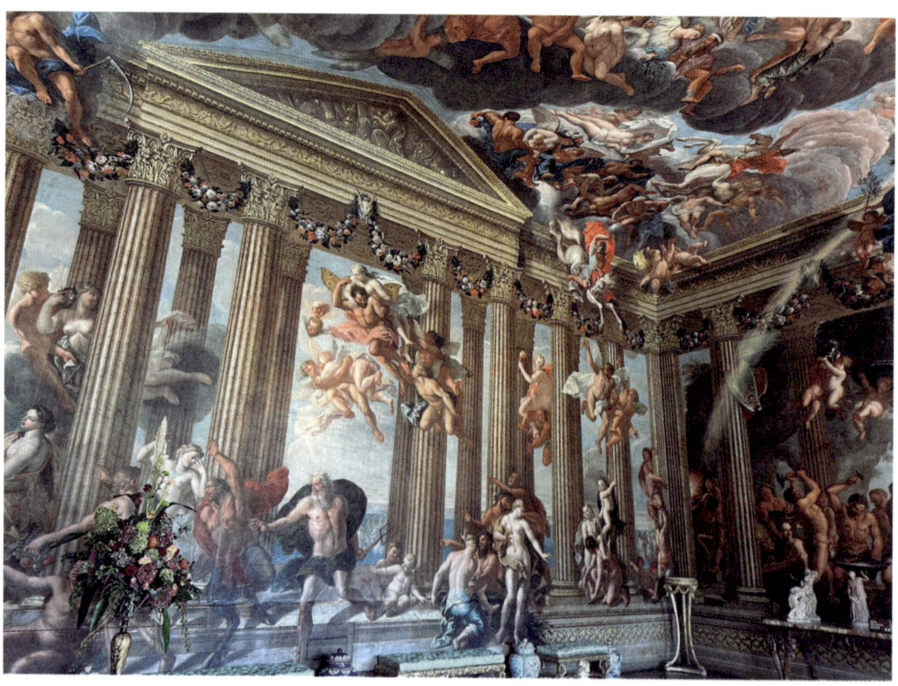

Antonio Verrio, Heaven Room mural, Burghley House, Lincolnshire, 1697–9

8

The unspeakable price of the Grand Tour
1660–1772

JUST BEFORE THE restoration of the monarchy in 1660, Mary Beale (1633–1699) painted a self-portrait (see overleaf). It is an assured work – ambitious, assertive and unconventional. Unusually for a self-portrait, it includes the artist's family – her husband Charles and son, Bartholomew. By 1660 Charles was her studio manager and assistant and Bartholomew was a frequent sitter, appearing in many portraits as well as in roles from a pipe-playing shepherd boy to a young Bacchus. Bartholomew would also become her assistant, as would his brother Charles, who was born in this year. But it is Mary Beale I am drawn to. She is the one meeting my eye, the one I want to know more about. She may be pregnant with Charles in this portrait – she disguises her stomach under drapery reminiscent of Van Dyck, a flounce of ochre silk over an indigo dress. Her husband looks sober by comparison, dressed in black with a hand on his son's shoulder, gazing into the distance. This passive role was traditionally the preserve of women in family portraits and Beale is consciously exploiting it, inverting it. Father and son form a linked unit through their touching hands, while Beale uses her own hand to point towards herself, just as Dürer had done in his 1500 self-portrait. She is the master (technically the mistress) at work here, the hand suggests.

Including her immediate family tells us something else about her. She had an unusual but loving partnership where husband and wife lived as equals. This is not conjecture – Beale spells this out for us in her 1666 book *Discourse on Friendship*, in which she advocates for equality in friendship and marriage. Eve, she writes, was created to

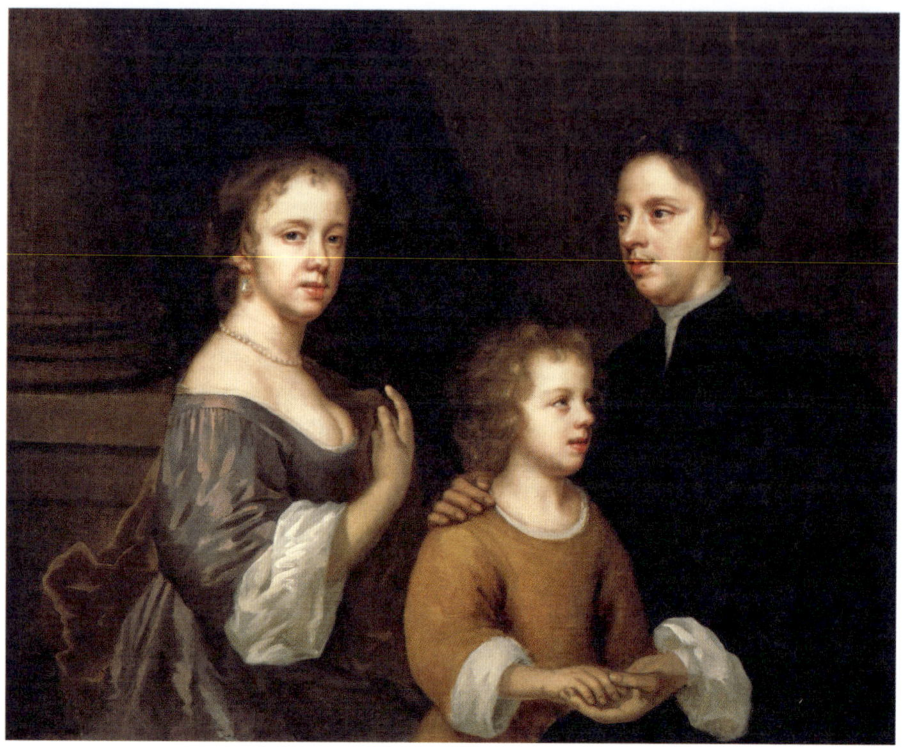

Mary Beale, self-portrait with her husband and son, oil on canvas, 1660

be Adam's 'wife and friend but not a slave'.[1] She represents this in her portrait by showing the two adults as a mirror image, turned towards each other and almost the same height. But her direct gaze lets us know with whom we should be dealing when it comes to painting.

By this date Mary Beale lived in a four-storey townhouse in Fleet Street, London. She had been born in Suffolk and her clergyman father, a keen amateur artist, may have taught her the fundamentals of painting. She also took instruction from those who had come before her – she borrowed Italian drawings from the king's collection and Old Master paintings from Lely. Ten years after this was painted, following a spell in Hampshire, the Beales returned to London and established Mary's 'painting room' in a new house on Pall Mall, on the corner of newly developed St James's Square. Charles Beale had left his job at the Patent Office and now worked for her full-time. He stretched her canvases, applied size (animal-skin glue) to tighten the weave and primed them with an initial layer of paint. He also kept a daily studio journal, detailing sitters, painting commissions and records of pigments and payments. Mary worked six days a week for a range of clients including earls and countesses, senior clergy, city professionals and the gentry. In 1706, just six years after her death, Bainbrigg Buckeridge wrote of Beale: 'She work'd with a wonderful Body of Colours, was exceedingly Industrious and her Pictures are much after the Italian Manner, which she learnt by having copy'd several of the great Masters of that Country, whose Pictures she borrow'd out of Sir Peter's [Lely] Collection.'[2]

VAN DYCK'S LEGACY

Beale was an artist who knew she had a talent and knew how to wield it to maximum success. She specialised in portraiture, following the traditions of Van Dyck, as did her peers Lely and Joan Carlile (*c.*1606–1679). Lely, Carlile and Beale serviced a need among their clientele to be painted as if they were stepping into the shoes of Van Dyck's sitters. Lely was the artist appointed to be Charles II's principal painter after the Restoration and he took Beale under his wing, even allowing her to watch him paint (for a price) until he realised she was a rival as well as a friend. Carlile was a generation older than Beale and had weathered the Civil War. Before the war King Charles I had presented her and her contemporary Van Dyck with a substantial amount of ultramarine and she was held in high regard. As Beale was painting her early self-portrait, Carlile was setting up a studio (short-lived, as it turned out) in Covent Garden, the artistic centre of London, turning out portraits of slender young women in white satin dresses, adapting Van Dyck's elegant compositions to suit her own needs. Lely also deferred to Van Dyck, purposefully translating the older master's poses for a new generation of women at court, creating his covetable series of 'Beauties', as his portraits of doe-eyed aristocrats were known.

Lely's portrait from around 1670 of Barbara, countess of Castlemaine (one of Charles II's many mistresses) mimics the pointing pose and outdoor setting of Van Dyck's *Portrait of Anne Kirk* (*c.*1637), even including its urn, dog and rosebush. This was one of the many Van Dycks Lely owned, allowing for close scrutiny of technique and composition. Through such paintings as *The Countess of Castlemaine* we see the immense impact of Van Dyck on British portraiture. This is why, when we look at portraits in stately homes, they often seem rather homogeneous (particularly Lely's interchangeable 'Beauties'). Artists adopted a successful flattering style and a Van Dyck composition to maximise sales. Beale was not immune to this, but in her self-portrait we feel we see the real her. She paints herself with the same scrutiny that William Hogarth (1697–1764) brought to bear almost a century later.

Beale, along with many other artists including the miniaturist Samuel Cooper (1609–1672) and Carlile, also offered another service – the copying of famous works of art so they could hang in more than one location at once. In an age before photography, the only way to acquire a likeness of a celebrated painting would be to buy the associated print or commission a copy by a leading artist of the day. Beale charged the same amount for a small copy of a painting by Van Dyck or Lely as she did for a three-quarter-length portrait: £10 (£1,100 today). These were not quick knock-offs but detailed and time-consuming recreations of the original. When Lely visited Beale in April 1672 he praised her small painting of a family portrait by Van Dyck, claiming it to be the best copy he had ever seen of Van Dyck's work.[3] Copies of Lely's work were sometimes commissioned by his own patrons – they may have been keen to have the copy in their townhouse with the original in their home in the country. The network between artists such as Lely and Beale was vital to ensure the copies were of a suitable calibre.

ANDIAMO IN ITALIA

With the dawning of a new century came the Hanoverians, starting with George I, who ascended the throne in 1714. He was the great-grandson of James VI and I, and the closest blood relative who was a Protestant following the death of Queen Anne (a new requirement following the Act of Settlement of 1701). Anne had presided over the formal unification of Scotland and England in 1707, when Scottish and English Parliaments drew up the Act of Union that created a united kingdom called Great Britain. But an increasing number of aristocrats were not living in the newly formed Great Britain, but were travelling across Europe en route to Rome.

While Lely and Beale were kept busy by patrons in the capital, an increasing number of young wealthy aristocrats were choosing to spend years travelling throughout Italy to immerse themselves in the ancient landscape and culture of their classical education. They expressed a particular love for Venice, where the internationally acclaimed Rosalba Carriera (1673–1757) would capture their likeness in pastel and they could admire altarpieces by Bellini, Dürer and Titian. They travelled across Italy, buying contemporary religious works and portraits at the studio of Carlo Maratta (1625–1713) in Rome and commissioning paintings from Carlo Dolci (1616–1686) in Florence.

Why should we look at Italian art in a book focused on the British Isles? Let's consider again the portraits of Endymion Porter and Elizabeth Cromwell from the last chapter. Both Dobson and Wright used classical reliefs to add meaning to these portraits. This suggests they felt viewers would have been able to read these, to understand why they were included. Those commissioning and looking at portraits were educated in the classical histories and mythologies of ancient Greece and Rome. Britain increasingly modelled itself on classical principles, from the Corinthian columns of Inigo Jones's architecture to the swags of fabric used by Lely and Beale to ennoble their sitters like Roman senators. Neoclassicism was the height of fashion.

The travel writer and priest Richard Lassels coined a term for this form of erudite travelling: the Grand Tour.[4] Both men and women embarked on such journeys, sometimes publishing accounts of their travels. Hester Lynch Piozzi's second husband was an Italian musician and in 1784 the couple joined the 'magic procession' of British travellers who ventured overseas.[5] For three years they toured Italy and Piozzi used her position as the wife of an Italian to get beneath the surface of daily life. She criticised the young men on the Grand Tour 'counting churches, pictures, palaces' and 'those who run from town to town, with no impression made but on their bones'.[6] She published her travel guide to Italy in 1789 and it was a bestseller.

The Grand Tour reached its zenith in the eighteenth century. Arriving in Rome, travellers could have their portraits painted by the Scottish artist Katherine Read (1723–1778). She had studied in Paris and Rome, met Carriera in Venice and painted self-portraits to display her skill to passing tourists. She was much in demand, painting a young Lord Fortrose with his tutor Dr Mackenzie in 1752 and a cluster of male aristocrats in wigs and frock coats lounging in front of the Colosseum around 1750 (see overleaf), and her paintings hang in drawing rooms in country houses across Britain to this day.

In Venice, the British consul Joseph Smith controlled the sale of *vedute* (view paintings) by Canaletto (1697–1768), acting as the artist's

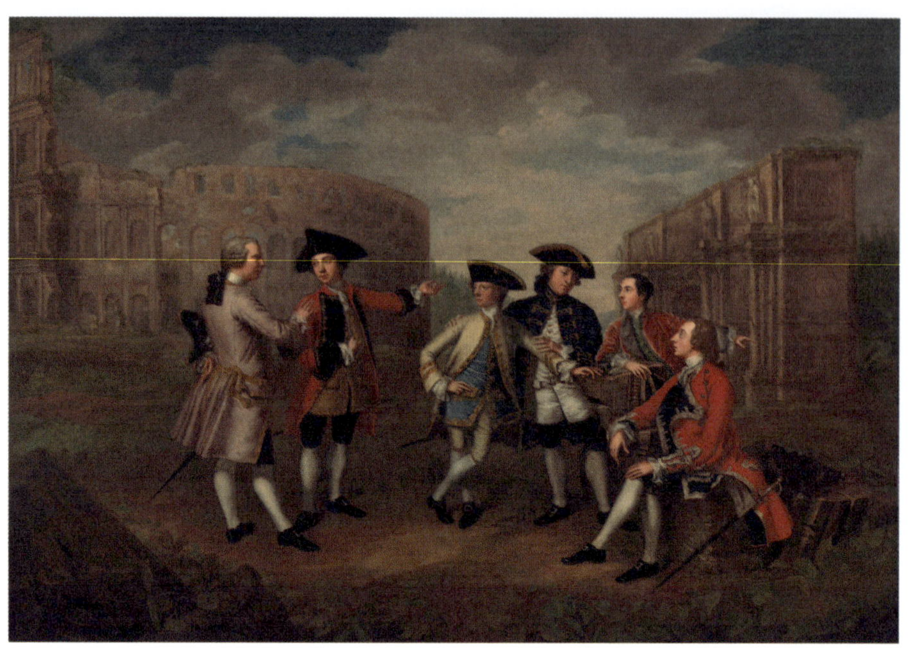

Katherine Read, *British Gentlemen in Rome*, oil on canvas, *c*.1750

agent for eager British collectors. These included Henry Howard, fourth earl of Carlisle, and John Russell, fourth duke of Bedford. They both bought so many that they were able to assemble dedicated Canaletto rooms in their respective homes of Castle Howard in Yorkshire and Bedford House in London. (The Canalettos were transferred to Russell's country seat of Woburn Abbey in Bedfordshire in 1800, where they hang to this day. The Castle Howard collection was subsequently sold.)

As the eighteenth century progressed, the excavations of ancient art in Rome and beyond increased. The buried Roman city of Herculaneum was discovered in 1738, followed by Pompeii in 1748. Volcanic ash from Vesuvius's massive eruption of 79 CE had preserved entire rooms of wall paintings and courtyards filled with busts and figurines. Marble sculptures including the *Discobolus* were discovered at Hadrian's Villa in Tivoli outside Rome, and in Rome itself ancient figures of Diana and Venus were unearthed. Many of these emerged headless or missing limbs. While some British collectors, such as Charles Townley, preferred to buy ancient sculptures as they were found, paying hundreds of pounds for undamaged figures, the majority bought works that had been heavily restored.

Henry Blundell from Ince Blundell Hall, Liverpool, was one of these collectors. The agent Thomas Jenkins claimed he worked for 'English *virtuosi* who had no value for statues without heads', and local sculptors would provide them.[7] A head from one ancient sculpture could also end up on a different body. Blundell set off on his Grand Tour unfashionably late, when he was in his fifties. He didn't have the reputation of having a knowledgeable eye. Instead, he bought in bulk through Jenkins, securing whole collections from those forced to sell, both in Italy and in the new British auction house established by James Christie in 1766. Blundell owned a fine ancient Roman sculpture of Athena, still intact, but he also bought a statue of Diana in 1786 that is now known to have been fabricated in the eighteenth century from an incredible 127 ancient fragments from a variety of sources. It is a pastiche of an ancient sculpture, a chimera, built for a market that had an insatiable appetite for all things antique.

Townley's collection, the most important of its kind, was bought by the British Museum after his death in 1805 for the significant sum of £20,000 (around £900,000 today). But his friend Blundell's collection remained at Ince Blundell Hall until 1959. Blundell first built a neo-classical garden temple to showcase highlights from his collection, but it is his second garden structure for which he is now remembered – a scaled-down version of Rome's Pantheon. The banker Henry Hoare had built a garden folly modelled on the Pantheon at his Stourhead estate in Wiltshire, but Blundell's included Roman relief sculptures mounted on the pediment and internal niches filled with classical sculptures. In total he amassed 600 works, including life-size figures of gods and goddesses, portrait busts of emperors, funeral urns, statuettes and grave markers. *Country Life* photographed the house in 1958 (see overleaf) and you can see his collection carefully laid out across the circular floor, with marble tables, plinths and columns displaying sculptures of all sizes underneath the central dome and oculus. (An oculus is a glazed circular aperture that lets in light; the Roman original is open to the elements.)

Today Ince Blundell Hall is home to a handful of octogenarian Augustinian nuns who used to run it as a nursing home. The Garden Temple and the Pantheon still stand but have been emptied of sculpture, which now belongs to National Museums Liverpool. Sister Gemma gave me a tour of the hall and grounds – the Pantheon now houses artificial flower arrangements rather than marble statues, and hospital beds have replaced the busts of Roman emperors. To see the collection

I had to visit the museum's stores, where antique friezes lie on pallets, gods are boxed up in packing cases and portrait busts are shrouded in cloth, parcel tags loosely tied around their necks. There's little appetite for Blundell's voracious level of collecting today, and we frown upon the heavy restoration that gives a statue of Apollo a whole left leg and head from a different sculpture. We are obsessed with authenticity, but in the eighteenth century, as in Roman times, it was the look of a thing that mattered to men like Blundell. If the original was damaged or unavailable then a copy would do just fine.

Neoclassicism only finally began to wane in the twentieth century, with the demise of the British empire. Latin was replaced by modern

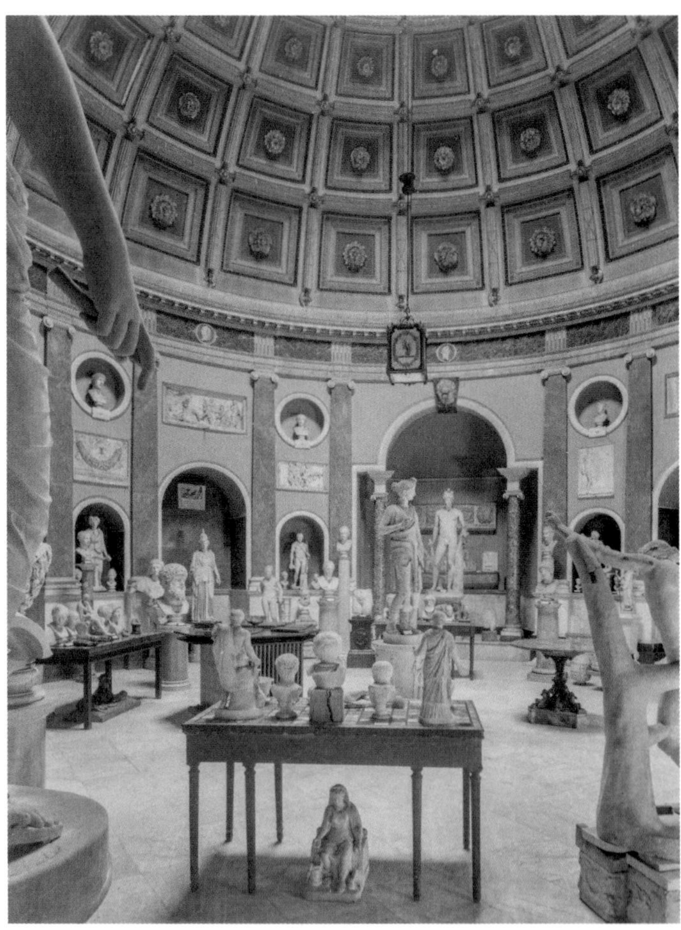

Henry Blundell's Pantheon at Ince Blundell Hall, near Liverpool, photographed for *Country Life*, 1958

Romance languages in the school curriculum, modern history supplanted Homer and Cicero and conceptual art replaced a grounding in classical form. The growing invisibility of classicism today is countered by a rise in visibility of all that was suppressed or brushed under the carpet during this period. Because much of the wealth of these Grand Tourists was derived from sugar plantations and slavery.

THE VISIBILITY OF BLACK BRITONS

Barbara Walker (born 1964) is a contemporary artist who was nominated for the Turner Prize in 2023. Her detailed drawings confront our collective past by suggesting new ways to view art history. Since 2018 she has researched paintings held in British public collections that feature Black subjects for her series *Vanishing Point*. The subjects she focuses on often occupy the far edges of canvases, their identities not recorded. They are young servants, maids and grooms, occasionally a biblical king in an ornate turban, and they perform a role on each canvas rather than being painted as and for themselves. Walker has used paintings by Paolo Veronese, Titian and Dolci as starting points as well as eighteenth-century portraits that have been included in important recent exhibitions such as *Black Atlantic: Power, People, Resistance* at the Fitzwilliam Museum in Cambridge in 2023–4 and *Entangled Pasts 1768–Now* at the Royal Academy in London in 2024. In reworking such paintings she refocuses our attention: the privileged white men and women become mere outlines, blind embossed on paper, while the Black figure leaps off the page, every detail of the face and clothes painstakingly drawn in pencil (a medium always threatened with erasure). As Walker says, 'I'm very interested in visibility and non-visibility in terms of marginalised communities. I use erasure as a metaphor for how the Black community is overlooked, ignored, and even dehumanised by society.'[8]

In eighteenth-century Britain there were thousands of Black men, women and children working in middle-class and aristocratic households.[9] Slavery was illegal in Britain but many of these employees received nothing but bed and board for their long days of service. They were often dressed in household livery and served aristocrats who considered owning a young Black boy or employing a Black servant to be the height of fashion. Advertisements for the sale of these 'employees' in the *London Gazette* and *Gentleman's Magazine* suggest the reality of such a life – the language used is that of ownership: 'A Black boy, twelve years of age, fit to wait on a gentleman, to be disposed of . . .'[10]

We see such servants in eighteenth-century paintings by Hogarth, Joshua Reynolds (1723–1792) and Johan Zoffany (1733–1810) as well as seventeenth-century portraits by Van Dyck, Lely and Dobson. Hogarth was the leading satirical artist of his day, creating cycles of paintings depicting the fall of rakish young men or fashionable couples who spent when they should have saved. In *Marriage à la Mode* (*c.*1743) Hogarth dresses his flighty young bride as a shepherdess who is hosting her lover and hangers-on in her bedroom in the fourth painting in the series, *The Toilette*. A young Black boy in quasi-Indian dress plays with family heirlooms on the floor while a Black servant attempts to serve hot chocolate, sweetened with plantation sugar, to his mistress.

Millions of Black men, women and children were involved with harvesting the tobacco that filled British pipes and cutting the sugar cane that was processed to sweeten tea imported from India. This workforce was not paid. Individuals were traded like animals, shackled

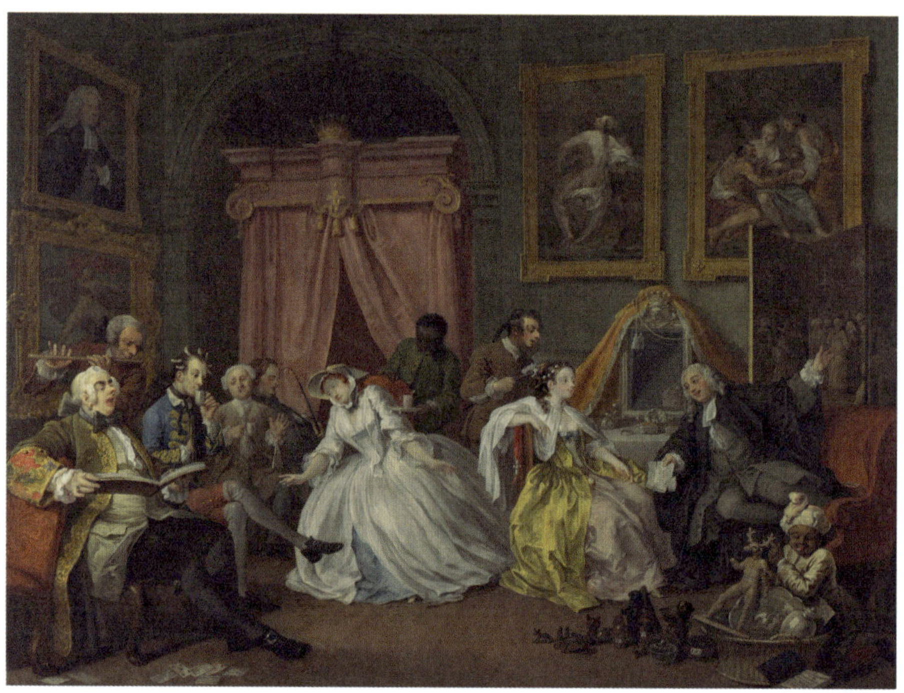

William Hogarth, *Marriage à la Mode: 4, The Toilette*, oil on canvas, *c.*1743

and shipped in cramped and fetid conditions from West Africa to the Americas, where they were expected to work for no wages in sweltering conditions with the constant threat of physical and sexual violence.

Britain had been involved in slavery since the sixteenth century but it was in the eighteenth that the Atlantic slave trade reached its peak. With a rapacious attitude to colonisation, Britain had appropriated islands in the Caribbean and land in South and North America to develop as plantations. Initially these were staffed by indentured (unsalaried) British servants, but the high labour demands of growing sugar cane in Barbados and Jamaica – both islands seized by the British in the seventeenth century – led to the transition to African slavery. By the time the trade was abolished for British companies in 1807 nearly three million Africans had been shipped to the plantations by what became known as the Middle Passage. (The equivalent of the total populations of Dublin, Manchester, Glasgow, Belfast and Cardiff being shackled and sold into slavery today.) This was the forced movement of enslaved Africans across the Atlantic on overcrowded and unsanitary slave ships, with many dying in transit.

Some of the Black men and women in Britain had been forcibly removed from West Africa as children, compelled to work on plantations before being transferred to new owners, often naval officers. Legally, once they were in Britain, they should not have been kept as slaves but the visual record suggests otherwise. A bust from around 1700 by John Nost the Elder (*c*.1655–*c*.1712), owned by Queen Anne, was described by a visitor as a 'bust of a Moor very well done from life' (see overleaf).[11] The man is dressed in a feathered turban with a jewelled chain across his shoulders. But it is the collar around his neck that we notice first. Who could do this to a fellow human being? The collar was originally locked with a padlock, suggesting that whoever held the key 'owned' the man. Slave collars resembled those used for dogs, a symbol of ownership that could be engraved with the 'owner's' name and any message, such as: 'The Lady of Bromfield's Black, in Lincoln's Inn Fields'.[12] This inscription was printed in an advertisement when the thirteen-year-old wearer of the collar ran away. A guinea was offered for his capture and return. We can also see these collars on the young Black boy who pours the tea in plate two of Hogarth's print series *A Harlot's Progress* (1732) and on the young page in the same artist's *Taste in High Life* (*c*.1742). When I first looked at Hogarth's prints and paintings in the 1990s I didn't notice these keenly observed details of contemporary life – it has taken a groundswell of new

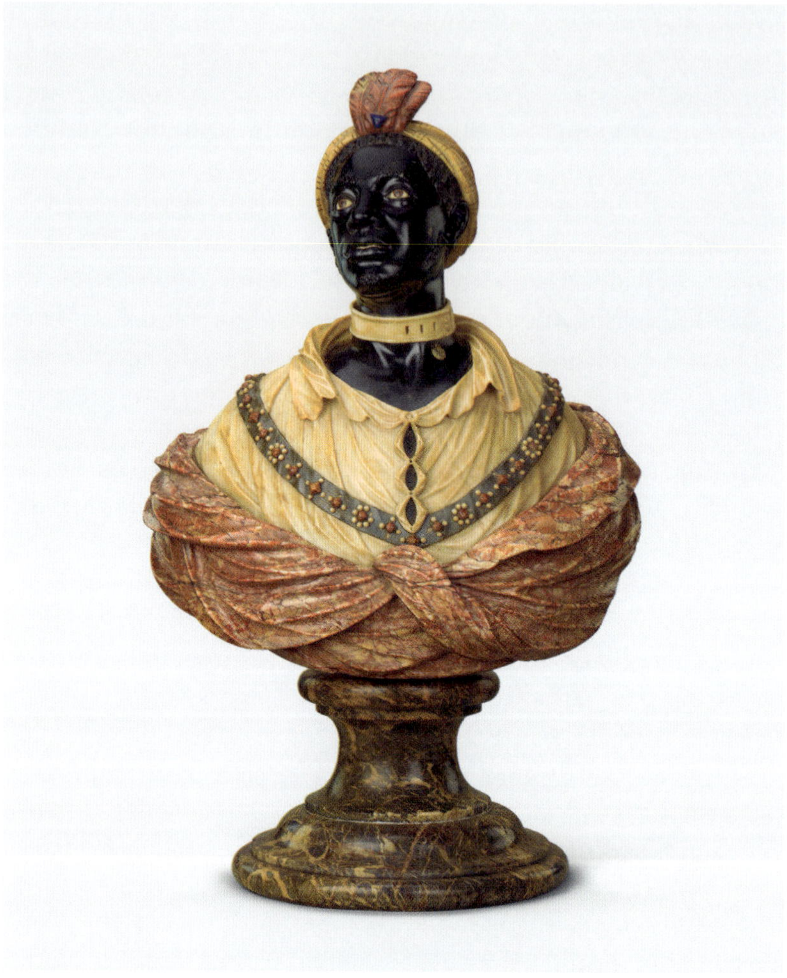

John Nost the Elder, bust of an enslaved man, composite marble, *c*.1700

research into Black Britons to help us see what was in front of our eyes all along.

Alongside this world of servitude were Black men and women who lived freely in the British Isles. Some arrived as sailors, others as soldiers from the American War of Independence. A few were the sons of African leaders, sent to Britain to be educated in European trade negotiation. The Black scholar Francis Williams was born in Jamaica around 1690 but educated at Cambridge, where he specialised in mathematics and Latin. He inherited his father's estate in Jamaica with its enslaved labour force but he did campaign for the rights for free

Black men. He left next to nothing in written form, but we can get a sense of him from his curious portrait in the V&A (*c.*1745–60). While it is amateur in execution, by an as yet unidentified artist, it is competent enough for us to see that he was a scholar who loved books and learning: an open volume lies under his fingers next to an astrological globe, and a further globe rests on the floor. There's a quill for writing and dividers for accurate measurement. Books line the wall behind him next to a window that opens onto his Jamaican estate. Despite the eccentric proportions of his body in the painting, with his improbably tiny hands and feet, we get a sense of the man who has risen to greet us. His left hand still marks his place in the text he is reading and his face is one of earnest concentration.

In London, some free Black men and women were employed as musicians, such as the violinist George Bridgetower, and others moved out of service into commerce like Charles Ignatius Sancho. Others published accounts of their lives, such as Olaudah Equiano (1789) and Mary Prince (1831), and in a few cases their portraits were professionally painted. The oval portrait of a man in a red waistcoat and black wig is the most enigmatic. It dates from the mid-eighteenth century and was once thought to be Equiano, but this has now been disproved. Despite his assured gaze and fine clothes no name was written on the portrait: we are left guessing as to his identity, but he was clearly a man of means and this is a nuanced and sophisticated portrait.

The English sculptor Francis Harwood (1726/7–1783), who worked in Florence and catered for British travellers on the Grand Tour, carved a bust of a now anonymous Black man in 1758. He was clearly a person of some significance to merit such a commission – his muscly naked torso suggests he may have been a sporting hero or someone known for his physique. But again, his name has not been passed down through time and his identity remains obscured.

William Hoare (1707–1792) painted Ayuba Suleiman Diallo in 1733 during his fourteen-month stay in London. Educated by his father (an imam of royal blood), Diallo had been captured in The Gambia, endured the Middle Passage and was sold into slavery in Maryland. A chance interception of a letter in London, asking his father for help, led to his release and he subsequently worked as an Arabic–English translator, mixing in intellectual circles while in Britain. Francis Barber, Samuel Johnson's servant and companion, was painted by Reynolds. He lived and worked with the writer and lexicographer for thirty-four years and inherited money and property upon Johnson's death.

Sancho was painted by the leading portrait artist Thomas Gainsborough (1727–1788) in 1768. Like Diallo and Barber, Sancho had also experienced slavery. He was born on a slave ship bound for New Granada in 1729. Both his parents died soon after the ship docked in South America, but Sancho survived and was sent to London, where he was 'gifted' to three sisters in Greenwich. He grew up in their care, although they did not seem to care for him at all and purposefully

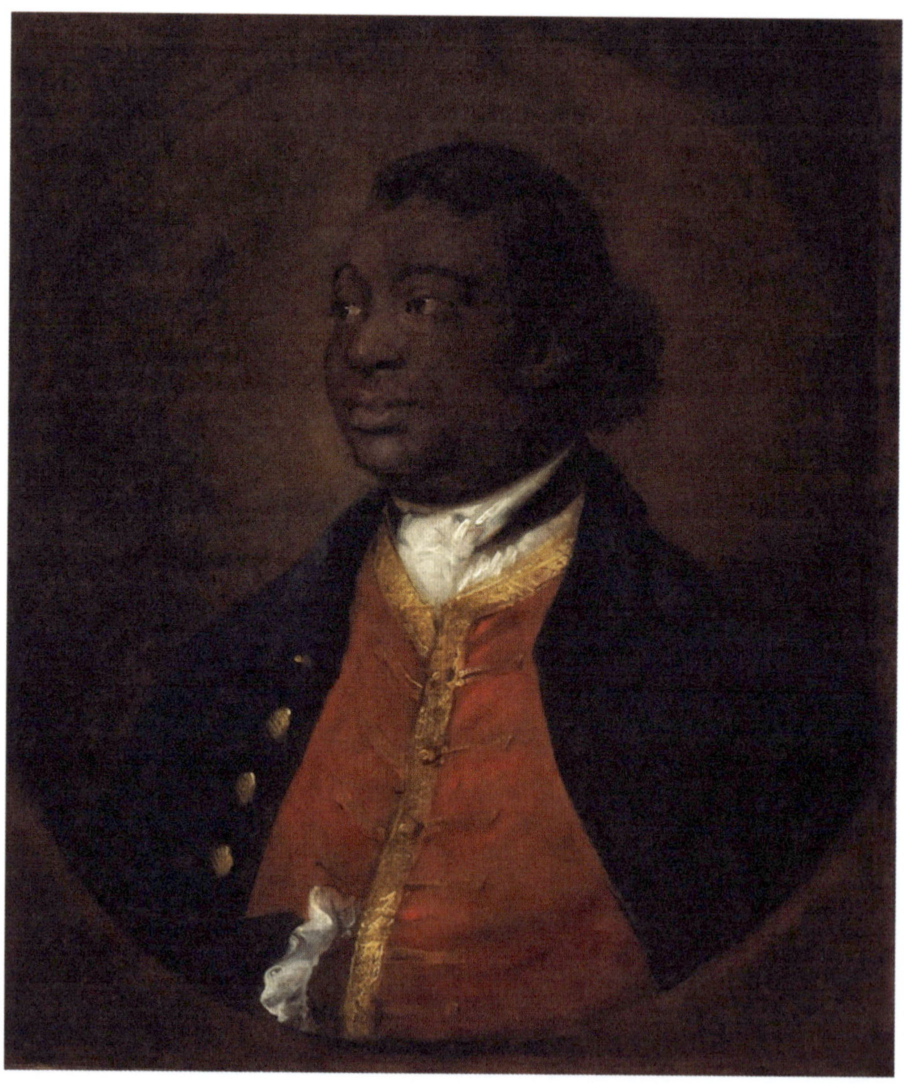

Thomas Gainsborough, portrait of Charles Ignatius Sancho, oil on canvas, 1768

tried to restrict his knowledge of the world. Luckily the second duke of Montagu taught him to read, and as an adult Sancho worked as a butler for the duchess of Montagu and later her son-in-law, the earl of Cardigan (later confusingly known as the first duke of Montagu), before setting up in business as a grocer. It was during his time working for the first duke that he sat for Gainsborough in Bath on 29 November 1768.

What do these portraits tell us? They give us a glimpse into the lives of a few of the Black men who called Georgian Britain home. Gainsborough spent fifteen years (1759–74) in the spa town painting a fashionable clientele who came to take the waters. Many of his portraits and family groups occupy vast canvases and he was revered for his breathtaking brushwork, as seen in *The Blue Boy* (1770) and *The Byam Family* (1760s). It was reported that his portrait of Sancho took Gainsborough under two hours and was completed in one sitting. I have a hard time believing this because it is a detailed and nuanced likeness, from the warmth of his eyes to his full mouth with its hint of a moustache. Through it we get a sense of Sancho, his lively spirit as well as his love of fine food and wine (eventually he had to give up working for the duke when his gout and corpulence demanded it). It is fortunate his portrait survives for he was the first Black man known to vote in Britain, able to do so because he owned property. His letters were published two years after his death – more than 1,200 subscribers ensured the first edition quickly sold out.

But where are the paintings of Black British women? There were fewer Black women than men in London at this time and most of the anonymous servants who appear in works by Hogarth and Zoffany are men. There were women working in service but when we see Black women from this period they are often sexualised in prints by the leading satirists of the day, such as Thomas Rowlandson (1756–1827) and James Gillray (1756–1815). But there is one painting that tells a very different story.

In Scone Palace, near Perth, hangs a large double portrait in a gilded frame from around 1776 by David Martin (1737–1797). Two young women gaze out, smiles playing across their lips. The setting is the grounds of Kenwood House on the outskirts of London, the country house of William and Elizabeth Murray, Lord and Lady Mansfield, where they spent their weekends and where this painting would have originally hung. One of the women sits on a green bench in a gauzy pink gown, a book held open in her lap, flowers in her hair. The other looks as if she is springing up from the arm of the bench, a platter of fruit held by her left hand as the right points to her slender face. She sports a turban with a dark ostrich feather and her white satin gown is complemented by a sheer Indian shawl. They both wear strings of pearls around their slender necks, tight like slave collars but indicative of wealth and freedom. What makes this portrait unusual is that the seated Lady Elizabeth Murray is white and her cousin Dido Belle is mixed race.

Both girls were great-nieces of Lord and Lady Mansfield. The Mansfields were a childless couple who agreed to raise the pair. Elizabeth's father was the ambassador to Austria and Paris, and when his wife died Elizabeth was still an infant. Dido's father was Sir John Lindsay, a captain in the Royal Navy. Dido had been born out of wedlock to Maria, variously identified as an African woman from

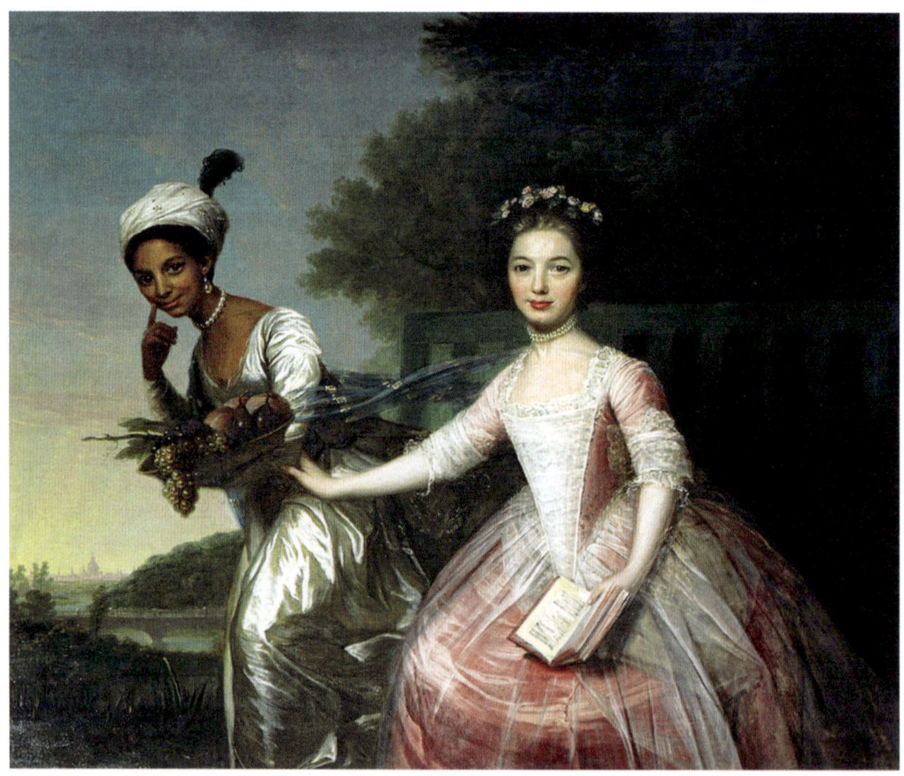

David Martin, portrait of Elizabeth Murray and Dido Belle, oil on canvas, 1778

Jamaica, a Cuban slave captured by the Spanish fleet and a free Black woman who was Lindsay's mistress and either had Dido on his ship as it headed back to England in 1761 or gave birth in London shortly afterwards. When Dido was a toddler Maria left England, and Dido entered the care of the Murrays around the same time as Elizabeth. Lindsay later married a different woman but he gifted Maria property in Florida and left Dido a substantial sum of £500 in his will (£55,000 today). Dido's great-uncle also left her the same amount and an annuity of £100 for life, suggesting she was a much-loved member of the family.

Yet despite the love the family showed to Dido and Elizabeth, visitors distinguished between the two women on racial grounds. Thomas Hutchinson, the former governor of Massachusetts Bay, took issue with Lord Mansfield's devotion to Dido, noting how he paid her 'the greatest attention' and 'called upon [her] . . . every minute for this and that'. Hutchinson's prejudices were such that he could not accept Dido as an equal, and clearly did not keep his opinions to himself, writing that Lord Mansfield 'has been reproached for showing fondness for her'.[13] Even in the portrait Elizabeth is shown as a quintessential young British lady while Dido is exoticised, dressed in a turban and Indian shawl, holding a platter of fruit as if symbolising the bounty of warmer colonial lands. However, the closeness of the black and pale green grapes could allude to the close sisterly friendship of the two girls, mirrored by Elizabeth's hand staying the energetic Dido just long enough for the portrait to be painted.

In spite of the prejudice she faced from some guests, Dido played a significant role in the development of Lord Mansfield's thinking. He was chief justice of England from 1756 to 1788. In 1772 his decision that James Somerset, a Black man who had been brought to England as a slave, could not be treated as a slave on British soil was the chink in the judicial armour that abolitionists had been waiting for. If Lord Mansfield's deliberations were protracted and he looked for every loophole before siding with Somerset, his final verdict was emphatic. Slavery was, he said, 'so odious, that nothing can be suffered to support it'.[14] Somerset was discharged a free man, and the abolition movement, growing since the 1760s, took a giant step forwards. But when would the government abolish slavery in the colonies? That was some way off yet.

It is important to insert these paintings of Black Britons into the story of eighteenth-century British art. For too long they have been written out of collective histories and it is only now, in the twenty-first century, that we see their contribution to history being acknowledged in rehangs of national museums and galleries such as Tate Britain, and in important temporary exhibitions like *Black Atlantic* and *Entangled Pasts*. There are those who consider this a 'woke' trend, as if inclusivity somehow devalues quality. Let me suggest instead that it is more akin to taking off blinkers and discovering you had previously been seeing the world in monochrome, instead of living in Technicolor.

9

AGE OF 'ENLIGHTENMENT'?
1727–1840

THE EIGHTEENTH CENTURY has often been referred to as the Age of Enlightenment, although today we may question just how 'enlightened' it was. As Britain increased its grip on colonial assets and reaped the financial rewards of slave-run enterprises, the wealth that accumulated was ploughed back into an obsessive level of consumption of all things associated with the country's far-flung territories. An early collector on a global scale was Hans Sloane. Much of his wealth came from slave-run plantations in Jamaica, as well as his work as a society physician in London. He acquired coins, weapons and shoes as well as gemstones and precious metals, corals, shells, plant specimens, insects, animals and books. Frederick, prince of Wales, visited his collection in Chelsea and stated: 'How great an honour will redound to Britain to have it established for publick use.'[1] Sloane's private museum of curiosities became the British Museum, which opened in 1759. Only in recent years have the museum's intimate connections with slavery and colonisation been explored, most notably by the sculptor Hew Locke in his 2024–5 exhibition *what have we here?*

Sloane had replaced Sir Isaac Newton as president of the Royal Society in 1727. This scientific body had been established in 1660 to further knowledge of the physical world (even though systemic prejudice meant Francis Williams was refused full membership on racial grounds). However, there was no equivalent society for artists and architects. Schools and academies had opened in London but all fell short of offering artists a place to train, exhibit and hold rigorous debates. Things came to a head in 1768 when an internecine rivalry between two architects in the Society of Artists caused mass resignations. In November of that year four former directors successfully petitioned King George III to establish a Royal Academy of Arts, and thirty-six founder members became the first Royal Academicians.

It must have been a political and partisan place when it first opened its doors in a small gallery on Pall Mall in London. Membership had been purposefully capped – successful painters from the Society of Artists such as Joseph Wright (1734–1797) had not been invited to join and only two of the founder members, Mary Moser (1744–1819) and Angelica Kauffman (1741–1807), were women. Leading portrait painter Reynolds had to be persuaded to become the first president and his rival Gainsborough was ambivalent about his membership. More telling is the number of European artists living in Britain who were included: one-quarter of the founder members had been born on the continent. Other founder members we would call international today were Benjamin West (1738–1820) from America, and George Barret (1730–1784) and Nathaniel Hone (1718–1784) from Ireland (both considered British colonies at the time). The inclusion of such a high proportion of overseas artists was mirrored by the number who were simultaneously members of art academies in Italy and France, including Kauffman, Reynolds and West.

When the Royal Academy moved to larger premises at Somerset House on the Strand in 1780, paintings by West and Kauffman were commissioned for the Council Chamber ceiling, under which new Academicians would be elected. These paintings epitomised the aspirations of the Royal Academy to be a place of intellectual rigour and one that could compete with the more established classical academies on the continent. Kauffman's allegorical paintings showcase the building blocks of art – invention, composition, design and colour – as personified by women. They are not portraits but represent the art of painting itself. In *Design*, for example, a young woman sits in front of the famous Belvedere Torso. It had been unearthed in Rome during the Renaissance and a plaster cast was now part of the Royal Academy's teaching collection. The importance of Rome couldn't be emphasised more in *Design*, from the classical columns behind the figure and the sculpture she draws to her Italianate sandals. Her left hand holds a drawing board and she sketches the muscles of the naked male fragment with her right. Her sleeves are rolled up and the movement of drawing

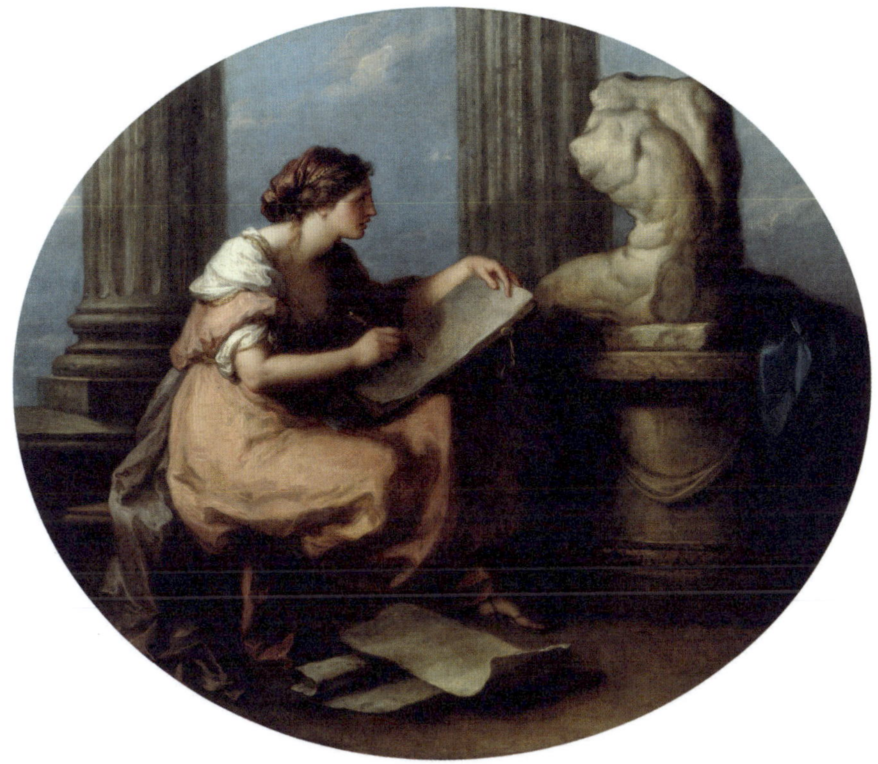

Angelica Kauffman, *Design*, oil on canvas, 1778–80

has dislodged her pink satin gown from her shoulder. Previous sketches litter the floor; she is steadfast in her relentless study of the antique. Kauffman's use of female figures to embody aspects of painting was a traditional one but the irony would not have been lost on her – women Academicians were not allowed to vote in the Council Chamber, just as they were not allowed into the life-drawing room.

SCIENCE MEETS ART

Those behind the foundation of the British Royal Academy were keen for it to match those on the continent, with their emphasis on studying classical sculpture first-hand and on creating an intellectual hierarchy for art that championed the moral rigour of history and mythological painting and belittled 'mere' portraits and still lifes. Perhaps this explains why Wright and George Stubbs (1724–1806) were not admitted at its inception. Wright was a successful portrait painter from Derby who was exhibiting in London, when the Society of Artists began to fracture. Stubbs had recently published his ground-breaking *Anatomy of a Horse* and was much in demand for his portraits of horses (and people). By the time they were eventually asked to join, in 1784 and 1781 respectively, they both refused – Wright felt slighted and Stubbs failed to submit a diploma work (the price of admission as a Royal Academician).

Wright was born in Derby and spent much of his working life there after training in London at the studio of the portraitist Thomas Hudson (1701–1779), who had previously taught Reynolds. Hudson followed the teachings of his father-in-law, the artist and theorist Jonathan Richardson (1667–1745), who wrote that 'a painter must not only be a poet, an historian, a mathematician &c, he must be a mechanick, his hand, and eye, must be as expert as his head is clear, and lively, and well stored with science'.[2] Wright was an accomplished portrait artist but he is best known today for his dramatically lit paintings of scientific experiments. He was fascinated by how things worked and built himself a viewing box in which he could stage mise-en-scène, studying how light fell and shadows pooled.

To further his career he began exhibiting at the Society of Artists. His large and complex paintings such as *A Philosopher Giving that Lecture on the Orrery, in Which a Lamp Is Put in the Place of the Sun* (exhibited 1766) and *An Experiment on a Bird in the Air Pump* (1768) were highlights of the Society's annual exhibitions and caused a reviewer in the *Gazetteer* to call Wright 'a very great and uncommon genius'.[3] Looking at the *Orrery* today I still feel the thrill of expectation as the scientific model is unveiled. Curious onlookers watch as the planets are shown to revolve around the sun. An oil lamp illuminates the eager children's faces, a young woman lost in thought, a diligent note-taking gentleman (Wright's friend, the cartographer Peter Perez Burdett) and the natural philosopher (scientist) leading proceedings in an eye-catching red gown. A silhouetted figure in the foreground offers us a shoulder over which to observe proceedings. To the right of the painting Wright has included a portrait of the naval officer Washington Shirley, fifth earl of Ferrers, who had his own orrery, and this strategic inclusion led to Shirley becoming the first owner of the paint-ing. Wright's training as a portraitist allowed him to create polished

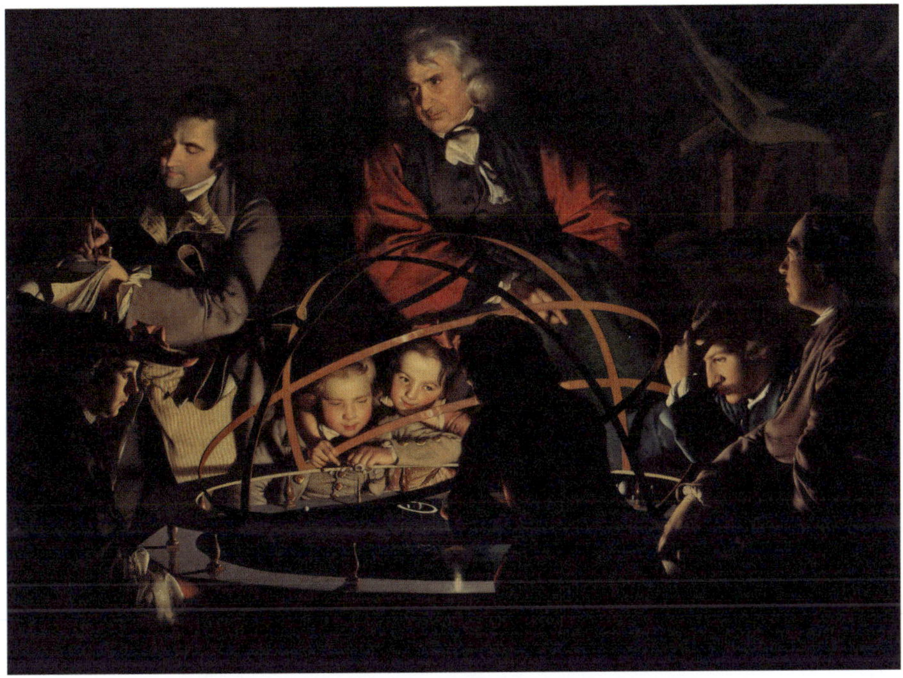

Joseph Wright of Derby, *A Philosopher Giving that Lecture on the Orrery, in Which a Lamp Is Put in the Place of the Sun*, oil on canvas, exhibited 1766

expressive faces, but it is the dramatic use of a central light source in an otherwise darkened room that adds the drama. This painting capitalised on the growing popularity of public science lectures and spliced together the British conversation piece with the theatrics of Caravaggio.

In the mid-1750s Stubbs spent eighteen months holed up in a barn in Horkstow in Lincolnshire with only a rotting horse carcass for company, sketching, measuring and studying each layer of muscle, sinew and bone from the front, back and side. He used a waxy substance injected into the blood vessels to help retain the horse's shape and held it up on a pulley system suspended from the barn's ceiling. His original drawings are in the collection of the Royal Academy. I carefully leafed through them in their Research Library and Archive, watching the horse shed its skin, muscles and organs to reveal its skeleton, a right foreleg raised as if it were still in motion. Stubbs transformed his anatomical drawings into a large portfolio of engravings and self-published the collection in 1766. His methodical and anatomically accurate studies allowed him to understand the horses he specialised in painting inside and out, whether he was creating imaginative works such as *Horse Devoured by a Lion* (1763) or commissioned portraits such as *Molly Longlegs* (1762).

Mary Delany (1700–1788) was never invited to become a Royal Academician. She made vividly coloured flower collages on black card, creating nearly 1,000 examples for her *Flora Delanica*, inspired by a visit to Joseph Banks where she viewed his collection of specimens. All are carefully labelled using the new classification system introduced by the Swedish naturalist Carl Linnaeus. Banks had accompanied Captain James Cook on his first world voyage (1768–71) and later became president of the Royal Society. He praised Delany's flowers as the only examples he would trust to 'describe botanically any plant without the least fear of

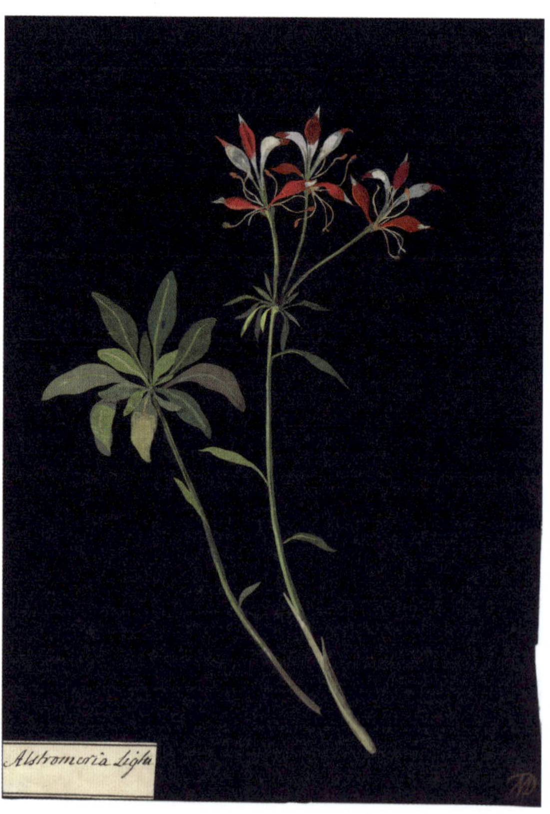

Mary Delany, *Alstromeria ligtu*, paper collage, 1779

committing an error'.[4] Cut freehand, the layers of coloured paper create a subtle three-dimensionality that enhances each flower's naturalism. Stamens dance over petals, sepals sit behind flowerheads, branches are knobbly with texture and fresh leaves appear to sprout from darker stems. If I had attempted these there would be gluey fingerprints everywhere, but Delany's collages are neat and precise. In *Achillea millefolium* we can make out the tiny white flowerheads that push up vertically from a central stem and slender fern-like leaves that circle the base above a short brown root. In *Alstro[e]meria ligtu* impossibly slender curls of paper represent stamens weaving between red and white petals while a cluster of variegated leaves is formed from seven or eight different greens.

Wright, Stubbs and Delany did not aspire to uphold Reynolds's goal of idealising nature. Instead Wright painted detailed scientific studies of light, Stubbs dissected an entire horse to better understand anatomy and Delany created scientifically accurate collages of flowers. They interrogated physical aspects of the world to create works of great accuracy and naturalism, reflecting the age of the scientific Enlightenment.

ARTISTS AS EXPLORERS

As a bullish Britain continued to exploit its colonies, the Royal Navy and Royal Society co-funded global journeys under the auspices of science. Captain Cook's first voyage across the Atlantic and Pacific oceans was to observe the Transit of Venus in 1769 and to search for Australia (then known hypothetically as Terra Australis Incognita). Banks was a wealthy man and paid for berths on Cook's voyage for himself, the artists Sydney Parkinson (*c.*1745–1771) and Alexander Buchan (died 1769), the naturalist Herman Spöring, fellow botanist Daniel Solander and four assistants. Cook circumnavigated the world in three years and the perilous journey claimed many lives. Parkinson died en route to Cape Town, and Buchan died in Tahiti, leaving Banks with no means of visualising his finds when he returned to Britain. So he recruited Stubbs to flesh out the new animals he had 'discovered', including a kangaroo and a dingo, giving him sketches, field notes and preserved specimens on which to base his paintings.

Banks understood the power of art to visualise his finds and circulate his ideas. Engravings appeared within a year of Stubbs's painting being completed, and his mouse-like marsupial with its head pivoted backwards was Britain's first glimpse of a kangaroo. Banks recruited the Royal Academician Zoffany to accompany him on Cook's second voyage (1772–5), but Banks's growing demands ended with him being refused passage.

Instead Cook's second voyage included the artist William Hodges (1744–1797). I've always been fascinated as to why artists would risk their lives to join expeditions like Cook's. Hodges must have known the fate of Parkinson and Buchan. But what the opportunity offered him was the potential for a vast array of exclusive new material. He was twenty-seven when the three-year journey began, a former pupil of the landscape artist Richard Wilson (1714–1782; another founder member of the Royal Academy). Wilson had visited Italy in 1750 and painted classical British landscapes in the seventeenth-century style of Claude Lorrain. Hodges painted in Wilson's style but with brand-new subject matter: views of Tahiti, Raiatea, Rapa Nui, Bora Bora, New Zealand and South Africa. And yet, when we look at his landscapes, they seem strangely familiar. War canoes appear to beach on Italian shores and the peaks of Tahiti are veiled as if seen through a hazy Claude glass (a small darkened mirror used by landscape artists and amateur painters to turn any view into a tonal Claudean scene). The indigenous population is reduced to decorative staffage, where interchangeable figures are inserted by landscape artists in the foreground purely to offer scale and touches of colour.

Hodges used aesthetic devices such as picturesque composition to help Western observers understand and 'enter' these new islands and countries. His painting of the barren island of Rapa Nui (Easter Island) features its iconic statues standing under a changeable European sky that throws into relief the pale stone of the figures with their red-stone topknots. Hodges added fallen boulders and human remains to stress the transitory nature of the civilisation who carved them. They represent the ruins of a former empire, recorded and repurposed for a British audience. He also painted several portraits. While these lack the confident brushwork of his landscapes, they offer perceptive likenesses of Cook and of Mai, a Raiatean islander living in Huahine near Tahiti who travelled back to Britain aboard Cook's second ship the *Adventure*, and who remained in London for two years before returning home with Cook as he embarked on his third and final global voyage.

The Bora Borans had conquered Raiatea when Mai was ten, killing his father and causing many – like Mai – to flee to Tahiti. Mai's reason for travelling to Britain was to acquire firearms, the Western weapon that he felt would give him the upper hand to recover his land. The life-size full-length portrait of Mai by Reynolds, formerly called *Omai* (1776), was the most celebrated painting of him, exhibited at the Royal Academy and circulated as an engraving. Mai stands in a barkcloth *tapa* that resembles a classical toga, his face Westernised by Reynolds for his British audience. His tattooed hands and turban

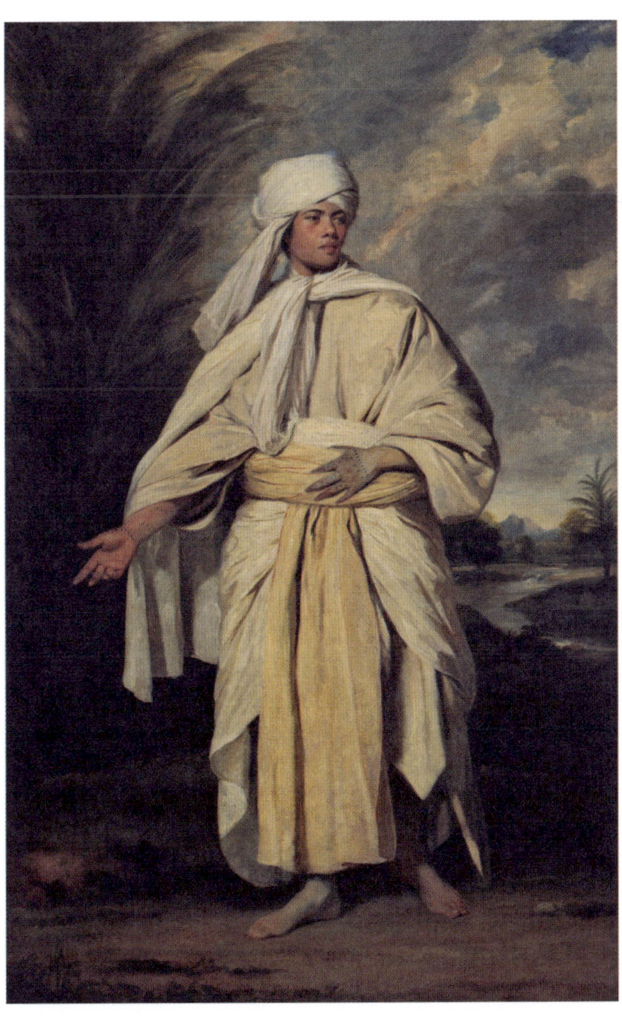

Joshua Reynolds, portrait of Mai, oil on canvas, *c*.1776

point to cultural difference, as does the token palm tree in Reynolds's generic landscape backdrop. However, accounts of Mai in London suggest he wore Western dress at all times and it remains unclear whether Mai or Reynolds was instrumental in choosing how he was depicted in the painting. Hodges's portrait of Mai appears to give a more closely observed physiological likeness. While the pose is awkward, it is countered by the artist's direct engagement with Mai. His wide nose and broad cheekbones have not been Westernised by Hodges and, in contrast to Reynolds, he pays particular attention to Mai's skin colour and the consistency of his thick black hair.

A large body of visual material acquired during Cook's three global voyages also made it back to Britain. The collections of Cook, Banks and the naturalist Johann Forster include a green nephrite pendant from New Zealand carved into a seated figure with shell inlay eyes, patterned barkcloth and wooden *ti'i* carvings from Tahiti taken from the prows of canoes. Cook's *ti'i* sculptures are of a man and a woman, their raised belly buttons shiny from repeated touching, their heads enlarged to stress their significance while their fingers have been reduced to shallow carved stripes. Hodges included such a *ti'i* carving, much enlarged, in his painting *Tahiti Revisited* (1776), disregarding its original purpose and placing it on the banks of a river, employing it as a sign of 'exotic' difference in his picturesque scene.

Although Banks is surrounded by many Polynesian items in his full-length portrait by West (1771–2), he gave many of his unclassified acquisitions away to friends and institutions. Cook gave his to patrons and King George III. Forster's collection was the best documented but it too was divided, with a selection given to Oxford University. Slowly, in the nineteenth century, the remains of these three collections gravitated towards the new Pitt Rivers Museum, which opened in Oxford in 1884. Today they are presented together in a single glass case on the first floor of the museum. These hugely significant artefacts are part of the story of art in Britain, from their first displays in private homes to their later assimilation into a public collection. In the early twentieth century, modernist artists working in Britain including Henri Gaudier-Brzeska and Henry Moore sought out sculptures from the Pacific islands, admiring their qualities that reduced the human body to its most essential form. But their current display does not acknowledge this aesthetic importance to Western art (we will look at this in Chapter 12).

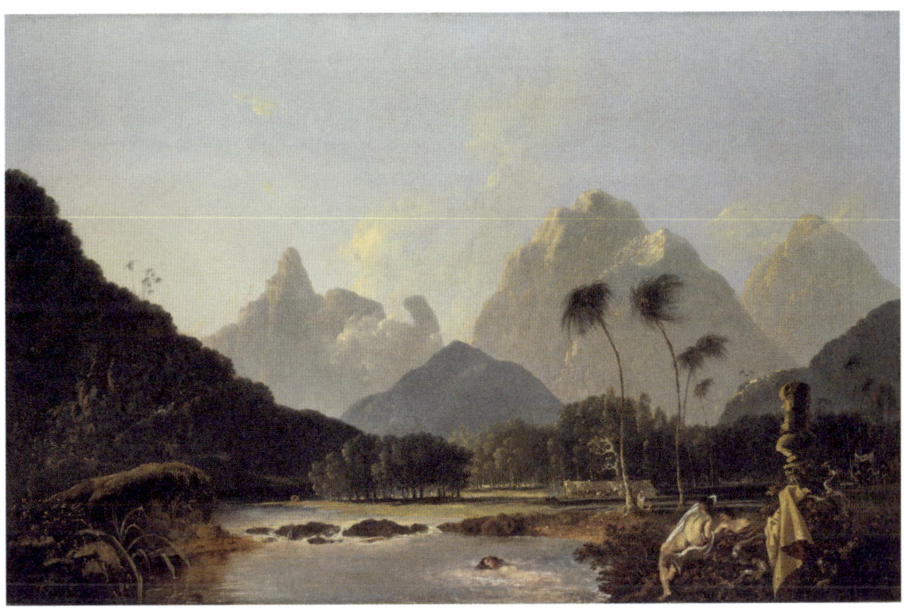

William Hodges, *Tahiti Revisited*, oil on canvas, 1776

NAWABS AND NABOBS

Context is everything. Art history as a discrete discipline coalesced in the eighteenth century, with discourses ranging from the beauty of the naked form in ancient Greek art (Johann Winckelmann) to the importance of education and hard work in achieving artistic genius (Reynolds). Art was never made in a vacuum, and understanding the climate of art's production at any given time allows us to make sense of why particular things happened – why Hodges turned every view into a Claudian arcadia, for example, or why Kauffman pushed on with history paintings instead of portraits. The context for artists' growing fascination with the subcontinent of India lies back in Elizabeth I's reign, when the East India Company was founded in 1600.

The East India Company started out as a joint-stock trading business, where investors pooled resources to ship wares from Asia (the 'East Indies') rather than the Americas (the 'West Indies'). Risk and reward were shared and the business model was a success – at its peak the East India Company controlled half the world's trade. But this control was bought at a high price. From its coastal trading stations in India the Company became greedy for control. It drove hard bargains with

Indian suppliers and provoked discord between the ruling parties, doing deals with local rivals and installing them as puppet leaders. It also invested in its own army and navy to protect its fleet of Indiamen, the merchant ships that carried produce back to British consumers.

The Company's headquarters were on Leadenhall Street in the City of London, and it employed artists to paint it in the best light. In the 1730s George Lambert (*c.*1700–1765) and Samuel Scott (*c.*1702–1772) embarked on a series of views of the Company's warehouses in the ports of Bombay (now Mumbai), Calcutta (Kolkata), Madras (Chennai) and Tellicherry (Thalassery) to hang in the directors' court room. Lambert and Scott did not visit any of these ports but based their paintings on second-hand accounts, maps and plans, as well as the Indiamen in dock in Deptford, London. In *Bombay* (1731) the Company's neoclassical warehouse gleams white behind the port wall as an array of British ships lies at anchor in the harbour. A white flare from a distant ship and a plume of spray next to the hull of an Indiaman suggest a level of competition from other parties keen to take the merchandise by force. Including this detail was purposeful – the threat of attack justified the growing fleet of gunships the Company kept stationed in India. Despite this dynamic inclusion, the British ensign flying from the fort at the harbour's mouth clarifies that the British remain in control.

In 1778 the Company commissioned Spyridon Romas (*c.*1735–1786), a Greek artist working in London, to design a large oval painting for the ceiling of the revenue committee room. *The East Offering Its Riches to Britannia* (*c.*1778) is not of the highest quality but its message was clear for all to see: Britannia's dominance over the world, thanks to the East India Company. Three women personify Britain, India and China. Britannia sits on a rocky outcrop with Old Father Thames at her feet. Beneath her, offering up a basket overflowing with strings of pearls, is bare-breasted India in loose-fitting *pajama*. Beside her China is ready to present a large blue-and-white porcelain vase and a crate of tea. The white-skinned Britannia, Union shield below her, also shows a titillating breast as she leans over, hands raised, examining the quality of the pearls on offer. Between the women, in the distance, an Indiaman in full sail brings the 'jewels' being offered back to Britain (in reality spices, tea, cotton and silk).

And yet, of course, these treasures were not being offered as gifts. What had started as a trading company had become a domineering behemoth with a private army bigger than Britain's own. If an Indian leader stood against it, the Company went to war. Robert Clive, who worked for the Company from 1743 to 1767, defeated the nawab of Bengal at Plassey, 145 kilometres north of the trading port of Calcutta. Clive, who became known as 'Clive of India', netted £234,000 for himself when he emptied the Bengal treasury, a tenth of the value of the hundred ships full of gold and silver that sailed back to Britain (£2.3 million, an astounding £270 million today). Francis Hayman (1708–1776) painted the 1757 *Battle of Plassey* for the hugely popular Vauxhall Pleasure Gardens in London just three years after it had taken place.

Hayman, Spyridon, Lambert and Scott never set foot in India. Theirs was an India of the imagination, a colonial fantasy. The East India Company was disbanded in 1873 (replaced by the British Raj), and the contents of its museum were dispersed later that decade. But through the art that remains we can conjure a vision of its employees swaggering through the London headquarters, pockets heavy with coin and heads filled with self-belief that Britain ruled the waves. This image leaves a bitter taste in my mouth, as I imagine the Georgian and later Victorian men who conducted colonial business under Spyridon's bare-breasted Britannia and tallied up their exploitative gains.

However, a number of artists including Hodges and Zoffany did travel to India. They toured the country, sketching the ancient remains and observing the interactions of Britons and Indians. Others based themselves in Company strongholds – London-born Tilly Kettle (1735–1786) set up his studio in Calcutta and Dublin-born Thomas Hickey (1741–1824) in Madras. Anna Maria Jones (1748–1829), the wife of William Jones, a British Supreme Court judge in Calcutta from 1783, was an accomplished botanical artist, but (until the nineteenth century) she was a rare exception to the rule as the British artists at work in India were predominantly men.

Hodges journeyed to India in 1780 following his three success-ful years with Cook. He spent a further three years exploring the Ganges, Bengal and Bihar, keen to paint the history of India into his landscapes. He cast an imperial eye over the country, focusing on the ruins of Indian mosques, captured forts and modern Western infrastructure, sketching and painting in situ for paintings such as *Tomb and Distant View of the Rajmahal Hills* (c.1782) and *A View of Marmalong Bridge with a Sepoy and Natives in the Foreground* (c.1780–1). Hodges was ambitious for his paintings, exhibiting them at the Royal Academy of Arts in London where he enjoyed considerable success. He capitalised on the lucrative market for foreign views by issuing a series of forty-eight aquatint prints called *Select Views of India, Drawn on the Spot* (1785–8). Such prints were valued for their perceived topographical accuracy and the picturesque glimpses they offered of distant lands (despite their clear imperial perspective). In his advert for subscriptions, Hodges emphasised that they were 'faithful representations of remarkable places in that remote country'.[5]

When Robert Clive returned to Britain he commissioned West to paint four huge canvases depicting his career in India for his dining room. West had never been to India and this series was never completed, but we can imagine them – one would certainly have been the *Battle of Plassey* that Hayman showcased at the Vauxhall Pleasure Gardens. By the end of the eighteenth century, enterprising artists were creating dramatic panoramic views of key battles in the aggressive imperial campaigns of the East India Company, which would lead to direct colonial rule of the entire continent by 1858. Robert Ker Porter (1777–1842) had never been to India either, but this didn't stop him painting a 36-metre-wide panorama of high drama, imagining the storming of the fort at Seringapatam (Srirangapatna) in 1799, a bloody finale to the reign of Tipu Sultan that ended the Mysore Wars. His 180-degree painting opened at the Lyceum Theatre in 1800, accompanied by a printed key so fee-paying visitors could keep up with the action and identify those involved, from subaltern lieutenants to the Tipu Sultan himself.

People like Clive were known as nabobs in Britain – men who had made their fortunes with the Company in India and exported their new wealth back to Britain, purchasing a landed country house or two along the way. Clive bought several houses including Claremont in Surrey and stuffed them full of Indian treasures. A 1771 inventory lists six Indian pictures among them; Clive's son Edward, who became governor of Madras, also collected Indian paintings for his seat at Powis Castle in Wales.

The British in India have often been depicted as steadfastly sticking to British rules of decorum and dress and only interacting with the 'locals' on the level of master–servant. But there is lots of evidence to the contrary. British scholars adopted Indian dress, Indian nawabs sought out British portraitists, Indian artists embraced Western painting methods and European artists responded to the intricate detail and high colour of Mughal painting. Art was used by both countries for diplomatic gifts and for strengthening ties between the two nations. Edinburgh-born George Willison (1741–1797) journeyed to Madras in 1774 with the help of his uncle George Dempster, a wealthy director of the Company. The nawab of the Carnatic (a kingdom of southern India) became a significant patron and Willison painted his entire family. An anonymous Indian artist painted *Mahadaji Sindhia Entertaining a British Naval Officer and Military Officer with a Nauch* (*c.*1815–20). It glossed over recent conflicts between the Sindhia dynasty and the East India Company to depict the late ruler Mahadaji and British officers seated side by side enjoying a dancing display, suggesting it was made for a British market.

Zoffany, in India from 1783 to 1789, painted an intricate scene of international relations in *Colonel Mordaunt's Cock Match* (*c.*1784–6). It captures a cockfight in action in the foreground, with Indian and British men holding spare birds. But while this may suggest a battle between the two sides, the outstretched arms of a slender John Mordaunt (in tight white breeches and waistcoat) and the stockier Asaf, nawab of Lucknow (in translucent *jama* and orange *pajama*), suggests otherwise. It was painted for Warren Hastings, former governor-general of Bengal, and

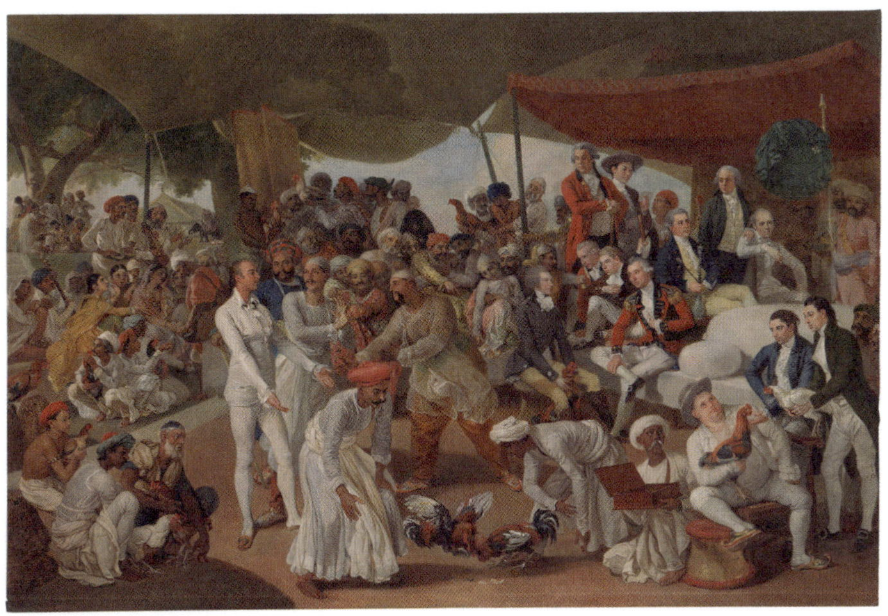

Johan Zoffany, *Colonel Mordaunt's Cock Match*, oil on canvas, *c.*1784–6

hung in his library at Daylesford House in Gloucestershire. Asaf had a copy made for himself as well, which was finished by a Lucknow artist.

'AM I NOT A MAN AND A BROTHER?'

Previous volumes on the history of British and Irish art have mostly ignored India as subject, source and inspiration. They have largely overlooked the artists who journeyed with Cook or explored distant lands for themselves. If the landscapes and portraits they produced were considered, it was without a rigorous exploration of just who was looking at what and how. The imperial context in which they were produced was ignored, as were the numerous examples of cross-cultural exchange between artists, when both should have been at the centre of our understanding. Edward Said noted in *Culture and Imperialism* (1993) that we cannot understand Western culture without understanding and acknowledging the importance of empire in shaping and conditioning that culture.[6] His hugely influential books on colonialism and culture opened the door for us to begin to see the complex connections – good and bad – between different communities and cultures.

Similarly, books on the history of the British Isles have often side-stepped any consideration of slavery, at home and in overseas territories. Yet it was endemic throughout the eighteenth century and was increasingly debated as the years progressed. From the 1760s British campaigns to abolish slavery laid bare the connections between the consumption of goods such as sugar and tobacco and slave labour. Lord Mansfield's ruling in 1772 that the bindings of slavery had no traction in the British Isles gave impetus to this nascent movement. Black American slaves heard of Mansfield's ruling and enlisted in the British army during the American War of Independence (1775–83) in the belief that in Britain, after the war ended, they would be free men. By contrast white American artists, as colonial subjects, could choose to move to Britain and avoid the fighting altogether.

Following in the footsteps of his mentor West, who had travelled to Britain via Italy in 1763 and never returned to America, John Singleton Copley (1738–1815) moved from Boston to Italy in 1774 for a year of study. He left behind a successful portrait business, but when the American War of Independence broke out, he too decided to relocate to London. Like West, who had also worked as a portraitist in America before switching to history painting in Britain, Copley enjoyed exploring the wide range of options available to a white male artist in eighteenth-century London. Following West's lead, he made a name for himself as a contemporary history painter, at times eschewing exhibiting at the Royal Academy (into which he was elected in 1779) to exhibit in hired rooms, charging the public a shilling a visit and working with leading print publishers such as John Boydell to ensure maximum dissemination of his images.

When Copley's *Watson and the Shark* was unveiled at the Royal Academy's annual exhibition in 1778, it was a terrifying and sublime success. It was a dramatic retelling of the rescue of the young British sailor Brook Watson from Havana harbour in Cuba thirty years earlier, when he was almost eaten by a shark after going for a swim. Copley packs the rescue boat with nine men, who pull on the oars and stab at the shark. Two lean far over the edge of the boat, hands grazing the green water, trying to grab Watson, who frantically reaches higher,

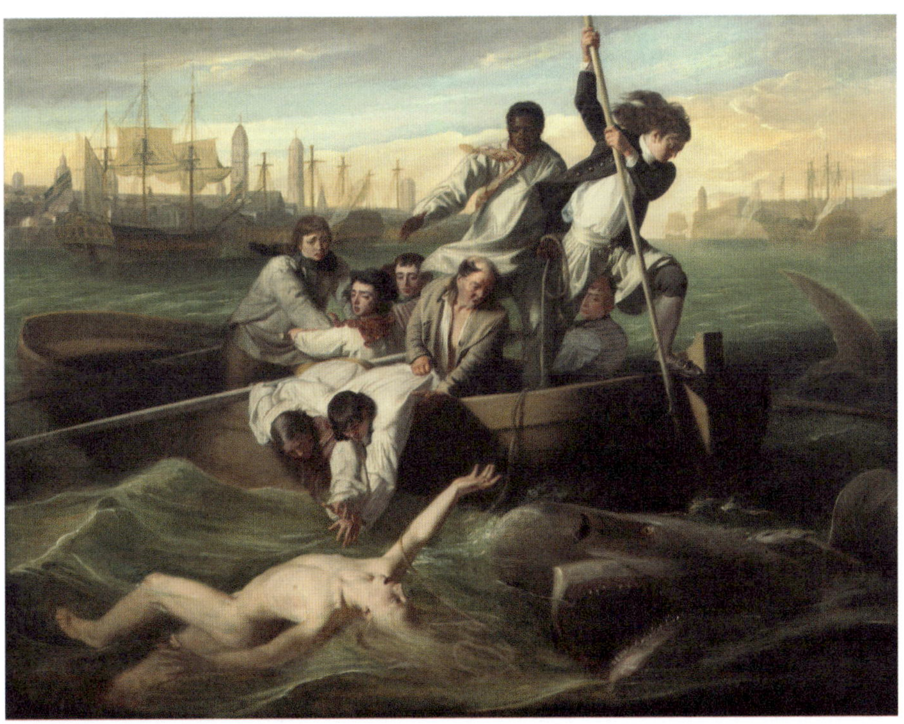

John Singleton Copley, *Watson and the Shark*, oil on canvas, 1778

upwards, to the man who stands at the highest point on the boat, rescue rope in hand. We can see he has thrown one end of the rope that is now coiled around Watson's outstretched arm and is about to pull him to safety.

Painting Watson's rescuer as a Black seaman was a last-minute decision for Copley, as his preparatory drawings show a white servant in the role. Some reviewers brought their prejudices to play and saw the figure as 'idle', despite the clear evidence that he is about to be the one to save Watson. They also failed to see that it is the dynamism of this man that gives the composition its drama. The diagonal thrust that begins with Watson's outstretched hand and rises up through the white-shirted bodies of the two men over the edge of the boat ends with the outstretched arm and smock of the standing sailor. It is this figure who will reach Watson and pull him to safety, the movement of his smock and scarf indicating that he is anything but static, idle or passive. (The young Romantic French artist Théodore Géricault must have known of this painting through circulating prints because, forty years later, his *Raft of the Medusa* uses a similar dynamic diagonal composition for his own sea rescue painting, with a Black sailor similarly being shown as the rescuer, waving his shirt to catch the attention of passing ships.)

So why did Copley change the identity of this figure at the last moment? With the American War of Independence raging, perhaps he was making a statement about the hypocrisy of a country fighting for 'freedom' while hundreds of thousands of Black men, women and children remained enslaved there. When he worked in Boston as a portraitist it is estimated that 60 per cent of his sitters would have owned slaves – through marriage he himself became a slave owner. Perhaps it was in response to the growing calls for slavery to end in Britain, or to represent the egalitarian position of all men, Black and white, when faced with disaster. While we do not know who Copley used as a model, the face is clearly based on careful life studies (unlike some of the more generic faces of the men rowing the boat).

Josiah Wedgwood (1730–1795) crafted a jasperware medallion showing a Black man in shackles pleading 'Am I not a man and a brother?' that became the official emblem of the newly formed Society for the Abolition of Slavery. Imagine holding this in your hand. A fellow human being kneels, hands clasped in desperate hope, heavy chains linking wrists to ankles. He is not asking for money or love but for the basic human right of freedom. Abolitionists took handfuls with them on tours of the British Isles. Women had them fashioned into brooches, bracelets and hairpins to advertise their allegiance to the cause, while men carried tobacco boxes inset with the medallion. (I fear the bitter irony of this was lost on them – tobacco was harvested by slave labour in Virginian plantations in America.) The fashion for young Black servants serving hot chocolate was slowly replaced by a growing understanding of the inhumanity of slavery. Former slaves including Equiano published candid accounts of the atrocities they had faced on the Middle Passage while being transported in shackles from their African homeland to plantations in the Americas, a journey lasting up to ninety days.

Equiano was a key member of the 'Sons of Africa' abolition movement, a group of twelve Black men who campaigned alongside white MPs William Wilberforce and Charles Fox and civil servant Granville Sharp. There are many oil portraits of these white abolitionists, and large marble monuments commemorate their lives such as that of Charles Fox, Britain's first foreign secretary, in Westminster Abbey. Carved by celebrated sculptor Richard Westmacott (1775–1856), it features a corpulent Fox expiring in the arms of a nubile Liberty, with Peace draping herself in sorrow over his feet. Kneeling by his bedside is an anonymous Black man. He is unshackled and clasps his hands to pray for Fox, who was instrumental in the abolition of the slave trade in Britain in 1807. The Black men and women who campaigned alongside white abolitionists such as Fox were not recorded in the same way and were subsequently overlooked by history until recently. Only now are they rightfully being reinstated.

Enslaved people tried to fight for their own rights but retribution was swift and severe. The visionary artist William Blake (1757–1827) contributed engravings to John Stedman's book on revolt in Surinam plantations in 1796.[7] Henry Fuseli (1741–1825), who specialised in supernatural scenes, turned his dramatic imagination to slavery for his 1806 engraving *The Negro Revenged*, which illustrated William Cowper's poem *The Negro's Complaint*. But the greatest cause of death was the Middle Passage itself. As late as 1840, J.M.W. Turner (1775–1851) chose to paint a historical slave-ship tragedy to focus attention on the first international convention of the British and Foreign Anti-Slavery Society, held in London that year to lobby other nations into renouncing slavery. In *Slave Ship (Slavers Throwing Overboard the Dead and Dying – Typhoon Coming On)* Turner depicted a horrific event that occurred on the Middle Passage in 1781, where the captain of the slaver *Zong* threw more than 130 shackled and sick slaves into the sea alive so he could claim compensation money for those 'lost at sea' in a storm (there was no payout for those lost to disease).

In the next chapter we will look at Turner's revolutionary approach to landscape, but this painting shows us that no artist exists in a vacuum and slavery touched everyone living and working in the British Isles, both directly and indirectly. As we enter the nineteenth century we must bear in mind Robert Winder's conclusion in *Bloody Foreigners*, that 'the fortunes founded on slavery . . . shaped the structure of British life as decisively and irrevocably as had William the Conqueror's gifts of land to his favoured knights'.[8]

10

RADICAL LANDSCAPES
1740–1860

IN THE ULSTER Museum in Belfast is a landscape that looks as if it belongs simultaneously to the past, present and future. I can see it is painted on vellum – the animal-skin ground used for medieval manuscripts and Tudor portrait miniatures – but it isn't that old, because the tiny figures wear clothes from the mid-eighteenth century. It is a painting of tall basalt columns of the natural phenomenon known as the Giant's Causeway in County Antrim. It's a subject that fits comfortably within the Age of Enlightenment and its fascination with the

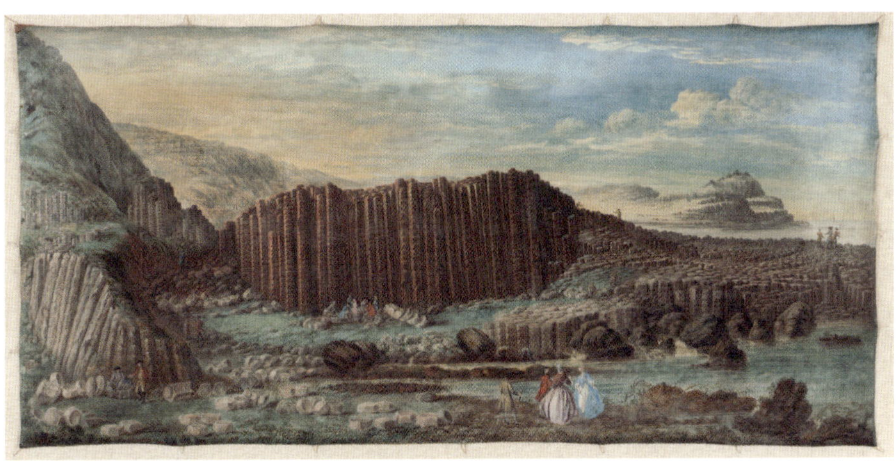

Susanna Drury, *Giant's Causeway*, watercolour on vellum, 1739–40

natural world. Painted in watercolour, a popular medium for eight-eenth-century artists who liked to paint outdoors, this detailed work also points the way to the future of landscape painting, when subsequent wars in Europe made travel beyond the British Isles nearly impossible and artists and travellers alike began looking to their own areas of natural beauty rather than those on the continent.

Susanna Drury (*c*.1698–1770) was the first artist to paint the Giant's Causeway with any degree of accuracy. Schematic maps of the site had been published around the time it was 'discovered' by British scientists in the late seventeenth century. Irish folklore held that it was a road built by the giant Fionn mac Cumhaill (also known as Finn McCool) to reach Scotland so he could fight his nemesis, the Scottish giant Benandonner, but Royal Society scientists saw a different history. The distinctive fac-eted columns are volcanic basalt, formed over fifty million years ago when a vast lava flow cooled and contracted, cracking into columns as it did so. Some 40,000 of them stretch along the coast, forming the Causeway's cliff-face and extending under the sea. But when they first came to the attention of the natural philosopher Sir Robert Redding in 1689 he noted: 'These Columns are so regularly ranged and fitted one to the other that it seems rather the work of art than nature.'[1] Ironically it would take an artist to convince people of their scientific significance.

Frustratingly little is known of Drury's career as an artist. She was one of five Anglo-Irish siblings and her brother Franklin was a mini-aturist, a limner. The level of detail she includes in her four Giant's Causeway paintings (1739–40), as well as her use of watercolour, suggest this was her training too. I don't know what led her to paint this scene, but I can see that she was committed. Mary Delany, the botanical artist we met in the last chapter, wrote admiringly that 'Mrs Drury . . . lived three months near the place, and went almost every day. I can do nothing so exact and finished.'[2] It is hard to imagine what the conditions must have been like for Drury. The Causeway was three miles from the nearest town of Bushmills, and there was no coast road until 1834. To reach the Causeway I walked along the cliffs and took a steep cliffside stair, 162 steps long, but I could have taken the easier tarmac road from the nearby car park. Neither was available for Drury. For her it would have been a muddy hike across exposed fields before she began the descent. And yet she sketched on site almost every day, and her final paintings suggest she conducted rigorous empirical research.

Five years after winning first prize in the Dublin Society competition with these paintings, she commissioned a suite of engravings. They were dedicated to John Boyle, fifth earl of Orrery and fifth earl of Cork, an Anglo-Irish writer who was friends with Samuel Johnson. This indicates she was a well-connected artist and so it is infuriating that hardly any other works by her survive and we know so little about her life. But her *Giant's Causeway* lived on through her prints, which were also used to illustrate Diderot's widely circulated 1765 encyclopaedia. The prints include tiny numbers and letters scattered across the landscape, with a key below explaining the scientific importance of each aspect of the site. These are based on Drury's field notes with measurements, colours and general observations. Many of the scientists at the Royal Society did not venture to see the Giant's Causeway for themselves but relied on Drury's paintings and prints to further understand the geology of the British Isles.

'I'LL *PROSE* IT HERE, I'LL *VERSE* IT THERE, I'LL *PICTURESQUE* IT EVERYWHERE'

The eighteenth century was when landscape found its voice and the nineteenth century is when it began to sing. This analogy is not as strange as it might seem, because landscape came to embody a wide range of human emotions as artists sought to convey fear, melancholy, love and happiness through the trees and vistas they painted. It was a time when Britain's imperial might was in the ascendant and ownership – of land, of people, of commodities – was reaching unprecedented heights. This is inherently connected with the growing interest in landscape painting for artists and collectors, as the land became a view to be shaped, controlled and – above all – owned.

Artists had been painting the landscape since Roman times, but it was always the backdrop, never the leading lady. It was only in the seventeenth century that artists such as Claude Lorrain in Italy and Jacob van Ruisdael in the Netherlands began to concentrate solely on the view itself. Welsh-born Richard Wilson spent seven years in Rome in the 1750s, crafting a style that led him to be seen as the father of British landscape painting. This concentration on the view echoed the findings of leading philosophers such as the Anglo-Irish Edmund Burke, whose 1757 enquiry into the sublime and the beautiful in landscape became hugely influential. An aspect of the beautiful was the picturesque, popularised by the Reverend William Gilpin (himself an artist) in his *Observations on the River Wye, and Several Parts of South Wales, etc, Relative Chiefly to Picturesque Beauty*, published in 1782. He defined the picturesque as 'that peculiar kind of beauty which is agreeable in a picture'.[3]

Gilpin searched for the picturesque in nature but readily admitted that 'nature is most defective in composition and must be a little assisted'. The 'natural' view was in fact a created one, by Gilpin and artists such as Hodges and Wilson (as well as by the leading gardener of the day, Lancelot 'Capability' Brown). As Gilpin admitted, to create his picturesque view he would 'take up a tree here, and plant it there. I pare a knoll, or make an addition to it.'[4] Trees and people in the foreground were positioned to catch your eye, their pointing hands or ruffling branches directing your gaze towards a stream or path that would glide from the foreground to the midground. Then there would be something of interest – a bridge or castle, a ruin or waterfall – before you were drawn further into the distance, towards mauve mountains or a receding townscape, all but lost in a misty haze. It never rains in a picturesque painting, but – as exemplified by Claude – the sun often infuses the pale blue sky with a peachy golden glow. Compare Wilson's *Pembroke Town and Castle* (1774) to George Barret's *The Waterfall at Powerscourt* (c.1762) or J.M.W. Turner's *Crossing the Brook* (1815) and you can see how pervasive the trend was. Views of Pembrokeshire, County Wicklow and Devon are homogenised by the picturesque, just as India, Rapa Nui and Tahiti were in Hodges's paintings. The landscape – any landscape – was rendered comfortably familiar and pleasing to the eye. A view could be recognised but so too could the picturesque style of painting that softened and made harmonious the entire British Isles (and beyond).

The small inconsequential figures (the 'staffage') in Drury's painting also indicate the exponential rise in tourism that was by now occurring. John Knox (1778–1845) painted *Landscape with Tourists at Loch Katrine* (c.1815–20) with elegant visitors standing on the bank of the loch in the heart of the Trossachs in the Scottish highlands. Transportation had improved, and those who could afford it were persuaded to travel by the growing number of guidebooks as well as references to beauty spots in contemporary novels and poems. Sir Walter Scott's *The Lady of the Lake* (1810) was responsible for a rapid uptick in tourism at Loch Katrine, just as Aidan Turner's bare-chested *Poldark* boosted the Cornish economy when the series first aired on television in 2015.

Thomas Rowlandson mocked the hordes of artists who battled the wind and rain to tour Wales in the hope of securing views. Turner visited Wales, as did his rival view-maker Thomas Girtin (1775–1802). Hodges captured its castles, as did homegrown talent Wilson. Rowlandson was a skilled portraitist but he is best known as a biting caricaturist and social satirist. In 1809 he produced a series of coloured engravings called *The Tour of Dr Syntax: In Search of the Picturesque* with verses by William Combe. He pokes fun at all those in rapture to the picturesque when Dr Syntax states the purpose of his tour:

> I'll ride and *write*, and *sketch* and *print*,
> And thus create a real mint;
> I'll *prose* it here, I'll *verse* it there
> And *picturesque* it everywhere.[5]

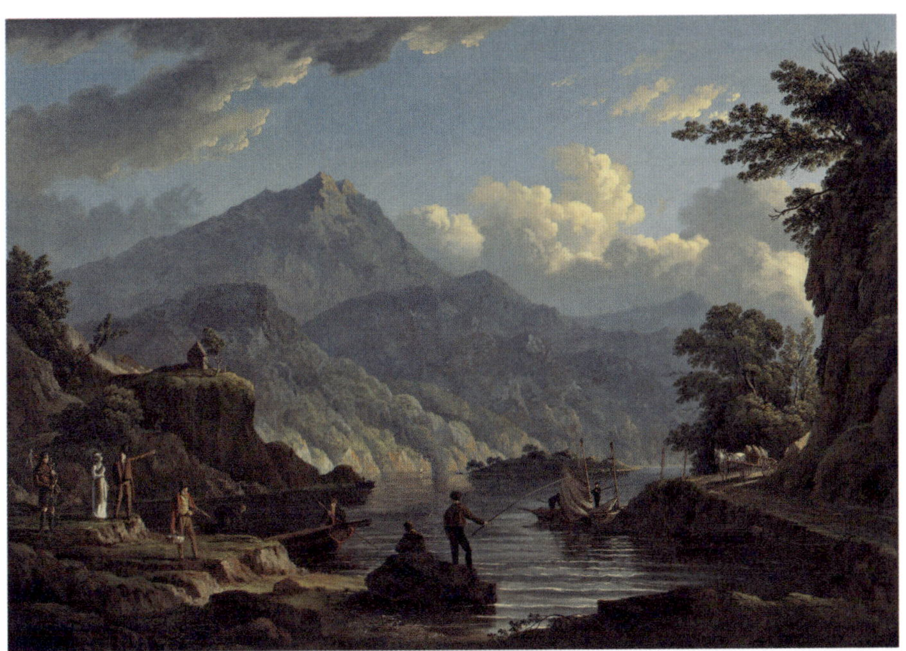

John Knox, *Landscape with Tourists at Loch Katrine*, oil on canvas, *c*.1815–20

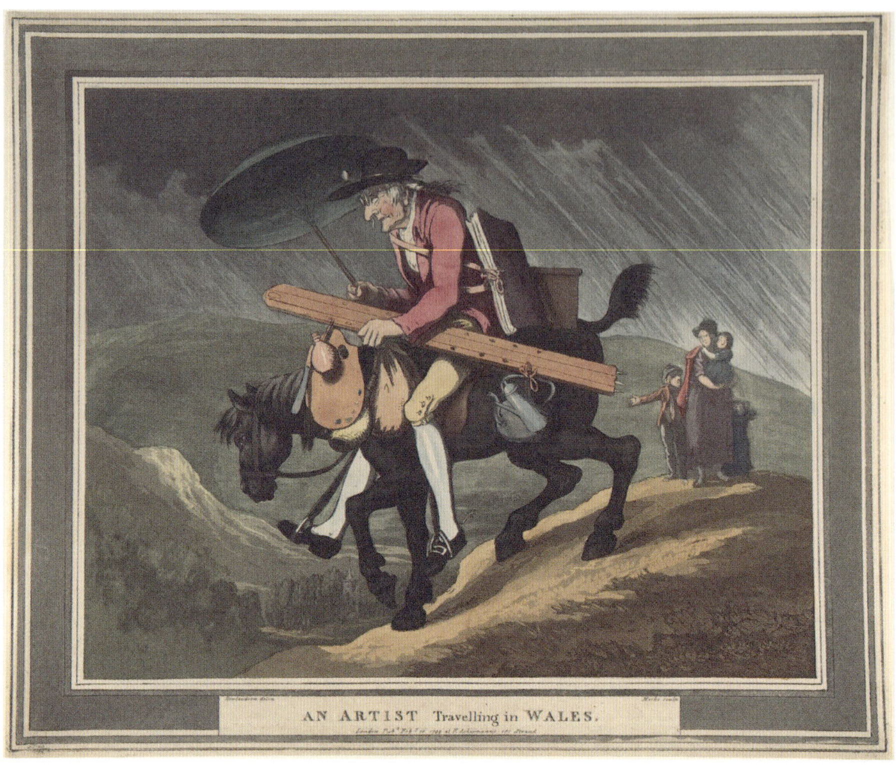

Thomas Rowlandson, *An Artist Travelling in Wales*, etching and aquatint with hand colouring, 1799

Rowlandson's 1799 aquatint print *An Artist Travelling in Wales* shows a man in frock coat and breeches balanced on the back of a long-suffering pony, surrounded by his collapsible easel, palette, sketchbook and supplies. This is the reality of searching for the picturesque view – I can imagine Turner embracing these conditions but Rowlandson's artist is ill equipped. The small green parasol does little to protect him from the cloudburst that drives rain diagonally across the barren hills towards him.

THE THRILLING TINGLE OF TERROR

If Rowlandson turned the picturesque into a lucrative verb, other nineteenth-century artists would turn the sublime into a shuddering juggernaut of emotional intensity. The sublime in landscape was also underpinned by theory, this time drawn from Burke's *A Philosophical Enquiry into the Origin of Our Ideas of the Sublime and Beautiful* (1757). Burke held that fear was at the heart of the sublime. The sheer power of nature could astonish and terrify. Waterfalls were no longer seen from a safe distance but thundered down in front of your eyes, drenching you in spray. Storms raged overhead rather than on the horizon; cliffs became vertiginous and landscapes apocalyptic. This terror was no longer external but internal, something that caused a physical response, the nerve-tingling thrill of absolute fear. 'No passion so effectually robs the mind of all its powers of acting and reasoning as fear', Burke wrote. 'Whatever therefore is terrible, with regard to sight, is sublime too.'[6] Today it might be a rollercoaster ride or boat trip under Niagara Falls – it's the moment when you can no longer rationalise your experience and instead you feel it with every nerve in your body.

Early incarnations of art approaching the sublime were spectacular. In 1781 Philippe Jacques de Loutherbourg (1740–1812) opened his *Eidophusikon* in Lisle Street in London. De Loutherbourg was a talented landscape painter who looked to Dutch rather than Italian antecedents. He was a member of the French Academy and had been the king's painter before moving to London in 1771 to take advantage of the growing market for landscape paintings. He carried with him a letter of introduction to David Garrick, the famous actor-manager of the Theatre Royal in Drury Lane. De Loutherbourg would work there for the next ten years as its chief scene designer. His sets included the use of puppets, lighting, pyrotechnics and sound effects and he was the most creative designer in Europe, but his *Eidophusikon* took this one step further. It was a stage set without actors and was designed to be an immersive experience, with different landscapes animated by sunrises, sunsets and storms. The audience sat on benches in front of a large ornate picture frame, 2 metres wide, within which each view was staged in turn. A harpsichord provided mood music, occasionally someone sang, and the viewer was transported around the world. Dawn broke across Greenwich Park followed by noon in Tangiers, sunset in Naples, a moonrise over the Mediterranean and, as a finale, a loud flashing storm that culminated in a shipwreck.

Only with video art and immersive installations in the late twentieth century did artists approach the complexity and ambition seen in De Loutherbourg's *Eidophusikon*. It pre-dated the first 360-degree 'panorama' painting by ten years and must have been a spectacular sight. William Henry Pyne, an artist who visited the *Eidophusikon* as a boy, remembered the moment the curtain rose on daybreak over Greenwich, 'so true to nature, that the imagination of the spectator sniffed the sweet breath of morn'.[7] But by the finale he was terrified, with the storm raging over the shipwreck a sublime act that was 'awful and astonishing'. Reynolds was a regular attendee and Gainsborough paid multiple visits. During one performance he noted that De Loutherbourg's version of a storm was superior to the one that was wreaking havoc outside at the same time.[8]

De Loutherbourg sold the *Eidophusikon* after a couple of seasons, and later in the 1780s he travelled to Switzerland for six months, returning to London to paint his masterpiece, *Falls of the Rhine at Schaffhausen* (1788), a tumultuous foaming waterfall that dwarfed the buildings and people nearby. De Loutherbourg knew how to harness the sublime and throw it full pelt at the public. This painting is 2 metres wide so it engulfs you as you approach, filling your range of vision. You wonder if Turner saw this when it was exhibited at the Royal Academy annual exhibition, where De Loutherbourg was a member. Turner would have been thirteen and would enrol at the Royal Academy Schools the following year, so it's a possibility. He would later frequent De Loutherbourg's studio, keen to learn how he made his saturated pigments, and De Loutherbourg's skill at painting with coloured light must have fascinated the younger artist.

Turner was quick to pick up on the latest trends in landscape painting. His early work is often picturesque in nature, but you feel it was the sublime that captured his heart and his imagination. Like the early paintings of Wilson, Turner began by including historical figures in his landscapes to elevate them in the eyes of the Royal Academy. But one look at his 1812 *Snow Storm: Hannibal and his Army Crossing the Alps* and you can see it is the raging storm that looms over the men on the mountain pass like a deadly tsunami that is his real subject. By 1842, when he painted *Snow Storm: Steam-Boat off a Harbour's Mouth*, the black hull of the foundering steamer is barely visible within a vortex of wind, waves and snow that whips around the entire canvas. This is a version of the sublime that I can see, taste and feel. That metallic taste in my mouth is fear as I am transported to the deck of the steamer in a violent squall or feel the snowstorm engulf me as I make my way along the Alpine pass, dwarfed by the enormity of nature.

These paintings are both over a metre wide, an ambitious scale for a landscape that ensured it wouldn't be overlooked in the annual Royal Academy exhibitions. But John Constable (1776–1837), Turner's contemporary, decided to emulate the scale of De Loutherbourg when he created his series of views that became known as his six-footers. Beginning with *The White Horse* in 1819, ending with *Salisbury Cathedral from the Meadows* in 1831, and including *The Hay Wain* (1821) and *The Leaping Horse* (1825), Constable's giant landscapes were a statement of intent. The size helped them stand out in exhibitions, of course, but by painting landscape on this scale he was implying that it deserved to be the dominant work on the wall, that landscape alone – without historicising or mythological elements – could hold its own. The scale allows you to step inside Constable's world, to see nothing else as you gaze on his breeze-tossed trees, the boats gliding over the glassy water surrounding his father's mill, the changeable skies overhead and the people working the land. Constable

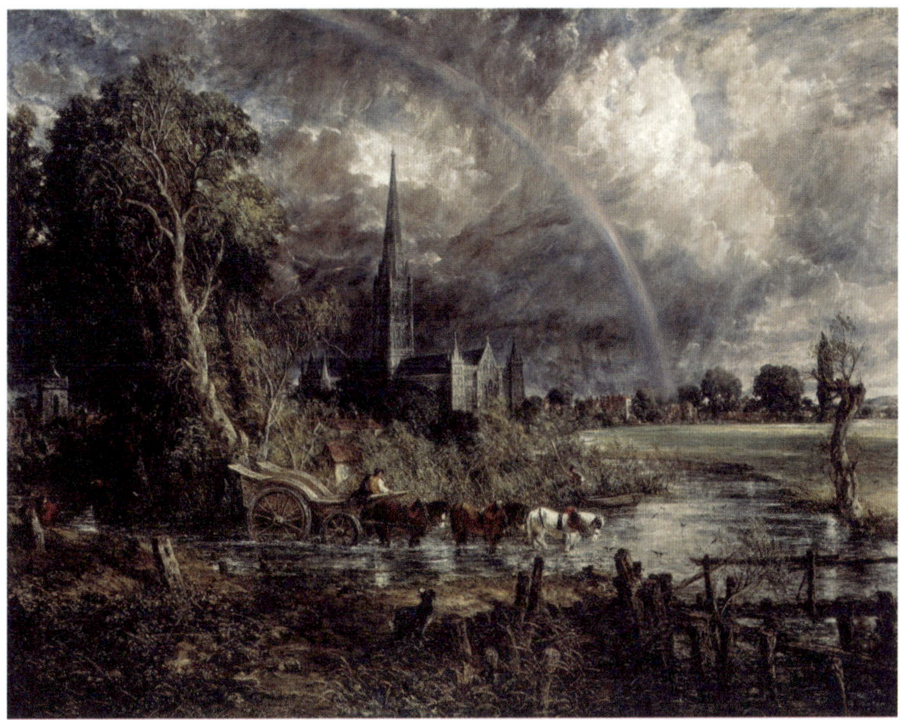

John Constable, *Salisbury Cathedral from the Meadows*, oil on canvas, 1831

gives us a counterpoint to Turner's sublime, a similarly immersive and emotive experience but one without the spine-tingling feeling of dread.

For Constable, the landscape was synonymous with feeling. He painted ephemeral fast-moving clouds like nature's moods and he loved a rainbow. In 1807 William Wordsworth wrote a poem dedicated to the same phenomenon: 'My heart leaps up when I behold / A rainbow in the sky'.[9] Wordsworth was a Romantic poet and for the Romantics the bond between nature and humankind was absolute. They stressed the importance of independent thinking at a time when the industrial revolution was picking up pace, when machines such as power looms and steam engines were taking the place of workers and animals. Constable and Turner's focus on capturing the transient moods of nature through the prism of their own emotions dovetailed with the beliefs of poets like Wordsworth, Percy Bysshe Shelley, Felicia Hemans and William Blake to create a pan-arts Romantic movement. This was a pivotal moment for how people looked at and experienced art. The art historian Jonathan Crary has described this as a 'modernisation of vision'. Vision went from being external, something fixed and timeless, to something internal, dependent on the person looking, making it personal and contingent.[10]

Blake was both poet and artist. In his watercolours and books he revealed a different connection between Romanticism and sublime nature. For him, and for several of his peers, nature and God were irrevocably connected. The artist was a conduit to expressing the beauty and terror of nature as conjured by the ultimate Creator. Blake's acolyte Samuel Palmer (1805–1881) employed the sun's warming rays to express the light of God in his modestly scaled but psychologically intense paintings. Both Blake and Palmer existed on the fringes of the London art world; Palmer was largely self-taught and Blake became his guiding light. But John Martin (1789–1854) would make a greater visual impact, exhibiting his vast canvases of biblical armageddon at the Royal Academy.

Martin took an unorthodox route to fine art by working as a painter for a coachman and then in a ceramics and glass business. He realised he would never make his name that way and so began painting landscapes in the style of Claude. But it was with his *Sadak in Search of the Waters of Oblivion* (1812) that he made his mark. It was nearly 2 metres tall and featured a dramatic rocky landscape illuminated by bolts of lightning. Sadak clings to a rocky outcrop as a waterfall tumbles around him. He is a spent figure, dwarfed by the fiery red rocks and black cavernous voids of this sublime landscape.

A reviewer in the *Examiner* offered a back-handed compliment with the conclusion that 'this subject would afford a sublime treat from the hand of Mr Turner'.[11]

Sadak was a character from *Tales of the Genii* (1764) by the British chaplain James Ridley but Martin soon switched to the Bible for his cataclysmic subjects. His vast canvases and prints (ensuring maximum circulation) depicted a host of scenes, from *Adam and Eve Driven Out of Paradise* to the *Seventh Plague of Egypt* and *Joshua Commanding the Sun to Stand Still upon Gibeon*. Martin didn't have the expressive brushstrokes of Constable or Turner, employed to such powerful emotive

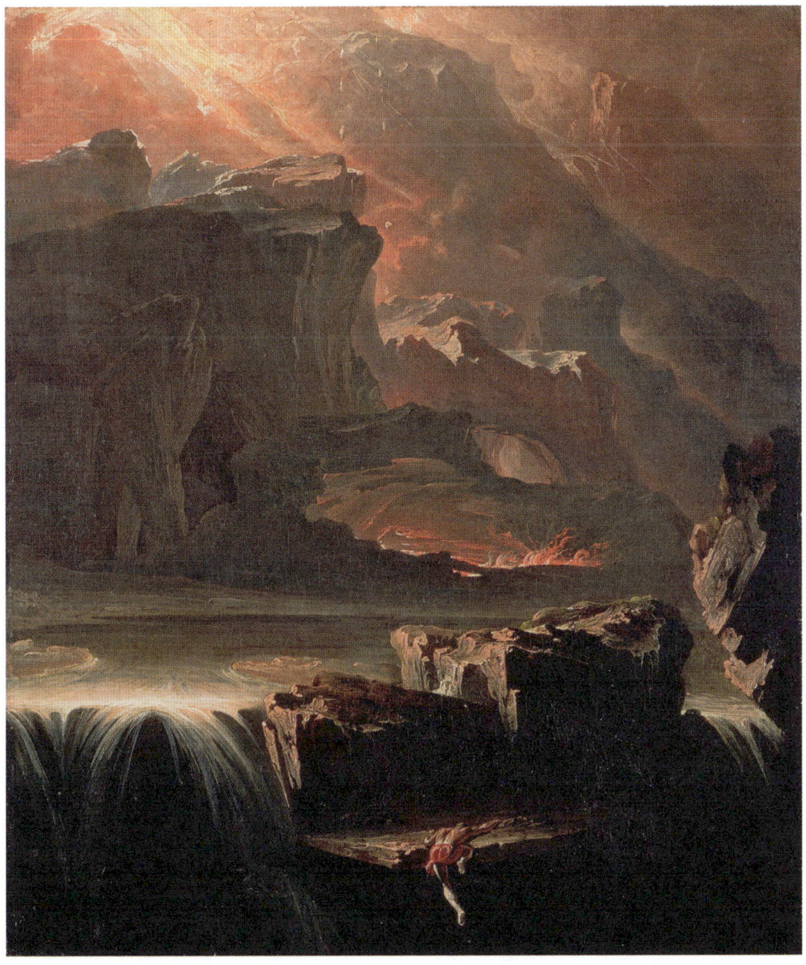

John Martin, *Sadak in Search of the Waters of Oblivion*,
oil on canvas, 1812

effect, but his commercial training meant he understood spectacle and scale just as De Loutherbourg had done. Dramatic lighting, epic storms, soaring rockfaces and figures dwarfed by historical and biblical disasters became his trademark, culminating in his three late masterpieces *The Last Judgement*, *The Great Day of His Wrath* and *The Plains of Heaven*, all completed in 1853, the year before he died. These canvases were each over 3 metres wide and toured the country following his death. Compared with the *Eidophusikon*, which cost five shillings a visit (£22 today), Martin's paintings could be seen for sixpence (£2). A flyer for their display in St George's Hall in Bradford claimed they were 'the most sublime and extraordinary pictures in the world' and noted they had already been seen by upwards of two million people.[12] Even today, in a world of blockbuster disaster movies, they still have the power to take your breath away.

WORKPLACES AND WAR

Romanticism and the sublime could be seen as a reaction to the unsettling times artists were living through. Martin was born in 1789, the year of the French Revolution, and for the first twenty-five years of his life it wasn't safe to travel to Europe from the British Isles because of the Napoleonic Wars. The American War of Independence had concluded in 1783 and these seismic revolutions showcase the power of disenfranchised people to effect systemic change. Liberal movements were on the rise in the UK, from the abolitionists to those campaigning for women's suffrage. The traditional values of the monarchy and Parliament were now up for debate, and while some Romantic artists retreated from contemporary issues, others used their brushes to advocate for recognition and change.

War, estate ownership, the changing use of land and rural poverty became subjects for some nineteenth-century artists, who responded to the groundswell of interest in political reform by addressing social issues. Parliament largely comprised landowners and passed a series of Enclosure Acts from 1773 to 1859. These saw common land – once used for grazing cattle, gathering wood for fuel, growing crops and keeping bees – legally folded into the growing country estates of wealthy families. With the reduction in common land, the rural poor were forced to move into paid labouring jobs rather than relying on their own crops and animals to support themselves. This flooded the labour market and drove down wages. The German theorist Karl Marx would later identify this as 'the conquest, enslavement, robbery, murder' caused by landownership in his first volume of *Das Kapital*, (1867), a coruscating critique of capitalism written in London, where he had lived since 1849.

Country estates were often bolstered by money coming from Caribbean sugar plantations, and the wealthy treated land and people as commodities to be owned. For centuries the legacy of sugar money was kept quiet, a distasteful side to the British empire that was brushed under the carpet. But increasingly today the history of Britain's colonial wealth is being explored, revealing the extent to which the slave trade touched British lives. For example, Henry Vaughan, the Victorian who gave Constable's *Hay Wain* to the National Gallery, inherited a fortune derived from slave-run South Carolina plantations, which funded his art purchases.

Since the time of Joseph Wright, who painted Derby's iron forges in the early 1770s, artists have captured industry in action. Iron had been worked for over 2,000 years, but the industrial revolution was fuelled by coal. The exponential rise in its use in the eighteenth century was propelled by the invention of machines such as the steam engine.

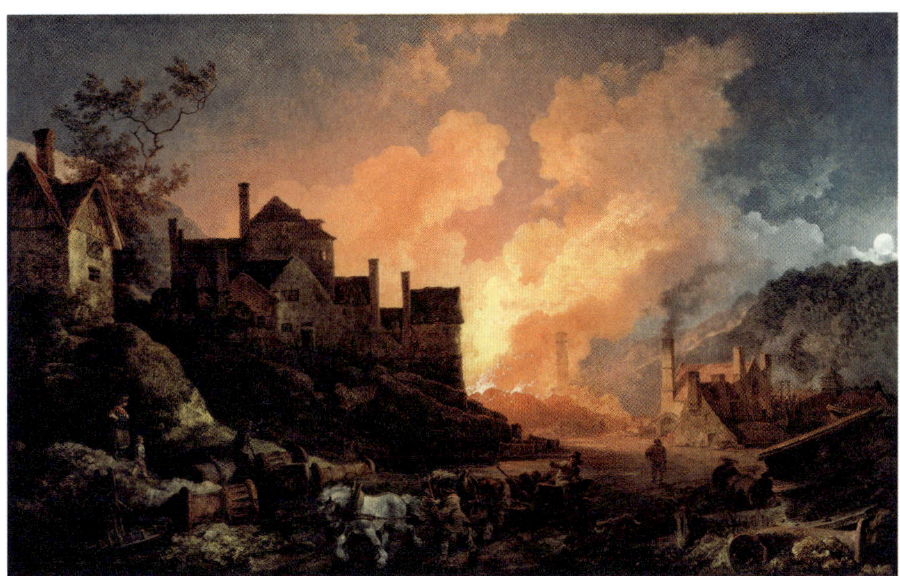

Philippe Jacques de Loutherbourg, *Coalbrookdale by Night*, oil on canvas, 1801

Turner painted Coalbrookdale in Shropshire around 1797, and De Loutherbourg completed *Coalbrookdale by Night* four years later (see previous page). Much as Wright had done before them, both artists lit their canvases from within by using the coal as their light source. Both framed burning fires with rustic buildings and wooded landscapes to emphasise the contrast between the rural past and industrial present, and both set their scenes at night, for maximum impact: industry never sleeps. Wright's portrayal of his friend Richard Arkwright's cotton mills by night in 1782 depicts glowing interiors lit by gas lamps, rivalling the moon that illuminated the scene from above. Wright captured the impact of gas lighting on production. It turned the working 'day' into a 24/7 possibility, in one stroke transforming the cyclical nature of work based on natural light into a regimented repetitive routine run by clock and lamp.

Turner celebrated the speed and dynamism of modernity in several of his paintings, most famously in *Rain, Steam and Speed* (1844), where the Great Western Railway's steam train roars along the track, outpacing a hare. But he also lamented its constant need to drive forwards. In *The Fighting Temeraire* (1839) the mighty warship appears ghostly and powerless, towed to the breaker's yard by a squat black steam tug belching fire as the sun sets on the era of sail.

Other artists chose to concentrate on the workers who had previously been anonymous staffage in landscapes. In the 1780s Stubbs painted *Haymakers* and *Reapers*, focusing on agricultural workers in the fields, while David Wilkie (1785–1841) painted a cluster of women, men and children gathered around a newspaper at the outskirts of a town, eager to hear about the latest events, in *Newsmongers* (1821). Wilkie epitomises this shift in direction. He was born in Pitlessie in Fife but moved to London in 1805 when he was nineteen. He exhibited *Pitlessie Fair* in his friend's shop. It is bawdy – a dog relieves himself over the artist's signature and a man does the same against a wall during the village's May Fair – but it quickly sold. Like seventeenth-century Flemish and Dutch artists Wilkie focused on the lower classes, their customs and parties, their fallings out, their hardships, their games and their weddings. Settings were village squares and city streets, flagged kitchens and dingy alehouses. *The Village Politicians* became the painting of the year at the Royal Academy's annual exhibition in 1806 and visitors queued for half an hour to see the artist's latest works.

For Wilkie it was about the authenticity achieved by painting from life. *Pitlessie Fair* was based on many sketches of the villagers in his father's parish in Fife. Writing to a friend while he painted it, he said, 'I now see how superior painting from nature is to any thing that our imagination, assisted by our memory, can conceive.'[13] But for all Wilkie's early proclamations of painting from nature, he ultimately became a genre painter, increasingly setting his characterful scenes in a rose-tinted past. In *The Penny Wedding* (1818) Scottish villagers dance to a fiddle in a barn while Scotland was experiencing the fastest rate of urbanisation in Europe.

The Village Funeral: An Irish Family by a Graveside during the Great Famine was painted by Daniel MacDonald (1821–1853) around 1850. It similarly reflected village traditions, but with a more sombre tone. Women express their grief as male gravediggers look on wearily and a dog digs desolately for its dead master. Cork-born MacDonald had previously exhibited *An Irish Peasant Family Discovering the Blight of Their Store* at the British Institution in London in 1847, one of the few contemporary depictions of the Great Famine that ravaged Ireland between 1845 and 1852. Potato blight had decimated the harvest and more than a million people died. This painting was largely ignored when it was first exhibited, however, reinforcing the widely held Irish belief that the British government was not doing enough to alleviate the dire situation. (In fact the British government brought the country close to bankruptcy trying to combat the famine.)

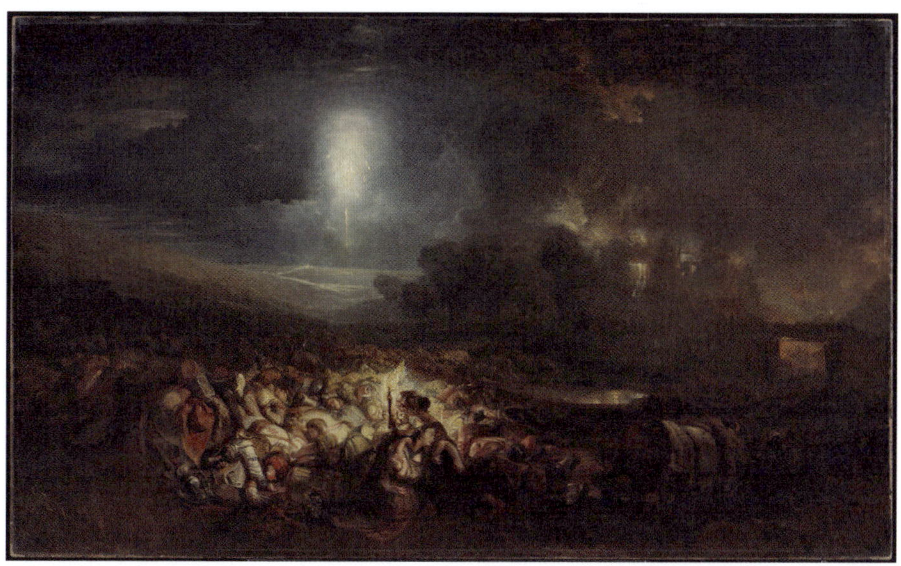

J.M.W. Turner, *The Field of Waterloo*, oil on canvas, 1818

War was another subject for artists intent on portraying contemporary life. Heroic battles had long been staged on canvas but traditionally they were set in the ancient past. The American artists Benjamin West and John Singleton Copley brought these battles up to date with the use of modern uniforms and portraits of those involved, but these paintings were still highly idealised, with death depicted as a spiritual beginning rather than gory end. Turner's *The Field of Waterloo* (1818), see previous page, offered a new approach. He had visited the site of the battle in 1817, sketching and taking notes. His final painting is still dramatic, with the field of battle shown at night, lit by the torches of women who looked for survivors. But it is also lit by Henry Shrapnel's devastating exploding shell that takes the place of the moon – it is this light that falls on the countless dead piled in anonymous heaps. There is no noble death here – Turner shows the human cost of battle, emphasising this by including a line on Waterloo from Lord Byron's *Childe Harold's Pilgrimage* (1812–18) in the catalogue when it was exhibited: 'Friend, foe, in one red burial blent!'[14] Turner's use of the deadly weapon that was instrumental in winning the battle – placed as an illuminating flare that replaced natural moonlight – creates a man-made apocalypse, an unnatural event where the skies burn brightly at night and youth lie dead on the ground.

Despite their grisly content, paintings of wars were crowd-pleasers at the Royal Academy. Elizabeth Thompson, Lady Butler (1846–1933) painted *The Roll Call* in 1874 and it had to be patrolled by a police-man to hold back the crowds. Soldiers from the Grenadier Guards line up after the Battle of Inkerman, a key moment in the Crimean War, some twenty years earlier. At nearly 2 metres wide, the stark reality of the wounded and exhausted soldiers, one lying lifeless on the snowy ground, hit home. Butler had interviewed survivors and used several as models for the painting, searching out Crimean uniforms to ensure the utmost accuracy. The painting subsequently toured the country and turned Butler into a celebrity.

The Crimean War had been fought between 1853 and 1856. It was reported in the British Isles through wood engravings in illustrated news-papers, theatrical panoramas, print portfolios, sketchbooks, paintings and book illustrations, as well as – for the first time – photographs. Through these black-and-white images we can witness the moderni-sation of vision that was occurring. Photographs fuelled the growing interest in the modern world, a world that was fast, transient and

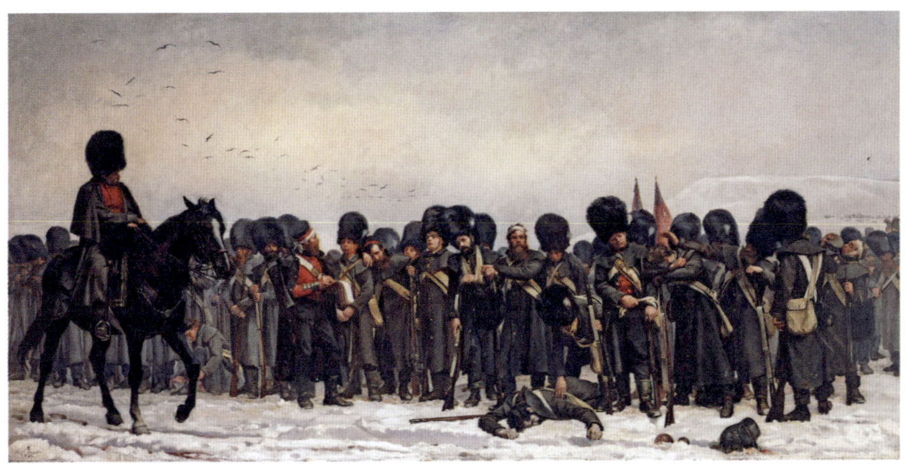

Elizabeth Butler, *The Roll Call*, oil on canvas, 1874

subjective. People no longer wanted to see mythological battles set in the ancient past but the real world, close up and dirty. The camera provided what appeared to be the perfect modern image, an indexical or mirror reflection of what was in front of it, captured on a glass negative in a matter of seconds.

Lancashire-born Roger Fenton (1819–1869) employed the picturesque to shape his landscape photographs from Crimea, most notably in *Valley of the Shadow of Death* (1855), where a track littered with cannonballs stretches into the distance. To today's eyes it is clear that many of the cannonballs have been placed strategically on the central path, fished out of the ditch into which they first rolled. But in the nineteenth century photography was seen as offering an unprecedented truth, a way of almost being at the scene yourself. 'We cannot doubt the evidence of the lens', wrote a reviewer of Fenton's Crimean photographs.[15] But this picturesque approach feels dated when you line it up next to a photograph by James Robertson (1813–1888).

Fenton photographed the ageing commanding British officers as they posed at tables covered in wine bottles, a servant hovering close by. By contrast Middlesex-born James Robertson and his assistant (and brother-in-law) Felice Beato (*c.*1832–1909) witnessed the fall of Sevastopol and camped with the British troops, selling their photographs taken in the field of battle directly to those who were fighting in it. Robertson (like Fenton) framed his early photographs as picturesque scenes, allowing potential buyers back in Britain to feel familiar with the manner in which the photograph was taken, if not with the Crimean landscape itself. But as he spent more time in the theatre of war his viewpoint shifted, possibly following Beato's lead, and his camera became part of the action. *Interior of the Barrack Battery* (1855) confronts us with a battery wall with defensive cannon seen from behind. There is rubble everywhere, broken wicker baskets for carrying shot and a stool with a broken leg. The sky has been masked out and appears flat and white. Nothing distracts from the foreground. This is a man-made dystopia, in stark contrast to the new Pre-Raphaelite paintings that filled the Royal Academy in the 1850s such as the leafy *Ophelia* (1851–2) by John Everett Millais (1829–1896), but with the same forensic eye for detail. Both dealt in death, but instead of the imagined suicide of a Shakespearean heroine we have the brutal reality of a war zone.

The difference between Fenton's *Valley* and Robertson's *Interior* is like comparing Romantic poet Wordsworth and contemporary rapper Stormzy. This seems extreme, but the difference is that marked. Both photographers were in the same theatre of war, but while Fenton presents us with a carefully orchestrated elegy of service and sacrifice, Robertson embeds us with the troops, situating us directly in the field of play. I can smell the sulphurous smoke from British muskets and hear the cold creak of ill-fitting leather boots.

STARS IN THE EAST

Can we believe what we see in these Crimean photographs? The influential Victorian art critic John Ruskin had urged the Pre-Raphaelites to 'go to Nature in all singleness of heart . . . rejecting nothing, selecting nothing, and scorning nothing; believing all things to be right and good, and rejoicing in the truth'.[16] The novelist W.M. Thackeray parodied the public's thirst for the truth in *Punch* magazine: 'What the nation wants is TRUTH. Truth pure, Truth unadulterated.'[17] You certainly feel as if you are inside the battery when you look at Robertson's image, as if this is what it was really like. But where are the men manning the guns? And where are the dead? Robertson's photographs from the Crimean War did not include any dead or wounded troops. While photographs from the theatre of war seemed to offer an instant facsimile of events, and were widely used by the illustrated newspapers as the basis for their engravings, the photographic artists who were framing the view were just as selective as their contemporaries exhibiting at the Royal Academy.

There was a rising desire to see the world, fuelled by a bullish empire and its rhetoric of imperial power. You could read about faraway places in the *Illustrated London News* and *The Graphic*, subscribe to print portfolios of the Holy Land by David Roberts (1796–1864) and Louisa Tenison (1819–1882), buy photographic albums of China by John Thomson (1837–1921) and view 'Orientalist' paintings by John Frederick Lewis (1804–1876), Richard Dadd (1817–1886) and Arthur Melville (1855–1904) at the Royal Academy.

British artists and writers supplied a growing market with words and pictures from the Ottoman empire, known at the time as the Near East, creating a fashion for Orientalism. Orientalism was a Western construct. At the time it was seen as offering an authentic view of faraway lands, but as Edward Said identified in the 1970s, Orientalism could also be seen as an emblem of domination and a weapon of power. Today postcolonial art historians offer new routes through this period, revealing instances of cross-cultural exchange as well as myriad examples of imperial exploitation. But in the nineteenth century Orientalism presented the 'Orient' as a European fantasy of heat, seduction and decay, with ruined cities and indolent locals, rather than a complex multicultural region that was rapidly modernising and engaging with the West on its own terms.

The Ottoman empire, centred on Constantinople (now Istanbul), had recently relaxed its borders as it became open to European industrialism and modernity. This led to a massive influx of archaeologists, surveyors, naturalists, writers and artists, all keen to transport the 'Orient', back to Britain in the form of ancient sculptures, maps, specimens, stories, photographs, prints and paintings. While artists recorded views of Turkey, Palestine and Egypt for a Western audience and the Royal Navy charted the region's coastlines and rivers, British (and French) archaeologists dug down into the earth and extracted its ancient history, shipping back entire temples, giant friezes and choice architectural fragments. Britain was attempting to understand the 'Orient' through ownership, whether conceptually (through maps and paintings) or physically (through archaeological finds that made their way into British museums).

Lewis spent ten years living in Cairo in the 1840s, painting its people and places for a British market. Wilkie would have been one of the first painters to capitalise on the opening up of the region, as he travelled to Constantinople, Jerusalem and Alexandria in 1840–1, but he died on the return journey. (Turner memorialised his passing in *Peace – Burial at Sea* the following year, showing Wilkie's body lowered over the side of the P&O steamer *Oriental* against a seascape blackened with soot from the steamer's chimney.) It was Roberts who became the first professional artist to travel independently to the region in 1838–9. He completed hundreds of sketches during his eleven-month journey. These sustained him for his entire career and led to his ambitious portfolio of lithographs, *Holy Land, Syria, Idumea, Arabia, Egypt and Nubia*, published by subscription from 1842 to 1849.

Dadd travelled to the Middle East in 1842 as the companion artist of Sir Thomas Philipps. He followed in the footsteps of Roberts, writing to the older man that he saw Lebanon through his eyes, because he had seen Roberts's paintings of the region in his studio prior to departure. He was not alone in this. When Thackeray travelled by steamship to the same region, he wrote: 'The view of Constantinople is as fine as any of [Clarkson] Stanfield's best theatrical pictures.'[18] Views by the earliest artists and writers to the region conditioned the expectations of later travellers and perpetuated Orientalist fantasies of sensuous women in harems and languid men with hookahs in the ruins of an ancient and great empire (unaware that their Ottoman hosts often exaggerated or parodied Western travellers' expectations). As Thackeray noted in his travel memoir: 'You may imagine that you have been in the place before, you seem to know it so well!'[19]

Philipps and Dadd travelled at breakneck speed and Dadd complained that he rarely had time to sketch or paint. They followed the route of the eighteenth-century Grand Tour through Europe and then set off by steamer across the Mediterranean. From Jerusalem they journeyed to the Dead Sea with a group of naval officers and midshipmen, who later offered them passage on the armed steamer *Hecate* from Jaffa to Alexandria. All this travelling took its toll on Dadd and he descended into what he called a 'nervous depression'.[20] On his return home his family sought help for him, but during a walk in Cobham Park in Surrey he stabbed and beat his father to death. The rest of his life would be lived out in mental hospitals including 'Bedlam', the Bethlem Royal Hospital in London, where he painted *The Artist's Halt in the Desert* (1845). This hallucinatory painting recollects his visit on horseback to the Dead Sea, where he waited for the moon to rise to enable his

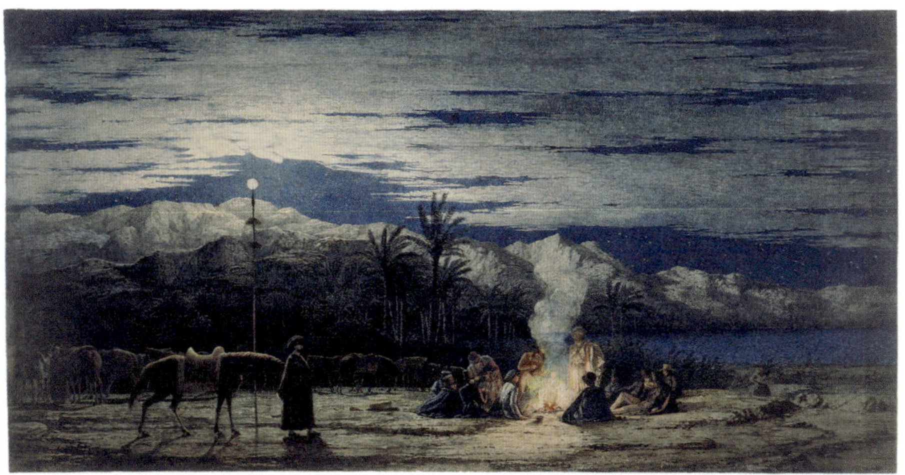

Richard Dadd, *The Artist's Halt in the Desert*, watercolour on paper, *c.*1845

party to ride back towards Jerusalem. The full moon looks as if it is impaled on the long standard that rises behind the silhouetted horse. Men gather around an open fire but it is the moon that illuminates the sky as if it is day.

Artists such as the Pre-Raphaelite William Holman Hunt (1827–1910) and the poet and artist Edward Lear (1812–1888) travelled to the same region in the 1850s. They were also drawn to the expansive skies and pastel hues of dawn and dusk as they played out across desert landscapes that were at the heart of Jewish sacred texts and Christianity's Old Testament. Tenison was also drawn to the Middle East. Her *Sketches in the East*, published in 1846, included more than thirty accomplished lithographs, based on her drawings depicting the ruins and ancient history of Luxor, Karnak, Petra, Mount Sinai, Jerusalem, Nazareth, Damascus and Baalbek. Gender was being seen (by women, at least) as no barrier to exploration or artistic achievement, and consequently the nineteenth century saw an explosion of ambitious women artists.

11

WOMEN'S WORK

1800–1914

THE NINETEENTH CENTURY was a watershed moment for women. At the beginning of the century, to be a middle-class woman was to be dependent on a man, either a father or a husband. Her property passed to her husband if she married; she had few legal rights and no protection against domestic abuse. She could only work at home, raising children, and she couldn't vote. But by the end of the century these women were typists and telegraphers, nurses and novelists, accountants and artists. Pressure was growing for women to be given the vote, bolstered by the founding of the London Society for Women's Suffrage (1867) and later the National Union of Women's Suffrage Societies (1897) and the Women's Social and Political Union (1903).

As we have seen in earlier chapters, women forged paths as artists before this period but often they were compelled to work as amateurs (that is, not sell their work). Those who pushed to exhibit in the academies of Europe most often came from artistic families, which allowed them access to proper training and a studio. Occasionally artists came along who were an exception to this rule of thumb, as was the case with Sarah Biffin (1784–1850). Biffin was a miniature painter who counted King George IV as a patron. She toured Britain, exhibiting in Edinburgh, Bristol, Dover and Newcastle, and had a studio on the Strand in London.

The fact that Biffin had been born with phocomelia, and had no arms or legs, didn't perturb her. She taught herself to sew using her mouth at the age of eight, making her own clothes by cutting fabric and threading needles herself. She then turned to painting, taking instruction from a Mr Dukes. From the age of twenty she lived with Dukes's family and the pair toured the country. In a way that seems wholly unacceptable to us, she was 'exhibited' as a curiosity at country fairs, where people paid a shilling (£2.50 today) to watch her paint, write and draw. In a print by Rowlandson of Bartholomew Fair from 1807 we can see a poster advertising 'Miss Beffin' alongside others for a juggler and a menagerie. If she later felt that Dukes took advantage of her financially – she never received more than five pounds a year – Biffin didn't regret the work. 'I feel a wonderful pleasure in being exhibited', she wrote, 'and will go so far as to say that I think it my duty. I do not regret my situation, I thank god that he has been pleased to make me as I am, nor do I envy the enjoyments of others.'[1] She used her fourteen years on the road to perfect her art, exhibiting in cities across Britain and picking up a significant number of collectors along the way.

By the time she painted this self-portrait in 1821 she was an accomplished artist running a successful studio. We see her sitting on a

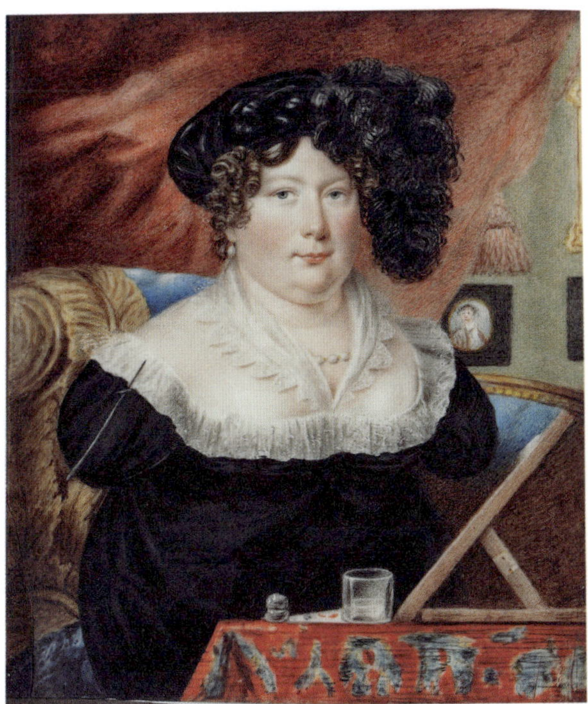

Sarah Biffin, self-portrait, watercolour on ivory, 1821

blue-and-gold chaise, her easel propped on a table in front of her. She wears a black feathered hat and matching black gown trimmed with fine lace. A tumbler of water and small ivory palette are just visible on the table. Biffin painted with her mouth, and we can see her fine brush attached to a loop on her right shoulder. Tiny feathery strokes rouge her cheeks and give soft undulations to the thick red curtain behind her, pulled up to show an example of her miniature commissions on the wall behind. She looks out confidently, aware of her talent. Working in watercolour on ivory, she painted the likenesses of royalty, naval officers, ladies at court and children, supplementing her income by taking on students during residencies in Birmingham, Brighton and Liverpool.

Biffin died in Liverpool in 1850 at the age of sixty-five. The art of the miniature was in steep decline following the invention of photography a decade earlier. This new technology, alongside many others, was showcased the following year at the Great Exhibition, London's answer to Paris's industrial fairs and the first world fair. It was held in a dauntingly large purpose-built glasshouse called the Crystal Palace, erected in Hyde Park. There were a staggering 100,000 exhibits from the British empire and forty-four other nation states, and more than six million people passed through its doors. Queen Victoria and her husband Prince Albert were regular visitors and the novelists Charlotte Brontë and Charles Dickens attended. It was a huge success and funded the establishment of the museums of 'Albertopolis' nearby: the Victoria and Albert Museum (V&A), the Science Museum and the Natural History Museum.

DEEDS NOT WORDS

Against this backdrop of industry and modernisation, women artists began working together and campaigning for access to life-drawing classes and admission to the Royal Academy Schools. They had to fight prejudice if they were ambitious and wanted to paint history or war scenes like Elizabeth Thompson. Barbara Leigh Smith Bodichon (1827–1891), herself a talented landscape artist, campaigned for a woman's right to work, launching the Society Promoting the Employment of Women in 1859. Two years earlier she had published *Women and Work*, an incendiary pamphlet that targeted young women. 'Awake!' she cried. 'Do not be contented to be charming and fascinating; be noble, be useful, be wise.'[2]

This same year, 1857, Emily Mary Osborn (1828–1925) exhibited *Nameless and Friendless* at the Royal Academy. Against a rainy London skyline a woman and her son stand in a picture dealer's shop as he scrutinises one of her paintings. Her son holds a portfolio of work under his arm – he looks directly at the dealer but the woman fiddles nervously with a piece of string and looks down at the floor. Is she a widow? Her black dress suggests she could be. Is she selling her family's heirlooms to stay afloat or is she the artist of these works, trying to make her mark in a patriarchal society? The men scrutinising prints behind her look up and study her as if she were the object on display, not her paintings. Another woman is about to exit the shop, her son behind her with a roll of drawings under his arm, suggesting the wealth of material such dealers had to choose from.

Nameless and Friendless was exhibited the year William Powell Frith (1819–1909) was hard at work on *The Derby Day* and his close friend Augustus Egg (1816–1863) was planning his moralising triptych *Past and Present*. There was a vogue for modern narrative paintings

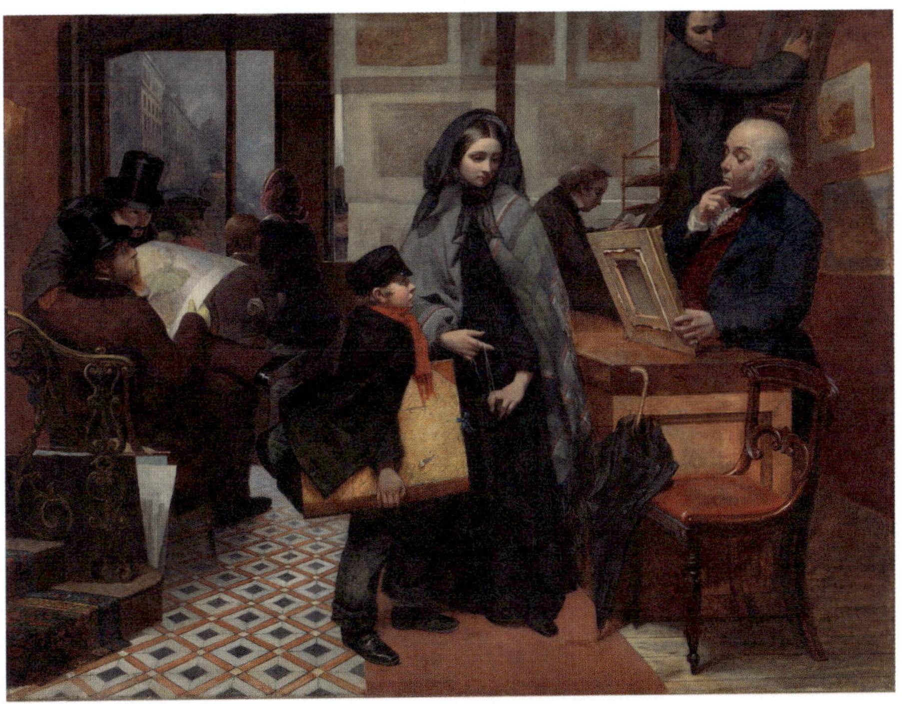

Emily Mary Osborn, *Nameless and Friendless*, oil on canvas, 1857

featuring all walks of life, and middle-class visitors couldn't get enough of seeing themselves reflected in Frith's meticulously detailed scenes or empathising with the women in Egg and Osborn's moralising and emotive paintings. But what was it like trying to make a name for yourself as an artist if you were a woman like Osborn (or Osborn's subject)? The Royal Academy was a collegiate boys' club – it wouldn't elect a third woman member until 1936. For well over a century it had enjoyed a stranglehold on many aspects of art production, from training to exhibiting to who could become the next Academicians. But chinks in its armour were beginning to show. Women were admitted into the Royal Academy Schools in 1860, after a sleight of hand by a female applicant who signed her work A.L. Herford, but they were still excluded from life-drawing classes until 1893. Private academies, however, were happy to take women students and in 1871 the Slade School of Fine Art was founded: it allowed men and women to enter on equal terms.

Women also banded together to offer each other support. Osborn painted Bodichon's portrait around 1884, while the artist Marie Spartali Stillman (1844–1927) modelled for the photographer Julia Margaret Cameron (1815–1879), posing as Hypatia, the Roman mathematician and astronomer, in 1868.

Cameron was one of the first people to use a camera to create art in Britain. Her works feature young models posing in elaborate costumes and she manipulated light, shade and the natural environment to create literary tableaux and atmospheric portraits. She held more than twenty exhibitions of her work in Britain and Europe but she failed to recoup her costs, and her ethereal photographs were not fully appreciated until after her death.

Cameron photographed the artist-explorer Marianne North (1830–1890) painting on the shady veranda of her house in Ceylon (Sri Lanka) when North visited in 1877. North began travelling beyond Europe in 1871 and she painted the flora, fauna and landmarks of every country she visited. Her limpid oil paintings include Chilean palms, Australian bottle trees and vanilla pods from the Seychelles. She carefully observed opium poppies and aloe plants as well as the Taj Mahal and Java's active volcanoes. Monkeys, kangaroos, butterflies and birds all make an appearance, often depicted with the fruits they eat or the vegetation they inhabit. She exhibited 500 paintings in London, keen to educate the public about the lands she had visited and the specimens she had seen and studied. Some of the plants she painted could not be identified

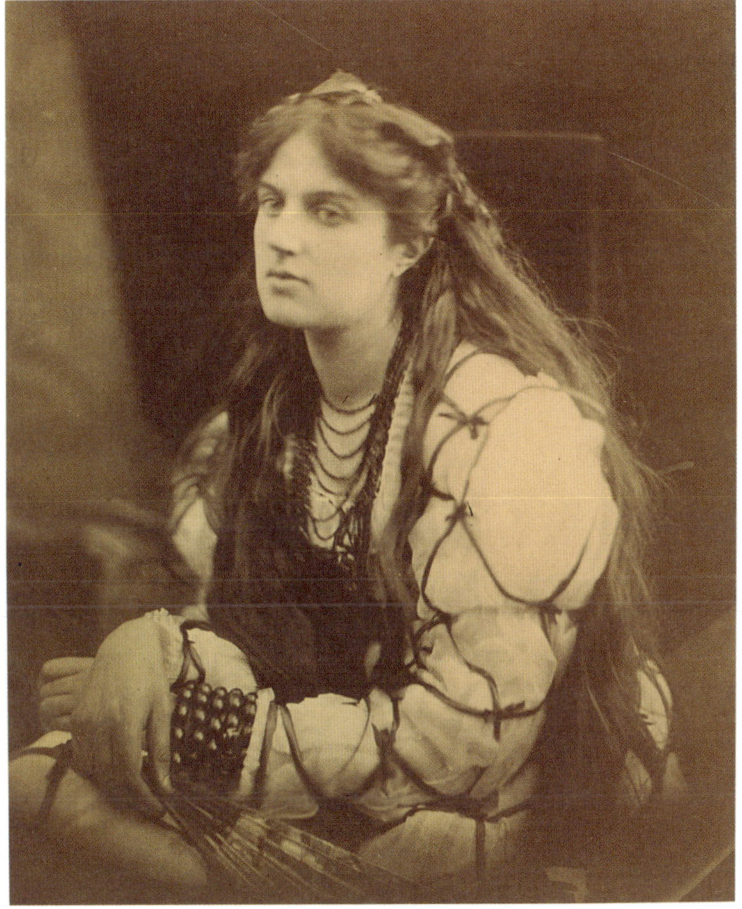

Julia Margaret Cameron, *Hypatia*, albumen print from glass negative, 1868

because she was the first to record them. She offered the entire collection to Kew Gardens and worked closely with the architect James Fergusson on the gallery she designed to house them. It resembles the place she was photographed in by Cameron, with a wide veranda held up by columns. It opened in 1882 with 627 of her paintings on display and was hugely popular (as it still is to this day). The *Daily News* reported: 'Few women and not a great many men have raised monuments to art by their own unaided initiative, energy and industry, such as that which Miss North has just presented to the nation.'[3]

While North painted to record the world around her, other artists were drawn to a growing belief in Spiritualism, turning to art as a means of communicating with the world beyond the grave. Georgiana Houghton (1814–1884) was one of Spiritualism's stars. Guided by the angels and archangels she believed she encountered while operating as a medium, she began drawing and then painting in gouache, water-colour and ink in the 1860s. She claimed spirit guides directed her hand, and the resulting images were looping tendrils of high colour that curled into fantastical peacock feathers, underwater plants and livid fireballs. She saw her drawings as spiritual flowers and fruits, embodying the energy of a particular person in the spirit world. She had lost many of her siblings to death and often named her drawings after them: *Zilla's Flower*; *Cecil's Fruit*. Decades before the Surrealists became interested in automatic drawing (done without the conscious input of the artist), or the rise of mainstream abstract art, Houghton created fantastically complex layered paintings of energy fields, freed from the constraints of figuration.

You may think Houghton must have existed a long way from the centre of the British art world, but that wasn't the case. In 1865 her work was accepted by the Royal Academy for the annual exhibition (although ultimately it wasn't shown) and she held her own exhibition at the New British Gallery on Bond Street, sending Queen Victoria the leather-bound catalogue *Spirit Drawings in Water Colours*. Her spirit guides had told her to hold the exhibition, and she explained that she had 'been entirely guided by invisible spirits, who could thus delineate what was beyond the human imagination'.[4]

Other women artists pushed against marital resistance to create works of immense scale and ambition. Phoebe Anna Traquair (1852–1936) was born and educated in Dublin before she married a Scottish palae-ontologist working there, Dr Ramsay Heatley Traquair. He eventu-ally took a job in Edinburgh and they relocated to Scotland. Phoebe Traquair had met Ramsay when he was looking for someone to illus-trate his research. She continued to do this for thirty years but her own ambitions led her also to become a successful book illustrator, textile designer and the artist responsible for the most ambitious cycle of murals in Edinburgh.

In 1893 she secured the commission to paint the interior of the Catholic Apostolic Church, built twenty years earlier. The architect had left room for a frieze along the nave and for paintings to fill both the 19-metre-high chancel arch and west wall. It was an epic undertaking, one that took her eight years and that she completed largely on her own, having to adjust her working patterns to ensure she always had the best natural light in which to work. The Apostolic Church believed the second coming of Christ was imminent, and Traquair transformed biblical scenes from Revelation and Ezekiel into rainbow-tipped celebrations, with angels filling heaven with golden music played on slender trumpets and harps. Despite the biblical subject matter, she staged each scene in the Irish landscapes of her childhood and used Celtic triskeles and ribbonwork as decoration. Today the church is an events space known as the Mansfield Traquair Centre, but the paintings still

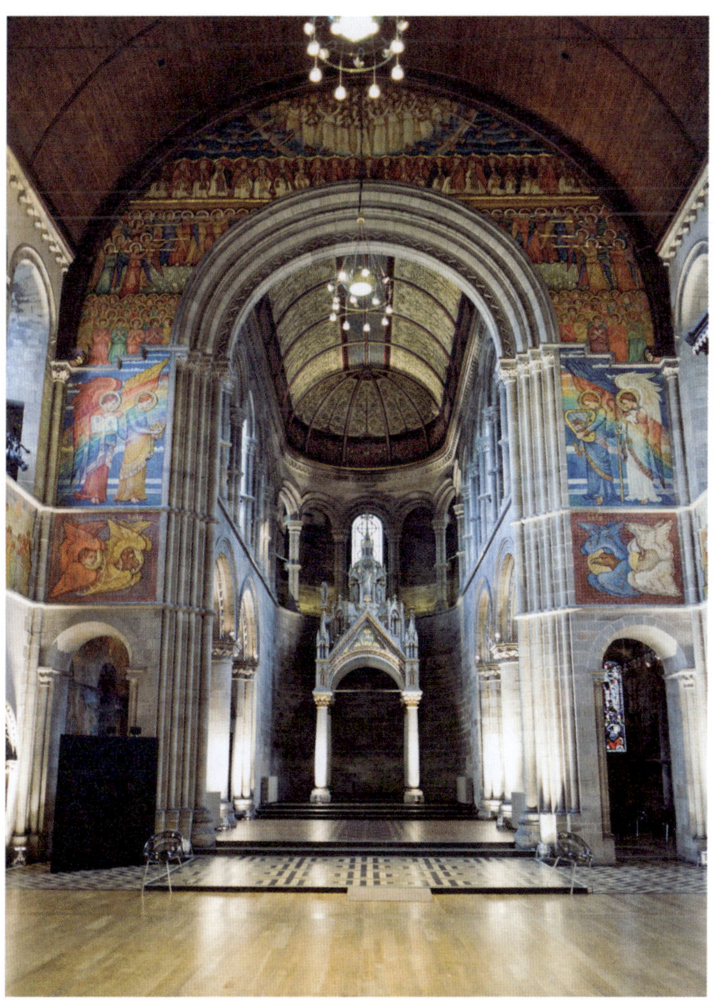

Phoebe Anna Traquair, murals for the Catholic
Apostolic Church, Edinburgh, 1893–1901

dominate as you enter, a complex testament to the artist's role in the Celtic Revival movement, indicative of Scotland's growing interest in its Celtic past.

Mary Seton Watts (1849–1938) similarly transformed an interior into an Arts and Crafts masterpiece, but she was instrumental in designing the building as well. The Watts Chapel is now part of the Watts Artists' Village which includes her home Limnerslease and the Watts Gallery, built to house the paintings of her husband G.F. Watts (1817–1904) the year he died. G.F. Watts was one of the country's leading artists by this time, known for his allegorical paintings such as *Hope* (1886). However, it was the chapel that was the clear highlight of my visit. Towards the top of a small grassy cemetery, a red-brick domed building is supported by pillars writhing with decoration. Mary Watts had trained at the Slade and taught terracotta classes on Thursday evenings in her drawing room to enable seventy local volunteers to make the chapel's decorative bricks. Her intricate designs include Celtic knots and complex ribbonwork, a nod to her Scottish ancestry (although, as we have seen, Celtic art was made across the British Isles). An arch of angels line the door, their eyes alternating open and closed as if occupying both the physical world and a spiritual one. Inside, red, green and purple angels hover over walls interlaced with roots and vines. The room feels alive as sinuous lines curve away and haloes and wings become three-dimensional, built up in gilded gesso. Every surface contributes to the overall effect, from the ornate wrought-iron gate to the slender blue-and-green stained-glass windows.

The Watts Chapel is the culmination of a way of working developed by members of the Pre-Raphaelite circle and epitomised by Morris & Co., the business of William Morris (1834–1896) and partners. Such collaborations between artists, designers, architects and others have often been written about in the past by sidelining the contribution women made in favour of a cleaner, neater, patriarchal story. But it is far more exciting to see how brothers and sisters, husbands and wives, daughters and sons worked side by side to create some of the most iconic works of art of the nineteenth century. What Traquair, Watts and North had in common was the ability to visualise their work on an unprecedented scale. Looking at it today, I could feel the ambition and steadfastness needed to mount the scaffolding or travel the world with paintbrush in hand.

THE SISTERHOOD

I have touched on the Pre-Raphaelite Brotherhood already – the influence of this small band of Royal Academy students is still felt in the unerring popularity of their paintings, from John Everett Millais's *Christ in the House of His Parents* (1849–50) to William Holman Hunt's *The Hireling Shepherd* (1851). Seven of them, including Dante Gabriel Rossetti (1828–1882) and his poet brother William, decided to band together in the late summer of 1848, a time when the rest of Europe (in total fifty countries) was in revolutionary fervour. Across Italy and the empires of Austria and Prussia, in Paris and Prague, people of all classes came together to campaign for workers' rights, for famine relief, for the abolition of serfdom and to demand government reform.

In London, the young members of the Pre-Raphaelite Brotherhood must have felt revolutionary as they began to sign their paintings with the initials PRB. They were being educated in a school that prized above all else the artists of the High Renaissance: Raphael, Leonardo,

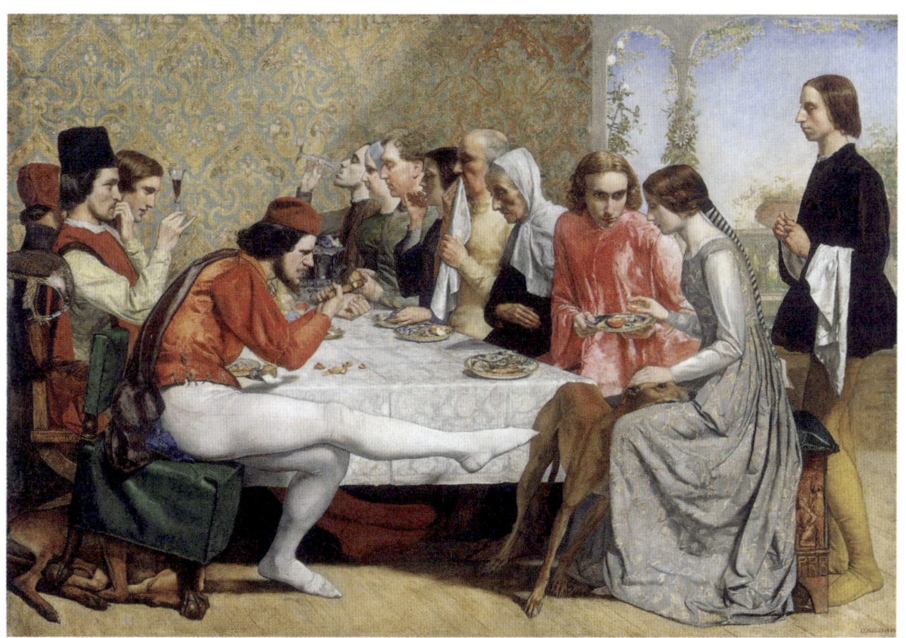

John Everett Millais, *Isabella*, oil on canvas, 1849

Michelangelo, Titian. But these young students felt that the polished finish of Academy paintings – think of Osborn and Egg – froze each scene in aspic. Where was the life? Where was the essential truth? Where was the truth to nature? Using the Nazarenes of Germany as their role models, they decided to turn to art from before the time of Raphael as their guide.

In 1849 Rossetti, Holman Hunt and Millais all had work accepted into the Royal Academy's annual exhibition. Millais submitted *Isabella* (see previous page), a secular Last Supper based on a fourteenth-century story (reinterpreted by the poet John Keats in 1818) where the doomed Lorenzo offers his lover Isabella a blood orange. The orange is symbolic of his blood that will soon be spilled by her brothers, who want to marry her off to a wealthy nobleman instead. There is a wealth of detail in the storytelling. Look at the way the dog cowers in Isabella's lap, victim of her brother's swift kick – he tips his chair forwards to extend his reach. He will be similarly brutal to Isabella soon enough, when he kills her lover. Millais paints a passionfruit vine winding around the window frame directly above her head to remind us of her love for Lorenzo. This plant is instantly recognisable, studied from life, as are the people who join the lovers at the meal, from the man with rosacea cheeks to the old woman with thinning grey hair and wrinkles.

The Pre-Raphaelites painted everything from life, using friends as models and working in situ to capture a stream's grassy banks or the messy floor of a carpenter's workshop, strewn with wood chippings. Sisters and lovers became the Virgin Mary; fellow artists posed for heroes and victims. But hold on just a moment. For those sisters and lovers who posed for the Pre-Raphaelite Brotherhood had what is known today as a Pre-Raphaelite Sisterhood of their own.

In 1856 Christina Rossetti wrote 'In an Artist's Studio'. This poem, unpublished in her lifetime, suggests she had been studying the paintings by her brother of the model and artist Elizabeth Siddal (1829–1862). Siddal had modelled for Millais's *Ophelia* but for the last four years she had posed exclusively for Dante Rossetti. 'One face looks out from all the canvases,' the poem begins, as it describes how the artist feeds upon his model day and night: 'Not as she is, but was when hope shone bright; / Not as she is, but as she fills his dream.'[5] The poem suggests that a model is an object for the artist, a conduit through which they convey what they want to say. Christina had been Dante's model for *The Girlhood of Mary Virgin* (1849) and *Ecce Ancilla Domini!* (1850)

but by 1856 only Siddal modelled for him. Both of them were creative in their own right and Christina's visualisation of the artistic feasting by the male artist on the female model is unsettling. Although Siddal had not been to art school, she became an artist herself and her Pre-Raphaelite watercolours have much in common with Dante's own, suggesting an aligning of interests.

John Ruskin praised the 1855 painting of the Anglo-Saxon Queen Elgiva by Joanna Boyce (1831–1861), and an increasing number of women artists were drawn to the Pre-Raphaelite commitment to nature and medievalism. William Rossetti championed their art in his exhibition reviews in the American journal *The Crayon*, praising the work of Boyce and Siddal.[6] A younger generation of artists would subsequently continue to develop the Pre-Raphaelite style, including Spartali Stillman, Eleanor Fortescue-Brickdale (1872–1945), Louise Jopling (1843–1933) and Evelyn De Morgan (1855–1919). G.F. Watts thought De Morgan was 'the first woman artist of the day – if not of all time'.[7] She had attended the Slade, and the influence of pre-Raphael artists such as Sandro Botticelli and Pre-Raphaelites such as Edward Burne-Jones (1833–1898) is clear to see in paintings such as *Venus and Cupid* (1878) and *Flora* (1894).

Perhaps buoyed by the liberal revolutions in Europe and the campaigns for reform across the British Isles, this period saw an unprecedented number of artists working collaboratively. William Morris joined forces with friends and family in 1861 to found 'The Firm', officially known as Morris, Marshall, Faulkner & Co. When William Morris married Jane Burden (1839–1914) in 1859 they commissioned the Red House in Bexleyheath near London from the architect Philip Webb. It was a medieval fantasy of steep roofs, round windows and a turreted well. William, a friend of Rossetti's, championed art and design that was well-made and authentic. When he couldn't find furniture to meet his standards he designed his own, and the idea for 'The Firm' was born. Jane ran the embroidery department and Burne-Jones was in charge of stained glass. William concentrated on bespoke furniture design, the antidote to industrial production, and later fabric and wallpaper patterns, and the business was a huge success.

Jane had trained in design and specialised in embroidery. Margaret Macdonald (1864–1933) would also work in textiles (and glass) but her training at the Glasgow School of Art gave her a solid grounding as an artist. The school was open to men and women and Macdonald attended with her sister Frances (1873–1921). There they met Charles Rennie Mackintosh (1868–1928) and James Herbert McNair (1868–1955). They became known as 'The Four' and worked collaboratively on a range of projects.

Margaret and Charles married in 1900. He wrote, 'If I had the heart, she had the head. Oh, I had the talent but she had the genius. We made a pair.'[8] Their collaboration on the Hill House (1902–4) in Helensburgh, 35 kilometres northwest of Glasgow, is exemplary in its attention to detail and design. Walking through the doors is like stepping into a *Gesamtkunstwerk*, a total work of art. From the handles, rugs and bedspreads to the wardrobes, fireplaces and even the fire tongs, the interior of the Hill House reflects and enhances Mackintosh's Art Nouveau architecture. I can hear the clatter of bespoke cutlery in the panelled dining room, the scrape of ladderback chairs as guests rise from the dining table. I can see the servants turning up the oil lamps in the brass wall sconces and folding back the hand-decorated eiderdowns.

The Hill House was designed for the publisher Walter Blackie, who commuted to work in Glasgow using the unlikely combination of a traditional horse-drawn carriage and the railway. His was a generation where the old hurtled into the new at an unprecedented rate. It was the turn of the century, and the *fin de siècle* saw the wealthy industrial city of Glasgow become a European centre for art, with the Macdonalds and Mackintosh helping to foster a 'Glasgow style'. They designed houses and tea rooms, furniture and textiles, paintings and typefaces, all in a distinct style that fused the sinuous lines of Art Nouveau – a pan-European trend – with the belief in quality materials and bespoke design.

Margaret's gesso relief painting *The Sleeping Princess* sits above the fireplace in the Hill House drawing room, a harmonious array of lines that coalesce into a woman's form and a shower of roses. There's a sense of the deep time of Celtic art as well as the flattened colour panels of Gustav Klimt's paintings, which the couple saw together when they exhibited at the Vienna Secession in Austria in 1900, where Klimt was president. The whole-building approach of the Macdonald–Mackintoshes resonated with the artists, designers and architects who had founded the Secession three years earlier to promote similar ideas of a 'total art'. Their position in Europe was assured – the Macdonald–Mackintoshes were seen as influential avant-garde leaders who inspired Klimt and received lucrative commissions from Austrian millionaires.

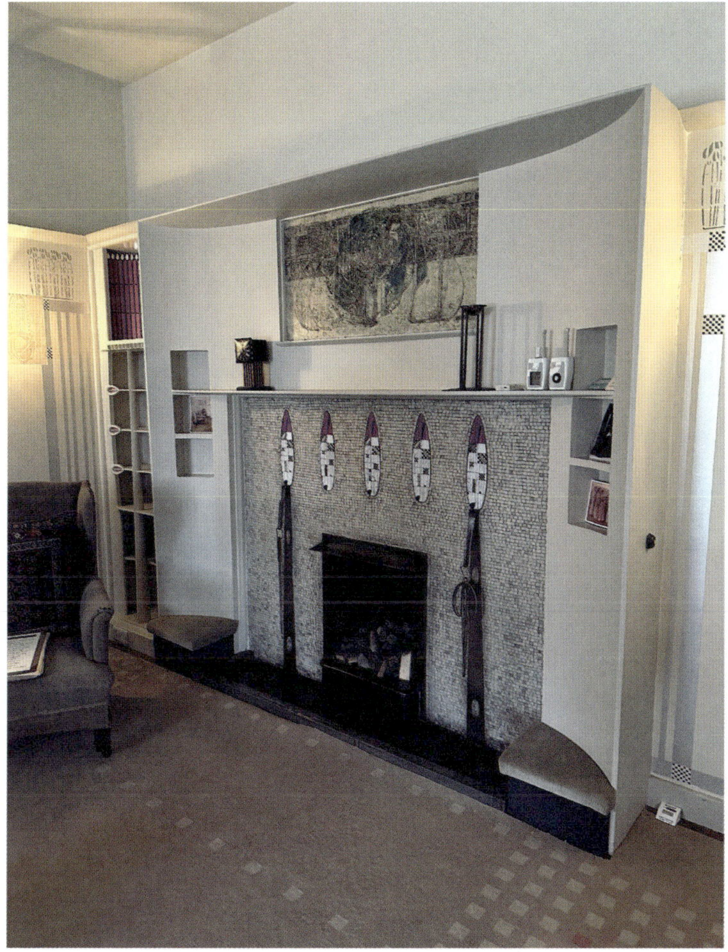

The Hill House featuring Margaret Macdonald Mackintosh's *The Sleeping Princess* above the fireplace, oil, gesso and wax on panel, 1908

A MONTH IN THE COUNTRY

In 1897 Mackintosh won a competition to design a new building for the Glasgow School of Art. By the 1890s it needed to expand, with record numbers of men and women applying to study there, their ambitions stoked by the success of the Glasgow Boys (and Girls). Several of the Glasgow Boys – James Paterson (1854–1932), George Henry (1858–1943) and Edward Arthur Walton (1860–1922) – had graduated from the Glasgow School of Art in the previous decades. They did not see themselves as a group or movement but they shared many of the same ideals. They despised the slick academic painting of the Scottish National Academy in Edinburgh, calling its practitioners the 'Glue-Pot School'.[9] Not for them polished narratives or heroic vistas. They wanted to stand their easels in cabbage patches and orchards and paint the lives of the men, women and children who worked the land as artists did in France. Although they used the growing rail network to reach such places, they wanted to turn their back on the industrial revolution and paint what they perceived to be the timeless traditions of farming and rural life.

Many of these artists, including Paterson, Belfast-born John Lavery (1856–1941) and James Guthrie (1859–1930), had spent time in Paris. They had seen first-hand the work of Barbizon School painters such as Jean-François Millet and admired the rural naturalism of Jules Bastien-Lepage. These French artists painted outdoors, *en plein air*, and concentrated on rural subjects. The artists who became known as the Glasgow Boys wanted to do the same, and so they ventured to the Scottish coast, to villages such as Cockburnspath and Kirkcudbright. Guthrie lived near Cockburnspath for three years and in summer nearly every house in the village had an artist renting an attic or barn. These artists painted children herding geese and picking apples, strings of onions and fishing nets hanging to dry, sheep in summer fields. In Guthrie's *A Hind's Daughter* (1883) we see a girl working in the fields. She stands at the edge of a sparse crop of brassicas, knife in one hand and cabbage in the other. 'Hind' was a Scots word for a farmhand, and his daughters and wife would also be expected to work the land. Guthrie uses the flat white light of a cloudy day to highlight the girl's bodice (tight above her hessian apron) and the brassica heads. Using a square brushstroke favoured by Bastien-Lepage, Guthrie builds his scene from small tonal blocks instead of the near-photographic polish of Scottish National Academy pictures.

Why were they so keen on breaking with the Academy's approach? Romanticism had given voice to the emotions of artists, to their own individual responses, a counterpoint to the growing mechanisation of the industrial revolution. And with the advent of photography, the role of the artist irrevocably changed. Now a tool – a camera – appeared to hold a mirror up to the world. Photographic studios replaced portrait artists, and photographers sold their views of the world for less than the price of a print. Yet this also liberated artists. They were freed from mimicry and for the first time could begin to explore conceptually (and perceptually) what it meant to use brushstrokes to create paintings.

A painting was increasingly seen not as a window through which to observe the world – either modern or ancient – but as an object in its own right. Its flat surface was part of its composition, and artists like Guthrie began to explore what this meant. The daughter's bodice, apron and the flowers that dot the earth behind her sit on the surface even while they coalesce into a scene, and the tree, sky and low-slung barn roof fuse together. The paintings of the Glasgow Boys were initially criticised for being unfinished but they reflected a modernisation of vision that was also seen in France at this time.

The Glasgow Boys were not alone in heading to remote coastal villages for inspiration. Artists' colonies had sprung up across the British Isles and Europe. The artists who lived there shared common values – a desire to paint directly from nature and to capture the ancient land with its 'timeless' customs. In Newlyn in Cornwall Frank Bramley (1857–1915), Walter Langley (1852–1922), Stanhope Forbes (1857–1947), Elizabeth Armstrong Forbes (1859–1912) and more than 100 artists worked alongside the town's fishermen and women, painting their catches and the losses at sea. 'Here every corner was a picture,' Forbes recounted in a rather patronising lecture he gave in 1900. 'The people seemed to fall naturally into their place and to harmonise with the surroundings.'[10] There was an irony to artists journeying to such 'remote' places as Newlyn – you could travel from London to nearby Penzance in nine hours by train from 1867 onwards. These artists were aware of the encroaching creep of modernity; this drove their nostalgia for an untouched and timeless past that in reality did not exist.

Cockburnspath was a temporary artists' colony but Kirkcudbright, like Newlyn (and neighbouring St Ives), became a permanent centre. Its sheltered harbour gave onto the estuary of the river Dee in Dumfries and Galloway, and this small coastal village attracted the likes of Edward Atkinson Hornel (1864–1933) and George Henry. They became increasingly interested in Scotland's Celtic history and collaborated on *The Druids: Bringing in the Mistletoe* in 1890. Bessie MacNicol (1869–1904), another alumna of the Glasgow School of Art (and Paris), was friends with Hornel and spent time in Kirkcudbright in 1896. In her *A Girl of the Sixties* (see overleaf), painted at the turn of the century, we see the influence of these Glasgow Boys. But MacNicol also expands on Guthrie's consideration of the surface as a flat space by drawing on Japanese prints that had been circulating in increasing numbers since the country was forcibly opened up to trade in 1854. Japanese prints employed a flattened perspective and flat blocks of colour to convey overall harmonies, and MacNicol reinterprets this for her painting of a young woman standing in the dappled shade of an oak tree. We can see how the dappled sunlight on her dress echoes the autumn leaves on the branch above her, while the white highlights on her sleeves are mirrored by those on the field behind. The paintings of MacNicol, Henry and Hornel connect to the post-Impressionism of Paul Gauguin and Paul Cézanne rather than the Barbizon School's *en plein air*. They also share links with the Aesthetic movement – a branch of the Arts and Crafts movement – and in particular the work of James Abbott McNeill Whistler (1834–1903).

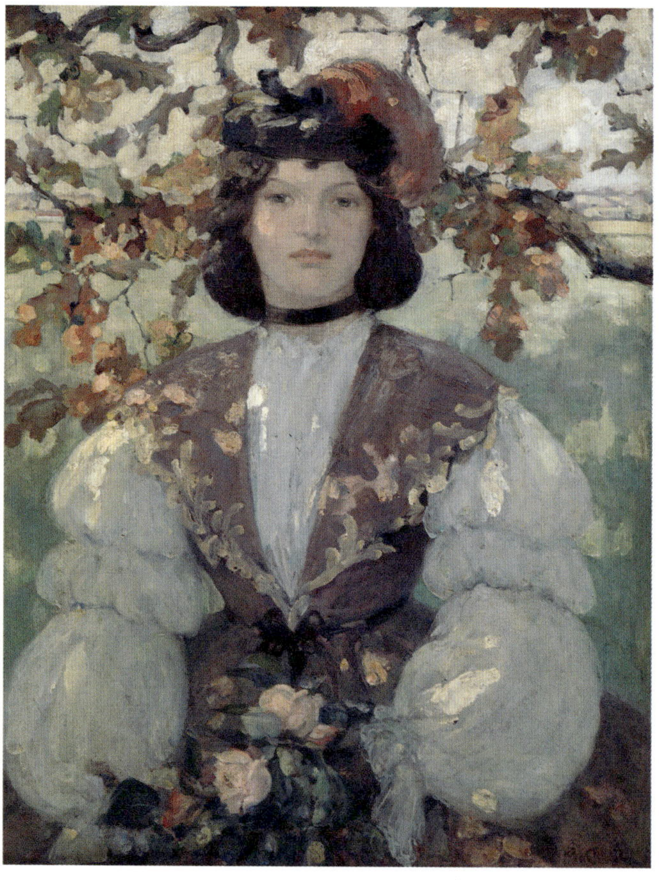

Bessie MacNicol, *A Girl of the Sixties*, oil on canvas, *c.*1900

It is easy to see how an artistic community could quickly develop if several artists lived and worked in a remote village, but in a city like London there was always going to be a number of choices or paths an artist could take. Would you toe the line at the Royal Academy or look to France's outdoor naturalism? Would you work alongside designers on Arts and Crafts buildings or be drawn to communing with the spirits? Or would you be bold and declare that art's sole purpose should be beauty? The poet Algernon Swinburne believed this to be the case and validated a painting by Albert Moore (1841–1893) by stating: 'Its reason for being is to be.'[11] Like the languid classical beauties of Frederic Leighton (1830–1896), Moore's handsome men and women in diaphanous togas were devoid of historical purpose or narrative but were there to be admired solely for their elegance of line and colour harmonies.

From 1860 until the turn of the century the British Aesthetic movement attracted some of the best painters of the day. Whistler arrived from the United States by way of a Paris education and brought with him a love of Japanese prints and porcelain. Moore and Whistler added branches of Japanese blossom to their paintings, flattening perspective and reducing their palette range until Whistler was painting monochromes of girls dressed in white, such as *Symphony in White No. 2* (1864). Their art was not about a story or a social message, it was about pure beauty expressed in colour and tone and pattern and line.

It was all too much for the ageing Ruskin. He had championed Turner's chromatic experiments and landscapes that had teetered on the brink of abstraction, but he couldn't fathom Whistler's *Nocturne in Black and Gold, The Falling Rocket* (1875; see overleaf) when it was exhibited at the newly opened Grosvenor Gallery, founded as an alternative venue to the Royal Academy and challenging its hegemony, just as the Impressionist exhibitions were doing to the official Salon in France. In 1877 Ruskin dipped his poison pen in his inkwell and wrote that charging 200 guineas for such a daub was like 'flinging a pot of paint in the public's face'.[12] Whistler sued him for libel and they ended up in court, although Ruskin was too ill to attend. Fellow artists including Frith, Burne-Jones and Leighton were drafted in to answer questions as to what constituted a work of art. In the end Whistler was victorious, but it was a pyrrhic victory – he was only awarded damages of a farthing, or quarter of a penny, and the cost of the case left him bankrupt.

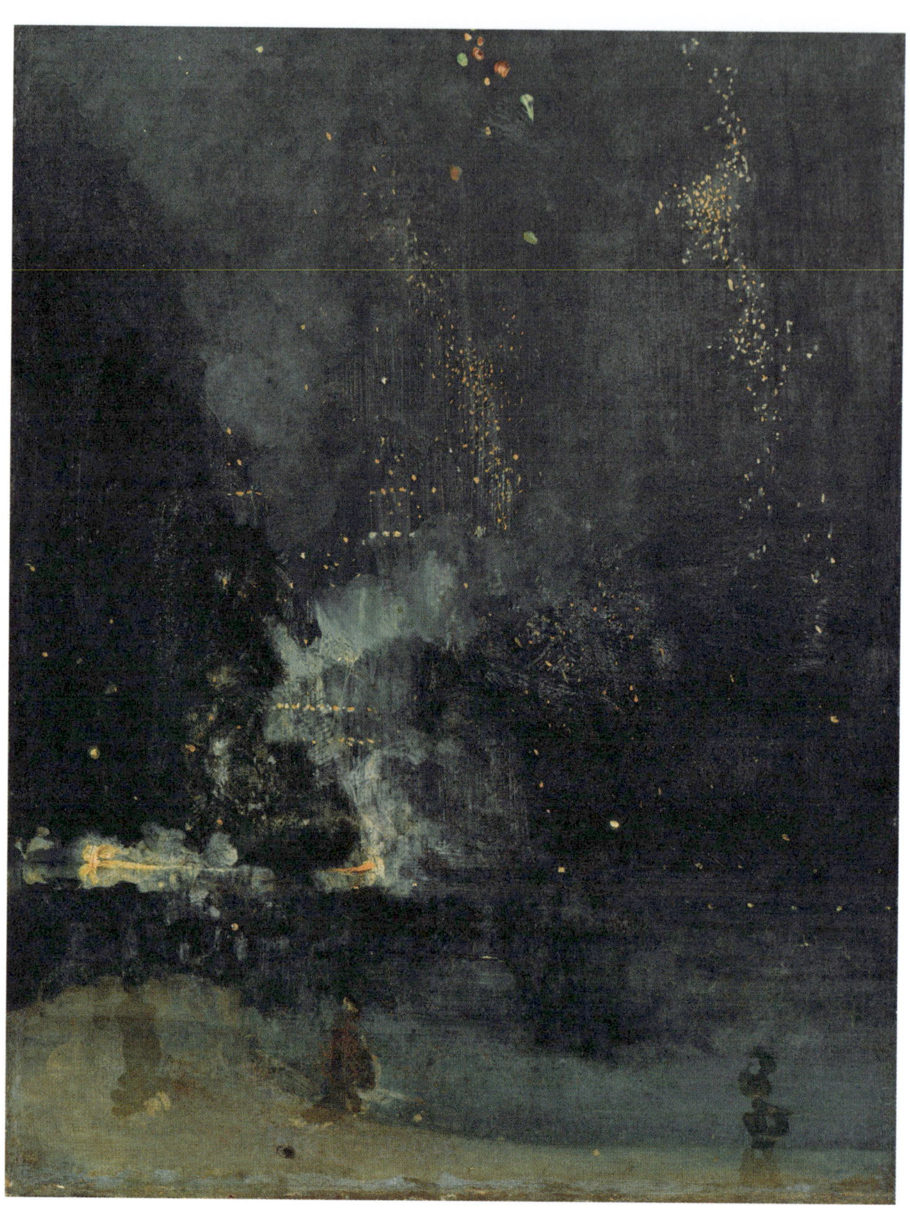

J.A.M. Whistler, *Nocturne in Black and Gold,*
The Falling Rocket, oil on panel, 1875

BEAUTY AS A FORM OF GENIUS

The allure of the Aesthetic movement attracted a slew of international artists to London. The French painter James Tissot (1836–1902) focused on middle-class fashion and leisure in the 1870s, while Dutch Lawrence Alma-Tadema (1836–1912) created languid classical scenes. Whistler hailed from the United States, and the society portrait painter John Singer Sargent (1856–1925) had been born in Florence to American parents. Working on commission, Sargent produced lively, spirited portraits such as *Ena and Betty, Daughters of Asher and Mrs Wertheimer* (1901). He had moved to London in 1886, taking Whistler's old studio on Tite Street in Chelsea. His vigorous style and breathy compositions were the complete opposite of the lifeless photographic polish of Royal Academy regulars. Sargent's brushstrokes had the energy of Velázquez and the freshness of *en plein air* painting. He had studied in Paris as the first Impressionist exhibitions were held. These artists, who banded together to exhibit away from the Salon, took the Barbizon School's method of painting outdoors to the next level. They concentrated on the way light sparkled on the river and dappled the dresses of dancers at open-air parties. They were not looking to capture essential truths of nature but the dynamic transience of life, the way the world changed with every moment.

During the Franco-Prussian War of 1870–1 many of these artists who would become known as Impressionists waited out the war in Britain. Claude Monet (1840–1926) painted views of the Houses of Parliament in London while Camille Pissarro (1830–1903) headed to the suburb of Crystal Palace. A few years later Berthe Morisot (1841–1895) spent time painting in the Isle of Wight and the south of England on her honeymoon with Édouard Manet's brother Eugène. The Impressionists tracked the haunts of Turner and their paintings in turn inspired a new way of looking at the world.

Today we think of Impressionism as Monet's exploration of light on water, Morisot's women at the theatre and Edgar Degas's ballet dancers seen from the wings. Degas (1834–1917) was a strong influence on Walter Sickert (1860–1942), who met him in 1883 when he was delivering Whistler's *Portrait of the Artist's Mother* to the Paris Salon. Sickert – born in Germany but raised in Britain since the age of eight – worked for Whistler in London but it was Degas who would have the biggest impact on his own work. Degas had painted cafe-concerts and ballets by expanding the view to include the men watching from the bar or dancers in the wings adjusting their shoes. Sickert had initially worked as an actor and many of his most successful paintings are of the stage. He also included the artifice of performance – the prompt side of the wings and the stage rail, for example – and he loved painting the cat-calling audience as much as the proscenium arch. As part of the Camden Town Group he displayed the seedy underbelly of the city as Degas had done in Paris, even painting a series called *Camden Town Murders* in response to the death of the prostitute Emily Dimmock near his studio in 1907.

Nineteenth-century artists had to travel to Paris to see works by Morisot and Degas, but as the new century dawned British and Irish collectors began to buy and show their work. Welsh philanthropists Gwendoline and Margaret Davies bought their first Impressionist and post-Impressionist paintings in 1908 and their collection – which included works by Monet, Pissarro, Manet, Van Gogh and Cézanne – inspired Samuel Courtauld to start buying similar work (he later founded the Courtauld Institute of Art; the Davies sisters left their collection to the National Museum of Wales). This same year Dublin-born Hugh Lane's Impressionist paintings went on show at the newly opened Municipal Gallery of Modern Art in Dublin. The British artist and critic Roger Fry (1866–1934) staged two important exhibitions of post-Impressionist work in 1910–11 and 1912.

Around Fry a circle of like-minded friends including Vanessa Bell (1879–1961) and Duncan Grant (1885–1978), were painting sun-drenched portraits and still lifes, channelling the Henri Matisse paintings seen in Fry's exhibitions. They lived in Bloomsbury and their work was the antithesis of Sickert with his earthy, grimy tones, love of the music hall and spartan bedsit. Fry had founded the Omega Workshops so the Bloomsbury Group could focus on making art together but it was short-lived, overshadowed by events on the continent. Britain entered the First World War on 4 August 1914.

12

WAR'S RAPID RATTLE
1914–30

ONE MONTH AND two days before Britain entered the First World War, a new magazine was published for the first time. The word 'BLAST' roared across the cerise cover like a clarion call to modernity. *Blast* was fiercely modern, its sans-serif capitals declaring the magazine's intent from the outset, the coloured cover differentiating it from the newspaper in your parlour. It was written by Percy Wyndham Lewis (1882–1957), the founder of a new group of artists who called themselves Vorticists. Born out of French Cubism and Italian Futurism, Vorticism was the British love-child that similarly fractured surfaces and embraced dynamism but claimed a discrete place for itself, beyond the remote analytical planes of Cubism and the Futurists' obsession with speed and cars. The Vorticists wanted to embrace the modern world by placing themselves at the epicentre of the vortex, deconstructing skyscrapers and street scenes and faces and recreating them in facets of vivid colour in their paintings and as black-and-white woodcuts within the pages of *Blast*.

Vorticism grew out of a disagreement between Lewis and Fry. Lewis tore into his ideals in the Vorticist manifesto, saying the Bloomsbury Group was not in touch with reality and lacked ambition. Its members had evolved from the Aesthetic movement by way of the latest French trends whereas the Vorticists revelled in being at the centre of contemporary London life. They were fuelled by the present, by the industrial cities where many of their parents worked and by the modern ports from which British warships would soon set sail. Artists who rallied to Lewis's

195

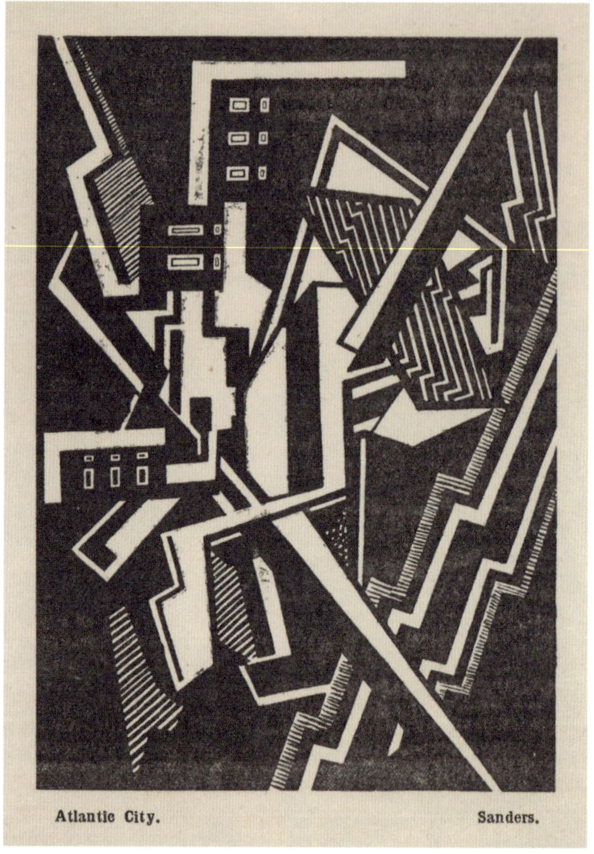

Helen Saunders, *Atlantic City*, illustration of her painting in
Blast magazine, 1915

call included David Bomberg (1890–1957), Helen Saunders (1885–1963),
Edward Wadsworth (1889–1949) and Jessica Dismorr (1885–1939).

Modernity fed on industrialisation and the consumption levels of the
rising middle class, and was whipped on by Britain's desire to compete
on a global stage. It was bullish, fast-paced, seemingly unstoppable.
And then came the war. The Vorticists were intransigent at first. 'That
the war will in any way change the currents of contemporary art, I do
not believe: they are deeper than it', wrote Lewis in the second issue
of *Blast*.[1] The French sculptor Henri Gaudier-Brzeska (1891–1915),
who had lived in London since 1911, sent his Vorticist despatch from
the trenches in northern France in the spring of 1915. 'This war is a
great remedy', he wrote. 'My views on sculpture remain absolutely the

same. It is the vortex of will, of decision, that begins.'[2] But by the time his views were published in *Blast* Gaudier-Brzeska was dead, killed in action during a charge at Neuville-Saint-Vaast.

THE FUTURE ISN'T BRIGHT

Many artists saw active service during the war. Bomberg served in the Royal Engineers and Lewis was a gunner. Their contemporary C.R.W. Nevinson (1889–1946) volunteered for the Red Cross in France. All three would go on to produce paintings based directly on their experiences, modifying their avant-garde style to suit the unremittingly bleak scenes they now found themselves confronting. Nevinson had been a Futurist before the war and had angered Lewis by including him in his essay 'Vital English Art', co-written with Futurism's founder Filippo Marinetti. In it the pair claimed that many English artists, including Lewis, had chosen to align themselves with the Futurist movement. Lewis was incensed, immediately founding the Vorticist movement and excluding Nevinson. And yet to me their responses to the war are not dissimilar. Both Nevinson's *La Mitrailleuse* (1915) and Lewis's *A Battery Shelled* (1919) use angular planes to construct noses and cheeks under steel helmets with backgrounds featuring mechanistic soldiers and a twisted array of barbed wire, smoke and trench supports.

Soon the spiky geometries of Vorticism lost their meaning for Lewis. The idea of art for art's sake, even when it drew upon contemporary life, suddenly seemed inappropriate. It was as if the war had followed art's lead and fragmented the world into shards, and artists across Europe began to retrench from such avant-garde positions and return to figuration. By 1917 Nevinson's Futurist dream of man and machine in ecstatic unison had also been annihilated. In *After a Push* we see him turn to a traditional form of naturalism to convey the fields of mud pitted with flooded bomb craters. The portrait artist William Orpen (1878–1931) employed a similar style when he was appointed an official war artist in 1917, but even in his most successful works such as *Zonnebeke* (1918) it feels as if he only experienced such scenes at one remove. He was chauffeured between front lines rather than being one of the troops, and it shows. Zonnebeke was the location for the Battle of Passchendaele, where 325,000 Allied men died. Orpen presents a solitary figure lying lifeless by a bomb crater, alongside a tree that has been reduced to a stump. Employing the picturesque, he draws us into the painting by joining the bomb craters into a serpentine body of water. Everything is present – the war-ravaged countryside, a dead soldier – and yet this picture conveys nowhere near the emotion we feel when we read the first four lines of the serving officer Wilfred Owen's poem 'Anthem for Doomed Youth' (1917):

What passing-bells for these who die as cattle?
– Only the monstrous anger of the guns.
Only the stuttering rifles' rapid rattle
Can patter out their hasty orisons.[3]

If we look at *We Are Making a New World* (1918) by Paul Nash (1889–1946) we come closer to the bleak futility of Owen's verse. In Nash's painting the landscape has become alien – trees are blackened stumps that reach into the sky like skeletal arms. The ground is an unpassable maze of hillocks and the sun, breaking through blood-red

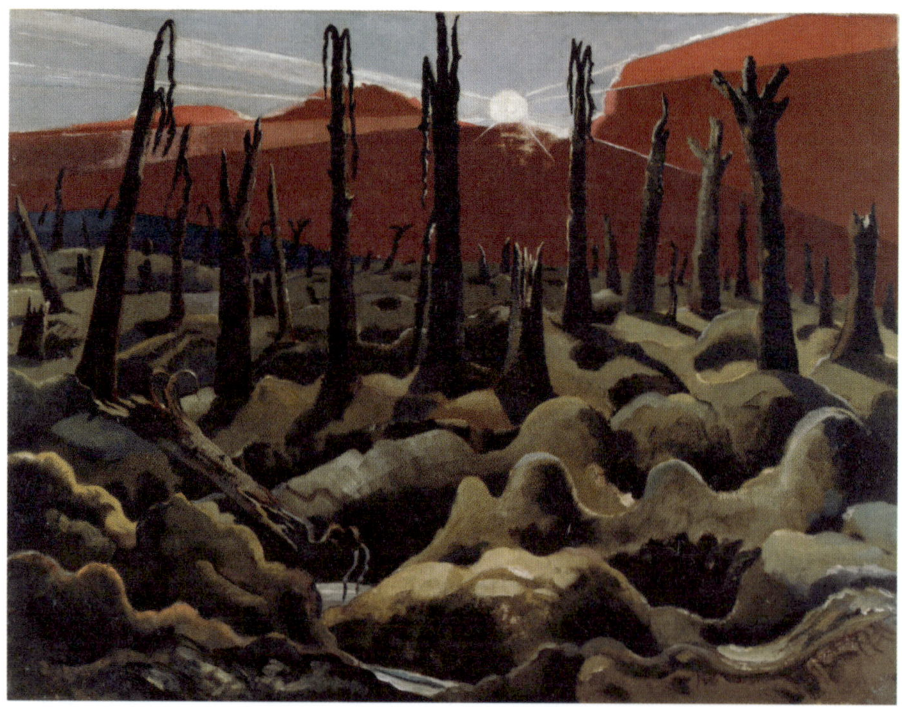

Paul Nash, *We Are Making a New World*, oil on canvas, 1918

clouds, shines on the scene like an enemy searchlight. The fallen tree trunk, with its splintered roots and amputated branches, stands in for all the soldiers who have died in this dystopic land. Perhaps this is why Nash's paintings still resonate with us today, because they connect with the war at both a personal and a universal level. This was a man who knew the trenches at first-hand, knee deep in mud with death around every corner. We feel this when we look at his paintings – instinctively we have a visceral response rather than an aesthetic one.

Like Orpen, Nash became an official war artist in 1917. Many of the artists who saw active service in the first half of the war subsequently became war artists and received official commissions from the British War Memorials Committee. Nash painted *The Menin Road* (1919) on the scale of a history painting, and his younger brother John (1893–1977) contributed *Oppy Wood, 1917* (1918) for a proposed Hall of Remembrance. Artists who hadn't seen direct action themselves were also asked to take part, and Sargent's *Gassed* (1919) reflected the war on an epic scale. It is over 6 metres wide and shows two columns of men walking towards a dressing station. Their eyes are bound, victims of mustard gas, and they hold the shoulder of the man in front like the biblical blind leading the blind. It is a damning statement on the wastage of war, on the unthinkable human cost. In the distance you can spy a few men in coloured shirts playing football on the edge of camp, the next crop of victims.

The Imperial War Museum was founded in 1917 and opened in 1920, originally in the Crystal Palace. Before it opened it set to work recording the war it was born into. Anna Airy (1882–1964), a former Slade student, was commissioned to paint the industrial reality of war on the home front. She visited factories and forges in Glasgow, Manchester and London, standing on 'an earth floor black hot, that burnt a pair of shoes off my feet'.[4] She made numerous sketches in situ and her detailed paintings take us to the heart of the action as shells glide by on chassis, red-hot from the forge. The workers are faceless, anonymous, but the ammunition is depicted in great detail. Clare Atwood (1866–1962) was on the Women's Work Sub-Committee at the museum, a body that commissioned women artists to record the war effort. Her own painting *Olympia in War Time: Royal Army Clothing Depot* (1918) has bales of clothes built up like fortifications across the floor of the Olympia exhibition hall in London.

LOST BUT NOT FORGOTTEN

On 11 November 1918 the First World War ended. The nation began to imagine how so much death and destruction could be commemorated. A symbolic solitary funeral for the Unknown Warrior attracted huge crowds in 1920. Villages and towns erected their own memorials to the fallen, as did institutions, churches and factories. As early as 1917 a Scottish National War Memorial was planned, to be sited on Castle Rock in Edinburgh, and it finally opened in 1927, dedicated to 'the Glory of God, and in memory of Scots who fell, 1914–18'.[5] It is a large architectural edifice, not unlike a church, with a Hall of Honour and a separate octagonal shrine. Photography is not allowed and the air is reverential. Around the edges of the shrine is a cast-bronze frieze by Alice (1877–1934) and Morris Meredith Williams (1881–1973). A procession of seventy-four soldiers, naval officers, nurses and ambulance drivers walk alongside tanks, planes, horses and dogs. The first thing I noticed was how young so many of them are. The clothes they are wearing denote their regiment or role, from snowshoes and spurs to hazard suits and goggles, kilts and tam-o'-shanters. There are generals and lieutenants but also privates and support staff. Six women, representing navy and RAF nurses, are squeezed into the outer reaches (it was unusual to have them there at all at this time). What makes this frieze particularly interesting today is its acknowledgement of the wider support for Britain in the war. There are privates from the South African Scottish and Canadian Scottish, a trooper from the Imperial Camel Corps and a piper from New Zealand's Auckland regiment. The frieze was designed to situate Scotland within the British empire as well as assert the Scottish diaspora.

Over three million people from across the empire and Commonwealth supported the British army during the First World War. Nearly half a million had enlisted from the Caribbean, Africa and India but their contribution was overlooked by the organisers of the 1919 Peace Day parade despite 20,000 troops from European Allied countries, America, China and Japan taking part. The inclusion of Commonwealth troops in the Scottish War Memorial was notable, but it too excluded Black Africans and Indians.

As well as public memorials to the fallen there was a proliferation of private ones, dedicated to a particular person or family group who had died during the war. One of the most ambitious is the Sandham Memorial Chapel in Burghclere in Hampshire, commissioned by John and Mary Behrend and dedicated to Mary's brother, Harry Willoughby Sandham, who had died in 1919 from an illness (possibly malaria) related to his service in the war. He had been stationed in Salonika (Thessaloniki) in Greece, where the artist Stanley Spencer (1891–1959) had also served as a medical orderly. Spencer had been thinking of embarking on a war memorial before he met the Behrends in 1923, but he didn't have the funds. Together they drew up plans for the Sandham Memorial Chapel and Spencer spent five years working on its cycle of paintings from 1927.

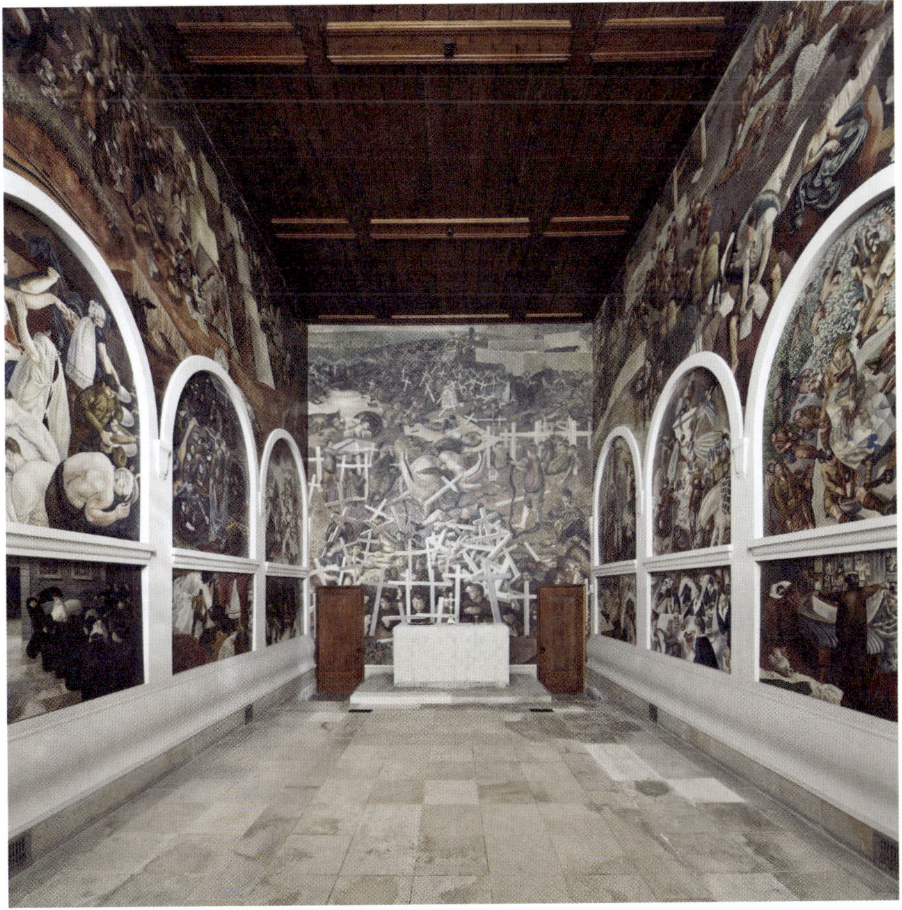

Stanley Spencer, murals for Sandham Memorial Chapel, oil on canvas, 1927–32

The chapel is based on the proportions of Giotto's Scrovegni Chapel (*c*.1305) in Padua, Italy. Spencer also drew on Giotto's treatment of the human form as a solid physical entity, not idealised but credible. Spencer, like many of his contemporaries including Lewis, Nevinson and Airy, had studied at the Slade under Henry Tonks (1862–1937). Tonks had trained as a surgeon before becoming an artist and he was rigorous in his teaching of the structure of the body.

For the Sandham Memorial Chapel, Spencer devised a scheme of nineteen paintings that drew upon his time as a medical orderly in Bristol and Macedonia in Greece, where he later enlisted in the infantry. He painted the mundane tasks he had to perform, such as scrubbing the floors and filling tea urns, combined with his duties looking after sick patients, changing bedsheets and washing lockers. His scenes of war are unsensational – a kit inspection, for example, or the filling of water bottles. It is as if he reserved all the drama for the huge mural on the back wall that greets you as you enter the chapel. It imagines the resurrection of soldiers on Judgement Day and features a proliferation of white crosses carried by the risen dead. In the dark gloom of the interior the crosses seem to glow. They are being returned to Christ, who gathers them up in the distance, outside the walled village of Kalinova in Macedonia. The men who carry them show signs of their injuries, with amputated feet taped up or tangles of barbed wire incarcerating them. Many of them look like Spencer, their dark hair neatly parted above pale faces, and the whole cycle feels like an externalisation of Spencer's own experiences of war. This repetition is uncanny, and I leave the chapel contemplating Wilfred Owen's anonymous men who die as cattle, faceless and interchangeable.

THE HUNT FOR ESSENTIAL FORM

In 1913 the sculptor Jacob Epstein (1880–1959) had created *Rock Drill* in his London studio. It was a futuristic figure straddling a drill bought from a Welsh quarry, a radical assemblage of a sculpture and a ready-made object that captured the essence of Vorticist modernity with its machine aesthetic. But the First World War had a significant impact on all artists, and within two years Epstein had mutilated it. He discarded the drill with its tripod legs, reminiscent of the Vickers Mark 1 machine gun (which could kill someone 2 miles away). The initial plaster figure, a robotic droid, was sliced in half, its legs discarded, its arms amputated. Only the small soft foetus at its core, nestled between its ribs, survived. Epstein placed the new amputee on a plinth, no longer in control of its own destiny.

In many ways *Rock Drill* is an outlier in Epstein's practice. Before the war he had been drawn to art from beyond Europe that could be seen at the British Museum, the Pitt Rivers Museum in Oxford and the National Museum in Scotland. It was not displayed as art but as exotic 'curios' taken from around the globe as Britain's imperial expansion continued. When the missionary and explorer David Livingstone died in Zambia in 1873, Africa was a largely unknown continent in Europe, beyond its coastal fringes. But within fifty years a handful of European countries – including Britain – had carved it up and taken ownership of its mineral wealth and its people. The Scramble for Africa, as it is now known, was a land grab of unprecedented proportions that culminated in the Berlin Conference in 1884–5 where Africa was carved up between European colonisers, resulting in the violent subjugation of many peoples and cultures. (Yinka Shonibare CBE RA (born 1962), whom we will meet in Chapter 17, reinterpreted this geopolitical event in his 2003 sculpture *Scramble for Africa* by dressing the Victorian European negotiators in African wax-printed fabric known as batik and beheading them.)

By 1897 large swathes of Africa were under British colonial rule. So when a British envoy and his party were killed in Benin City, retribution was swift and merciless. The British sacked the city, systematically looting everything they perceived to have value before setting the whole place on fire. British forces took what are now known as the Benin Bronzes. Created in the fifteenth to nineteenth centuries, the brass and bronze plaques and ivory sculptures record the life of the Benin king, the Oba, and his court. The looters didn't catalogue their 'finds' but heaped them in large piles in the central courtyard before shipping them back to Britain to be sold to the highest bidder. (This was not the first time the British had done this – in 1860 they looted and burnt the Summer Palace in Beijing, and in 1868 they did the same in Abyssinia in modern-day Ethiopia. While these events were condemned at the time, cultural material still made its way to Britain and into British museums.)

The Benin Bronzes began entering museum collections within a few months. They were not displayed as art, even though now we consider them to be. They were not respected as spiritual objects, despite many being found in shrines. Instead they were grouped with other objects from Africa, often ahistorically and without contextualisation. But for artists working in Britain who sought them out, they showed a level of sophistication on a par with anything produced in the West, one that challenged Western stereotypes about African art.

Artists working in Britain became fascinated by sculptures from Africa, Oceania and the ancient civilisations of Assyria, Egypt and the Maya. They began to haunt the less visited corridors of national museums – Epstein would visit the British Museum regularly with the sculptor Eric Gill (1882–1940). The pair were looking for sculptures that had a raw energy, ones that offered them a completely new way of thinking about the body, a new way of seeing. They were drawn to sculptures that expressed the essence of their subject rather than a surface likeness – the blocky strength of bent legs or the pronounced features of mask-like faces with large almond eyes. At the time artists referred to this as 'primitive'. It was not the pejorative term it is today but conveyed a sense of an intuitive rightness of form that came from within. It was the antithesis of the cold scientific naturalism of the classically rooted Western world with its commitment to mimicry and one-point perspective. Fry, in his influential collection of essays *Vision and Design* (1920), wrote about a recent exhibition of African art he had seen: 'Without ever attaining anything like representational accuracy they have complete freedom.' This, he noted, gave the forms a 'disconcerting vitality, the suggestion that they make of being not mere echoes of actual figures, but of possessing an inner life of their own'.[6]

Epstein had lived in Britain since 1905 after studying in New York and Paris. His *Tomb of Oscar Wilde* (1908–12) in the Père Lachaise cemetery in Paris, carved from a single 20-ton block of Hoptonwood stone, has a monumentality reminiscent of the human-headed winged bulls from Assyria (710–705 BCE) he had seen in the British Museum. Gaudier-Brzeska saw Wilde's tomb in Epstein's London studio. It gave him the impetus he needed to take direct inspiration from the sculptures he was also looking at in the British Museum and the V&A. His *Red Stone Dancer* (*c.*1913) seems to grow out of her stone base, gyrating as she does so: her whole body is in movement. Her face is reduced to a triangle, her fingers to simple incised lines. She is born of stone, not humankind, but she conveys the essence of movement like no classical sculpture ever could.

Works like *Red Stone Dancer* gave young sculptors the courage to experiment further and they became committed to 'truth to materials'. They advocated direct carving, a way of working with a block of stone or piece of wood to allow the material to help shape the final form. Barbara Hepworth (1903–1975), Ronald Moody (1900–1984) and Henry Moore (1898–1986) believed that truth to materials offered a way to create authentic, essential forms. As a teenager Moore had joined the Civil Service Rifles, experiencing life in the trenches and a mustard gas attack. But in September 1919 he became a student at Leeds School of Art and later the Royal College of Art (RCA) in London. He too was inspired by non-European sculpture that he sought out at the British Museum after reading Fry's *Vision and Design*. Pre-Columbian Chac Mool sculptures from Mesoamerica informed his Horton stone *Reclining Figure* (1929) and he was inspired by everything from Egyptian funerary sculpture to the Benin Bronzes.

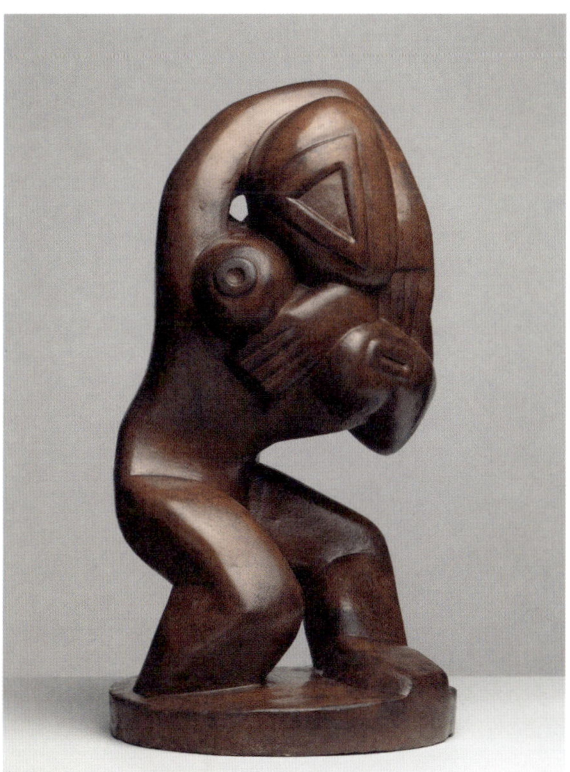

Henri Gaudier-Brzeska, *Red Stone Dancer*,
red Mansfield stone, *c.*1913

Moody, who had moved to Britain from Jamaica in 1923 to train as a dentist, also frequented the Egyptian galleries. It was during a visit to the British Museum in 1928 that he resolved to pursue his dream to become a sculptor. 'The use of the material, the massive forms treated with such amazing skill, sensitiveness, delicacy and daring, and lastly, the spirit behind it was strangely sympathetic,' he explained on the BBC's *Calling the West Indies*. 'From that moment I felt I wanted to do sculpture.'[7] Working in wood like Moore and Hepworth, he responded to the material's organic nature. The shape of the tree trunk, the knots and burrs and grain he turned into contours, mapping the swell of cheekbones and breasts. His carved elm-wood figures, such as the larger-than-life *Johanaan* (1936), share similar qualities with the hieratic Egyptian statues made 3,000 years earlier that he had seen at the British Museum, with their static poses and far-seeing blank eyes.

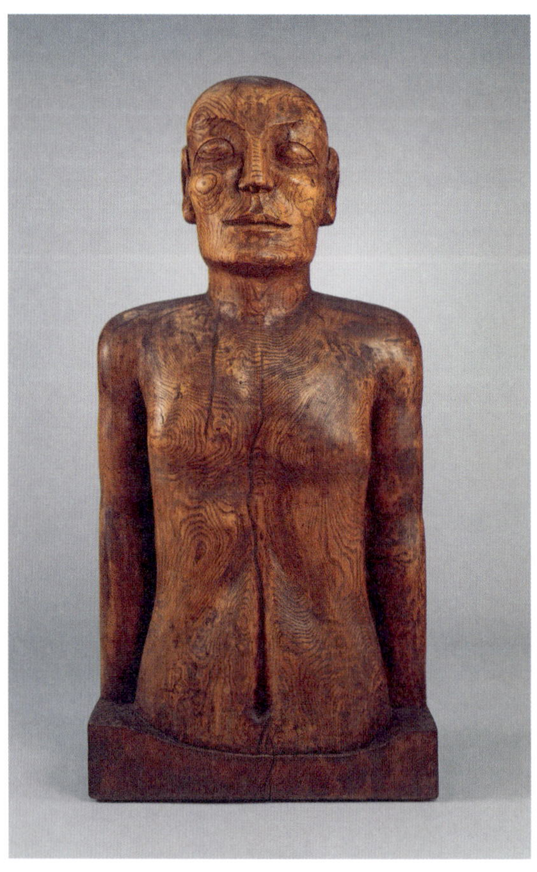

Ronald Moody, *Johanaan*, elm wood, 1936

By looking at sculpture from beyond the Western tradition, artists found what Moore called a 'common world-language of form'.[8] Hepworth employed direct carving and reduced form to its essential qualities to tease each sculpture from the material she was working with. 'Carving is interrelated masses conveying an emotion', she wrote in 1934: 'a perfect relationship between the mind and the colour, light and weight which is the stone, made by the hand which feels. It must be so essentially sculpture that it can exist in no other way.'[9] She carved torsos from pyinkado wood, using the grain to swell breasts and hips. Her rosewood *Kneeling Figure* from 1932 crouches on blocky stylised legs with an integral plinth that indicates the original circumference of the tree trunk it was carved from. In 1935 Moody exhibited his oak sculpture *Wohin* at the *Negro Art* exhibition at the Adams Gallery in London. The show featured new British sculpture by Epstein, Moody and others alongside West African sculpture, including bronze plaques from Benin. Moore attended the opening, supportive of fellow sculptors pursuing a similar path and keen to see further examples of African art.

FRENCH COLOUR

We will return to Moore, Moody and Hepworth in subsequent chapters. For now we must further interrogate the links between France and the British Isles during the first decades of the twentieth century. We have seen how British artists visited and studied in France while others relocated to London from Paris. In 1924, at the Galerie Barbazanges in Paris, an exhibition was held of four Scottish painters' work. The gallery was known for showing paintings by the avant-garde – Pablo Picasso, Natalia Goncharova, Matisse. It billed the show of work by J.D. Fergusson (1874–1961), S.J. Peploe (1871–1935), F.C.B. Cadell (1883–1937) and Leslie Hunter (1877–1931) as *Painters of Modern Scotland*. We know them today as the Scottish Colourists. These four men, all born in the 1870s and early 1880s, had studied and lived in Paris before the First World War, spending summers painting in the South of France, in Cassis and La Rochelle. They all hailed from Scotland but, like their predecessors the Glasgow Boys, were seduced by developments in French art, from the *en plein air* Impressionists to the bold and unexpected colours of the post-Impressionists and, in particular, Matisse and the Fauves.

The Fauves had been experimenting with colour to such an extent that a critic who reviewed their paintings in the independent Salon d'Automne exhibition of 1905 called them *les fauves* or wild beasts. We can see the impact of their work on the Scottish Colourists if we consider two paintings by J.D. Fergusson. The first, *Hat with Bird*, was painted in 1907, while *The Pink Parasol* dates to a year later. *Hat with Bird* is an assured portrait of the American artist Anne Estelle Rice, who lived in Paris. Fergusson had moved to Paris the year before and his use of black in this painting, along with his gestural brushwork, brings Manet to mind (as well as the monochrome tones of Whistler). But look at *The Pink Parasol: Bertha Case*. It is a riot of colour, from the pink rose on Case's hat to the way the white brushstrokes

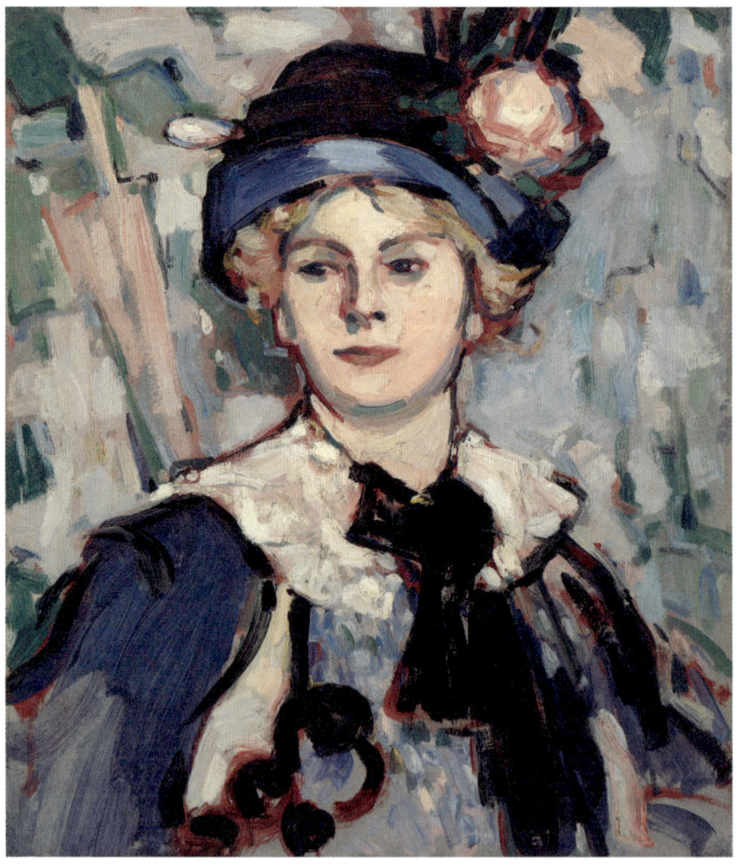

J.D. Fergusson, *The Pink Parasol: Bertha Case*, oil on millboard, 1908

dance over greens and blues to form the background. Fergusson has used bold green stripes to add shadows to her peach face, something that Matisse had been criticised for when he exhibited *Woman with a Hat*, a portrait of his wife, in 1905. But fellow artists quickly realised Matisse's approach was based on an authenticity of looking – not painting the colour he knew the face to be but the colour it appeared at that instant. Fergusson is clearly responding to Matisse's painting and this allowed him to take a bold approach to the figure in future.

Fergusson was embedded in the avant-garde scene in Paris and when Peploe arrived in 1910 he found a ready-made group to socialise with and learn from, but by the outbreak of the war they were back in Britain. Peploe's early lively landscapes gave way to more contemplative still lifes, channelling Cézanne's slow accretion of *taches* (patches of colour) as he painted vases of roses, pot plants and fruit. In *The Brown Crock* (*c.*1925) he uses a swathe of blue fabric to recess the wall behind a table of upended objects. We have to work hard to separate the forms at times (as we must do in Cézanne's still lifes), as they oscillate between appearing as pure patches of pink and orange and coalescing into a fan or a piece of fruit.

A ROOM OF ONE'S OWN

I cannot help thinking of the artist Cecile Walton (1891–1956) when I imagine these four men travelling the length of Britain, taking a boat across the English Channel and proceeding to Paris or Marseille. Walton was twenty years younger than Peploe, the daughter of the Glasgow Boys painter Edward Walton (1860–1922). She trained in Paris and Edinburgh; by the age of eighteen she was exhibiting at the Royal Scottish Academy and at the Royal Academy in London shortly after. Her misstep was marrying the alcoholic artist Eric Robertson (1887–1941) in 1914. They had two children but had divorced by 1927; he drank himself to death and corroded the Edinburgh Group, of which she was a member along with Dorothy Johnstone (1892–1980) and Mary Newbery (1892–1985). The cost of her marriage was her painting career – she subsequently worked as a writer, set designer and BBC producer as she brought up her two sons alone.

The price of motherhood for ambitious women artists is articulated succinctly in Walton's 1920 painting *Romance* (see overleaf). You can feel the bitterness as she chooses its ironic title. She paints herself lying in after the birth of her second son Edward. A nurse gives her a sponge bath as her older son Gavril stands at the end of the bed, observing her. She purposefully uses the composition of *Olympia*, Manet's notorious painting of a white prostitute and Black servant exhibited at the 1863 Salon des Refusés in Paris. Manet's model, the artist Victorine Meurent, looks out at the viewer, her hand spreadeagled over her sex, blocking access, fully in control of her own body. Walton, by contrast, does not meet our eyes and instead looks towards her baby. Sex has given her children, not financial independence, and now she is incapacitated and not painting. Her artist husband is missing from the scene, but the small framed painting on the wall and the screen behind the bed imply he is out there somewhere, still working. As with Manet's painting, Walton's is all about the gaze – the fierceness of her scrutiny causes the baby to turn away. The nurse also averts her eyes, as does the doll Gavril clutches. He stares ahead, strangling his baby substitute, ignoring the roses shedding their petals on the floor beneath the bed, symbolic of his mother's life and youthful bloom ebbing away.

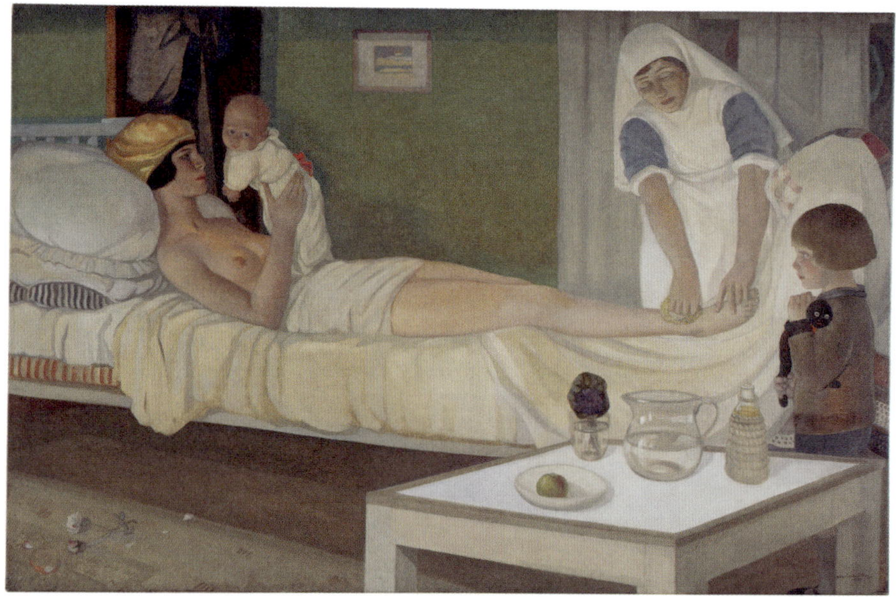

Cecile Walton, *Romance*, oil on canvas, 1920

Gwen John (1876–1939) offers another perspective on being a woman artist. She was born in Wales but studied in London then Paris, at Whistler's Académie Carmen. Whistler's influence on her was significant but so too was the dynamic climate of the Parisian avant-garde. Unlike her bohemian artist brother Augustus (1878–1961), Gwen John preferred Paris to London. She modelled for the celebrated sculptor Auguste Rodin (1840–1917), who became her lover for a time, but she remained childless. She saw how difficult motherhood was for her friend Ida Nettleship, who had married Augustus. For Gwen John, her art was her baby, and when she sold work she described herself as a *maman* (mother) placing her children in a good home.[10]

Gwen John lived in France from 1907 until her death in 1939. Her quiet paintings of women in interiors have a stillness about them that we gaze upon like a balm for our busy lives today. Paris was jumping with colour and ideas at this time, but within that climate John found a way to move from painting portraits of individuals to a calm distillation of womanhood in *The Convalescent* (*c*.1923–4). An anonymous woman sits in a cane chair reading a letter, a pot of tea close by. All extraneous detail has been removed to leave only the essence of the woman, a study in marine blues and greys, surrounded by the warm ochre tones of the chair, table and teapot. The artist Celia Paul (born 1959) wrote a book of letters to Gwen John in 2022. She described this painting as 'fragile and robust as an egg', marvelling that 'the structure of the composition holds everything in place; this delicate painting will endure'.[11] Gwen John was aware of this, as she wrote in a letter to her friend Ursula Tyrwhitt: 'I cannot imagine why my vision will have some value in the world – and yet I know it will.'[12]

John's women sit alone, in rooms of their own, engaged in private activities such as reading. They do not engage in the domestic sphere; they do not look after children. In their own solitary way they offer resistance to the male expectation that they should aspire to motherhood. Some are nuns, others convalesce, most are young. They represent the women Virginia Woolf was imagining in *A Room of One's Own* (1929). John herself could be Woolf's heroine, steadfastly ploughing her own furrow, creating work as a woman, rather than work that apes that of men. She is the antithesis of the other women Woolf laments, the mothers such as Walton: 'For all the dinners are cooked; the plates and cups washed; the children sent to school and gone out into the world. Nothing remains of it all. All has vanished.

No biography or history has a word to say about it.'[13] Walton's gaze in *Romance*, painted nine years before Woolf published these words, seems to convey this future as she contemplates her new baby.

The immediate post-war years were a time of rapid development within European art as artists began tipping over into abstraction, previously only seen in the work of Spiritualists such as Georgiana Houghton. Abstraction for its own sake, not driven by spiritual guides but by an artist's conscious engagement with form, colour and line alone, began to gather momentum. The Russian painter Wassily Kandinsky published *Concerning the Spiritual in Art* in 1912 (it appeared in English translation by 1914), and it became a lodestone for artists looking to push their work in this exciting new direction. Ireland's first modern abstract artists entered this territory as the country finally broke free from British colonial rule in 1922.

13

THE SEARCH FOR SELF
1920–39

IMAGINE NEVER HAVING seen a work of non-figurative art before. Imagine every painting you have ever seen has been a representation of something, whether a portrait or landscape or mythological scene. And now imagine standing in front of *Decoration* (1923; see overleaf) by Mainie Jellett (1897–1944). Its title does it a disservice, but I wonder if it was acquired as a way to soften its entry into the world. Don't be troubled by me, it suggests; see me as something integral to the room rather than shocking and new.

Decoration was the first abstract painting to be exhibited in Ireland. It took its cues from Renaissance paintings of the Madonna and Child, and when you know this you can see hints of it in the shaped panel it is painted on, in the use of rich gold and blues, in the large curved outer forms that somehow protect the small brighter forms within. Its heritage is the Christian faith of Jellett's upbringing in Dublin, but this was not recognised when it was first exhibited. It was met with utter disbelief. The *Irish Times* called it 'an insoluble puzzle' and a 'freak' picture, and Jellett's work was later denounced by the critic George Russell as 'subhuman art', a form of 'artistic malaria' caught from Cubism.[1]

In fact identifying Cubism as an influence was correct. Like many of the artists we looked at in the last chapter, Jellett studied in Paris, first in the studio of André Lhote and then with the prominent Cubist Albert Gleizes. She had attended the Metropolitan School of Art in Dublin but it was in France that she found her direction. Gleizes taught

213

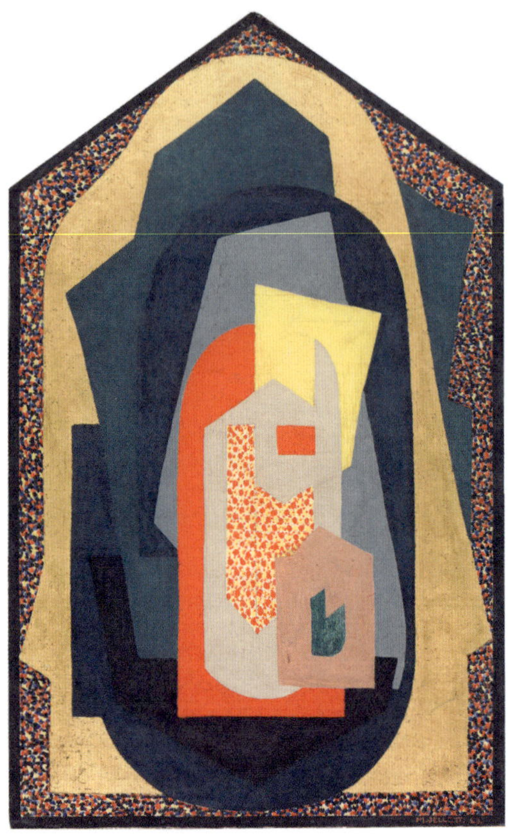

Mainie Jellett, *Decoration*, tempera on wood panel, 1923

Jellett and Evie Hone (1894–1955), and the three of them explored
the Cubist technique of 'translation and rotation' together.[2]

Jellett returned to Dublin fired up with her progression beyond figuration and into abstraction, and she was excited to share her modernist
discoveries with an Irish audience. She felt that European modernism
best offered a way to communicate everything there was to say about
contemporary life. So, despite almost blanket incomprehension, she
persevered, adding clearer figurative hints to later works such as *Homage
to Fra Angelico* (1928), compromising her radical beginnings to allow
a home audience to begin to appreciate her modernist approach to
religious imagery. She saw in her work a deep connection with her
Celtic roots, particularly illuminated manuscripts, but this didn't
initially resonate with her Irish audience.

Why did her paintings, and those of her peers Hone and Mary Swanzy (1882–1978), seem so alien to Dublin critics? They would have been aware of the latest developments in Paris through publications, and Hugh Lane's collection of Impressionism was exhibited in Dublin from 1908. To better understand this we need to add more context. For *Decoration* was exhibited at the Society of Dublin Painters in the autumn of 1923, at a time of tumultuous change for Ireland as it broke free from its union with Britain and struggled to become an independent country once more.

A FRACTIOUS INDEPENDENCE

Following invasions by the Normans in the twelfth century and Henry VIII's declaration that he was king of Ireland in 1541, James VI and I sent English and Scottish Protestants to colonise Ireland in the seventeenth century. Despite Ireland officially becoming part of the United Kingdom of Great Britain and Ireland in 1801, there had always been resistance to this muscling in from its colonising neighbour. The perceived lack of support from Britain for Ireland during the Great Famine in the 1840s and the treatment of Irish workers who subsequently migrated to England looking for work led to rising tensions and a growing call in southern Ireland for devolution and independence. However, Unionist families in the north advocated staying with Britain. Armed campaigns such as the Easter Uprising of 1916 led to an escalation of violence and many Irish men died fighting on both sides, either with the government troops or with the nascent Irish Republican Army (IRA). This ongoing conflict led the British government to propose a partitioned Ireland, with one government to oversee the twenty-six counties of the south and another to speak for the six Unionist-controlled counties of the north.

The Anglo-Irish Treaty was drawn up in December 1921 and the Irish Free State formally came into being a year later. But the compromise for Irish Republicans had been a clause that insisted they swear allegiance to the British Crown and accept the partition of Ireland. Some, who formed the new government, believed this bitter pill could be swallowed for now and regurgitated later. Others in the IRA found they could not stomach the decision at all. Civil war broke out and Irish men and women again died on both sides before the IRA finally laid down its weapons in the spring of 1923.

Modernism, and in particular abstraction, was seen as a threat by some of Ireland's artists and critics. At a time of enhanced nationalism anything that drew on ideas from overseas could be thought of as unpatriotic. The *Irish Times* critic George Russell's own position exemplified the climate in Ireland at this time. In 1899 he had publicly called for an exhibition of international art, so you would think he would have responded positively to Jellett's abstract painting. It was hardly revolutionary – even excluding the Spiritualists from the nineteenth century, abstract paintings by artists across Europe had been exhibited for a decade by this point. But Russell's issue was more specific. By 1923, following everything that had unfolded in Ireland, he now believed that art should be accessible, not esoteric, and it should promote some idea of Irishness, not link arms with those overseas.

The women pursuing the latest directions in European art were therefore often overlooked in favour of their male compatriots. Jellett, Hone and Swanzy didn't see borders, only opportunities and exciting future possibilities. But their male counterparts were acutely aware of the geopolitics of Ireland. These men, who included Seán Keating (1889–1977), John Lavery and Paul Henry (1876–1958), painted figuratively. They used muscular brushstrokes to convey visions of western Ireland and armed patriots, as in Keating's *Men of the South* (1921–2). The irony is not lost on us today – no artist exists in a vacuum and the style these men embraced also had its roots overseas, in academic British figuration seen at the Royal Academy in London for decades and channelled through the work of William Orpen (born in Stillorgan in County Dublin). But for a country that had endured a painful rebirth this easy-to-understand figurative style was believed to best articulate patriotic subjects, independence and Irish culture. Jellett had been striving to make her painting the 'object in itself'[3], by contrast Henry – who had also trained in Paris – employed a well-trodden style to deliver rugged views of windswept landscapes. Ireland was both subject and object as artists like Henry tried to conjure a clearly defined cultural identity of their homeland. The London-born Irish painter Jack B. Yeats (1871–1957) was feted as coming closest to harnessing modernity and Irishness. In the 1920s he painted shootings and funerals with a naturalism reminiscent of James Joyce's Dublin, as in *Singing 'The Dark Rosaleen', Croke Park* (1921), only becoming an expressionist painter in later years.

A SURREAL WORLD

The First World War had led to a return to figuration across Europe. In the new United Kingdom of Great Britain and Northern Ireland (UK) artists including Laura Knight (1877–1970) and Ethel Walker (1861–1951) continued painting naturalistic scenes that were highly acclaimed at the Royal Academy's annual exhibitions. Knight was made an associate of the RA in 1927 and a full member in 1936, the first woman to be elected since the foundation of the Academy in 1768. The luminous real women of Dod Procter (1890–1972) were also hugely successful. In her painting *Morning* (1926) a young woman in a simple white nightdress is asleep on a single bed. It is hot – she lies on top of the crumpled sheet – but the composition gives little else away. The cool grey light of early morning illuminates the figure but the tight crop does not include any windows, so we cannot orient her or ourselves. This painting won 'Picture of the Year' at the Royal Academy, was bought by the *Daily Mail* and gifted to the Tate Gallery, from where it toured twenty-three art museums across the British Isles over the following two years. Compared to abstract paintings, audiences found such works easier to engage with. There's a mesmeric stillness to the women she paints, a timelessness even though the bob of their hair or a scarf tied casually around a neck tethers them to the twentieth century.

The people in *The Deluge* (1920; see overleaf) by Winifred Knights (1899–1947) seem both startlingly modern and similarly timeless. This painting was completed in just eight weeks and scooped her a coveted Rome Scholarship. It is nearly 2 metres wide and features the rising tide of biblical catastrophe. Grey waters cascade over walls and flood the streets as people begin to climb the banks to escape God's wrath. A boxy ark floats on the waters behind but there is no sign of a rescue. Knights seems to have drawn on the work of Spencer for her biblical palette and Poussin for the figures' mannered poses, and yet she creates something strikingly original in doing so. The stiff geometries of the buildings are counteracted by the diagonals of the panicked hands stretching into the air as people flee. Her prize was a three-year stint at the British School in Rome and a stipend of £250 a year. She was the first woman ever to win.

In 1918 women over thirty who owned property became eligible to vote, a major breakthrough in women's suffrage. Ten years later this

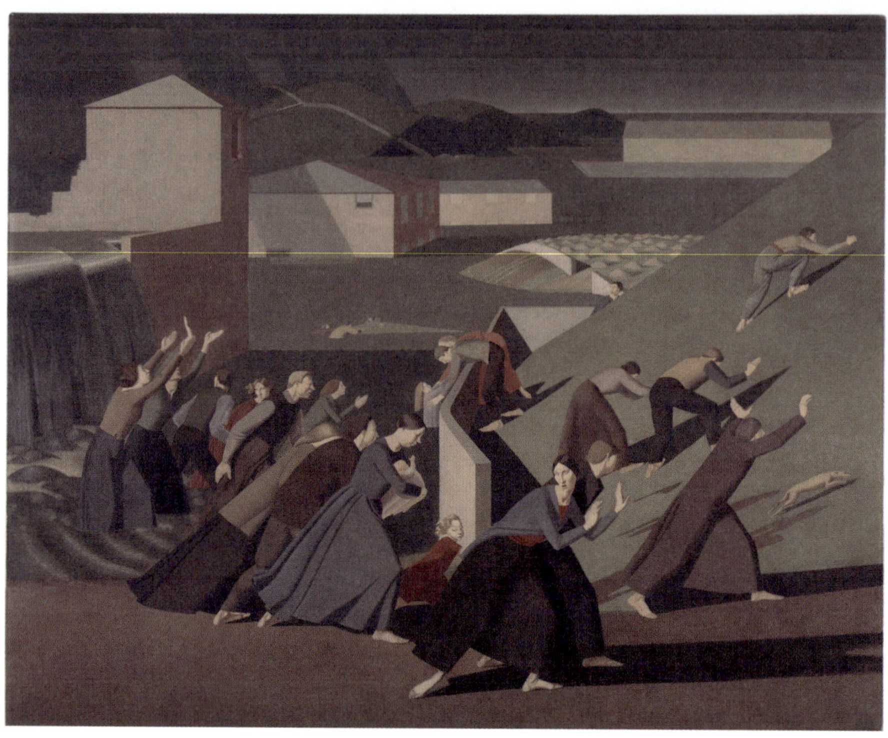

Winifred Knights, *The Deluge*, oil on canvas, 1920

was amended to allow all men and women over twenty-one to vote. Women such as Knights, Procter and Knight were breaking glass ceilings in these inter-war years, but we have to ask why their work and their names are not as well known as Spencer, Cadell or Wyndham Lewis. These women were accepted into largely male enclaves during their lifetimes, but the men who later shaped British art history, such as Ernst Gombrich and Anthony Blunt, operated as if they had never existed.

The relationship between the playwright Nesta Obermer and the self-styled Gluck (Hannah Gluckstein; 1895–1978) offers insight into the complexity of being a woman in the early twentieth century. Nesta (born Ella Ernestine Sawyer) had been pushed into marriage by her diplomat father, but the love of her life was Gluck, a British artist who dressed stylishly in men's clothes and whom Nesta called 'Darling Tim'.[4] In 1936, the year they fell in love, Gluck painted *Medallion*, a double profile portrait to mark their secret 'marriage'. Both women wear their hair cropped and brushed back off their faces, their strong jawlines emphasising Nesta's optimistic upward gaze while Gluck looks resolutely forwards. Some of those who saw the painting commented on the apparent closeness of the couple, but while Gluck could be provocative, she generally deflected such analysis with affected naivety.

Gluck said the shortening of her name was so her paintings could be judged for what they were, without gender bias. By wearing men's clothes she took herself out of the husband market, much to her parents' discomfort, and indicated her sexual orientation. Being a lesbian in the 1920s was not illegal. In 1885 'gross indecency' between two men became a criminal offence with a prison term, but it was never extended to women. In the inter-war period homosexual artists such as John Minton (1917–1957), Keith Vaughan (1912–1977), John Craxton (1922–2009), Robert Colquhoun (1914–1962) and Robert MacBryde (1913–1966) had to keep their sexuality hidden from the wider world, but artists like Gluck – while being seen as an outré outsider – could be more public (although not when it came to being in love with a married woman).

Gluck kept a studio in Cornwall, as did Marlow Moss (1889–1958), another woman painter who adopted men's dress and an androgynous name. Cornwall offered a refuge from London where artists could concentrate on work without interruption. Moss soon moved to Paris, inspired by the Neoplasticism of the abstract artist Piet Mondrian (1872–1944) whose style she adopted, not returning to Cornwall until 1940. But Ithell Colquhoun (1906–1988; no relation to Robert) would make the Cornish village of Lamorna her home for forty years.

Ithell (pronounced eye-thell) was her middle name. Like Gluck, she had her own trust fund, which gave her independence. Woolf saw an independent income as vital to women's emancipation. Also like Gluck (and Moss), choosing the name Ithell over Margaret was a way of controlling her own identity. She had been born in Shillong, India but grew up in England and attended the Slade before taking a studio in Paris in the early 1930s. Here she came face to face with Surrealism. The international movement focused on accessing the psyche through the subconscious, using the psychoanalysis of Sigmund Freud, and it chimed with her growing interest in the occult. Her early botanical watercolours morphed into human body parts as Surrealism strengthened its hold on her. In *Scylla* (1938) two craggy thighs poke up above a still body of water, with seaweed replacing pubic hair and a pointed

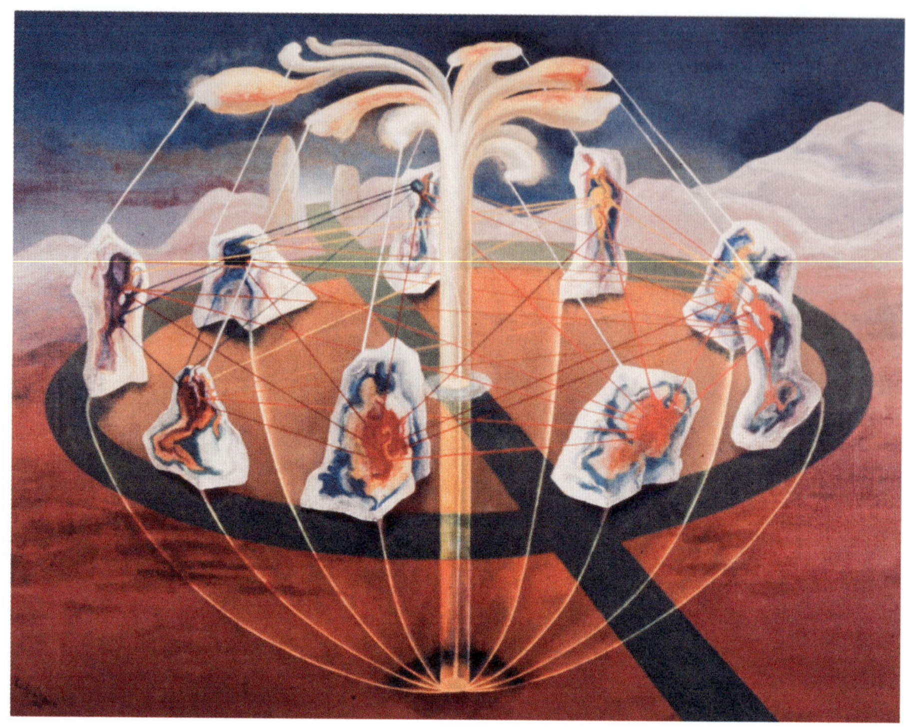

Ithell Colquhoun, *Dance of the Nine Opals*, oil on canvas, 1942

boat just visible between the legs, a hint of future sexual penetration. She contemplated Britain's Celtic past through the prism of Surrealism and in her paintings knees became flooded islands housing stone circles and bodies fuse with ancient standing stones, as in *Dance of the Nine Opals* (1942). In this painting the rocks seem alive, dancing around a maypoled tree of life, connected in this world and through all time, above ground and underground, in equal measure.

Her lifelong study of the occult and her fascination with sex magic, Kabbalism and esoteric research led her to being ejected from the British Surrealism movement. This may also have been because of her honest confrontation of sexuality in her work (she herself was bisexual). This was something that Surrealism was famous for, as in the work of Hans Bellmer and Salvador Dalí, for example, but was unexpected and perhaps shocking in the work of a woman.

In June 1936 the *International Surrealist Exhibition* opened in London. Surrealism as a self-contained movement had been launched in

Paris twelve years earlier, when the French poet André Breton declared Surrealism to be 'pure psychic automatism'.[5] Its membership had grown exponentially and in 1936 it was at its zenith, with major exhibitions in London, New York and Paris. Breton was in London for the opening, as were Max Ernst and Man Ray, and Dalí gave the opening speech wearing a metal diving suit that nearly suffocated him. It electrified the thirty-year-old Colquhoun, who had work included in the show. The young poet David Gascoyne and the artist and collector Roland Penrose (1900–1984) had organised the exhibition and they included the work of Eileen Agar (1899–1991), Paul Nash (whose ancient landscapes had taken a surreal turn) and Colquhoun alongside work by international Surrealists Ernst, Dalí, René Magritte, Meret Oppenheim and Man Ray. Sheila Legge (1911–1949), Britain's first performance artist, walked around Trafalgar Square on the opening day in a floor-length white satin gown and a mask that turned her entire head into a bouquet of paper roses (see overleaf). Critics found the whole experience variously 'decadent and unhealthy', 'serious nonsense' or 'thrilling, horrifying, puzzling'.[6] Agar, who exhibited her *Angel of Anarchy* (1936) at the exhibition, found in Surrealism 'the interpenetrating of reason and unreason'.[7]

When Penrose was selecting work for the *International Surrealist Exhibition* he visited Agar's studio and selected three paintings and five objects. *Angel of Anarchy* is a mannequin's head over which Agar attached coloured feathers and cowrie-shell braids. She placed diamanté highlights across the nose and lips and bound much of the face, including the eyes, in patterned silk ribbons. This blinding replicated the French Surrealists' famous group photograph when each member posed with his eyes held shut around Magritte's painting *Je ne vois pas la (femme) cachée dans la forêt* (I do not see the (woman) hidden in the forest) in *La Révolution surréaliste* magazine in 1929. It represented the inward gaze of the Surrealists, the desire to access subconscious thought through dreams and automatic writing.

Leonora Carrington (1917–2011) was nineteen when the *International Surrealist Exhibition* opened. She was one of its 23,000 visitors and felt particularly drawn to the paintings of Ernst. Within a year she was in a relationship with him in Paris. For Carrington, Surrealism was 'the belief that nothing is ordinary; that everything in life is extraordinary'.[8] She became Britain's quintessential Surrealist, despite spending her working life in France, Spain and Mexico, where she lived from 1942

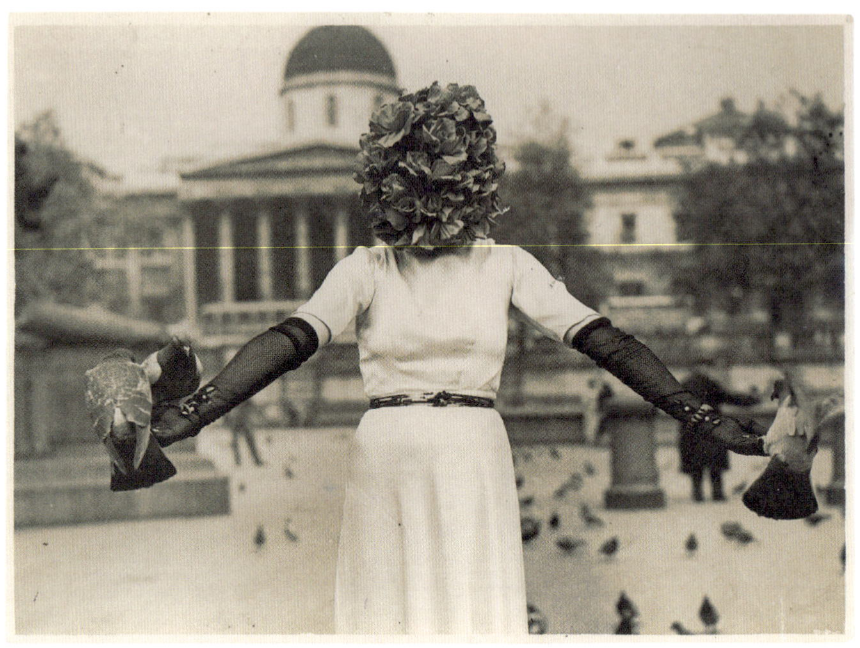

Sheila Legge, performance in Trafalgar Square, London, 1936

(at the age of twenty-five) to her death in 2011. In her *Self-Portrait /
Inn of the Dawn Horse* (*c*.1937–8) she sits on a small blue chair in a
bare room, whose only adornment is a large picture window swagged
in yellow drapes through which we see a white horse galloping across
a manicured park. Behind her head another white horse, this time on
rockers, floats in front of the wall, as if tangled in her wild mane of
chestnut hair. A striped lactating hyena approaches her outstretched
hand. 'Do you think anyone escapes their childhood?' she once asked.
'I don't think they do.'[9] The rocking horse from her own nursery trans-
forms into the horse outside offering her a form of escape, a release
she found through painting. Her white jodhpurs suggest she is ready
to leave at any moment.

BRITAIN AS REFUGE

Carrington and Moss both left the country of their birth, looking for
greater freedom in France; by 1940 Carrington had fled to New York

and Moss had returned to the UK. The Second World War evicted them from their creative lives in France, but for other artists the need to relocate happened years earlier. In 1933 Adolf Hitler, leader of the Nazi Party, assumed power in Germany. The rise of the Third Reich and its persecution of Jews, Black and Romany people and those who were gay, disabled or held opposing political views was unprecedented. During the six years preceding the war many Jewish artists, writers, architects and scientists left Germany for the British Isles. German artists who had been included in Hitler's *Entartete Kunst* (Degenerate Art) exhibition of 1937, such as Hans Feibusch (1898–1998) and Kurt Schwitters (1887–1948), arrived as refugees. Foreign artists who had also been denounced as 'degenerate' by the Nazis such as Mondrian also chose to move to Britain. Future artists, including Lucian Freud (1922–2011) and Frank Auerbach (1931–2024), arrived as children and trained in British art schools. Others travelled across Europe looking for safety before settling in England, such as the German expressionist Hilde Goldschmidt (1897–1980) and the political photomontage artist John Heartfield (1891–1968).

Heartfield and Mondrian both chose to live in the London suburb of Hampstead, five miles from the city centre. This may seem a strange place to have gravitated towards. But in the 1920s and 1930s it was at the centre of British modernism. The Russian Constructivist Naum Gabo (1890–1977) moved there in 1936, living alongside Ben Nicholson (1894–1982) and Barbara Hepworth, Henry and Irina Moore, and the Hungarian painter László Moholy-Nagy (1895–1946). Mondrian and Gabo had met Nicholson and Hepworth through Abstraction–Création, an association to promote abstract art founded in Paris in 1931. They were all members and when the sixty-six-year-old Mondrian moved to London he went to live in Hampstead, where Nicholson had organised accommodation for him.

Throughout the 1920s Ben and Winifred Nicholson (1893–1981) had been inseparable, living in Italy and then London and Cumbria. She was an assured painter with a deep sense of colour, pairing simple flower arrangements with views through windows, carefully observing how the light was refracted through a vase or became shadow between leaves. But in 1931, when their third child was just weeks old, Ben Nicholson began an affair with Hepworth, who was also married to an artist, John (Jack) Skeaping (1901–1980). Together Nicholson and Hepworth pursued abstraction as they divorced their first partners, had triplets together in 1934 and married in 1938. (Winifred moved to Paris in 1932 with her three children to retain her connections with the French avant-garde and, presumably, to distance herself from Ben and Barbara.)

The pursuit of abstraction in the UK was bolstered by the arrival of the founder of the iconic Bauhaus art school, Walter Gropius, who moved into the new modernist Lawn Road Flats designed by Wells Coates in Hampstead. Gropius had founded the Bauhaus in 1919 in Weimar, Germany, and it was the beating heart of modernism until its demise under the Nazis. It espoused the International Style, celebrated Constructivism and influenced everything from stage design to graphic art across Europe. But by the time Gropius arrived in London in 1934 the Nazis were closing art schools and banning modernist work. Meanwhile, in Russia, the birthplace of Kandinsky and Gabo, the communist government would only allow one art style to remain – Socialist Realism. It was tuned to the propaganda needs of Stalin and promoted an idealised society at work for a united purpose. Avant-garde artists had been exploring pure form, inspired by industry, newness and the future, but now governments were restricting artistic freedoms and dictating house styles.

Imagine what a contrast Hampstead was, with its artists continuing to explore the possibilities of organic abstraction. Moore's early Mayan-inspired figures became attenuated and distorted, as in *Composition* (1931). Hepworth's sculptures of female forms were reduced to slender marble columns; when she gave birth to triplets she completed *Three Forms* (1935), a sphere and two ovoids resting on a marble base, an abstract interpretation of motherhood (she is the base, the support). Ben Nicholson's early paintings had been replaced by all-white reliefs that relied on simple geometry and shadow to create form, as in *Quai d'Auteuil* (1935). It looks like the facade of a modernist building, like nearby Lawn Road Flats, with its sheer white 'walls' and circular 'windows' (although its title refers to the Parisian street where Winifred Nicholson lived with their children).

These Hampstead artists exhibited together as the 7 & 5 Society and in the newly formed Unit One group at the Mayor Gallery on Cork Street. The magazine *Axis* was founded, the first British title dedicated to abstraction, with Myfanwy Evans at the helm. Exhibitions such as *Abstract & Concrete* (1936) showed the work of British abstract artists alongside Mondrian and Alberto Giacometti and toured to

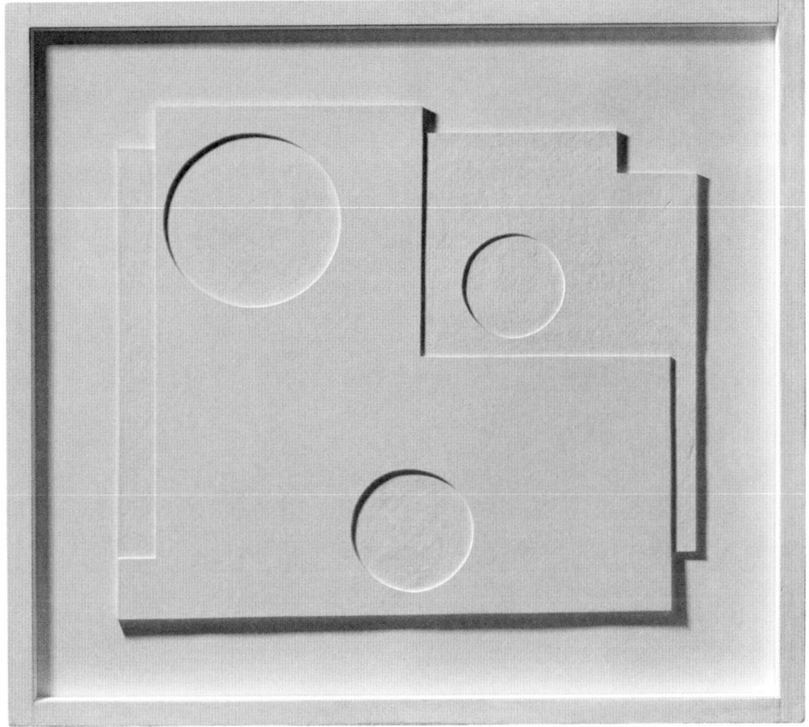

Ben Nicholson, *Quai d'Auteuil*, carved painted white relief, 1935

Oxford, Liverpool, London and Cambridge. But simultaneously there were artists working away from the bright lights of city galleries. As fascism gripped Europe these artists focused on the lives of the British working class.

ALL THE LONELY PEOPLE

Bill Brandt (1904–1983) was born in Germany but spent his working life in the UK, where he photographed class disparity throughout the 1930s. The Great Depression that struck America in the 1920s became a global downturn and more than two and a half million British people were unemployed by 1933. The hardest-hit areas were those of industry and mining, such as South Wales and the north of England, and Brandt set off with his Rolleiflex camera to capture the realities of working-class life. He photographed miners eating at cramped kitchen tables still blackened with coal dust and sticky-faced children playing in the streets. In his book *The English at Home* (1936) he contrasted views of terraced houses and homeless shelters with top-hatted race-goers, cricket matches and maids folding starched napkins for dinner. He was a realist, but he also turned the industrial landscape of Britain into something striking, even monumental.

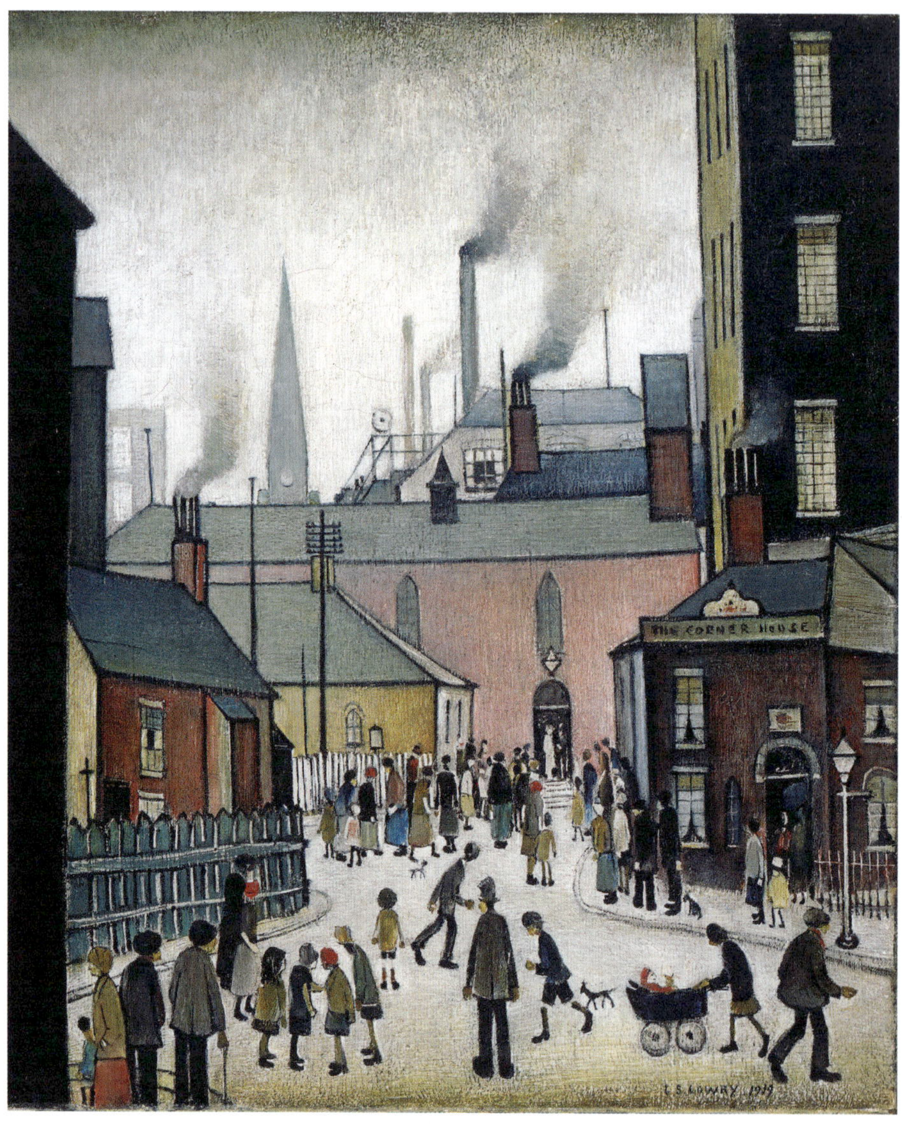

L.S. Lowry, *After the Wedding*, oil on canvas, 1939

Fifty kilometres southwest of Halifax was Manchester, the home of L.S. Lowry (1887–1976), arguably the most famous artist to depict working-class life between the wars. Lowry's 'matchstick' men, women and children walking in streets shadowed by mills and chimneys are instantly recognisable. He was a shy and secretive artist who only enjoyed commercial success in his later years. Painting in the attic of his family home at weekends and evenings after his full-time work as a rent collector, he documented the world he saw around him as he went door to door in Old Trafford, Hulme and Withington. He painted imaginary parades and weddings, fights and football matches, all conducted under clouds full of soot, smoke and rain. He peddled myths about his childhood, about being pushed into art as a teenager because he wasn't fit for anything else. The reality was crueller – his mother endeavoured to conform to middle-class expectations and wouldn't accept art as a proper career. He joined the workforce as a clerk at the age of fifteen, only able to take life-drawing lessons and painting classes at evening school.

Due to a reduction in circumstances, his family were forced to move to the industrial suburb of Pendlebury in 1909. This provided Lowry with direct access to the cityscape that became his main subject for the rest of his life. In *An Accident* (1926) he painted a crowd that had gathered after a woman drowned, framed by a claustrophobic backdrop of workers' houses, factories and belching chimneys. In *After the Wedding* a road snakes between factories, houses and churches. His palette has lightened a little, his skies now dirty white. A throng of people have gathered to witness a bride and groom leaving chapel. Lowry's style remained resolutely out of kilter with the broader trends of twentieth-century art, despite his having been taught by Adolphe Valette (1876–1942), a talented French artist. However, there was a growing interest in his paintings, and his first exhibition in London in 1939 resulted in a significant number of sales. But this was the year the shutters came down – Britain was at war with Germany again and no artist remained untouched by what became a brutal six-year assault on democracy.

14

RUINATION AND REBIRTH
1939–58

THUMBING THROUGH BACK issues of British *Vogue* from the Second World War is a strange experience. The subscription-only magazine continued to be printed throughout the war despite paper rationing, the destruction of *Vogue*'s pattern house and a direct hit on its head office in London's New Bond Street. The British photographer Cecil Beaton (1904–1980) dominated its pages and, as the Blitz began, his fashion shoots were interspersed with the occasional photograph of London's charred buildings, classical columns holding up nothing but sky. However, it was another photographer, an American called Lee Miller (1907–1977), who was to give *Vogue* readers on both sides of the Atlantic their closest view of war.

Miller had lived with the Surrealist Man Ray in Paris in 1929 and they worked together on experimental nude photography. A peripatetic adventurer with a taste for the new, Miller funded her travels by modelling for *Vogue* before opening her own photographic portrait studio in New York and then abruptly marrying the Egyptian businessman Aziz Eloui Bey. But as war began to threaten Europe, Miller followed her heart to London, where she moved in with the Surrealist Roland Penrose in Hampstead.

Miller disliked Beaton but warmed to *Vogue*'s new editor Audrey Withers, and together they created articles that highlighted the war effort: women operating a searchlight battery, models posing in fire masks, Wrens training in Scotland. Miller wanted to get closer to the action and, using her US citizenship, she became a war correspondent in 1944, sending photographs and reports back to Britain from the front line. She wrote long features on US Army field hospitals, the battle to reclaim Saint-Malo and the liberation of Paris, bringing the war directly into British homes. She wrote of snow-covered battle-lines and of men who 'pared bread and cheese with fighting knives' and drank coffee from shell cases: 'I'll never see acid-yellow and grey again like where shells burst near snow without seeing also the pale quivering faces of replacements, grey and yellow with apprehension. Their fumbling hands and furtive, short-sighted glances at the field they must cross.'[1] She followed Allied soldiers as they captured towns from the retreating Germans and ended up in Munich. It was here, in Hitler's apartment, that she had herself photographed in a surreal tableau. On the day Hitler and his partner, the photographer Eva Braun, committed suicide we see Miller the war correspondent stripped of her dirty uniform and washing herself in Hitler's bathtub. Her eyes turn towards a small sculpture of a nude woman and she mimics her pose; Hitler's portrait is balanced precariously on the lip of the bath behind her. This

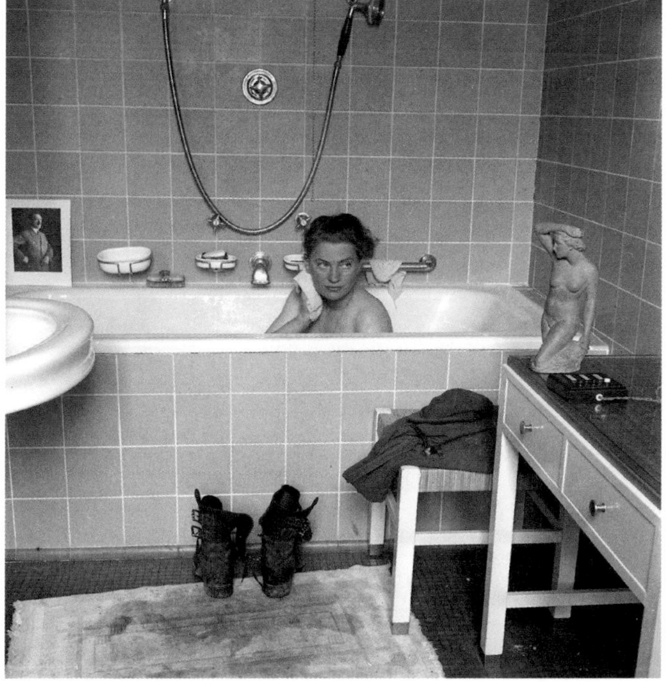

Lee Miller in Hitler's bath in Munich, Germany, 1945

photograph was used to illustrate Miller's *Vogue* article 'Hitleriana' but it took me some time to find it, as it was tucked away in the overmatter pages, alongside advertisements for maternity wear and tips for making jam.[2] Today it is one of the most memorable images from the end of the war, but it must have been a moment of light relief for Miller and the photojournalist David E. Scherman, who took the photo. For it was taken on the day they also entered the Nazi concentration camp at Dachau for the first time.

BELIEVE IT

Miller's photographs of Dachau and Buchenwald concentration camps still shock us today. She was one of the first photographers to enter. Through her lens we see emaciated dead bodies piled in heaps, gaunt men in striped prison-wear ranged in bunk beds, corpses and those clinging to life with shaved heads, knees wider than thighs, ribs poking through skin. We cannot come close to imagining the conditions the millions of prisoners were subjected to in such camps. Miller's photographs exposed the brutal, unprecedented cruelty of the Nazi regime, and they can still bring us to tears. But only one made it into British *Vogue*'s 'Victory Issue' in June 1945. Captioned 'Horrors of a concentration camp, unforgettable, unforgivable', it is a close-up crop of a pile of dead prisoners, legs crushing the faces of those below.[3] It is a printed small photograph, only 4 centimetres across, dwarfed by the ruins of Aachen Cathedral that dominate the page. Miller recounts the horror of entering the camp, of seeing prisoners who couldn't stomach regular meals because their stomachs had shrunk, of seeing piles of bodies outside the crematorium because the Nazis had run out of fuel the week before and could no longer burn them. In camp records she saw they had been killing between 5,000 and 6,000 inmates a month. But British *Vogue* didn't have the stomach to publish more than one of her concentration camp images; it was American *Vogue* that printed a wider selection the same month with the headline: 'Believe It'.

Miller was embedded with US troops because the British army would not sanction female war correspondents on the front line. However, women artists recruited by the British War Artists' Advisory Committee (WAAC), including Mary Kessell (1914–1977) and Doris Zinkeisen (1897–1991), also witnessed the horror of a concentration camp following the liberation of Bergen-Belsen by the British in April 1945. More than 60,000 prisoners were found inside with no food, water or sanitation, alongside 13,000 corpses.

Zinkeisen was one of fifty-two women artists commissioned by the British government to record the war. She was the first to arrive at Bergen-Belsen as she followed the relief work of the Red Cross. She remained at the camp for three weeks until it was burnt to the ground. In *Human Laundry, Belsen: 1945* we see well-fed women in pristine white uniforms helping grey shadows of men who are stretched out on hospital tables. They are on the edge of death; it is only because one sits up that we know we are not in a morgue. In *Belsen: April 1945* we are confronted by those who did not survive, their striped prison-wear rucked up to reveal deep cavities between ribcages and jutting hip bones, their glazed eyes unseeing in gaunt faces.

Evelyn Dunbar (1906–1960) was employed full-time by the WAAC but most women were offered short-term contracts, or sold their work

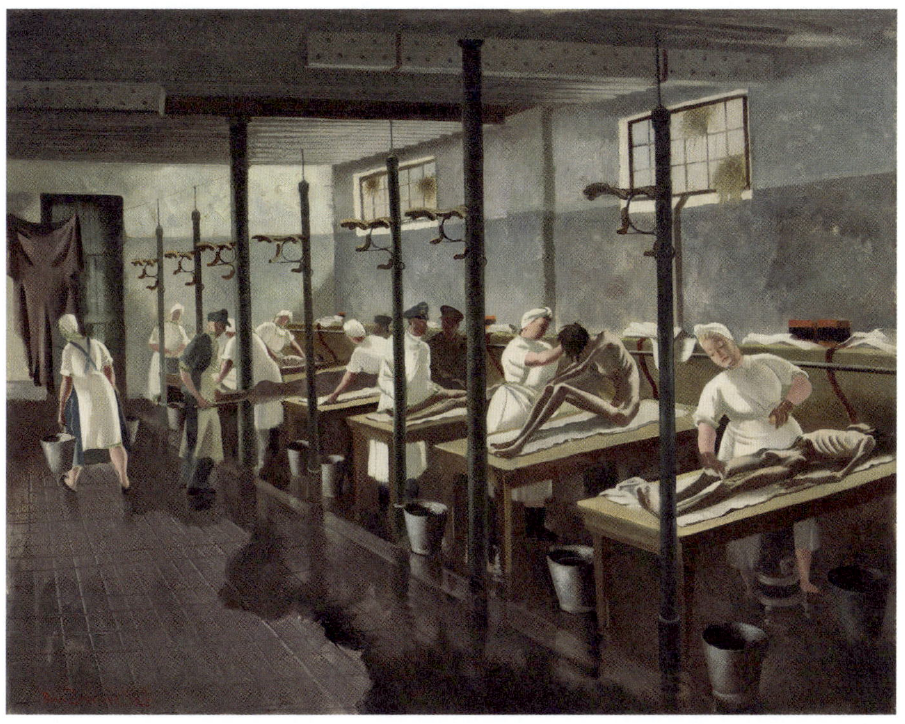

Doris Zinkeisen, *Human Laundry, Belsen: 1945*, oil on canvas, 1945

to the committee at a later date, like Zinkeisen. Laura Knight recorded many scenes of war, including the Nuremberg trials, but her most widely publicised image was *Ruby Loftus Screwing a Breech Ring* (1943). A young woman leans over a workbench in a factory, machining a component of the Bofors breech gun. It was a highly technical job, one that – before the war – required years of training, but she had quickly become the first woman to master it. She wears a blue boiler suit, her hair neatly curled under a green hairnet. She was symbolic of the female war effort where women stepped boldly into worlds that had formerly been the preserve of men. (Steve McQueen's 2024 film *Blitz* took inspiration from this painting, and those of Knight's peers, to focus on the world of women's war work.)

Of the 402 war artists, 350 were men. Miller photographed several of them for *Vogue*, including Spencer, Nash and Moore. She followed Moore into London's Tube platforms at night when he observed those using them as air-raid shelters, and she was angry when the magazine didn't give them significant space. Paul Nash and his brother John held salaried war artist contracts in 1940, the year Paul began *Totes Meer*. Under a waning moon a field of crashed German planes becomes a grey-green sea, their wings cresting waves that break against England's defences. This is the 'dead sea' of the title, given in German to emphasise that these were Luftwaffe planes, first seen by Nash piled up in an Oxfordshire field.

Some of the war artists had formerly been serving officers, such as John Worsley (1919–2000), who began the war as a midshipman in the Royal Navy Reserve. An appointment by the WAAC meant being removed from active duty and Worsley recorded events in the Mediterranean. Being a war artist did not protect him from being captured, and he ended the war sketching conditions in a German prisoner-of-war camp. Other artists travelled further afield. Edward Bawden (1903–1989) painted armed Muntafiq women in Iraq, while Leslie Cole (1910–1976) worked in Malta, Egypt and Greece before travelling to South East Asia Command and the Burmese jungle.

By the end of the war the WAAC had amassed 6,000 works. The collection was split between British museums, government departments and a few Commonwealth museums. Some works were lost in transit or in fires, such as *Devastation 1941: East End Street, Houses of the Poor* by Graham Sutherland (1903–1980). Sutherland had worked as a full-time war artist, recording the Blitz as well as regional industries such as tin and coal mining. Unlike the assertive figuration of Knight and Dunbar, Sutherland framed the war through his affinity with neo-Romanticism. Neo-Romantics presented a personal and poetic view of the world rooted in nature. He painted the landscape scarred by industry but still monumental, and transformed ruined streets into theatrical sets lit by moonlight. There are rarely any people, just the twists of gnarled tree stumps or the long sharp points of spiked branches. Sutherland's *Thorn Tree* (1945–6) became Christ's crown in his 1946 *Crucifixion* as his post-war career began, leading to his largest ever commission.

A TONIC TO THE NATION

Francis Bacon (1909–1992) did not fight in the Second World War on account of his asthma, but neither did he become an official war artist. He was thirty when the war broke out and once the Blitz was over he spent much of it in London. In 1944 he completed his visceral triptych *Three Studies for Figures at the Base of a Crucifixion*. It is a guttural howl for humanity, as powerful and disturbing today as when it was first exhibited at the Lefevre Gallery in 1945. Human hybrids bay in the grass and leer, blinded, on tripod legs, each isolated against a fiery orange ground. The bandages and missing limbs suggest they are wounded but they prowl and stalk the surface like beasts still hunting prey. Bacon was fascinated by anatomy and in particular mouths, copying examples from old medical textbooks. Pages torn

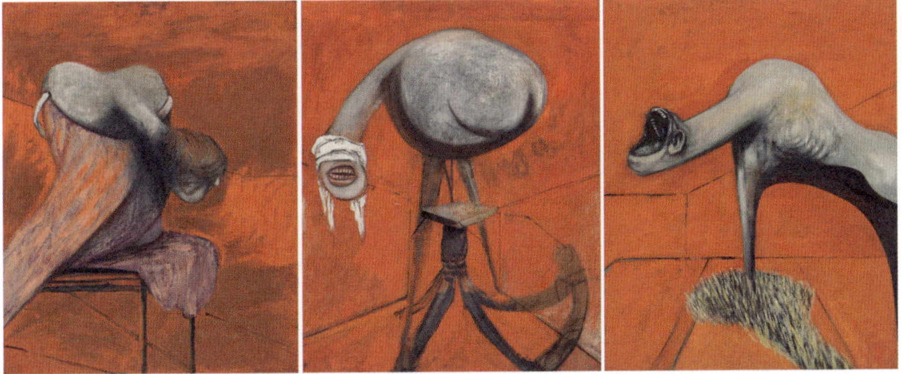

Francis Bacon, *Three Studies for Figures at the Base of a Crucifixion*,
oil on board, 1944

from magazines and black-and-white photographs littered the floor of his chaotic studio, all feeding into his raging canvases that expressed raw emotion.

As the war ended, galleries such as Lefevre tried to restore a sense of pre-war order. But for many artists the war had changed everything – studios had been bombed, artist groups had disbanded and international stars such as Mondrian had moved to America. The WAAC no longer offered salaried positions to artists. The Labour government of Clement Attlee, elected in 1945, remained in power until 1951, and life was hard, with continued rationing and a housing shortage. However, the immediate post-war years saw the establishment of the welfare state and a number of major commitments to body and soul, from the inauguration of the Arts Council in 1946 to the founding of the NHS in 1948. Those charged with rebuilding the UK were also evangelical about the role art could play in creating social spaces, and in the 1950s a number of major architectural projects had art at their core.

The 1951 Festival of Britain brought together the brightest architects, designers and artists to create an uplifting and futuristic national celebration of creativity and offer a 'tonic to the nation'.[4] Events were held across Britain, with a major exhibition on the South Bank in London that attracted eight and a half million visitors. The Royal Festival Hall is all that remains, but at the time you could walk around the Dome of Discovery, marvel at the soaring Skylon and eat lunch at the Thameside Regatta restaurant in front of a swirling abstract mural by Victor Pasmore (1908–1998) and the wiry *Birdcage* sculpture by Reg Butler (1913–1981).

The artists commissioned for the South Bank exhibition included giants such as Epstein as well as the new greats Moore and Hepworth. But a raft of new talent was also included, and many of these younger sculptors, including Butler, Lynn Chadwick (1914–2003), Geoffrey Clarke (1924–2014) and Eduardo Paolozzi (1924–2005), were dubbed 'Geometry of Fear' artists by the critic Herbert Read when they exhibited together the following year. They were not a coherent group but many of them used metal and wire to create attenuated figures and animals, instead of carving wood and stone like Moore and Hepworth. Their work chimed with the existentialism of Giacometti and Germaine Richier in France; work by other young British artists such as Elisabeth Frink (1930–1993) also fitted Read's description of this 'iconography of despair, or of defiance' that 'is close to the nerves, nervous, wiry'.[5]

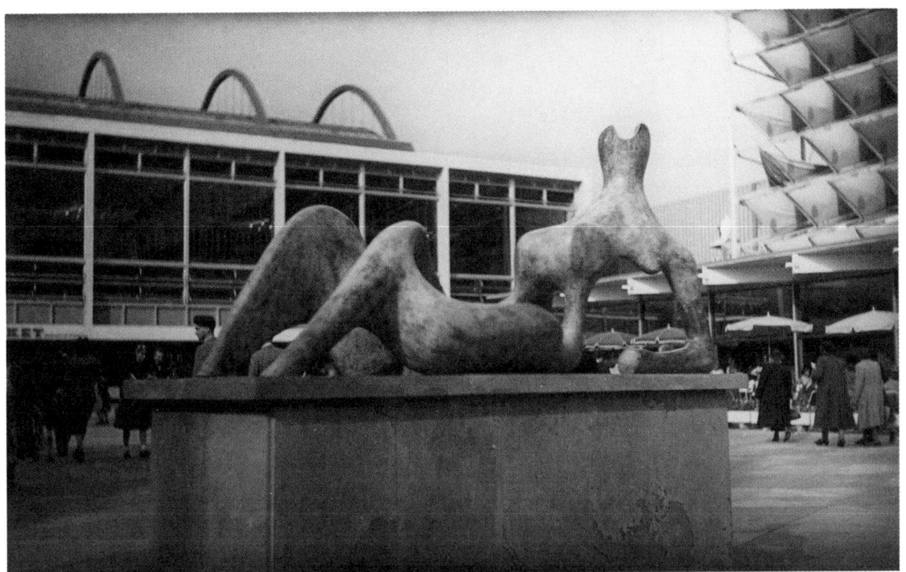

Henry Moore's *Reclining Figure* at the Festival of Britain, Southbank exhibition, London, 1951

Clarke was selected to create the high cross for the altar of the new Cathedral Church of Saint Michael in Coventry. The medieval cathedral had been destroyed by German bombs in 1940. John Piper (1903–1992), an artist, writer and stage designer, had been sent to paint the ruins by the WAAC. Fire had scorched the stones and its tracery windows were now open to the elements, with smouldering timbers all that remained of the roof. In 1952 the architect Basil Spence won a competition to rebuild it. He left the medieval ruins as they were and built a modern cathedral adjacent to them. The main entrance faced these ruins, emphasising the continuity of faith and resurrection. It took ten years to complete the new building before it was consecrated in May 1962. Piper was commissioned to create the baptistery window and today the entrance remains dappled in its coloured light while the soaring nave ends in Sutherland's vertiginous green tapestry, 23 metres tall, *Christ in Glory in the Tetramorph* (see overleaf). Frink's eagle lectern stands in front of three tall pottery candlesticks by Hans Coper (1920–1981). Epstein's *St Michael and the Devil* hovers on the porch that connects the old and new cathedrals. Art and architecture created a new beginning for Coventry Cathedral, while never forgetting its past – the ruins are always present, seen through John Hutton's southern screen wall, the glass etched with a host of saints and angels.

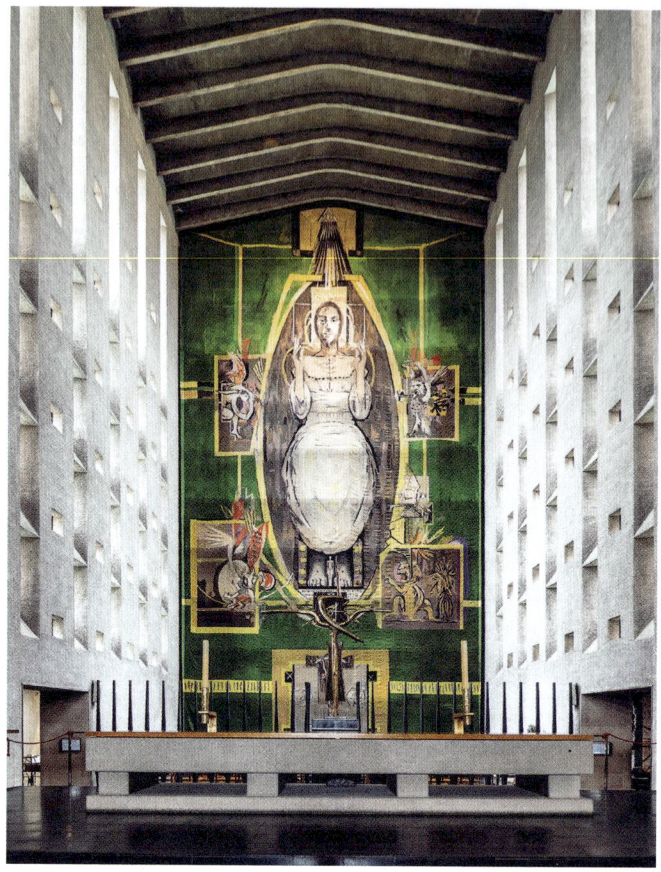

Graham Sutherland, *Christ in Glory in the Tetramorph*,
tapestry, installed in Coventry Cathedral, 1962

Post-war architects began to use modern sculptures (not statues) to articulate public spaces in new towns such as Harlow, where Hepworth's *Contrapuntal Forms* – first seen at the 1951 South Bank exhibition – still stands. Other artists who participated in touring exhibitions for the Festival of Britain now received their own major commissions. A *Still Life* by William Scott (1913–1989) had travelled across the UK alongside Freud's *Interior at Paddington*, which won the Arts Council Prize. Scott was chosen as one of two artists to create work for a new hospital built on the outskirts of Derry in Northern Ireland. Altnagelvin was the first NHS hospital in the UK, and in 1958 the architecture firm Yorke, Rosenberg and Mardall commissioned Scott to make a large mural.

Scott was of Irish and Scottish descent. He had been born in Scotland but spent his teenage years in Enniskillen in County Fermanagh and studied at Belfast School of Art before moving to London and enrolling at the Royal Academy Schools in the 1930s. After active service he returned to painting and concentrated on still life, turning saucepans, eggs, glasses and cups into increasingly abstract forms. The fifteen-panel mural for Altnagelvin is a rhythmic pulse of blue and ochre forms against a white ground. Fragments of a spiral remain in the central panel, a nod to Ireland's Celtic past and the triskeles we first saw at Brú na Bóinne in Chapter 2.

The architects gifted Scott's mural to the hospital shortly after it opened in 1960. But the hospital itself paid for the bronze *Princess Macha* (1957; see overleaf) by F.E. McWilliam (1909–1992), which originally stood outside the hospital entrance. Art could create a strong focal point for a building and foster a sense of community, and many architects and town planners embraced the vision that a public space could become a gallery where the general public would happen upon the finest examples of contemporary art. McWilliam, like Scott, had lived in England since the 1930s but he had been born in Banbridge in County Down. McWilliam's post-war sculpture had been attenuated and spiky like the work of the Geometry of Fear artists, but now he busied the surfaces by pressing small objects into clay before casting in bronze, giving them an overall design that had affinities with Celtic patterning. This could be seen to refer to a time when Ireland was unified but also when Ireland and Britain were part of the Celtic diaspora, a period of connectivity as well as nationalism.

The totemic *Princess Macha* welcomes patients with her arms outstretched, seated on an ornate stool. A diadem rests on her small head and her slender arms and legs push through her decorated gown. A dove sits on her left hand, a symbol of St Columba who cared for Derry's sick at his monastery in the sixth century. Macha herself was believed to have created the first hospital in Ireland in 300 BCE. Today she occupies a high plinth inside the hospital's new entrance, lit by blue LEDs. Scott's mural has been raised high above the reception desk opposite, out of harm's way, and has lost its human scale, the sense of walking along it, of being part of it. We can no longer see the textured brushwork or absorb the richness of those deep blues with darker forms floating within them. But this new entrance has clearly been sensitively designed with these works of art in mind, and offers a continuation of the relationship between art and wellbeing that was recognised when this first NHS hospital was built.

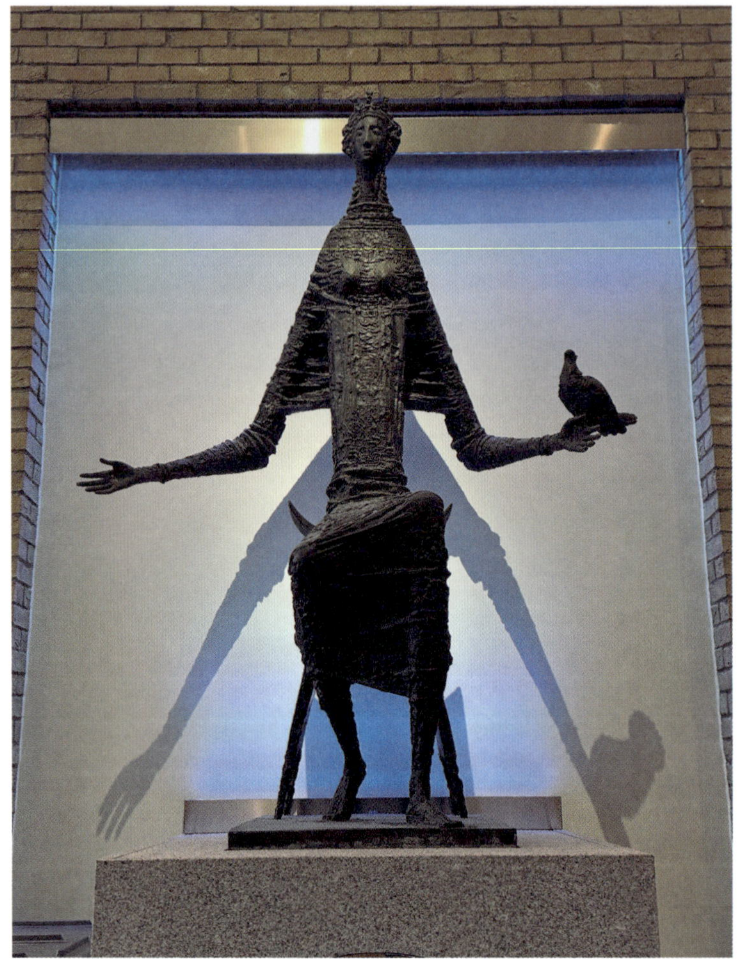

F.E. McWilliam, *Princess Macha*, bronze, 1957

OPPORTUNITY KNOCKS?

In 1948 the government passed the Nationality Act, which allowed anyone born within the British empire to travel and live permanently in the 'mother country'.[6] The Conservative MP David Maxwell Fyfe went on record to say 'we are proud that we impose no colour bar restrictions . . . We must maintain our great metropolitan tradition of hospitality to everyone from every part of our empire.'[7] But, as the historian David Olusoga has pointed out, there were many who did not agree with this and they quickly sought to limit migration.

In 1948 the *Empire Windrush* docked in Tilbury in Essex with 492 Caribbean passengers on board, all looking to begin a new life in Britain. Many had served in the war and wanted to be back on British soil. In the late 1940s only a thousand or so chose to migrate from British territories in the Caribbean each year, but by the 1950s this figure began to rise, peaking at 46,000 in 1956. Sam Selvon's novel *The Lonely Londoners*, written in creolised English and published that year, brought to life the prejudices and difficulties Caribbean people faced when they stepped off the boat train at Waterloo station. 'We is British subjects,' Moses rails when he is turned away from a restaurant run by a Polish man. 'We have more right than any people from the damn continent to live and work in this country, and enjoy what this country have, because is we who bleed to make this country prosperous.'[8]

Initially the artists who moved to Britain from the British Caribbean enjoyed a level of success. Aubrey Williams (1926–1990) relocated from British Guiana (now Guyana) in 1952, and within two years Frank Bowling (born 1934) and Donald Locke (1930–2010) had done the same. Williams had studied art but worked as an agricultural field officer before moving to London. Despite its Caribbean-style plantations, British Guiana was part of South America and Williams had spent time in the Hosororo rainforest with the indigenous Warao people, an experience that was instrumental to his development as an artist. He drew on their ancient petroglyphs to create energetic canvases that hover on the boundary of abstraction. In *Summer* (1956) spectral forms dance across the surface, throwing shadows to the ochre edges of the canvas, veined with seams of red. In *Guyana X*, painted three years before Guyana became an independent country in 1966, it is as if we are looking down on a river that runs red (see overleaf). The surface is encrusted with smears of paint that look as old as time, as if they have been excavated from the earth. Both paintings are resolutely abstract and yet communicate Williams's interest in ancient cultures, spirituality and deep time.

Williams held his first exhibition in London in 1954 and by 1958 he was showing at the New Vision Centre Gallery. At this time there were race riots in Notting Hill, where many from the Caribbean diaspora had settled, and Black families had to deal with racist graffiti telling them to 'Go Home' and 'Keep Britain White'.[9] Bowling became a student at the RCA the following year, winning the silver medal on graduation in 1962 – David Hockney (born 1937) took the gold. They

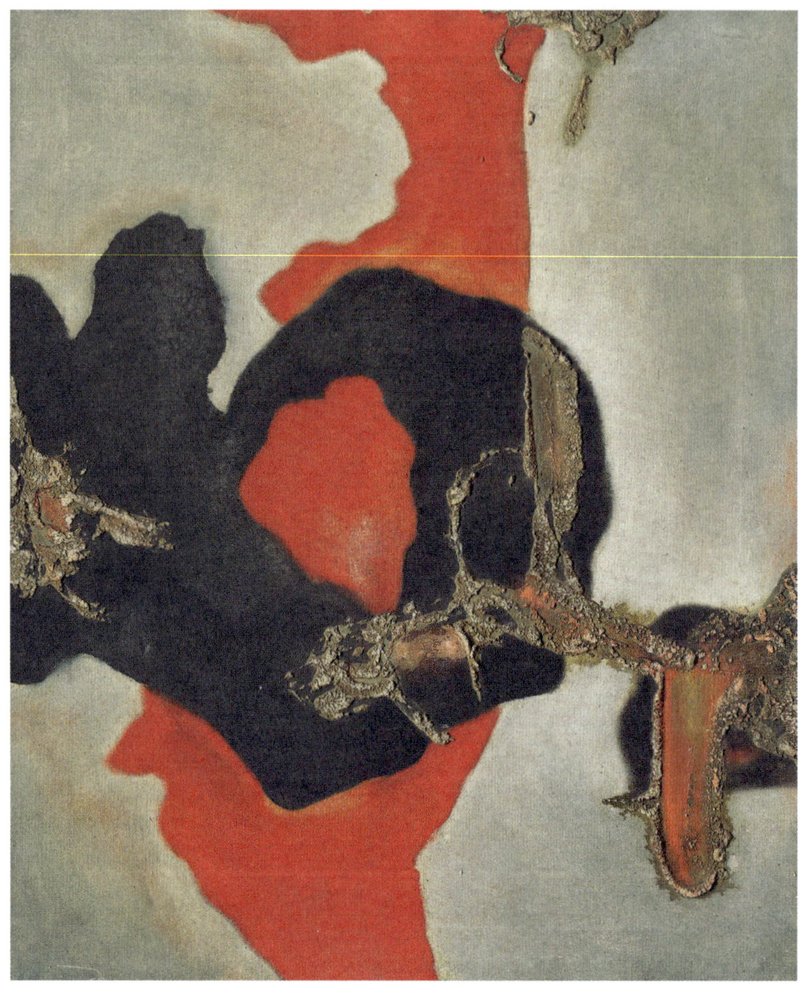

Aubrey Williams, *Guyana X*, oil and mixed media on canvas, 1963

exhibited together in *Young Contemporaries* and the Arts Council bought Bowling's Baconesque *Birthday* (1962). He became increasingly interested in the bright consumer colours of Pop, which he intercut with his own history in *Mother's House with Beware of the Dog* (1966). But his career didn't progress as he had hoped and he was made to feel his race was to blame. Williams felt the same: 'After two years all my shows were ignored,' he said.[10] Both artists eventually moved to America, where Bowling's later colour-field canvases and Williams's myth-infused abstracts chimed with the tenets of Abstract Expressionism.

Shortly after the Second World War ended, British rule in India came to a swift end with the bungled partition of the country. This was put in place over the summer of 1947, ostensibly to avoid civil war. Pakistan was cleaved off the western edge of India and denoted a Muslim country, as was East Pakistan (now Bangladesh). Punjab was split in two and millions of Muslims, Sikhs and Hindus hurried to cross the new borders before they were finalised. Up to two million people died in the ensuing religious violence.

Francis Newton Souza (1924–2002) had been expelled from the Sir J.J. School of Art in Bombay (now Mumbai) in 1945 for joining Gandhi's 'Quit India' movement, which demanded an end to British rule. He co-founded the Progressive Artists' Group in 1947, which worked to fuse India's artistic past with Western modernism. But he grew frustrated with India, feeling his country 'despises her artists and is ignorant of her heritage'.[11] He arrived in Britain in 1949 hopeful of finding a receptive audience for his art, but it wasn't until 1955 that he held his first solo show in London at Gallery One, a significant venue for international artists, along with the New Vision Centre Gallery. His muscular figurative style aggressively confronted the Catholicism of his youth. In *Crucifixion* (1959) Christ appears spreadeagled across the surface, as if nailed to the frame. Thorns protrude from his legs like arrows and his arms arc up as if avoiding the spiky headwear of the two men who stand beneath him. Souza identified with St Sebastian, often painting himself with arrows protruding from his neck. In *Crucifixion* Christ also has feathered barbs protruding from his limbs. Did Souza also identify with Christ and feel martyred by the fervent religion of his youth? He struggled with it as an adult and it was a constant motif in his paintings.

Anwar Jalal Shemza (1928–1985) was nineteen when Pakistan was created. He attended the Mayo School of Art in Lahore after studying philosophy and became a successful author and artist, editing the bi-weekly magazine *Ehsas*, publishing novels, teaching art and becoming a founder member of the Lahore Art Circle. He decided to further his art education in the UK when he was twenty-eight, enrolling at the Slade in 1956. Having achieved recognition in Pakistan, he was shocked when his art was not understood in London and his confidence was badly shaken. It took him time to recover, until he found inspiration in the Islamic art he saw at the British Museum and the soft geometric watercolours of the Swiss artist Paul Klee.

The Wall (1958) is a key early work of Shemza's. It combines the calligraphic style of Islamic art with Western modernism and a formal interest in repeated shapes and motifs. Against a scumbled gold-and-white ground the surface is dominated by interlocking brown squares

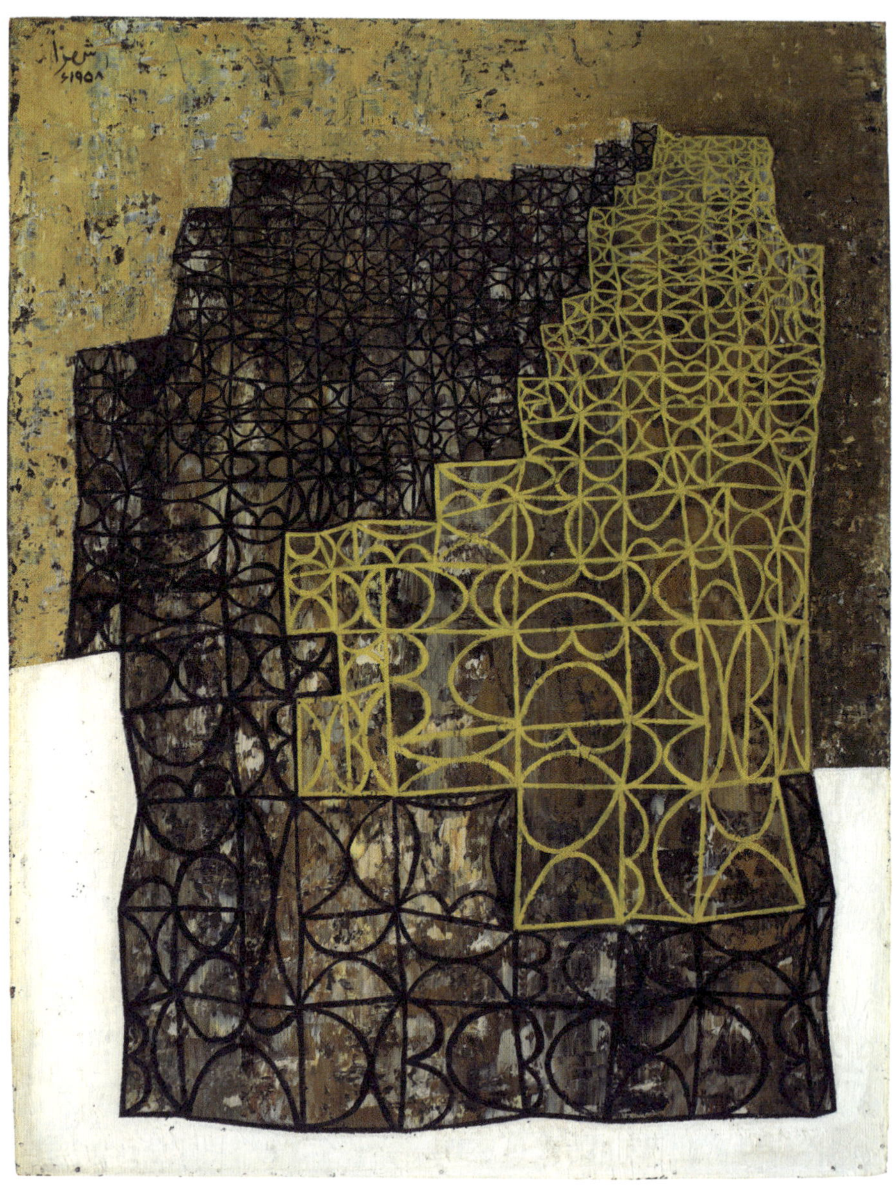

Anwar Jalal Shemza, *The Wall*, oil on board, 1958

covered with black-and-gold arabesques. Shemza later identified this new way of painting as: 'One circle, one square, one problem, one life is not enough to solve it.'[12] The wall he paints obstructs our view but also offers a sense of recession and depth as the squares reduce in size. In later paintings the boxes cover the entire surface, as in *Magic Carpet* (1961), but the surface still pulses with life, created by the oscillating size of each component.

Despite the presence of these artists in London in the post-war years, and supportive galleries such as the New Vision Centre Gallery, many of them felt overlooked or subjected to prejudice. After an initial post-war period of overseas recruitment to fill voids in the job market, the government (now Conservative) backtracked. From 1962, with the Commonwealth Immigrants Act, those carrying British colonial passports were subjected to immigration control and Britain shut the door on free movement across its former empire. Many of the artists who had moved to the UK from the British Caribbean or newly liberated India and Pakistan did not stay. Bowling, Williams and Souza left Britain for America in the 1960s. Shemza did stay, but only after failing to find employment in Lahore and because his wife, Mary Taylor, was a British artist. Moody, who had arrived in Britain from Jamaica in 1923 (as we saw in Chapter 12), spent time in Paris and his work was well received in America before the Second World War. But with the advent of war he returned to Britain and increasingly focused on portraits, and was elected to the Council of the Society of Portrait Sculptors in 1959.

Today these artists are rightly being written back into the narratives of post-war art in the UK, but during their lifetimes many experienced a form of ghosting, of being passed over and feeling they were not being offered the same opportunities as their white peers despite living and working in the same city. Simultaneously, other London-based artists chose to remove themselves from the noisy brouhaha of the capital. In doing so, they made a small fishing town in Cornwall an international centre for post-war abstract art.

15

ART'S EXPANDED FIELD
1939–73

WHILE THIS CHAPTER pursues art into the 1960s and 1970s, it begins with the story of a man who worked as a curator at the Tate Gallery in London in the 1920s and 1930s. He lived in Hampstead (of course) and amassed an outstanding collection of art. After retiring to Tangiers in bad health he returned to Britain in 1956 and embarked on converting four derelict cottages in Cambridge into a living gallery. The result was Kettle's Yard.

Kettle's Yard now boasts a state-of-the-art exhibition space, shop and cafe, but originally it was simply the house of Jim and Helen Ede from 1957 to 1973. The cottages had to be renovated and converted into a single property. 'So far it's all holes, skeleton floors, dismantled chimneys', he wrote. 'I begin (in mind) to hang pictures, to place a goblet here & a flower there.'[1] Jim had become friends with Ben Nicholson and Christopher Wood (1901–1930) while at the Tate, and began buying their work. He was also fascinated by the paintings of the untrained Alfred Wallis (1855–1942), a retired fisherman in St Ives in Cornwall, whose paintings of boats appear all over Kettle's Yard, from the bathroom to the library.

The Ede collection included glass jars, shells and spirals of pebbles as well as paintings by Scott and Ben and Winifred Nicholson, drawings by Hepworth and sculptures by Moore and Gaudier-Brzeska. A lemon was always displayed on a pewter platter close to *Tic Tic* (1927) by Joan Miró, the pitted skin matching the small yellow sphere in the painting, and *Prometheus* (1912) by Constantin Brancusi was balanced

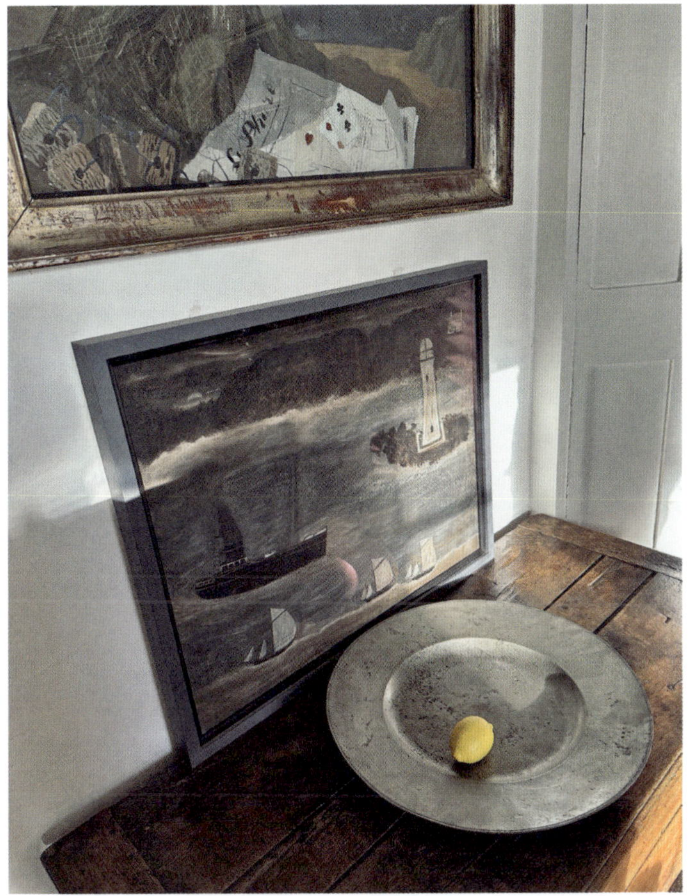

The sitting room of Kettle's Yard, Cambridge with Alfred Wallis's
*Seascape – ships sailing past the Longships, c.*1928, oil on canvas

on top of the grand piano. Jim curated the art and objects in thought-
ful arrangements, wanting people to happen upon them in a domestic
setting, to feel at home looking at them. If you pulled on the doorbell
any term-time afternoon Jim, in his signature beret, would give you a
tour (starting with *Tic Tic*) and then a cup of tea from a silver teapot.
And if you were a student at the University of Cambridge, he would
let you borrow a painting or sculpture to brighten up your digs until
the end of the academic year.

Ede had been tipped off about Wallis by Ben Nicholson, who nosily
knocked on his open door in St Ives in 1928. He could see his paintings of pilchard ships and fishing boats nailed to the walls of the front
room and was intrigued. Wallis had been born while the Crimean War

was raging and only took to painting aged seventy after a lifetime on the seas around St Ives. He used ship enamel and household paint and painted on old cereal packets and the back of advertisements. Nicholson told Ede about him and they began corresponding; Wallis eventually sent Ede more than 900 paintings from which he made a judicious selection, sending him two or three shillings a painting (£5–7 today).

Nicholson thought of Wallis as a 'primitive', someone untrained but who captured the essence of a subject. He was revered in the same way that the early modernists admired the sculptures in national museums from Africa and Oceania, for displaying the essence of his subject without the affectation of a fashionable style. Wallis's paintings are thought of as outsider art today – Nicholson and his peers saw him as the British Henri Rousseau, an untrained French artist known as 'Le Douanier' who worked as a customs officer and whose paintings were celebrated by Picasso. Ede would go on to display Wallis's works alongside those by Nicholson and Hepworth, both of whom also made St Ives their home.

THE COLOUR OF LIGHT

Hepworth and Nicholson lived together in St Ives for nearly twenty years. They first moved to neighbouring Carbis Bay in 1939, staying with the painter Margaret Mellis (1914–2009) and her husband Adrian Stokes. Naum and Miriam Gabo joined them there as they waited out the war. Gabo continued making his Constructivist sculptures, such as *Construction in Space (Crystal)* (1937–9). He framed the air using Perspex panels and taut wires, inspiring Hepworth to begin adding strings to her organic sculptures such as *Two Figures* (1943) and *Pelagos* (1946). She harnessed the natural forms of waves and sea-worn pebbles, piercing her carved forms to connect front to back. In October 1946 she was interviewed by *The Studio* – the slim magazine placed *Pelagos* on its cover. 'The carving and piercing of such a form seems to open up an infinite variety of continuous curves in the third dimension,' Hepworth said. 'Here is sufficient field for exploration to last a lifetime.'[2]

Nicholson oscillated between abstraction and figuration, painting the boats in St Ives harbour in 1943 but flattening tabletop and bottle in his Cubist *Still Life* of 1945. The colours of St Ives infused his palette – not the turquoise translucence of the sea but the lichen that

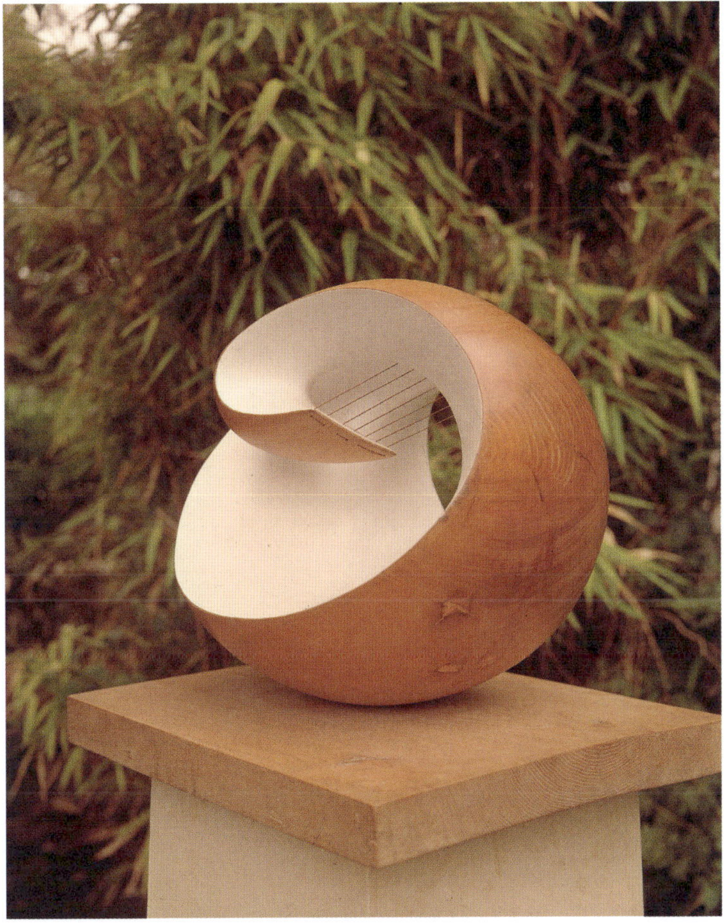

Barbara Hepworth, *Pelagos*, elm wood and strings on oak base, 1946

grew on the slate roofs, the off-white of seagull feathers and above all the clarity of light that is still unique to the town, intensified by sunlight reflecting through the shallow waters of its four beaches and tidal harbour. It is the reason the town is still full of artists. Each time I visit I am in awe of the light, from sunrise over Porthminster beach to sunset over Porthmeor, where studios still look out directly over the sands. The quality of light makes leaving difficult, as if you are turning your back on something nourishing.

Peter Lanyon (1918–1964), a young St Ives artist, had taken lessons with Nicholson before joining the RAF in 1940, and after six years in active service, he returned home. He was passionate about the Cornish landscape rather than its crystalline light, feeling that only someone born in the county could truly understand it. Lanyon had loaned his studio to Gabo during the war and continued to be inspired by the Constructivist's explorations of space, calling himself a 'disciple of Gabo'.[3] He had also taken lessons from the respected maritime painter Borlase Smart, but it was the land itself that spoke to him and he wanted to convey the experience of being immersed in the countryside he had grown up with. 'I paint places but always with the Placeness of them', he wrote in 1952.[4] Taking a Cubist approach of multiple simultaneous viewpoints, he painted abstracted aerial views spliced with rock formations, wave patterns and local landmarks, as in *Porthleven* (1951). Circles and shafts evoke the tin mines that still dotted the landscape, while ovals and curves brought to mind boats and pebbles. The paint crescendos to a peak, both peninsula and hill-top, the ground behind both foaming sea and scudding sky. Lanyon was inside, above, under and part of the land. His paintings embodied Jacquetta Hawkes's aspirations for her new book *A Land*, published the same year: 'The image I have sought to evoke is of an entity, the land of Britain, in which past and present, nature, man and art appear all in one piece.'[5]

By 1951 St Ives was buzzing with modernist artists. Wilhelmina Barns-Graham (1912–2004) had been there since 1940, and Terry Frost (1915–2003) and Bryan Wynter (1915–1975) relocated in 1946. Patrick Heron (1920–1999) had spent significant amounts of his childhood there and rented a house in St Ives each summer before buying Eagle's Nest in nearby Zennor in 1955 and moving there permanently. Lanyon and Wynter were among a group of artists who began exhibiting in the crypt of a deconsecrated chapel in 1946; after three exhibitions the Crypt Group joined with Hepworth and Nicholson to form the Penwith Society. These groups purposefully stood apart from the more traditional academic artists like Smart, who exhibited with the St Ives Society of Artists. The Penwith Society still exists today, with a large gallery in a former pilchard-packing factory a few doors along from Porthmeor Studios, where Heron, Frost, Lanyon and Barns-Graham worked. These studios front the wide expanse of Porthmeor Beach, with its Atlantic barrel waves and voluminous light. The paintings completed in these studios attracted the likes of the Abstract Expressionist painter Mark Rothko, the American art critic Clement Greenberg and New

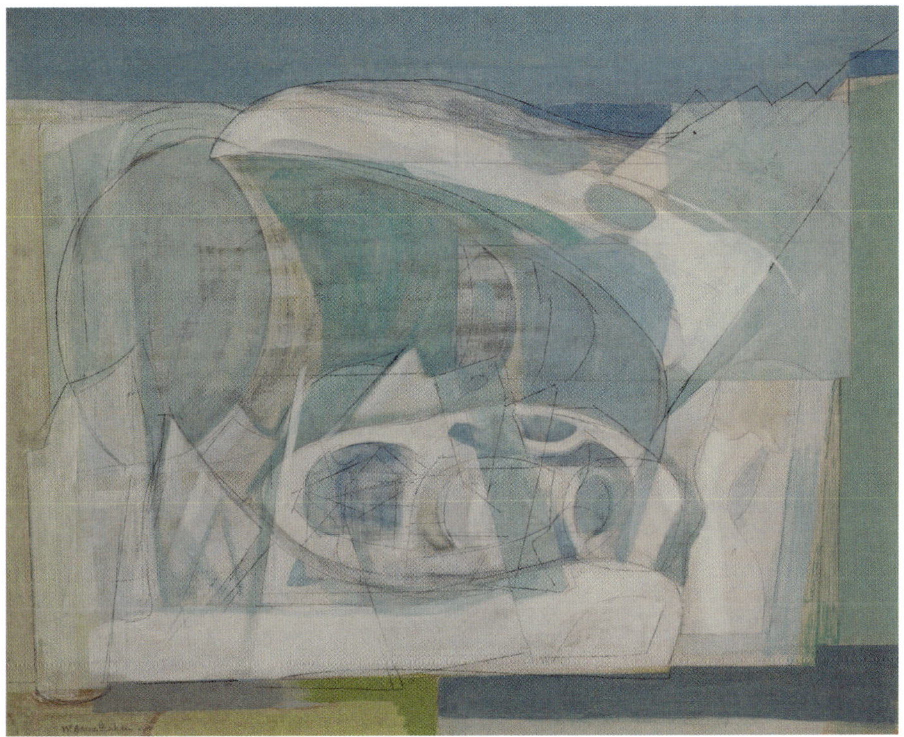

Wilhelmina Barns-Graham, *Upper Glacier*, oil on canvas, 1950

York dealers, who all embarked on the nine-hour drive from London to check out the latest developments in St Ives.

What was it about the post-war paintings made in St Ives that made them so beguiling? Early visitors were drawn by Hepworth, who moved into her Trewyn studio a few steps away from the harbour in 1949. She eventually took over the St Ives Palais de Danse to make her largest sculptures, which graced the courtyard of the United Nations in New York and the flagship John Lewis store on Oxford Street in London. The annual exhibitions of the Penwith Society also drew attention. Lanyon, Nicholson, Heron and Wynter had exhibited in the Festival of Britain's touring exhibition *60 Paintings for '51*, but it was the women artists who stormed the Penwith 'Festival of Britain' competition, with Hepworth winning the sculpture category and Barns-Graham winning best painting.

Barns-Graham lived in St Ives for much of her life, but it was the Grindelwald glacier in Switzerland that inspired some of her most successful paintings. She spent a day walking across its translucent surface, climbing its craggy peaks, studying the colours in melt holes, listening to it crack and moan, feeling it to be a living, organic entity. She saw it through Gabo's eyes, as a frozen moment of space and time, and painted it with Hepworth's understanding of natural form. In *Glacier Vortex* (1951) she pierced its oval depths and in *Upper Glacier* (1950) turned its peak into a giant wave. She brought the cold ice of Switzerland alive with a St Ives palette of ochre, grey, turquoise and white, creating veils of colour so multiple layers show through, revealing sculptural forms hidden within.

Patrick Heron's response to St Ives was not driven by the rugged land-scape that surrounded Eagle's Nest, the deep time of Zennor Quoit or even its more recent industrial past. In 1955 he wrote: 'The exhilaration of stating truly his purely pictorial discoveries will be the painter's only touchstone . . .'[6] His paintings and prints – sometimes figurative, sometimes not – resonate with colour and form, loops and whorls. It was colour that drove him, the zing of a red next to a green, the zip of yellow next to lilac, the shape of a purple pool as it lies on a red ground in *Porthmeor 1965, Rumbold 1970* (1970). While he became one of the most famous of the St Ives painters, his work was rooted in the colour harmonies of Matisse, Pierre Bonnard and Georges Braque. Yet there was something about St Ives – its remoteness, its light, its cluster of like-minded artists, its colours – that kept Heron nearby for the rest of his life.

In 1957, when Heron was in London visiting an exhibition he had organised at the Redfern Gallery, he bumped into the artists Roger Hilton (1911–1975) and Sandra Blow (1925–2006). He invited them to Eagle's Nest for Easter – Hilton would later move to nearby St Just with his artist wife Rose (1931–2019), and both their practices responded to the paintings they saw in St Ives. It only took a few weeks for Blow to give up her London flat and rent a cottage near Heron for a year. Blow, like Heron, took inspiration from European art. She had spent time in Rome with Alberto Burri and her abstract canvases had a muscular, material quality unlike any of the other St Ives artists. Even though she only spent a year in Cornwall, it changed her way of working and thinking. She started painting outdoors, propping her boards against a barn wall, and it's tempting to see a maritime bent to *Cornwall* (1958), with its loosely woven sacking hanging on the canvas like a fishing net out to dry, the brown shapes crowding in like the cheek-by-jowl fishermen's cottages of Downalong in St Ives.

THE WORLD GOES 'POP'

The St Ives artists worked in parallel to London-based practitioners, but remained independent of those who created what we now know as British Pop. These young artists turned their back on traditional art and focused on anti-art, technology and science in the early 1950s. Richard Hamilton (1922–2011), Eduardo Paolozzi, Nigel Henderson (1917–1985) and Magda Cordell (1921–2008) were part of a diverse group of artists, architects and writers who held lectures at the Institute of Contemporary Arts (ICA). Despite the ICA itself only being a few years old, this new cluster of artists was initially known as the 'Young Group' to differentiate

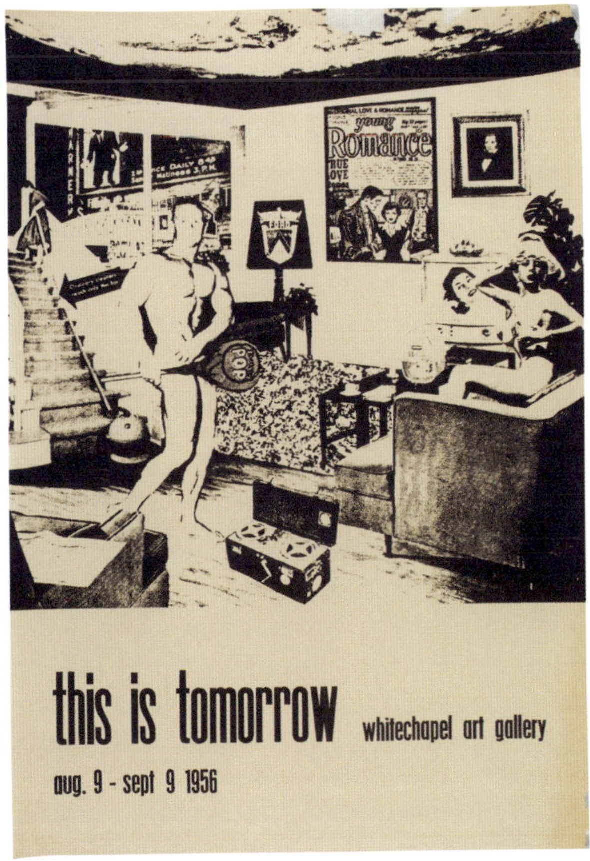

Richard Hamilton, *This Is Tomorrow*,
screen-printed poster, 1956

it from the ICA's founders Roland Penrose, Herbert Read and E.L.T. Mesens (1903–1971). The Young Group held its first meeting in 1952, at which Paolozzi presented *Bunk!*, a rapid-fire visual lecture of a vast array of American advertisements (anti-art) he had collaged together.

The Young Group ultimately became known as the Independent Group. There were no lectures on traditional art – Hamilton talked about white electrical goods and the critic Reyner Banham discussed car styling. They believed in a breakdown of traditional hierarchies between fine art and mass culture: comic strips, science fiction, advertisements. Couldn't it all be art? In 1956 the Whitechapel Art Gallery held *This Is Tomorrow*. Twelve mixed groups of artists, architects, editors and writers were commissioned to create an interdisciplinary vision of the future. What an exciting project to be involved with. Paolozzi was in Group 6 with the Brutalist architects Alison and Peter Smithson; Hamilton was in Group 2 with the artist and theorist John McHale and architect John Voelcker. McHale was studying at Yale University in Connecticut and sent trunkfuls of Americana back to Hamilton. Hamilton created an intricate collage, building on Paolozzi's *Bunk!* images of women incongruously cleaning show homes using the latest appliances. Hamilton's iconic image inserts a bodybuilder and a provocative nude into a modern home, feeding them with an oversized tin of ham and lacing the collage with popular culture (see previous page). The television is on, a comic book takes the place of fine art and an advert for *The Jazz Singer* can be seen through the window. It's a humorous image – the bodybuilder lifts a Tootsie 'Pop' lollipop instead of a dumbbell – and it became one of twelve posters to advertise the show.

Paolozzi's collage *I Was a Rich Man's Plaything* (1949) had featured a cartoon hand shooting a gun that exploded 'POP!' in the face of a female pin-up. In 1957 Hamilton used the term 'Pop Art' to define the group's new approach in a letter to the Smithsons, identifying their art as youthful, witty, transient, low-cost and mass-produced. His paintings from this period are fragmentary and seductive. In *$he* (1958–61) the soft curve of a peach shoulder sits alongside an open fridge door, where Hamilton's fascination with white goods also extends to a two-slot electric toaster. Money makes life easy and available, he seems to say. Everything is a commodity.

British Pop preceded American Pop by several years. As Andy Warhol and Roy Lichtenstein scaled it up in New York, a new generation of British artists were exploring consumer culture and the proliferation of images. When the Whitechapel Art Gallery held a Jackson Pollock retrospective in 1958 a young David Hockney hitchhiked from his home in Yorkshire to attend. Within a year he was living in London, studying at the RCA alongside Frank Bowling. His head was turned by America and he would live in Los Angeles from 1964, but it was not the macho action painting of Pollock that seduced him. A visit to New York in 1961, while still a student, opened his eyes to a new way of living with 24/7 culture and an established gay scene. His subsequent

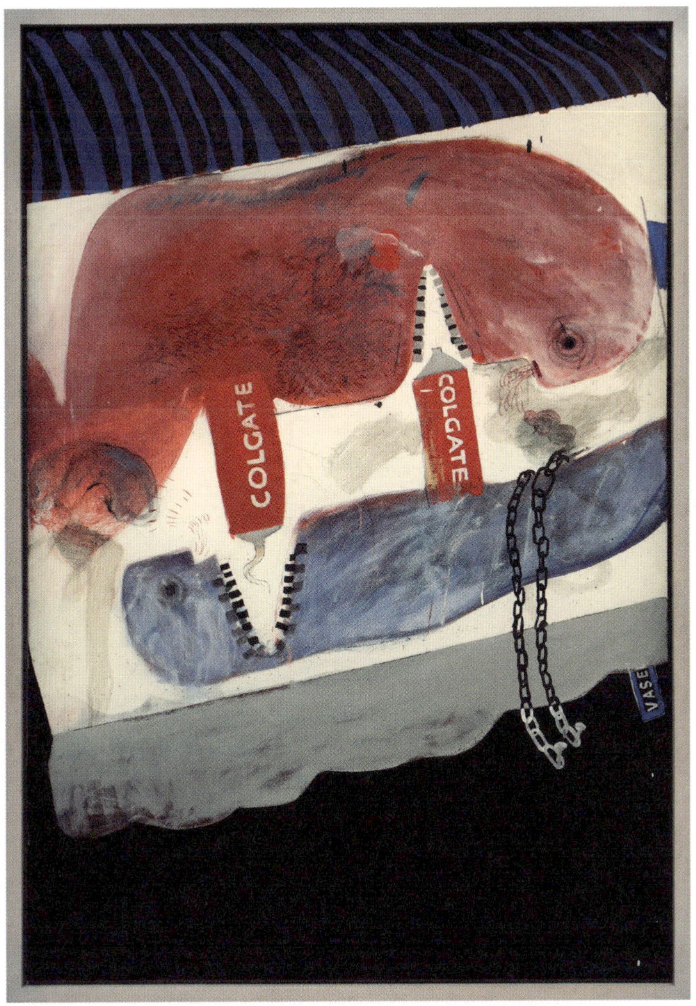

David Hockney, *Cleaning Teeth, Early Evening (10pm) W11*,
oil on canvas, 1962

paintings can be seen as British Pop, with their bright colours, product placement and inclusion of consumer goods. But paintings such as *We Two Boys Together Clinging* (1961) and *Cleaning Teeth, Early Evening (10pm) W11* (1962; see previous page) are also highly charged in a society that still imprisoned men for homosexual relations.

Peter Blake (born 1932) also studied at the RCA, graduating before Hockney arrived in 1956. He was a huge fan of American music, from the Everly Brothers to Little Richard, and went on to create the artwork for the Beatles album *Sgt Pepper's Lonely Hearts Club Band* (1967). In his 1961 *Self-Portrait with Badges* he holds a photograph of Elvis, with dozens of pop badges pinned to his denim jacket, and his baseball boots and jeans profess his love of American culture. He became a mentor to the younger RCA artist Pauline Boty (1938–1966), who also explored American culture and celebrity through her paintings of Marilyn Monroe. Boty had performed as Marilyn in student revues and she painted her repeatedly. In *The Only Blonde in the World* (1963) and *Colour Her Gone* (1962) you sense a purposeful slippage between the film star and the artist herself. While Boty's work is associated with Pop Art through her fascination with celebrity – she also painted Christine Keeler and the French actor Jean-Paul Belmonde – her work was becoming increasingly political before her early death from cancer in 1966.

No longer on a pedestal

After the wiry nervousness of the Geometry of Fear the bright, flat colours of Pop must have seemed as bold and brazen as the GIs dishing out chocolate and stockings during the war. But not all artists embraced Pop's fascination with a glossy American utopia. Jean Cooke (1927–2008) was married to the abusive 'Kitchen Sink' painter John Bratby (1928–1992). He only allowed her to paint for three hours a day and her domestic scenes see her valiantly trying to assert her presence, even allowing us to see her black eye in *Mad Self-Portrait* (1954). Joan Eardley (1921–1963), meanwhile, painted the children of Glasgow tenements, capturing their haunted gaze and guarded stance in *Brother and Sister* (1955) and bony rangy bodies as they sit on the edge of the pavement in *Street Kids* (c.1949–51). These paintings touch us emotionally, the paint flushing the cheeks of the abused Cooke, cooling the bare knees of Eardley's street boys. Pop, by comparison, was a rictus grin of excess, consumption and celebrity. It fed into the buoyant mood of the sixties with the boom in rock and roll, rising hemlines, the end of conscription and an increased awareness of civil rights.

Sculpture did not escape this new confidence emanating from America. Anthony Caro (1924–2013) began working as an assistant to Moore in 1951 and graduated from the RCA the following year. His early work is figurative, but he visited America for the first time in 1959 and saw the welded metal sculptures of David Smith. Smith's belief that he could place his work directly on the ground, without the need for a plinth, as with his series *Sentinels* (1956–61), was revelatory. We are so used to seeing sculptures occupying our space in this way today that we barely think about whether something is on a plinth or not, but at the point when Caro saw Smith's work Western sculpture had always been presented on some kind of raised platform. This kept it separate from our space, the space we lived in. It assigned the label 'art' to it and encouraged us to look at it in a particular way, at one remove. So what happened when you took it off the plinth, when it nestled in the grass outside a gallery or stretched across a parquet floor?

Caro abandoned the figure and began working in industrial materials. He coloured steel girders and I-beams bright yellow, red and black, welding them together into larger and larger constructions, placing them directly on the floors of galleries. *Early One Morning* (1962; see overleaf) and *Swing* (1965) were Pop-bright and in your space – they appeared to change shape as you walked around them, requiring time to get to know them. The flat panels and extended beams were like marks on a three-dimensional canvas that were constantly in flux. There was no Geometry of Fear here, just a bold confidence in form and colour and line.

By teaching on the advanced sculpture course at Saint Martin's School of Art, Caro became hugely influential. He taught Phillip King (1934–2021), whose brightly coloured abstract sculptures carried light-hearted names such as *Rosebud* (1962) and *Tra-la-la* (1962–3). *Rosebud* was like an inverted coffee filter, its conical form painted pale pink and split down one side to reveal a dark green interior. *Tra-la-la* seems to be an impossibility, an oversized twist of wire the colour of marshmallow resting on a Skylon-shaped slender almond all balanced on the tip of a powder-blue cone. King's sculptures were also floor-bound (no one could put that genie back in the bottle) and used industrial materials such as fibreglass, resin and plastic to create

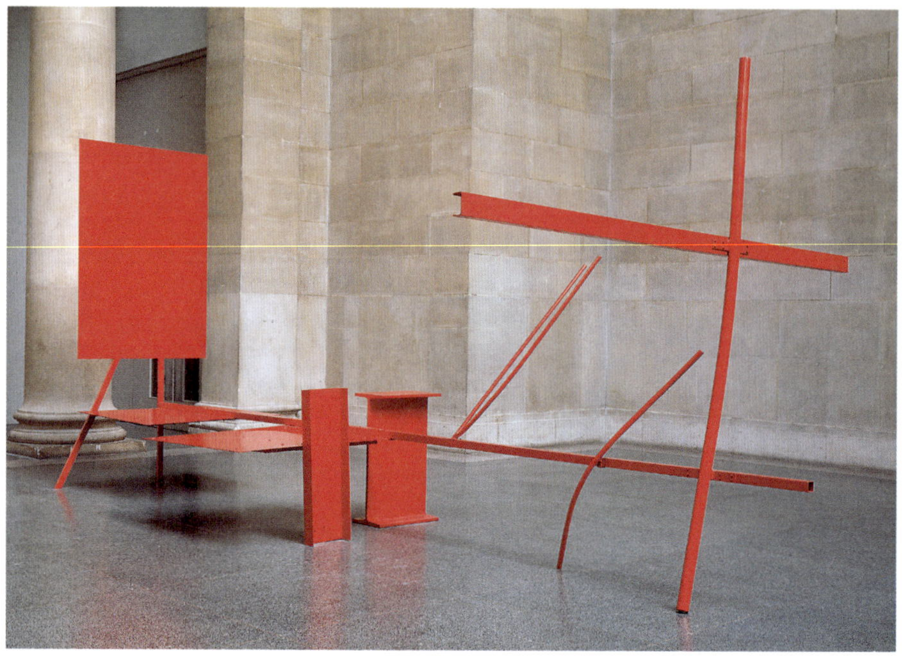

Anthony Caro, *Early One Morning*, painted steel and aluminium, 1962

such complex shapes. There was no communing with wood grain for these sculptors. They willingly embraced modern materials in order to create larger and more complex forms.

Mary (1907–1969) and Kenneth Martin (1905–1984) were Constructivist artists following Gabo's lead. They too worked in industrial materials but their work was geometric, not lyrical. In the early 1950s they had struggled to find places to exhibit but in 1963 the Arts Council staged *Construction England*, a touring exhibition that put them on the map. Mary Martin's relief sculptures use geometric tessellations and light to play with form, questioning our perception like the Op Art canvases of Bridget Riley, whose mind-bending stripes were swiftly commandeered by fashion designers including Mary Quant.

Kim Lim (1936–1997) approached sculpture from a different angle. She was born in Singapore, a British colony until 1957, and studied at Saint Martin's, where she was taught by Frink, before transferring to the Slade. She found the teaching too restrictive in both schools, with its emphasis on the figure, and instead used her travels to non-European countries and her interest in architecture to inspire her thinking. Her work has a solidity to it, a need to stand alone in the middle of a room, and a sense of repetition that is not contained within a set of rules like Martin's but rather offers itself as something temporary, in flux, as if it may reassemble at any moment. Lim and Martin, King and Caro all explored the new possibilities for sculpture now that it had leapt off the plinth and into our world. But nothing could have prepared them for what came next.

It's all in the mind

You never forget the first time you see *An Oak Tree* (1973; see overleaf) by Michael Craig-Martin (born 1941). It forces you to recalibrate everything you think you know about art. It looks like a glass of water on a high shelf. But an accompanying question-and-answer text tells us that it is in fact an oak tree. 'What I've done is change a glass of water into a full-grown oak tree without altering the accidents of the glass of water', Craig-Martin writes. The anonymous interviewer could be us, struggling to understand. It looks to all intents and purposes like a glass of water, but Craig-Martin says it isn't, that his intention has precipitated a change and that what we now see is an oak tree presented in the form of a glass of water. After raising multiple questions about perception, language and the emperor's new clothes, the interviewer asks: 'Do you consider that changing the glass of water into an oak tree constitutes an artwork?' The reply is emphatic: 'Yes.'[7]

An Oak Tree is the most iconic work of conceptual art made in the British Isles. Craig-Martin is right when he says he is more of a 'perceptual' artist than a conceptual one, but this work encapsulates a central tenet of a new way of thinking that surfaced in the 1960s and has been with us ever since. It is a switch in emphasis in art of such magnitude that it questioned millennia of art-making. By prioritising the idea over the made object it undermined the mantra of 'truth to materials' and the modernist emphasis on form, colour and line. These things didn't matter to the conceptual artist – front and centre was the idea.

Conceptual art became voiced as a new approach in the late 1960s in both North America and the British Isles. Two hotspots in Britain were Central Saint Martins in London, where Caro taught, and Coventry College of Art in the West Midlands. Artists in these institutions replaced

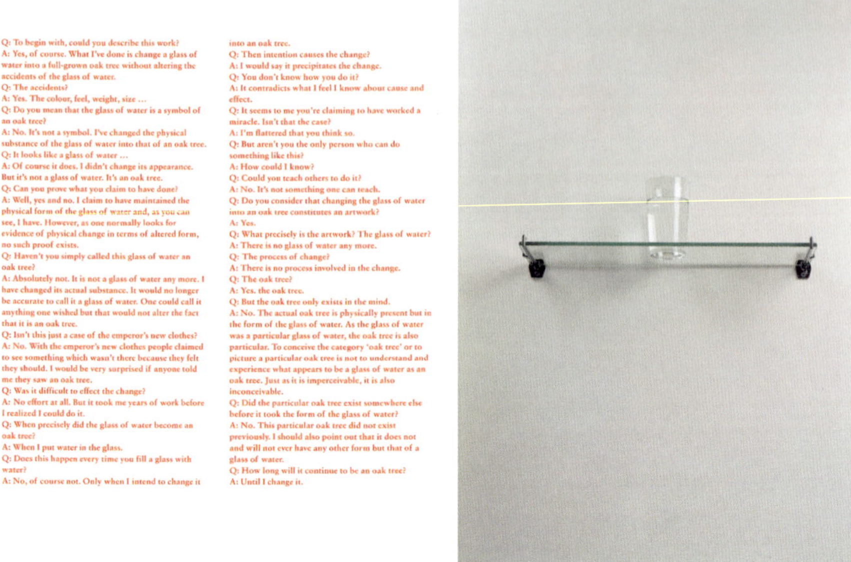

Michael Craig-Martin, *An Oak Tree*, glass, water, shelf and printed text, 1973

the focus on materials – wood, steel, paint – with a focus on time and duration. The audience became integral to the process of making each piece, from contemplating Craig-Martin's *An Oak Tree* to following the cues of *All Criteria* (1970) by Victor Burgin (born 1941) which asked viewers to consider different subsets and groupings, such as 'all criteria by which you might ascribe individuality to things other than objects'.[8]

Burgin and Craig-Martin had both studied at Yale and witnessed first-hand the rise of American Minimalism, an approach that relied on everyday materials and geometric repetition to explore form and how it is perceived. Maurice Merleau-Ponty's *Phenomenology of Perception* (1945) was central to their thinking and it directly informed Burgin. The book explored the perceptual instability of an object and placed the viewer at the centre of perception because it was how an individual looked at something that ultimately shaped its identity.

The Coventry group Art + Language, which included Terry Atkinson (born 1939) and Michael Baldwin (born 1945), questioned how modern art had been codified and how language shapes understanding. Its members explored the relationship between words and our expectations in early works such as *Painting/Sculpture* (1966–7). Two grey panels hang on a wall, both the same size and shape. On the left panel the word 'Painting' is written in capital letters, while on the right is the word 'Sculpture'. The art exists in the viewer's interaction with the words, rather than any particular visualisation. Our mind completes this by questioning our expectations for art when the words we use to describe it are shown as interchangeable at best and possibly redundant at worst.

Much conceptual art centred around the use of typed sheets of words and black-and-white photographs. It was art of the mind, not of the eyes. Only occasionally did it include visual representations – Susan Hiller (1940–2019) explored missing identity in her enquiry into those who photographed and hand-tinted seaside postcards in *Dedicated to the Unknown Artists* (1972–6). Following a line of thought to its conclusion over time became a dominant mode of working. John Latham (1921–2006), an incendiary artist, nearly lost his teaching job at Saint Martin's because he 'distilled' a library copy of Clement Greenberg's *Art & Culture* (1961) to a liquid in a stoppered phial. To conceptual artists Greenberg's intransigent position on modernism – with its sole focus on aesthetics and form – was anathema. Latham, his students and friends tore pages out of the library book and chewed them to a pulp before he squashed the remains into a flask, using acid and yeast to break them down. The library was not happy when he sent the phial back instead of the book, and he was forced to apologise. The art in Latham's version of *Art & Culture* (1966–9) existed in the performative aspect of Latham's actions and the concept. The phial was the residue.

Richard Long (born 1945) and Hamish Fulton (born 1946) had been students of Caro's at Saint Martin's in the 1960s. Caro had expanded the thinking on what constituted a sculpture but his students increasingly felt that he was imprisoned by his own modernist rhetoric. He still believed in the materiality of sculpture, but what if art could be made from nothing more than an experience? One of Long's first time-based works was *A Line Made by Walking* (1967). He took a train from Waterloo station and hopped off as soon as he entered the countryside. He then found a field and proceeded to walk methodically backwards and forwards until he had pressed a line into the grass. The time it took to make the piece and the experience of changing the environment in this way were where the art resided. Long had the foresight to take a photograph of the temporary path receding into shrubland and this became the residue of the work, like Latham's phial. Fulton similarly gave the viewer scant evidence of the art he had made. At times a single photograph and a few pithy words were the only record of a walk that covered hundreds of miles, as in *The Pilgrim's Way* (1971). The words became a residual haiku – 'A hollow lane on the North Downs / Ancient paths forming a route between Winchester and Canterbury' – and the viewer had to employ them, along with the photograph, to conjure the sensation of walking for days and days along ancient paths cut into the landscape.

This radical exploration of what art could be and an increasing focus on the making and process of art (not the final result) led a growing number of artists to use their own bodies as material. In November 1966 the Japanese American Fluxus artist Yoko Ono (born 1933) was invited to exhibit at the new Indica Gallery in London. As a preface to this, in September, she performed *Cut Piece* (1964) at the Africa Centre as part of the 'Destruction in Art' symposium. The London audience could experience for itself the power of *Cut Piece*, a work that had left those who saw it in America in tears. Today it is seen as an important proto-feminist work, and we will explore feminism shortly in the next chapter, but it has a conceptual root. Ultimately it exists as a set of instructions for a single performer, either male or female, who sits on a stage with a pair of scissors in front of them and allows audience members to come up one by one and cut off small pieces of the performer's clothing to take away with them. The collaboration with the audience is central to the work – while Ono conceived of it as a way to represent selfless giving to others, archive footage of the various stagings of the performance has a menacing quality, as men and women file on stage and cut Ono's suit to ribbons before snipping away at her bra strap and slip.

The year after Ono's performance in London, Gilbert Prousch (born 1943) and George Passmore (born 1942) met as students at Saint Martin's. They were also taught by Caro but were influenced by the rise of conceptual art and performance, and they began to utilise their own bodies to make art. Unlike Ono with her instructions for a single performer (any performer), Gilbert & George – as they became known – turned themselves into the work. They were living sculptures, painted bronze and performing the music-hall number 'Underneath the Arches' like automatons while standing on a rickety table (like a plinth) in *The Singing Sculpture* (1969). To this day they exist as a living sculpture, wearing matching three-piece suits and adopting a genteel persona that makes their sculptural (and photographic) practice a connected and ongoing work of art. Gilbert & George explore their concerns through a judicious use of their own bodies. This performative approach was also central to feminist art in the 1970s.

16

STAND UP AND BE COUNTED
1968–98

THERE HAD BEEN a sea change in how art was made in the 1960s. It no longer had to be concerned with materiality – with the creation of some kind of object – but was free to explore time, space and ideas. A temporary line trampled in a field, an oak tree that resembled a glass of water, artists who became their own artwork – art was liberated from the shackles of 'thingness'. The only problem was it seemed increasingly difficult to identify where the 'art' now resided.

In 1975 the writer Rosalind Delmar reviewed *Women and Work: A Document on the Division of Labour and Industry* for the feminist magazine *Spare Rib*. This complex piece was made by Kay Hunt (1933–2001), Mary Kelly (born 1941) and Margaret Harrison (born 1940), who had collaborated for two years to bring it to fruition. It was based on the men and women who worked in a metal-box factory in Bermondsey in London and was both artwork and exhibition, archive and databank. It was a sociological study as well as an exposé of the inequalities in pay found in industrial labour in the year the Equal Pay Act came into force. Delmar explained that the processes used were those of the historian, cartographer, archivist and activist rather than those traditionally associated with fine artists. The data they gathered was presented in typed tables, with black-and-white photographs, audio interviews and films of men and women working on the factory floor.

An early criticism of the piece was that it was 'arid', and even now this significant work can seem hard to grasp at first glance. It requires serious commitment on the part of the viewer, who has to read through the lists of earnings of double seamer operators and machine setters, study the maps showing where each worker lived and process visual, audio and textual data to tease out the inequalities the artists found. 'Its aura is one of a deliberate under-statement, an invitation to discovery rather than an overt declaration of findings', Delmar concludes. You can feel her rooting for the artists but struggling to see the 'art' in it herself, concluding it is 'a stimulating and thought-provoking experiment'.[1] She justified it as art because it was presented in a gallery in a particular way. But the art was in the very idea of it. The art was the concept devised by the three artists, who wanted to expose ongoing inequality as part of their commitment to what Delmar calls the 'women's liberation movement'. Today we would call this feminism.

WOMEN UNITE

The women's movement coalesced following the civil rights movement in America and the student uprisings that spiralled through Europe in 1968. Artist groups consisting entirely of women were formed in the British Isles, such as the Women's Liberation Art Group (1970), and feminist art programmes were launched at universities. Germaine Greer published *The Female Eunuch* in 1970, a scathing attack on the oppression of women, and two years later *Spare Rib* was founded. Greer acknowledged that the feminists of 1970 were standing on the shoulders of the suffragettes, the first wave of feminists, who had been imprisoned for their actions as they campaigned for the vote. However, Greer continued, women hadn't capitalised on the gains the suffragettes made: 'The cage door had been opened but the canary [the emancipated woman] had refused to fly out.'[2] And so now, she said, the emphasis had shifted. 'Then genteel middle-class ladies clamoured for reform, now ungenteel middle-class women are calling for revolution.'[3]

In the late 1960s and 1970s women took matters into their own hands. If men wouldn't cover their art in established magazines then they would form their own and write each other's reviews. If men wouldn't exhibit their work in museums and galleries they would band together and mount their own shows. There was strength in numbers and power in collectives. They reacted to the latest thinking by writers such as Laura Mulvey and John Berger, who exposed how women had been objectified in films, advertisements and popular culture.

Feminist art historians including Griselda Pollock, Rozsika Parker and Linda Nochlin began making visible historical women artists, revealing how male authors had sidelined them or written them out of the history books. Women artists began making work about how femininity and womanhood was constructed. They built on Simone de Beauvoir's landmark feminist text *The Second Sex* (1949) and her belief that women were not born but made. They also began using their own bodies in their art to assert a new kind of agency over the female nude and they chose to make work about the invisible aspects of womanhood, everything from weaning a new baby and household chores to giving birth and orgasms.

Kelly, one of the three artists behind *Women and Work*, had moved to London from Beirut in 1968. An American by birth, she lived in the UK throughout the 1970s, becoming interested in the jobs women did that were never talked about in history books. As part of the Berwick Street Film Collective she made *Nightcleaners* (1970–5), a film about the campaign to unionise the women who cleaned office blocks at night, who were exploited and underpaid. In *Post-Partum Document* (1973–9) she tracked the first five years of her son's life, from first words and first steps to the food he ate and the nappies he wore. She framed his scribbles alongside her diary entries that revealed the psychological complexity of raising a child and her theoretical interpretation of it. When the work was first shown at the ICA in 1976, the liners from her son's dirty nappies sent the national press into a tailspin. There were 135 elements to the work, each framed the same way to create a wall-based installation whose visual repetition chimed with the monotony of motherhood, despite all the tiny markers of development captured on the pages within each frame.

Throughout the 1970s Alexis Hunter (1948–2014), Monica Sjöö (1938–2005), Rose Finn-Kelcey (1945–2014), Linder (born 1954) and many other women continued to explore gender, the patriarchy, the commodification of the female body and the invisibility of women's work. In the 1980s Jo Spence (1934–1992) explored the complexity of womanhood in her photographic series *Remodelling Photo History* (1981–2). She worked with Terry Dennett to present her own body as a counterpoint to the male objectification of women in magazines, wanting to complicate readings of poses we had been conditioned to understand in a particular way. She does not pose like the young topless models on page 3 of the *Sun* newspaper (a feature introduced in 1970 to boost circulation and only cancelled in 2015). Instead, in *Colonization*, she stands in a doorway, wrapped in a towel and naked from the waist up, her full breasts adorned with a chunky necklace, holding a broom as if she is about to sweep the front step. In *Subordination* she lies spreadeagled in front of a car by a closed gate with a sign saying trespassers will be prosecuted. Spence challenges the history and practice of photography, 'the function they have had in constructing and encouraging particular ways of viewing and telling about the world'.[4] *Remodelling Photo History* is her riposte, a way of destabilising expectations of photographic nudes and reclaiming the female body for herself.

Others used new technologies to take control of the representation of their own bodies. Liz Rideal (born 1954) used a photobooth to deliver a new take on self-portraiture. In *'Think Pink' (aka booth wank at NPG)* (1985) she relied on periodic shutter timings to capture her facial expressions as she brought herself to climax and orgasmed, playing with notions of power as her body's reaction to stimulation took her beyond control but her recording of it allowed her to take ownership of her response.

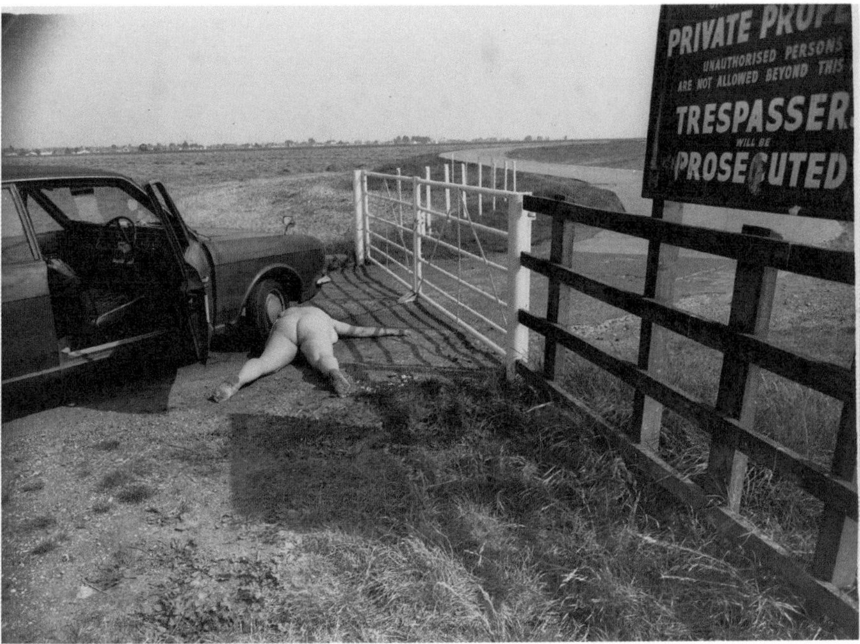

Jo Spence, *Remodelling Photo History: Subordination*, gelatin silver print, 1982

Similarly, Helen Chadwick (1953–1996) used an office photocopier with blue toner to create twelve composite images of her own naked body surrounded by fecund plants and animals in *The Oval Court* (1986). Like a fallen ceiling dedicated to a fertility goddess, or an elaborate *vanitas*, her body lay in various positions on the ground with five gold spheres balanced on top while columns pinned to the walls created a temple-like installation. In the photocopies she arcs her back over a trotting lamb and gorges on cut fruit. Strings of pearls swirl like semen near the suggestive underbelly of a ray. Its original companion piece, *Carcass*, was a fermenting column of all the organic material she had used. It offered a grim reminder that mortality was the endgame for all living things, but a leaky tank meant this morbid doppelgänger didn't last long.

These women were all feminists, but they were also all white. The Black woman artist Lubaina Himid (born 1954) was acutely aware of this at the time: 'The indifference of the initial feminist notion of sisterhood to the differences that structure our experiences in terms of race, in terms of class, in terms of age, in terms of culture, in terms of being mothers and non-mothers, in terms of a whole variety of differences, that seems to be a very important shift . . . It seems to me black women have a powerful charge to put against white feminism for precisely its failures, its indifference.'[5]

THE THIN BLACK LINE

If traditional methods of display are closed to you then the only way to be seen is to organise your own exhibitions. This is what Himid did throughout the 1980s. These shows are legendary now, but at the time Himid remembers it was an uphill struggle. *Five Black Women* was held at the Africa Centre in London in 1983 and included Himid, Sonia Boyce (born 1962), Veronica Ryan (born 1956), Claudette Johnson (born 1959) and Houria Niati (born 1948), artists of African and Caribbean heritage who lived and worked in the UK.[6] The Africa Centre had staged Yoko Ono's *Cut Piece* in 1966 but Himid's show was the first major exhibition of women's art ever held there. While there was funding in the British Isles for Black and Asian artists it was often tied to community or 'ethnic' arts, these terms used patronisingly (even pejoratively) to suggest the art of 'Afro-Asian' artists was in some way amateur or 'other' to Western fine art.[7]

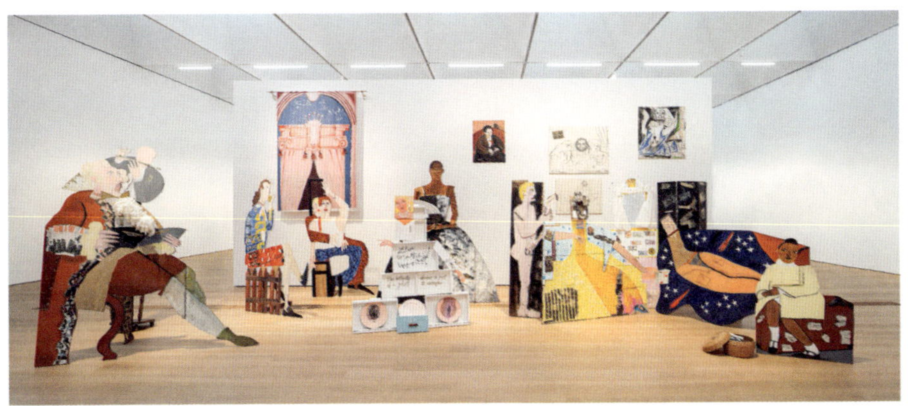

Lubaina Himid, *A Fashionable Marriage*, mixed media installation, 1986

Himid curated *Black Women Time Now* at the Battersea Arts Centre later in 1983. Around this time she was invited to talk at the University of Leeds, by Griselda Pollock who was a lecturer there. The impetus for the invitation had come from an ambitious young artist, Sutapa Biswas (born 1962), the only Indian British student in the whole art department at Leeds. Biswas also asked for Sonia Boyce to visit the department and Himid brought both Biswas and Boyce together in the third show she curated, *The Thin Black Line*, in 1985.

The Thin Black Line was held at the ICA. It included *Good Housekeeping I* (1985) by Marlene Smith (born 1964), a harrowing wall installation of a family photograph and textured portrait of Dorothy 'Cherry' Groce, who was paralysed after police raided her home in Brixton and shot her. Along the wall are the words: 'My mother opens the door at 7am. She is not bulletproof.' (The work is now lost but was recreated for the exhibition *Women in Revolt! Art and Activism in the UK 1970–1990* at Tate Britain in London in 2023–4. It had lost none of its impact.) For the women artists in *The Thin Black Line*, having their work exhibited at the ICA meant art-world validation, even though the exhibition space Himid had been given was far from optimal: a corridor rather than an endpoint. Ultimately, for Himid, this didn't matter. In the catalogue she makes her position clear: 'We are claiming what is ours and making ourselves visible. We are eleven of the hundreds of creative Black Women in Britain today. We are here to stay.'[8]

Himid's own work was concerned with supplanting colonial stories with new Black ones. In *A Fashionable Marriage* (1986) she reimagined Hogarth's *Marriage à la Mode: The Toilette* (*c.*1743), with a 3-metre-tall Black woman artist replacing the anonymous Black servant serving his white employer's hot chocolate. Her characters are painted on plywood, like theatre flats, and are arranged to fill the room into which you step. They become actors involved in a restaging of history – politicians (Margaret Thatcher and Ronald Reagan) supplanted Hogarth's lovers and the castrato became a male art critic (Brian Sewell perhaps?). It looks as if he is beruffled in flaccid condoms, a purposeful emasculation as she sought retribution for the impotence such critics possessed when it came to analysing the work of Black artists. Walking among them, you become part of history as it is being rewritten. What is your role going to be?

The three exhibitions curated by Himid between 1983 and 1985 announced the arrival of many of the Black and Asian artists who today are among Britain's most successful practitioners. Biswas's *Housewives with Steak-Knives* (1985) was included in *The Thin Black Line*. It's a confrontational image of a powerful Asian woman taking on the form of Kali, the multi-armed Hindu goddess of destruction and rebirth. She looms towards you waving a bloody machete and holding the skinned face of an older white man (representative of the British Raj), while around her neck are the heads of earlier victims (including Adolf Hitler). The flag she holds is the image of Artemisia Gentileschi's *Judith Beheading Holofernes* (*c.*1620), mirroring the actions of this fierce domestic goddess who decapitates men. Biswas painted this while still a student but it shows her coming out swinging, creating a talisman for the strong matriarchal South Asian community she grew up in. 'We are all goddesses,' she says, 'we are all heroines, we are all gods. And our histories can be within our own hands.'[9]

A precursor to Himid's women-only exhibitions was the Caribbean Arts Movement (CAM), which operated from 1966 to 1972. This interdisciplinary group was founded by Caribbean writers; the artists in it included Ronald Moody, Aubrey Williams and Paul Dash (born 1946) as well as the designer Althea McNish. Despite its non-visual bias – it focused largely on literature and music – the group was important for presenting a shared sense of belonging and engaging with Caribbean history in an unwelcome climate.

A decade later and the efforts of Himid in London were matched by a group of Black artists from the West Midlands who launched the first National Black Art Convention in 1982. They were known as the

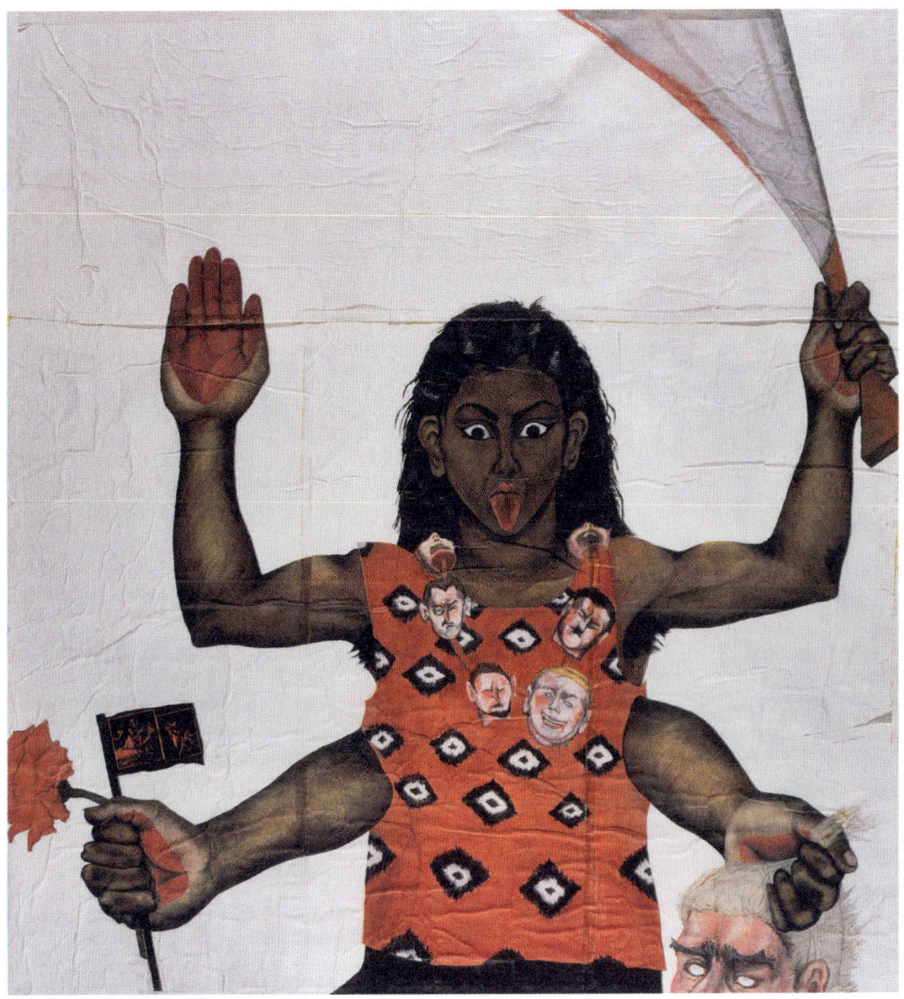

Sutapa Biswas, *Housewives with Steak-Knives*, acrylic, pastel and Xerox collage on paper mounted on canvas, 1985

Blk Art Group and included Keith Piper (born 1960), Eddie Chambers (born 1960) and Donald Rodney (1961–1998), who had all met at Nottingham's Trent Polytechnic, as well as Himid, Boyce, Johnson and Maud Sulter (1960–2008). Stuart Hall was their inspiration and champion. He advocated a multicultural approach to British identity, one that was alive and mutable, not stagnant and resistant to change. 'We are always in the process of cultural formation', he wrote. 'Culture is not a matter of ontology, of being, but of becoming.'[10] The Blk Art Group was part of the wider Black Arts Movement, an umbrella term for diverse artists who exhibited together and explored race, gender, politics and sexuality against a backdrop of discrimination, high unemployment and institutional racism.

But if many Black and Asian artists actively engaged in a postcolonial exploration of identity and visibility based on their own personal histories, there were others who wanted to be seen first and foremost as modernists. They felt that their paintings and sculptures should be viewed alongside those of their Western counterparts and were frustrated when critics would 'other' them or use derogatory language such as 'derivative' when comparing work. Rasheed Araeen (born 1935) had trained as a civil engineer in Karachi in Pakistan and his geometric abstract sculptures often have complex structural components. He moved to London in 1964 to escape Pakistan's conservative art scene but he found that opportunities for Asian artists such as himself were limited in the UK. He became politically active, joining groups such as Artists for Democracy, and launching journals including *Black Phoenix* and *Third Text*. In 1978 he began working on *The Other Story*, an exhibition that was finally staged eleven years later and toured to the Hayward Gallery in London, Wolverhampton Art Gallery and Manchester City Art Gallery and Cornerhouse.

Araeen's goal was to introduce artists from the Asian, African and Caribbean diasporas into the art-historical story of modernism as equal players. Artists included Shemza and Souza, Bowling and Locke, Araeen and Williams. Only four of the twenty-four artists included were women – Boyce, Himid, Kumiko Shimizu (born 1948) and Mona Hatoum (born 1952) – and criticism was levelled at the show for this. But largely the white male critics of the national press attacked it for its perceived reliance on earlier Western models. Andrew Graham-Dixon called it 'tame and derivative',[11] while Brian Sewell, writing in the *Sunday Times Magazine*, said 'Afro-Asian' artists in the West were 'no more than a curiosity, not yet worth even a footnote in any history of twentieth-century western art'.[12] These critics didn't grasp that influence worked both ways, and that modernist models exported to British colonies led to new offshoots and developments that in turn fed back into the art system when artists such as Araeen relocated to the UK.

Araeen selected only six individuals from the younger generation of Black and Asian artists working in Britain – four of these were the women listed above. Piper was another. This younger generation understood semiotics and the power of imagery to convey loaded messages. Piper's *Go West Young Man* (1987) comprises fourteen black-and-white panels featuring photographs, illustrations, typography and handwritten accounts. The first panel includes a print of the interior of a slave ship showing hundreds of bodies laid head to toe to maximise capacity. It was originally published in 1788 as part of the abolition movement to show how the Liverpool-registered slave ship *Brooks* treated humans as cattle. In Piper's work the print is surrounded by the phrase 'Go West Young Man', a nineteenth-century rallying cry for the colonisation of America.[13] Piper worked with the tension created between this phrase and this image: the idea of travel as adventure is contradicted by the print of the *Brooks*'s hold. The subsequent panels explore Black masculinity through images of bodybuilders, skull shapes and historical photographs. References to the father emphasise the importance of family history as the brutal history of slavery is evoked by 'the weight of the chain and the whip' and 'we had made the transition from humanity to commodity'.

The Other Story was not the whole story. There was no Black Audio Film Collective, founded by John Akomfrah (born 1957), Lina Gopaul (born 1959) and others. There was no Marlene Smith, no Nina Edge (born 1962), no Rita Keegan (born 1949). Several artists, including Kim Lim, Anish Kapoor (born 1954) and Shirazeh Houshiary (born 1955), refused the invitation to be included, preferring to present their work in exhibitions that did not focus solely on artists from outside 'the West'. Lim believed that 'to participate would be to self-consciously place myself in a situation of "otherness"'.[14] But even with the omissions and refusals it was an assertion of presence, a demand to be heard, and today is seen as a pivotal moment in the history of Black and Asian art in Britain and in postcolonial studies, a form of resistance to the exhibition programmes of major galleries and a protest at the ongoing invisibility of these successful artists in the mainstream media.

THE ONLY GOOD ONE IS A DEAD ONE . . .

Protests can be successful but they can also be deadly. In 1967 the Northern Ireland Civil Rights Association (NICRA), a bipartisan Christian group, was founded to campaign for the rights of Catholics who had been discriminated against. This was the time of the burgeoning civil rights movement in the United States and the campaign for race equality, and Catholics in Protestant-run Northern Ireland wanted to rebalance the status quo. They wanted a fairer voting system and an allocation of housing that wasn't so biased. They wanted the violent 'B-Specials' police unit to be disbanded and to be treated as equals in their own country.

Northern Ireland had been run by Protestant Unionists since the partition of Ireland in 1922. Electoral boundaries had been massaged to ensure Catholics would not receive the majority of the vote; they were therefore kept out of public office and many felt emasculated and frustrated. Marches were planned to protest at the injustice they experienced, and Protestants marched alongside Catholics under a 'Civil Rights Association' banner. But in October 1968 a second march was banned by the government, which claimed that NICRA was really a front for the IRA. When it went ahead the RUC (Royal Ulster Constabulary) used extreme violence to break it up. Seventy-seven people were injured. In January 1969 a civil rights march from Belfast to Derry was attacked as it approached its destination, and RUC officers and B-Specials marauded through Derry's Catholic Bogside area. Residents fought back, declaring the Bogside to be 'Free Derry'. What became known as 'the Troubles', Northern Ireland's thirty-year sectarian war between Unionists (Loyalists) and Nationalists (Republicans), had begun. (Loyalists are Protestant Unionists who believe in using force to preserve the union with Britain. Republicans are Catholic Nationalists who believe in a united Ireland at any cost. They are both subsets of their respective larger groups, but their approach is extremist in that they believe in success at any price.)

Belfast and Derry were at the centre of the violence between government forces, the British army and the Provisional IRA, particularly along fault lines between staunchly Catholic and Protestant areas such as the Falls Road and Shankill in West Belfast. The IRA killed a British soldier in 1971; thousands of suspected IRA volunteers were imprisoned without trial. NICRA organised a peaceful march to protest about the internment on 30 January 1972, a day now known as Bloody Sunday, after British paratroopers opened fire, killing thirteen.

By 1980 those imprisoned went on hunger strike, led by the IRA member Bobby Sands (who, while incarcerated, had recently been elected to Westminster as an MP). He was the first of ten men to die in the Maze prison near Belfast. This sparked a proliferation of public protest art, the largest ever seen in the British Isles, as thousands of political murals appeared across Northern Ireland.

Unionist and Loyalist areas in Belfast had hosted murals since 1908, painted to mark the anniversary of the Battle of the Boyne or to celebrate the British royal family.[15] But it wasn't until the hunger strikes that Nationalists and Republicans realised the power of using the sides of houses and shops for political expression. Murals could be seen by those who drove or walked by and were clustered in contested areas where their visibility maximised their impact. They were rarely painted by professional artists and remained largely anonymous, painted from within the communities in which they were located, reinforcing sectarian differences or commemorating the fallen. A 1981 mural on the Donegall

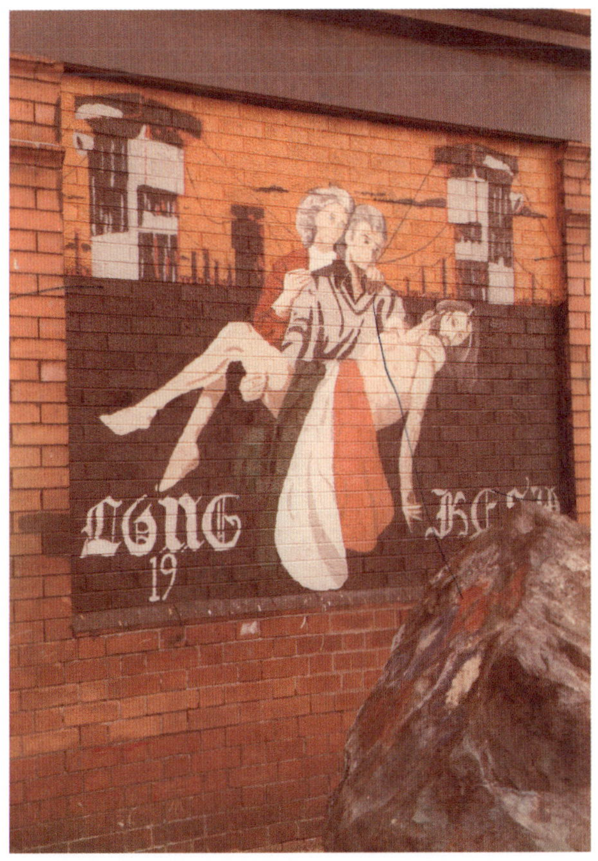

Mural of dead hunger striker Bobby Sands, photographed on Donegall Road, Belfast in 1981

Road in Belfast showed Bobby Sands being carried from the Maze prison at Long Kesh like Christ in the Deposition. The national flag of Ireland was draped over his naked body like a loincloth as prison watchtowers kept up their unrelenting surveillance behind him. Another mural from the same year depicted two paramilitaries loading a rocket launcher under the headline 'Victory to the IRA'.[16] The Loyalists of Shankill retaliated with murals such as a 1984 example that featured an armed UVF (Ulster Volunteer Force) militiaman in a balaclava, carrying an automatic rifle, under the banner 'This is Loyalist West Belfast / Shankill / No Surrender'.[17] In Derry early Nationalist murals similarly showed men aiming guns to the sky in a salute against a fiery phoenix backdrop, suggesting a united Ireland was ready to rise from the flames.[18]

The murals painted during the Troubles sat at the heart of the communities who experienced the ongoing war on a personal level. Many artists lived in these areas, such as Gladys Maccabe (1918–2018). She was known for her paintings of everyday life but as the violence escalated her subject matter became darker, as in *After a Car Bomb Explosion – Ulster Village* (1973). In *Funeral of a Victim* (1969) a group of anonymous mourners walks behind a hearse. It is a bleak scene – the trees are leafless and the sky heavy and grey. The only chink of colour is the flower display on the car's roof. Catherine McWilliams (born 1940) similarly painted scenes of the Troubles. Neither was a political painter, but they couldn't ignore the changes they witnessed in their communities. In 1975 McWilliams painted *Sunday, Tied-Up Swings*. To protect the sanctity of the Sabbath, Belfast was known for closing down all its leisure options, from pubs and cinemas to playgrounds. In this painting the children's swings are tied up, out of use for the day. Our eye, however, is drawn beyond them to the Nationalist graffiti that reads 'IRA Provisionals', written in large white capital letters against a flame-red wall under a burning orange sky.

Other artists responded to events whose aftershocks could be felt on an international level. F.E. McWilliam, whose *Princess Macha* we celebrated in Chapter 14, was not a political artist but the IRA bombing of the Abercorn cafe in Belfast on a Saturday afternoon in March 1972 led him to create a body of work shaped by the deaths of two women inside the cafe. His *Women of Belfast* (1972–3) is a series of violently dynamic bronze sculptures of women with their arms and legs outstretched, as if thrown backwards by an explosion. I first saw these at the F.E. McWilliam Gallery and Studio in Banbridge, County Down, the artist's home town and itself subject to a major IRA attack in 1998.

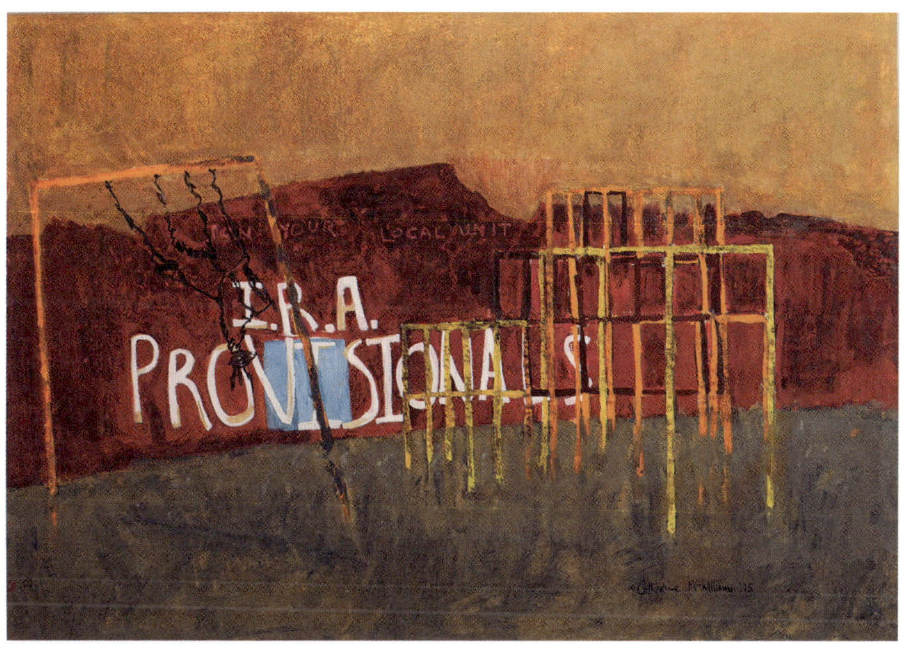

Catherine McWilliams, *Sunday, Tied-Up Swings*, acrylic on paper, 1975

Their limbs are spiky like flying shards of glass and their clothes have crumpled like twisted metal. Their faces have been blanked out, covered by flying debris that makes the women anonymous, representative of all caught up in sectarian violence.

All three of these artists were born in Northern Ireland. But what was the view from Ireland? The conflict was often coded as binary, but the real problem was prejudice on all sides. The Irish poet Seamus Heaney encapsulated this in his poem 'Whatever You Say, Say Nothing':

'Religion's never mentioned here,' of course.
'You know them by their eyes,' and hold your tongue.
'One side's as bad as the other,' never worse.[19]

This poem was inspired by an English journalist he met who was trying to understand 'the Irish thing'. Heaney contrasts the media's incendiary language of 'hate' and 'polarization' – the war seen from the outside – with his experience of living through it. The Irish 'thing' was one of 'Manoeuvrings to find out name and school, / Subtle discrimination by addresses', where 'whatever you say, you say nothing' and where daily life now included passing internment camps, bomb craters and machine-gun posts.

In 1972 the Irish Exhibition of Living Art (IELA) committee held *Living Art* at the Project Arts Centre in Dublin. The IELA had been set up by Mainie Jellett and others in 1943 to support abstract and avant-garde art. Exhibitions were held each year and in 1972 artists included Brian O'Doherty (1928–2022), Robert Ballagh (born 1943) and Les Levine (born 1935), all of whom had been born in Dublin, and all of whom made work in response to the Troubles.

Living Art was held ten months after Bloody Sunday and Ballagh's contribution was visceral. He chalked the outlines of thirteen figures onto the gallery floor, pouring blood into them. Thirteen people had died in Bloody Sunday and Ballagh employed the tools of policing – white outlines demarcating bodies in a murder scene – to evoke the brutality of the attack. Chalking them on the floor of a gallery made them vulnerable; over time, the figures were walked upon and destroyed, referencing how those lives were lost and gone. A print made by Ballagh four years later offers an echo of the installation and still invokes a powerful physical response. Gritty sand forms a ground that stretches across the paper apart from the outline of the figure, arm raised in defence, legs bent where they fell. A viscous red liquid appears to spill

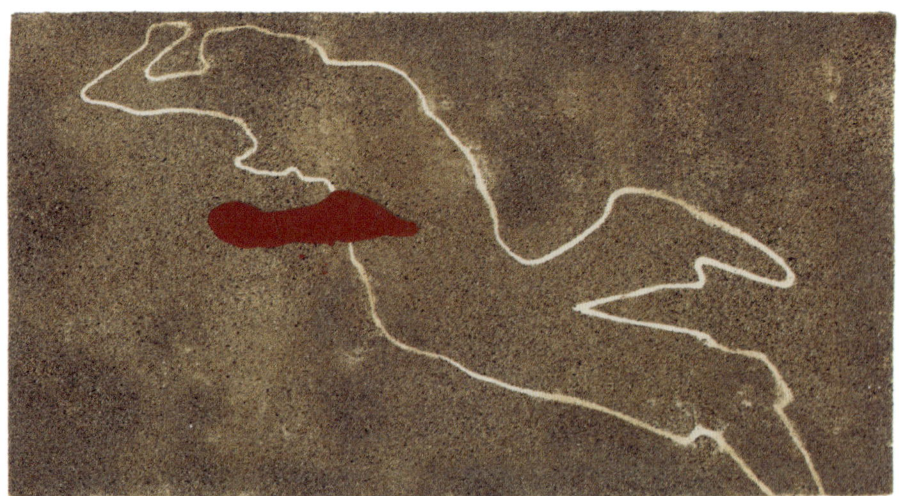

Robert Ballagh, *Northern Ireland: The 1,500th Victim*, print with incised sand surface and wax, 1976

from the body, pooling on the ground around waist height like blood from a bullet wound.

Artists living and working in Northern Ireland and the Republic of Ireland experienced bombings, arrests, internments, deaths, riots, raids, searches and surveillance as part of everyday life. The Troubles lasted nearly thirty years and fed into the work of artists as diverse as the Belfast-born figurative painter Rita Duffy (born 1959) and the Derry sculptor Locky Morris (born 1960) in the 1980s. Paul Seawright (born 1965) and Willie Doherty (born 1959) used photography to address the conflicted landscape where wire barriers, concrete roadblocks, cages and walls severed communities.

Doherty was born in Derry and represents the Venn diagram complexity that is Northern Ireland. Those born in the North can claim citizenship of both the UK and Ireland, and Doherty has represented Ireland in international art exhibitions. In 1994 he was also nominated for the British Turner Prize and later represented Britain in the São Paulo Biennial. As a thirteen-year-old he witnessed Bloody Sunday and it gave him a lifelong distrust of 'truth' because he became acutely aware of the manipulation of words and images. In his early work he married black-and-white photographs of the landscape and urban environment with specific words that influenced the viewer's reading of it, such as *Protecting/Invading* (1987). A view of a country lane seemed pastoral and timeless with the word 'protecting' printed on it, but a view through a hedgerow to a town across a valley became threatening because of the word 'invading', as if you were looking through the binoculars of a paratrooper or IRA operative.

His two-screen video installation *The Only Good One Is a Dead One . . .* (1994) uses narration to alter your emotions, turning you from attacker to victim as the film tracks the same stretch of country road through a car window at night. Doherty doesn't allow you to occupy one side or the other of a divide – you see things from both perspectives and have to navigate the complexity for yourself. Doherty's work was informed by his personal experience of the Troubles, but because of his choice of words and images it can always be read more generally, as relating to all conflict.

Doherty's photographs and films are professionally staged and reframe the personal as universal in a way that speaks to people across the world. The deeply political murals in Derry were originally the opposite: homemade, site-specific and burning with a partisan position.

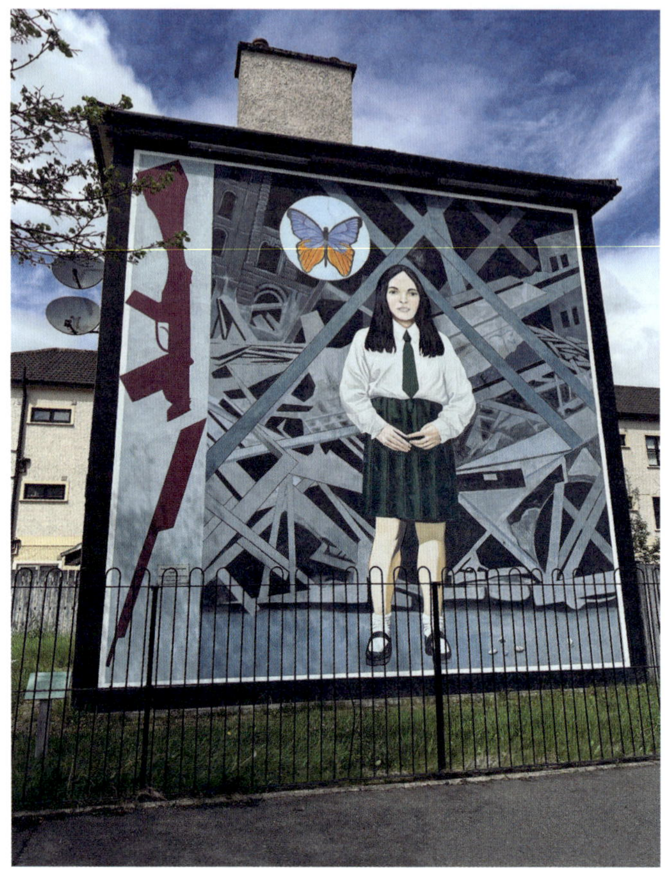

William and Tom Kelly and Kevin Hasson, *Annette* mural from
The People's Gallery, Bogside, Derry, 1994–2008

But today they form part of the city's heritage, with those who grew
up in the Bogside employed as tour guides. Twelve house-sized murals
tell the story of the Troubles from the civil rights protests to Bloody
Sunday, police brutality and hunger strikes. Known as *The People's
Gallery*, this mural cycle ends with negotiations for the Good Friday
Agreement, which came into place in 1998, and a large painting of a
dove, known as the peace mural. The cycle was painted by Bogside
artists between 1994 and 2008 and offers a counterpoint to the violent
and aggressive paintings of the 1980s, many of which have subsequently
been painted over.

The People's Gallery reframes the city's past, including scenes that
reflect violence and resistance but with no visible armed militia or

loaded weapons. Following the Good Friday Agreement, the giant gun in the mural *Annette* – depicting a schoolgirl who was caught in crossfire – was repainted, symbolically broken in two. The co-founders of the anti-sectarian SDLP, John Hume and Ivan Cooper, were added to the *Civil Rights* mural in 2015.

When I toured the walls in 2023 my guide, Gleann Doherty, talked with pride of the city's Peace Bridge, completed in 2011, and showed me the commemorative plaque that stands alongside the 'You are now entering Free Derry' wall. Doherty has a degree in Irish history and his tour ended at the memorial to Bloody Sunday. His father was the twelfth man killed on that day, when Gleann was just a young boy, and I can see his name carved into the stone. You feel the undertow of Northern Ireland's brutal history rising up as you notice that the spotlights surrounding the monument occupy metal cages for protection. And when I looked at my photographs later I noticed that under the 'Free Derry' message is another, fainter one. I had thought it white-washed over during the tour, but looking again I saw that some of the letters had been repainted. They are white on white, a ghostly rebirth for the statement 'GFA 25 – Partition is Injustice'.[20]

In Belfast, on a similar tour, there are still a lot of Bobby Sands murals but now he is as likely to appear campaigning for Ireland's union as he is as a Christ-like martyr. The mural walls on the Falls Road are now a tourist spot. Tours are conducted in the black cabs that used to be the only mode of transport when the buses stopped running following riots during the height of the conflict. Since the Good Friday Agreement, murals have been repainted to remove the giant skeletons that held machine guns and the armed paramilitaries in favour of a shared history.

On the other side of the 'Peace Wall', through gates that are still locked at night, is the Shankill Road, the heartland of Loyalists. My tour took place just five days after King Charles III's coronation but already there was a huge new mural featuring his portrait and the words 'God Save the King'. It was hard for me to see it because of all the red, white and blue bunting and Union flags strung the length of the road, way more than I have ever seen in mainland Britain. My (Catholic) tour guide, Patrick who also drove the taxi, said he wouldn't stop on the Shankill Road and pulled over instead on the Catholic side of the 'Peace Wall', a 10-metre-high metal fence that still occupies sections of Belfast, dividing Catholics from Protestants, Nationalists from Unionists, Republicans from Loyalists. During the tour we saw holes in buildings from sniper fire during the Troubles, rubber bullets the size of bricks and back yards that remain caged because of missiles periodically thrown over the wall to this day. The peace that holds out feels fragile, something constantly in a state of becoming or unravelling, depending on your perspective. Heaney's words still reverberate: 'O land of password, handgrip, wink and nod / Of open minds as open as a trap'.[21]

17

COOL BRITANNIA?
1980–2025

IN SPRING 1981 the American art critic Douglas Crimp declared 'The End of Painting'. He believed it had painted itself into a cul-de-sac from which there was no escape. The Pop artists of the 1960s had broken down boundaries between traditional 'high' art and popular culture. With the rise of conceptual and lens-based art in the 1970s time could now be folded into a video or a performance, something Crimp believed painting could never match. Conceptual artists even questioned the role of the artist as creator. What was left for painting but to accept its 'terminal condition', something that now seemed 'impossible to ignore'?[1]

This type of academic posturing took place on both sides of the Atlantic as writers and theorists struggled to keep up with the ever-widening field of art-making. Wrapping your head around art after 1970 was like trying to comprehend the big bang, with art expanding outwards with no visible borders at an unprecedented rate of change. Curators drew lines in the sand, trying to make sense of it all. In the same spring that Crimp declared painting dead, three Europeans – Christos M. Joachimides, Nicholas Serota and Norman Rosenthal – staged an ambitious exhibition at the Royal Academy in London. They called it *A New Spirit in Painting* and it featured thirty-eight artists, largely drawn from Germany, Britain, the United States and Italy. Picasso and Warhol were represented alongside Bacon, Hockney and Freud, and the show was dominated by the neo-Expressionism of the German painters Georg Baselitz and Anselm Kiefer. It was not without its critics, who lamented the exclusion of artists such as Karel Appel and Richard Diebenkorn.[2] But the organisers argued that this selection revealed how 'the creative imagination' had now replaced the 'puritan [conceptual] approach devoid of all joy in the senses'.[3] In the catalogue essay Joachimides confirmed: 'The new spirit in painting is one which has swept aside unnecessary convention to establish a new relationship between image and reality through a painting of intense poetic force and piercing imagination.'[4]

Looking at the roll call of names in this exhibition today, there are glaring omissions. Where is Bowling or Williams or Souza? And where are all the women? The exhibition's organisers didn't frame this as a man-only show, and reviewers didn't criticise it for its monoculture. Despite all the inroads made by women artists and Black and Asian artists in the 1970s, this show was curated as if they didn't exist. Why not show Blow's hefty abstracts or Barns-Graham's vortexed landscapes? The exhibition included freighted history paintings by Kiefer and Malcolm Morley (1931–2018) but nothing by Boyce or Himid. Howard Hodgkin (1932–2017) was represented by four paintings of remembered people and places including *Portrait of Terence McInerney II* (1980) but there was nothing by his contemporary Gillian Ayres (1930–2018), whose abstracts such as *Mons Graupius* (1979–80) employed a similar range of motifs. Energetic portraits by Maggi Hambling (born 1945) did not sit next to those by Freud, and distilled urban landscapes by Prunella Clough (1919–1999) did not form a counterpoint to Hockney's saturated California panorama *Mulholland Drive* (1980).

It is easy to criticise an exhibition with hindsight, but these blinding omissions do help us to understand how frustrating it must have been if you were not part of the white art-world patriarchy. By 1981 a woman could be prime minister, so it seems preposterous that not one woman artist was considered suitable for this exhibition. Following a decade of feminism and the collective voices of organisations such as the Caribbean Arts Movement, this purposeful selection of artists strives to assert that painting – what the catalogue described as the 'oldest form' of art – is only produced by artists who are overwhelmingly white and male. Yes, many feminist artists had turned their back on this traditional method of making art (specifically because of its association with male-dominated histories). But there were those who still believed in its power, such as Paula Rego (1935–2022), Rose Wylie (born 1934), Thérèse Oulton (born 1953) and Celia Paul. It is their work that convinces us that painting in the British Isles was anything but dead in the 1980s.

THE POWER OF PAINTING

Rego was born in Portugal but studied at the Slade and returned to London in 1974, where she lived and worked for nearly fifty years. Her early paintings featured cartoon-style animals playing out human roles, beating their loved ones or telling their parents they were pregnant. There was a dark edge to her paintings, a sense of foreboding, a threat

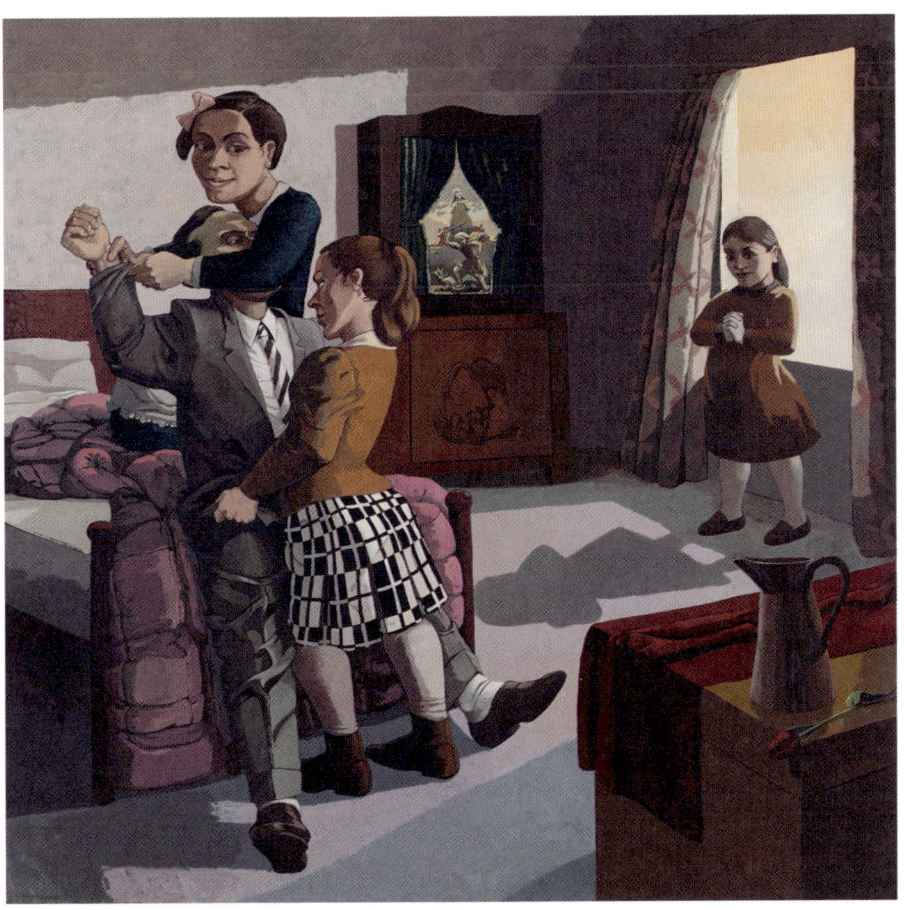

Paula Rego, *The Family*, acrylic on paper on canvas, 1988

of sexual violence, of secrets kept. She started to paint young women and they in turn began to take their revenge. In *The Family* (1988), a man is pinned to the edge of a single bed. He is gagged by the close proximity of one woman's arm while another woman stands between his legs, tugging at his suit. She threatens him despite her diminutive size – we can see the whites of his eyes and his legs are rigid with fear. A third woman, framed by the window, flexes her knuckles in both prayer and anticipation, catching our eye knowingly as she watches on.

Oulton meanwhile graduated from the RCA in 1983 and within a year had held her first solo exhibition, *Fool's Gold*. There's a soaring drama to her early works: crests of paint swell like a storm surge and walls of paint emerge from the distant past. They are suggestive of vast spaces yet her brushstrokes simultaneously dance across the surface. Within three years Oulton had been nominated for the Turner Prize, established in 1984 by the Patrons of New Art at the Tate Gallery with the objective to raise the profile of contemporary art in the UK.

The Turner Prize awards ceremony was televised and millions tuned in to watch the announcement of the first winner, the painter Malcolm Morley. There was no female winner in the 1980s, and whole groups of artists were again overlooked.[5] Painting dominated the prize initially, but in 1987 there was a change of heart. Oulton, one of two women on the six-strong shortlist alongside Chadwick, lost out to the young sculptor Richard Deacon (born 1949). Sculpture would go on to become the prize's default setting for nearly a decade.

THE RETURN OF MATERIALITY

Deacon, Alison Wilding (born 1948), Bill Woodrow (born 1948), Tony Cragg (born 1949), Kapoor, Houshiary and Antony Gormley (born 1950) are all associated with New British Sculpture, a reawakening of the medium after the visual reduction of conceptual art in the 1970s. Many of these artists showed at the Lisson Gallery in London – only Wilding and Gormley did not – but they were not a tight unit. Rather, they shared a growing interest in a return to materiality and making objects. Deacon created organic constructions from bent plywood and rivets with poetic sensory titles such as *For Those Who Have Ears #2*

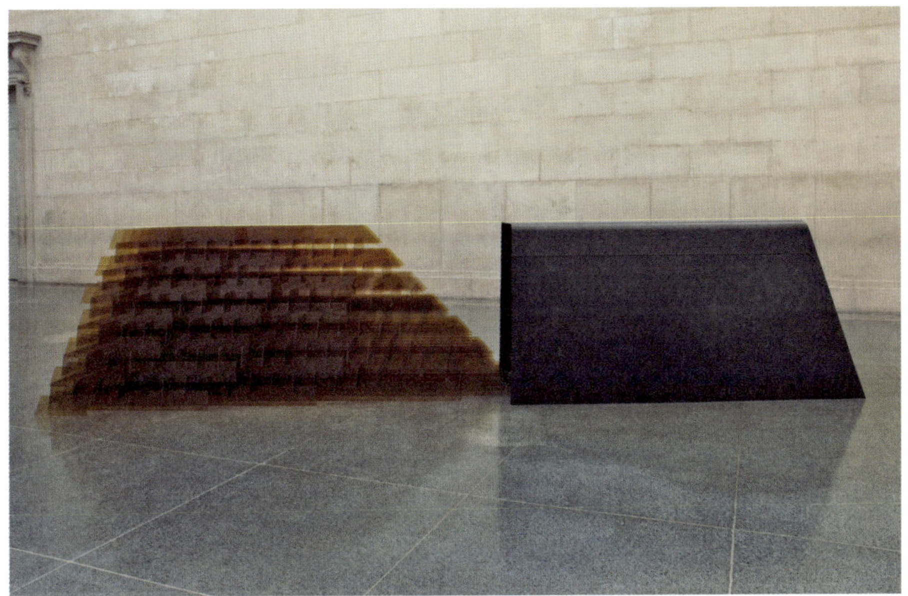

Alison Wilding, *Assembly*, powder-coated steel and PVC, 1991

(1983) and *Double Talk* (1987) while Houshiary welded zinc seams and coaxed plywood panels into complex points in *The Earth Is an Angel* (1987). Wilding investigated the relationship between materials, often pitting plastic sheeting against steel, as in *Assembly* (1991), using a flexible or organic material juxtaposed with a cool industrial one. Although they are largely abstract, her sculptures often feel bodily on a material level. Forms encircle each other, offering recesses and entry points, or work in pairs as if they are two bodies in space. They occupy our world (no plinths for any of these artists) and ask us to relate to them.

Other artists associated with the group used very untraditional materials. Cragg collected plastic detritus for his *Britain Seen from the North* (1981) and Woodrow cut up domestic appliances, transforming them into a guitar, a bicycle frame, a giraffe. Gormley made his earliest sculptures out of white bread, eating the shape of his body from a bed-sized block of slices to create a yeasty double sarcophagus in *Bed* (1981). Kapoor worked in pure pigment, initially shaking red, black and yellow powder over abstract geometric forms as in *White Sand, Red Millet, Many Flowers* (1982). He explored spirituality and belief by using pigment to transform these forms into weightless beings sprouting from the floor like temples of the mind. He began sinking holes into walls, floors and rocks, covering the interiors in dense black pigment that reflected nothing, leading the viewer to feel like they were contemplating infinite voids.

These artists showed in commercial galleries in London (mostly at the Lisson) but were also quick to receive exhibitions at the ICA and Serpentine Gallery. By 1982 they were showing abroad, first in Europe and then as far afield as the São Paulo Biennial and the Art Gallery of New South Wales in Sydney. In 1984 Kapoor, Deacon, Cragg and Woodrow were included in an exhibition at the Museum of Modern Art in New York; in 1987 Wilding had her first international solo show there. This level of success for a group of artists who were all in their late twenties and early thirties was unparalleled. It also laid the foundations for an even larger international phenomenon that was centred on the British Isles – the rise of the Young British Artists, or YBAs.

FREEZE FRAME

Richard Wentworth (born 1947) and Julian Opie (born 1958) were associated with New British Sculpture and showed at the Lisson, but in many ways their work feels connected to what came next. Opie had his first solo show in 1982, the year he graduated. His early sculptural works were simulacra of reality – an air vent, a stack of paintings – and he reduced buildings and cars to blocky forms like early computer graphics. Wentworth was a decade older and had taught Opie at Goldsmiths' College in London. He converted found objects into surreal sculptures by filling wellington boots with concrete (*Guide*, 1984) and floating a sardine tin in a steel bath (*Toy*, 1983). His ongoing series, *Making Do and Getting By*, looks at how we adapt objects to suit our needs. He photographed chance encounters he happened upon: chairs, cups and shoes holding open windows and doors; plates stacked in a grate as if on a draining board; a bollard engulfed in hoardings. Wentworth's irreverent mix of sculptural materiality and conceptual wit, and Opie's bold questioning of reality, were to inspire the YBA generation, who became known for their punchy one-liners and offbeat humour.

Wentworth taught at Goldsmiths from 1971 to 1988, alongside Michael Craig-Martin. Head of the art department was Jon Thompson (1936–2016), whom Craig-Martin described as 'a visionary and radical educationalist'.[6] Thompson allowed students to work in different media, rather than in the painting *or* sculpture school, and mixed up the year groups. Craig-Martin and Wentworth were successful practising artists and inspired their students to act professionally and make an impact. As Lisson had been intrinsic to New British Sculpture, Goldsmiths now became the breeding ground of the YBAs.

There's a photograph of Goldsmiths students from 1988. They are standing behind a table set with wine glasses on a sunny evening in August at the private view of the exhibition *Freeze*. Ian Davenport (born 1966) wears braces and a tie; Fiona Rae (born 1963) smiles in shades. Sarah Lucas (born 1962), Anya Gallaccio (born 1963) and Gary Hume (born 1962) look like they are sharing a joke. Only the man standing behind Davenport looks nervous, unsmiling. He is the curator of the exhibition, held in the derelict Port of London Authority Building in Rotherhithe facing what would become Canary Wharf, the legacy of Thatcher's capitalist dream. Sixteen artists exhibited in *Freeze*, all of them students. The curator's own work – coloured cardboard boxes fixed high up on a wall and a spotty mural – did not overwhelm, but his ambition, chutzpah and ability to stage the impossible couldn't

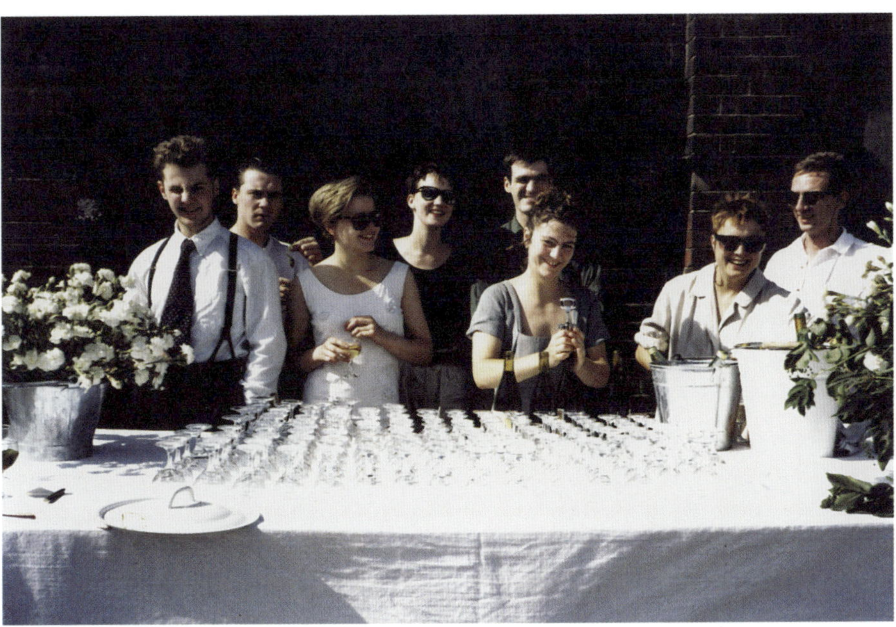

Participants in *Freeze*, 1988

fail to. For the curator was Damien Hirst (born 1965), ringmaster of the YBA generation.

Many of the artists who were in *Freeze* are now household names. Other artists quickly became associated with the movement as they graduated from different art colleges: Tracey Emin (born 1963), Rachel Whiteread (born 1963), Jake (born 1966) and Dinos Chapman (born 1962). Their early art could be deeply personal. Emin stitched the names of all the people she had shared a bed with on the walls of a tent in *Everyone I Have Ever Slept With 1963–1995* (1995). Gillian Wearing (born 1963) asked strangers to reveal their inner thoughts by writing them down on sheets of paper in marker pen so she could photograph them: a yuppie with quiff and tie wrote 'I'm Desperate'; a windswept bespectacled man held up 'Everything is connected in life, the point is to know it and understand it'.[7]

Much of the art by the YBAs was big and bold and brash. Hirst made giant tanks for colonies of flies and rooms filled with butterflies; Hume painted life-size hospital doors in household gloss paint; Lucas recreated body parts using fried eggs, doner kebabs, melons and cucumbers. The Chapman brothers turned shop mannequins into disquieting conjoined sculptures with penises for noses and anuses for mouths. Gallaccio created walls of freshly cut gerberas that putrefied, splattering the floor with organic waste, and Marc Quinn (born 1964) confronted death by turning ten pints of his own blood (the average amount contained in a body) into a frozen bust of his own head. Douglas Gordon (born 1966) slowed down Hitchcock's *Psycho* so it lasted twenty-four hours (the knife attack in the shower now stretched to ten grisly minutes). YBA art was front-page news, in Britain and overseas, and exhibitions supported by the British Council toured the world. Alongside the music rivalry of Oasis versus Blur, this group of artists was a fundamental part of making the British Isles 'Cool Britannia' for much of the 1990s.

At times YBA art became a matter for national debate, as with Whiteread's *House* (1993). Shortly after graduating from the Slade in 1987, Whiteread cast the inside of a hot-water bottle, pouring plaster down its neck then peeling away the rubber mould to leave a softly contoured shape reminiscent of a small body. Progressing to domestic furniture such as wardrobes, baths and chairs, she cast the space inside and under them, using the imperfections of the original to convey ideas of time passing and memories imprinted in the finished casts. In 1990 she created a plaster model of the inside of a front room much like the one she had grown up with in North London. By using the room as a mould everything was inverted. Light switches now sank into the wall but the fireplace bulged out, sooty residue dirtying the white plaster. She presented these panels turned outwards, recreating the size of the room but showing us the space in which memories were created, the lived space of home.

Working with the ambitious art facilitators Artangel, Whiteread took this a step further in 1993 by casting an entire house in concrete. For nearly three months *House* stood on a patch of scrubland that had once formed a terraced street in the East End of London.

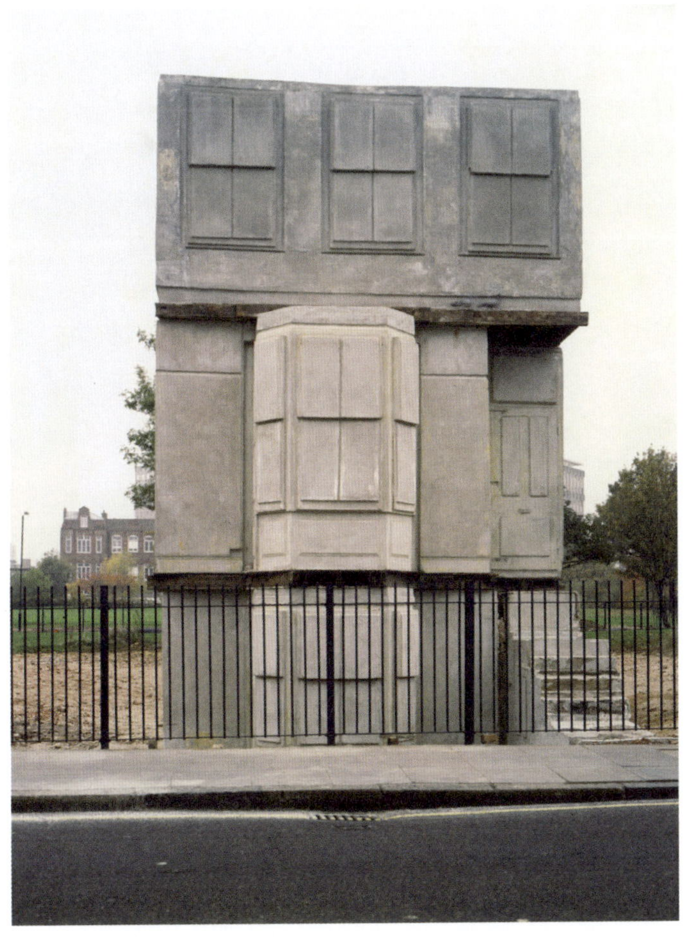

Rachel Whiteread, *House*, concrete cast, 1993

The space inside each room had been solidified, a tomb to memory, the windows now blank unseeing eyes. It was an echo of a home, an uncanny doppelgänger that stood mute and blinded as a media war raged around it. Many visitors wanted it to stay forever; others saw it as an eyesore. 'If this is art then I'm Leonardo da Vinci', railed the *East End Advertiser*.[8] It was bulldozed in January 1994 and, fittingly enough, now exists only as a memory.

Quite a few artworks pressed people's buttons in a polarising way. *The Holy Virgin Mary* (1996) by Chris Ofili (born 1968) had been exhibited in Britain without incident but when it was shown at the Brooklyn Museum in New York in 1999, it swiftly became caught up

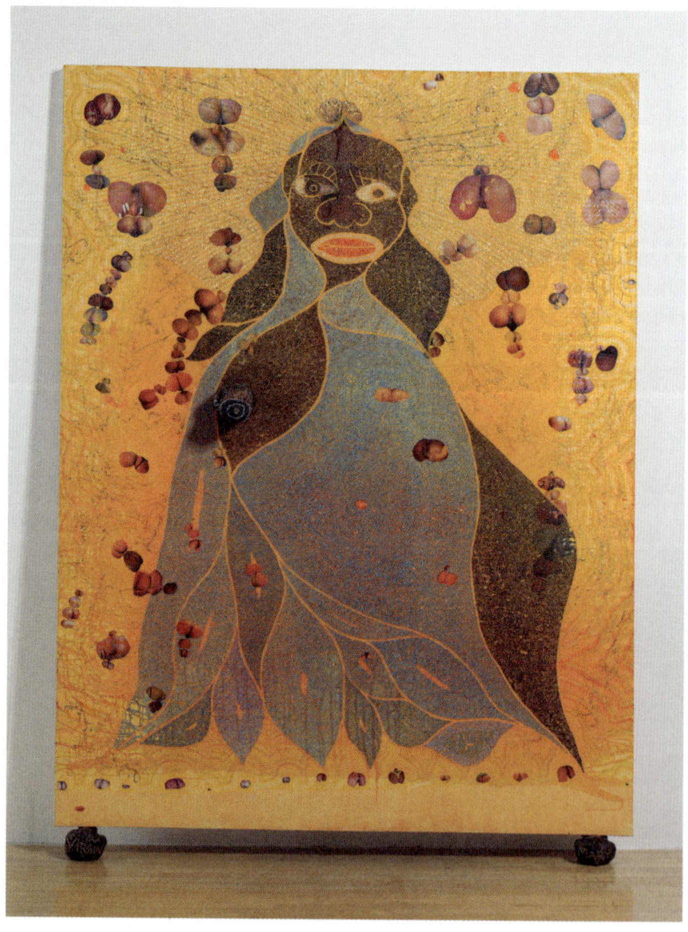

Chris Ofili, *The Holy Virgin Mary*, acrylic, oil, polyester resin, paper collage, glitter, map pins and elephant dung on linen, 1996

in a political row regarding the perceived desecration of religion. This led to the museum being threatened with the withdrawal of public funding and even closure by the conservative mayor Rudy Giuliani (who was trying to appease his Catholic voters). Ofili's rich yellow-orange painting, covered in resin and glitter, is nearly 2.5 metres tall. It sits on two balls of varnished elephant dung with a further ball attached where the Virgin Mary's breast would be. She is dressed in the blue robes of history and looks straight at us, her black face surrounded by a constellation of black bottoms like winged putti (cherubs) but cut from porn magazines.

In Britain the 1990s YBA scene was supported by dealers such as Karsten Schubert and Jay Jopling (and his gallery White Cube), and by curators including Iwona Blazwick, Julia Peyton-Jones and Ann Gallagher. But the conflation of Hirst's ambition and the collector Charles Saatchi's deep pockets led to some of the most iconic works. The Saatchi Gallery was originally located in Boundary Road in St John's Wood, London, and was a temple to contemporary art. It opened in 1985, originally showcasing Saatchi's collection of American Minimalism, and its vast warehouse-scale spaces and sleek lines were like nothing else in London at that time. It was here that Hirst's pickled tiger shark (funded by Saatchi) was first presented. It greeted visitors with a toothy smile and a cod-philosophical title: *The Physical Impossibility of Death in the Mind of Someone Living* (1991). Saatchi would buy entire bodies of work by YBAs and he was an intoxicating if elusive figure, notoriously not attending his own private views or giving interviews.

Just nine years after *Freeze*, Saatchi's collection was exhibited as *Sensation* at the Royal Academy. Billed as the 'first definitive survey' of YBA work, it included forty-four artists who ranged from the figurative painter Jenny Saville (born 1970) and hyperrealist sculptor Ron Mueck (born 1958) to the conceptual jester Gavin Turk (born 1967) and video artist Sam Taylor-Wood (now Taylor-Johnson; born 1967). There was work by Ofili (including *The Holy Virgin Mary*), Whiteread, Hirst and Emin. There was no coherent centre to the movement, or even a shared set of values; there was just an all-encompassing confidence that their art mattered. I remember that at the time this show felt like equality – there was work by women and men, Black and white, side by side. Artists were not talked about because of their gender or ethnicity but because their work was sensational. But let's drill down into the list of exhibiting artists a little. Of the forty-four artists exhibiting, eleven were women.[9] One-quarter. Equality? No. But an improvement on Britain's history of showing women artists in major galleries? Definitely.

Mona Hatoum was one of the eleven women in *Sensation*, but I wouldn't categorise her as a YBA. She is a decade older than most of them, and exhibited alongside artists such as Cornelia Parker (born 1956) and those associated with New British Sculpture in the 1980s. Her works are complex, probing and thought-provoking, often invoking feelings of unease, as in *Incommunicado* (1993), where the bars of a cot bed have been replaced with cheese wires. Hatoum was born into a Palestinian family living in Beirut but has spent her adult life in Britain. Her work often suggests displacement and discomfort rooted in bodily experience and her earliest works were performances, such as *Roadworks* (1985). For this she tied black Dr Martens to her ankles and walked barefoot through the streets of Brixton in London, the boots marching in time behind her like someone was monitoring her, keeping her under surveillance. Brixton, home to a large Afro-Caribbean community, was at the centre of riots in 1985 after a local Black woman was shot by police (as seen in Marlene Smith's *Good Housekeeping I* in the last chapter). Hatoum's work is rooted in the personal but she welcomed this connection to the people who witnessed her performance, who felt that the predatory boots meant she was being followed by the police.

Parker also began exhibiting in the 1980s, exploring how the life and meaning of objects could morph and change. In 1991 she blew up a garden shed, complete with its contents, with the help of the British army. She painstakingly collected the fragments of timber and plastic and reimagined them as a suspended cube for *Cold Dark Matter: An Exploded View*. Lit from within, the remnants of neglected domestic items formed larger-than-life shadows on the walls – the curve of a bicycle seat, the strings of a tennis racquet, the spout of a watering can. Parker wants us to think about residue and loss but also transformation and rebirth, whether she is blowing up a shed, gathering up the waste silver when a name is engraved on a school cup or drawing with a red-hot poker, burning the paper as she goes.

In parallel to the YBAs, artists from the Republic of Ireland and Northern Ireland including Daphne Wright (born 1963), Siobhán Hapaska (born 1963), Kathy Prendergast (born 1958) and Dorothy Cross (born 1956) were also making their voices heard in London.

Their work enjoyed wide exposure in British galleries and Prendergast and Cross also represented Ireland at the Venice Biennale. Prendergast began her *City Drawings* series in 1992 and she exhibited forty-nine of them in Venice in 1995. They are feathery drawings of the world's capital cities, each drawn on the same-sized sheet of paper and completely without textual markers. The cities float like amputated hearts, their roads like trailing veins and arteries. They reduce entire populations to single entities, like networked hives, exploring identity – sameness, difference – on a global level. Cross works at the other end of the spectrum, using deeply personal family objects in her sculptures. In *Virgin Shroud* (1993) a cow hide is draped over her grandmother's satin

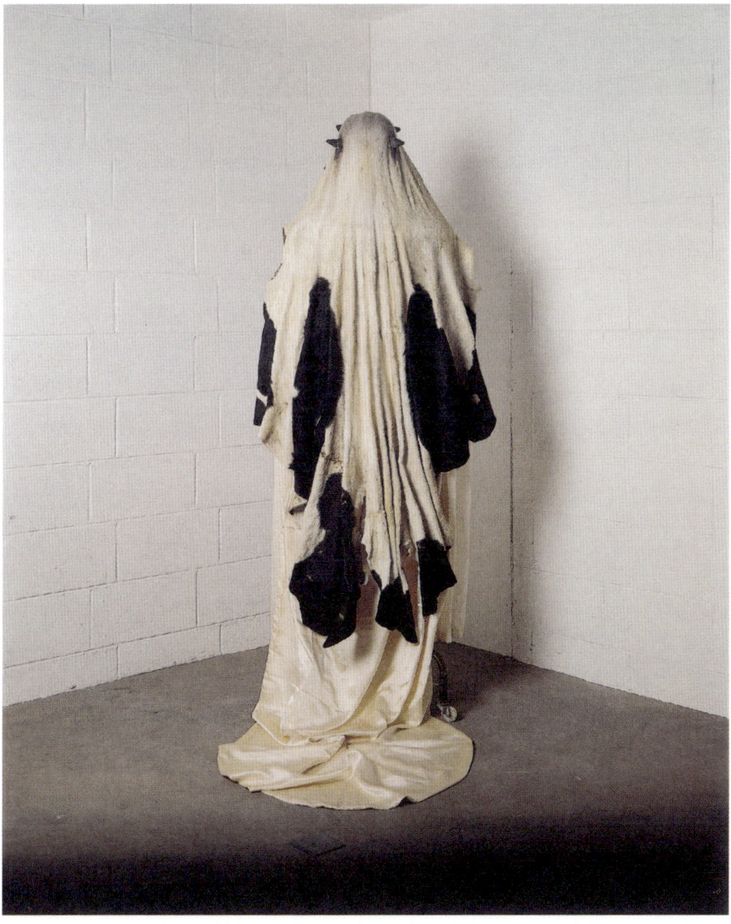

Dorothy Cross, *Virgin Shroud*, cowhide, muslin, satin, wood, plaster and iron, 1993

wedding dress on a mannequin. With the mannequin positioned in the corner of the room we see the back view, as if a person is standing there motionless, awaiting instruction (or punishment). Fertility, ancestry and ritual are stitched together in this intimate work. The cow's teats ring her head like a crown and the hide falls down her back in deep folds, like the drapery on a medieval sculpture of the Virgin.

KNOW YOURSELF

The 1990s was an exciting decade. It felt as if art from the British Isles was at the centre of everything. Exhibitions funded by the British and Irish governments toured overseas while the rapid rise in art biennials meant artists were exposed to the widest international audience possible. By 2000 there were around 300 biennials worldwide, some attracting more than a million visitors each. Often held in industrial spaces or purpose-built exhibition halls, these temporary exhibitions brought together new art from all over the world. Works were commissioned directly by the organisers and artists had to scale up to fill these vast spaces, hence the proliferation of room-sized installations.

In the UK, National Lottery funding led to a flurry of building work, with the New Art Gallery in Walsall opening in 2000 and the Baltic Centre for Contemporary Art in Gateshead in 2002. These purpose-built spaces became part of a growing contemporary art network across the British Isles. They connected with established venues such as the Arnolfini in Bristol and Modern Art Oxford and were augmented by major new museums opening, such as the Irish Museum of Modern Art in Dublin (IMMA) in 1990 and the Gallery of Modern Art (GoMA) in Glasgow in 1996. The Tate Gallery expanded with the opening of Tate Gallery Liverpool (1988), Tate St Ives (1993) and Tate Modern and Tate Britain in London (2000). Open-air venues followed the lead of the Yorkshire Sculpture Park, established in 1977, and sculpture trails opened in the Forest of Dean in 1986 and Castlewellan Forest Park in County Down in 1992.[10]

Contemporary art had also become big business for auction houses and by 2000 more money was spent on contemporary art than on Impressionist paintings at both Christie's and Sotheby's. The year 2000 was also when major foreign gallerists, starting with Larry Gagosian, opened up in London for the first time, joining important

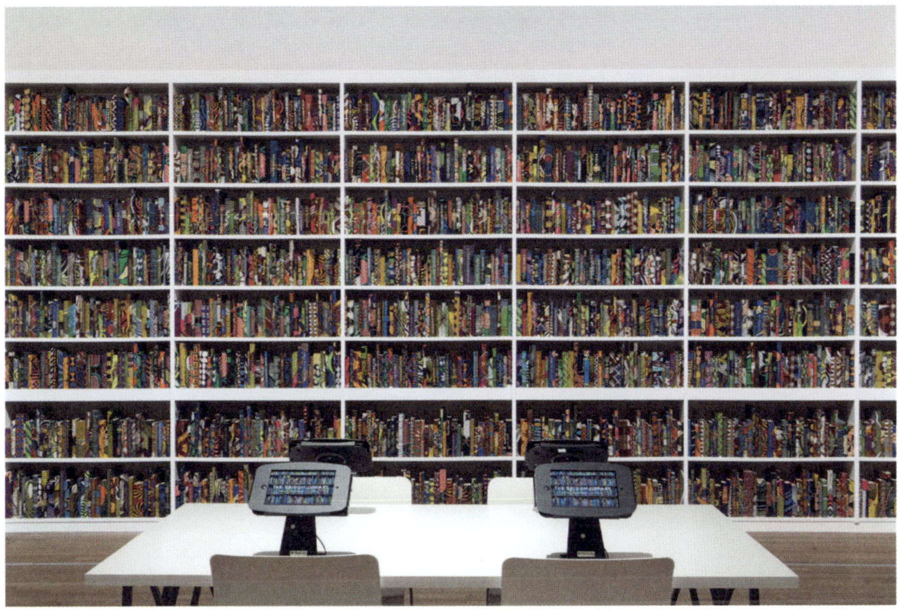

Yinka Shonibare CBE RA, *The British Library*, mixed media installation, 2014

British commercial galleries such as Victoria Miro, White Cube, Lisson, Maureen Paley and Frith Street.

In the twenty-first century, our century, this international network for art has provided a ready-made platform for artists who scrutinise the complexity of identity. Today we celebrate our collective hybridity but, as we have seen, this has not always been the case. Hybridity is something the critical theorist Homi K. Bhabha identifies as challenging the outmoded binary 'us' and 'them'.[11] Instead it offers a third approach, a difference 'within', 'a subject that inhabits the rim of an "in-between" reality'.[12] This is something that a growing number of artists working in the British Isles can identify with. Sometimes born in one country but working in another, or born and working in one country but with cultural heritage from others, artists now feel empowered to use their own stories of hybridity to inform their art.

British Nigerian Yinka Shonibare CBE RA uses batik fabric in all his sculptures, paintings and prints. As a student one of his tutors at Goldsmiths said, 'Why aren't you producing authentic African art?' and he asked, 'Well, what is authentic African art?'[13] He began to consider the question and went to a fabric shop in Brixton in South London. The women running the shop explained to him that batik was an

Indonesian-inspired fabric produced by the Dutch and sold into West Africa. He thought, 'Well, that's more-or-less the identity of a lot of the diaspora, because so many connections make up African identity.'[14] Colourful batik fabric had become popular with the African diaspora in the UK in the 1960s, adopted as a symbol of African allegiance. 'It was a way to show that you're a proud African,' Shonibare notes. 'You are not subject to Western ideas and you have your own independence.'[15] He has subsequently used this material to create colonial-era bustles and frock coats for headless mannequins, to rig HMS *Victory* and the *Mayflower* with batik sails and to cover entire libraries of books.

For *The British Library* (2014; see previous page) Shonibare purchased more than 6,000 second-hand books and wrapped each one in different-coloured batik fabric, creating a new identity for each volume. For him the fabric becomes a leitmotif for everything he wants to say about identity, politics, colonialism and postcolonialism. It represents the complex history of African people and symbolises a new independent future. 'A person from the African diaspora should be free to live anywhere in the world and absorb things in the way that colonial history has, which took in different identities and cultures,' he says.[16] On nearly half the spines are written the names of first- or second-generation British immigrants in gold lettering: writers Zadie Smith and T.S. Eliot; composer George Frideric Handel and singer Alesha Dixon; artists Hans Holbein, Donald Locke, Fiona Rae and Anish Kapoor. There's the actor Helen Mirren, the architect Zaha Hadid, the footballer Didier Drogba, the economist Amartya Sen and the dancer Darcey Bussell. Interspersed are the names of those who have opposed immigration, including Oswald Mosley and Nigel Farage. These provocative inclusions are designed to spark debate, and central to the work's installation is a table with tablets and chairs so people can sit and talk about their own stories of inclusion or exclusion, identity and nationhood.

Library of Exile (2019) by Edmund de Waal (born 1964) considers what it means to be uprooted from one community and establish yourself in another. The titles that once filled De Waal's library – 2,000 volumes written by authors in exile over the last 2,000 years – have now been transferred to the University of Mosul in Iraq, whose own library was obliterated by ISIS in 2014.[17] The inscribed porcelain walls of *Library of Exile* are now permanently sited in the Warburg Institute in London. The Institute's own library lives in exile in London after it was smuggled out of Nazi Germany to protect the

Jewish art historian Aby Warburg's personal collection of books on cultural memory.

Art centred on identity can be complex and expansive, as in the elegiac film *Out of Blue* (2002) by Indian Ugandan Zarina Bhimji (born 1963) who lives in London. It is a love letter to her Ugandan homeland, which she was forced to flee in 1974 following the expulsion of the Asian community by President Idi Amin. It is also a visual diary of the crumbling infrastructure, a metaphor for the regime that became so intolerant. Identity is inflected by race, class and gender, by hybridity and the difference 'within', by persecution and acceptance, making some films centred on identity difficult viewing. One such film is *Electrical Gaza* (2015) by Rosalind Nashashibi (born 1973).

Electrical Gaza was filmed in the weeks leading up to Israel's Operation Protective Edge, a military offensive against Gaza in 2014. Nashashibi presents the charged atmosphere of Gaza, the Palestinian territory bound by heavily guarded borders and the Mediterranean Sea. Nashashibi was born in London to a Palestinian father and Northern Irish mother. She was commissioned to film in Gaza by the Imperial

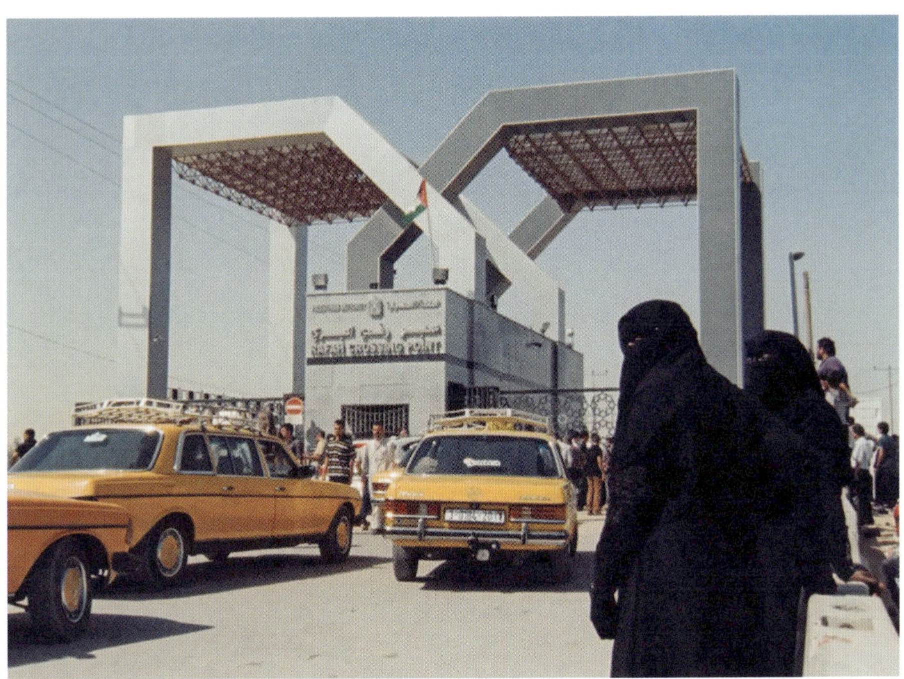

Still from Rosalind Nashashibi, *Electrical Gaza*, 2015

War Museum and it took four years to negotiate access. Using her perspective as an outsider, she filmed from the back of cars and seated in houses she was invited into. The atmosphere was charged, electric, as if Gaza's inhabitants knew an escalation of violence was coming. Within a week she was told to leave by the British consulate, something she felt was 'beyond shameful' because the people she had filmed could not do so.[18] *Electrical Gaza* was edited in the UK as the conflict escalated. She added a black spot that expands to cover a street scene towards the end of the eighteen-minute film to represent the growing threat of future violence.

As an ongoing site of tension and unspeakable violence, Gaza has been documented by many photojournalists and film crews. Nashashibi wanted to offer a view of life under siege, of boys cooling horses down in the sea, of women comforting children at home, of men singing together. Intercut with scenes of the closed gate at Rafah, the border between Gaza and Egypt, these domestic scenes heightened the sense of what was to be lost if the violence returned.[19] Sometimes people ask what art can bring to conflicts that are so heavily documented by the media. The answer is provided by films such as *Electrical Gaza*, ones that offer a sense of interwoven cultures presented in a moving and complex framework that allows for multiple viewings and readings. The viewer's own identity and experience also come to bear on films like these, as in Bhimji's *Out of Blue*.

Like Nashashibi, Hetain Patel (born 1980) was born in Britain but reflects on his cultural hybridity by making art centred on his Indian Gujarati heritage. His film *Trinity* (2021) was included in the *British Art Show 9*, which toured the UK throughout 2021 and 2022. Filmed like a Hollywood movie, *Trinity* explores language, communication and the different expectations for Indian women across the generations. Two women – one deaf, one wearing headphones – come together to battle using a *Matrix*-style martial art. Through this new hybrid language they learn to communicate and transform themselves. In an early performance of *Mathroo Basha* (*Mother Tongue*, 2024) Patel used his own body to dance to a soundtrack created from conversations with his aunt, mother and niece.[20] They flit from Gujarati to English as they discuss their Indian heritage and the loss of the Gujarati language among the younger members of the family. He hand-tufted a circular replica of his grandmother's patterned carpet that they all remembered, and he danced alone on this small stage – part ballet, part Bollywood, part rave – until he drew the carpet up around him like a skirt, twirling like a dervish as memories of his grandmother fused with his own British Indian identity. His work engages with a freedom of expression away from otherness and towards an acceptance of hybridity as part of lived identity. We all have different access points, Patel says, 'but we can still meet somewhere in the middle and understand each other'.[21]

Patel was included in the *British Art Show 9* alongside Hurvin Anderson (born 1965) and Michael Armitage (born 1984). Anderson's paintings of a Birmingham barber's shop, such as *Back* (2008) from *Peter's Series*, captured the community 'centre' of his father's generation of Caribbean immigrants to Britain. Armitage, who was born in Kenya and lives in London and Nairobi, uses the prism of East Africa to construct his paintings, which are painted on Ugandan lubugo cloth. Anderson and Armitage use their own cultural heritage to create their compositions but they also draw on the history of Western art, showing a deep engagement with British painters such as Hockney and Peter Doig (born 1959).

Anya Paintsil (born 1993) creates rug 'portraits' using Ghanaian figurative textiles and Welsh craft techniques to explore her heritage as a Welsh Ghanaian artist working in England. In *Blod* (2022) she

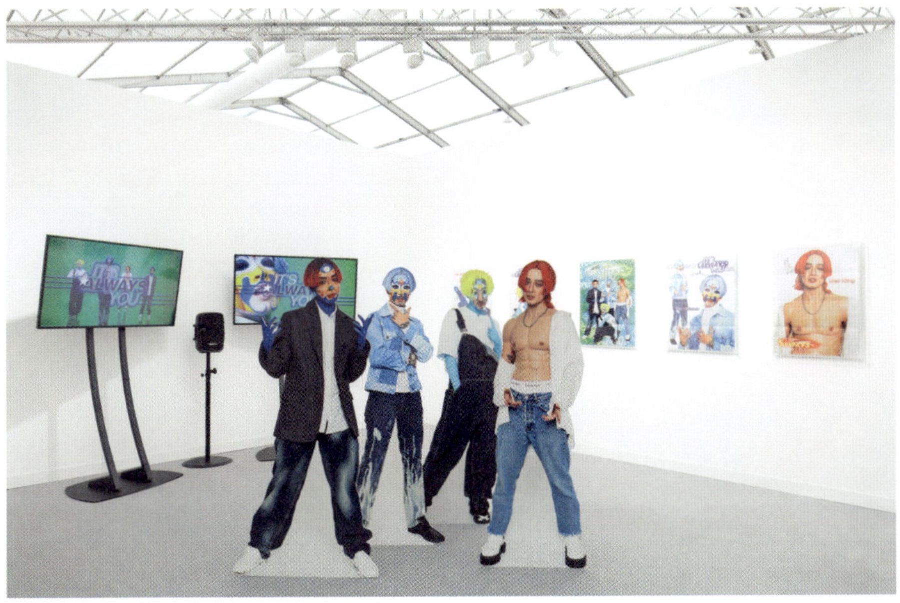

Sin Wai Kin, *It's Always You*, installation view, 2021

portrays herself as Blodeuwedd, a mythical Welsh woman made from meadowsweet and broom who has been transformed into a Black woman with tendrils of woolly hair and flowers dotted across her body. Sin Wai Kin (born 1991) also creates multiple versions of themselves for their videos, such as *It's Always You* (2021; see previous page). Their body carries multiple non-binary identities, manifested as four young singers in a boy band in *It's Always You*, from the redhead in Calvin Klein briefs with a faux six-pack to the one sporting face paint, blue hair and a bleached denim jacket. In *Today's Top Stories* (2020) they say: 'It is no longer possible to live one narrative. In the telling there is a dividing.' Their videos repeatedly ask us to question what is real and to break with binary patterns. 'To have a truly feminist, queer, post-colonial practice you must be constantly open to change. No one is going to be right their whole life through, that is not the narrative we live in.'[22]

It certainly didn't feel like there was anything right about the most divisive referendum of my lifetime: Brexit.

18

THE FUTURE NOW

In 2016 THE UK voted to leave the European Union (EU). Ireland remained in the EU, connected to continental Europe through a shared infrastructure, trading agreements, freedom to travel and the euro. This singular decision reversed forty-three years of greater connectivity with the world at large. The campaign group Led by Donkeys captured the sentiments of many who had opposed Brexit, with their projection onto the white cliffs of Dover where a gold star shone above the words: 'This is our star. Look after it for us.'[1]

Shortly afterwards, as Covid crippled the world, Layla Curtis began making new map collages, splicing European cities alongside their British counterparts to make new imagined geographies. Across a sheltered bay Lisbon, Amsterdam, Leeds and Malmö now shared a coastline with Gdansk, Valencia and Manchester. Called *United Kingdom + European Union*, the series culminated in small collages on board that Curtis sold through Matthew Burrows's Artist Support Pledge scheme, founded in the UK in March 2020. This global programme was designed to support artists during lockdown: individual works were sold on Instagram for the modest sum of £200 – and when an artist sold five of their own works they bought one by a fellow artist.

Why did Brexit happen? Tacita Dean (born 1965) and her artwork *Remain* asked us to 'VOTE for a future not a past', but 'Leave' politicians tugged on (false) histories of British superiority, of an image of Britain as a medieval castle with the drawbridge raised to halt immigration. The Leave campaign traded on a hankering for a Britain that never existed, as Hannah Rose Woods explains in *Rule, Nostalgia: A Backwards History of Britain*: 'It is a nostalgia for the spoils of imperialism (both psychic and material) without the wish to run an empire – an insistence on having one's cake and eating it, taking moral credit for having decolonised while retaining the bullish superiority of an imperial power.'[2] But time and again in this book we have seen that it was immigrants who shaped and defined the British Isles, as Jeremy Deller (born 1966) pithily expressed in his road sign *Stonehenge: Built by Immigrants* (2019, see page 11).

Concerns about immigration and racial tension are not unique to the UK. It was the killing of the unarmed Black man George Floyd in May 2020 in America that led to the Black Lives Matter movement. This quickly became transnational, and protests were held across the British Isles. In Bristol they culminated in the toppling of the statue of Edward Colston, an eighteenth-century merchant who had been actively involved in the transatlantic slave trade. Nearly three million Africans were shipped to the Americas by British slavers over the course of 150 years, and yet the plinth for Colston's statue made no mention of this. Instead it praised him as 'one of the most virtuous and wise sons' of Bristol. His statue had been erected in 1895, 170 years after his death, by the publisher James Arrowsmith. For a century campaigners had tried to have it removed. Black Lives Matter was the tipping point – on Sunday 7 June 2020 the statue was not only pulled down with ropes but also defaced with graffiti and dragged to Narrow Quay, where it was rolled into Bristol harbour.

History reinvented

David Olusoga wrote that 'few acts of collective forgetting have been as thorough and as successful as the erasing of slavery from Britain's "island story"'.[3] The toppling of the Colston statue brought this to national attention via the media. Contrasting views were presented as to the removal of statues in this way. Prime minister Boris Johnson took the position that Britons cannot, should not, edit their past.[4] He would say that – up until very recently the country's past had been shaped into history and written by men like Johnson (white and privileged). Today we understand that history is and will always be constantly in flux – new groupings and theories surface and new voices retell past stories from new perspectives.

Colston's statue was fished out of the water and can now be viewed by taking a tour of the stores of M Shed, part of the Bristol Museums. Seeing John Cassidy's sculpture of Colston in frock coat and breeches lying on its side, covered in spray paint, is an emotional experience. You sense the anger that enabled this larger-than-life bronze figure to be toppled from its high plinth and dragged along the road from Colston Avenue (yes, the same Colston) to Narrow Quay. The figure looks humbled now, tagged and dethroned. Presenting it in this way offers a new approach to dealing with contentious public monuments. It helps us ask the difficult but necessary questions about who our statues praise and why, and how we deal with other problematic figures still standing in cities across the British Isles today.

Artists such as Marc Quinn offer us another way to consider the history of statuary. He was quick to erect a black resin 3D-printed sculpture of Black Lives Matter protestor Jen Reid on Colston's empty plinth, her right fist raised high in the air, re-enacting the pose she adopted on 7 June when she first climbed on top of the base. Quinn's sculpture appeared without council permission and was removed twenty-four hours later, but in this digital age it lives in perpetuity on the internet, a statement of defiance against the faceless bureaucracy of a government that doggedly refused to remove the Colston statue for decades. (Not everyone believes Quinn's motives were altruistic. Black British artist Thomas J. Price (born 1981) described Quinn as a modern-day 'trophy hunter' seeking to capitalise on the moment.[5])

Hew Locke (born 1959) has spent his entire career considering the role of statues such as Colston's. He was born in Edinburgh, the eldest son of the sculptor Donald Locke. The family moved back to Guyana as it became an independent country once again and Hew Locke spent twenty-two years there before returning to the UK. In Georgetown, on his way to school each day, he would walk past a larger-than-life statue of Queen Victoria, a throwback to British Guiana and colonial rule. Richard Hope-Pinker's sculpture of the monarch had been unveiled in 1894, one of dozens shipped to colonial capitals to visualise the authority of the British Crown. Subsequently, in Locke's sculptures and works on paper, he has investigated the complex histories between colonisers and the colonised, often fusing histories together, as in *Hinterland* (2013), where he transposed Hope-Pinker's statue to the Guyanan landscape and surrounded it with indigenous ghosts.

In 2022 Locke realised his ambition to work with such a statue in the UK when he was commissioned to make *Foreign Exchange* to mark the Commonwealth Games in Birmingham. In Victoria Square a bronze cast of Thomas Brock's 1901 statue of Queen Victoria looks out from a tall plinth. Locke reimagined the sculpture as floating in a small boat above the square, accompanied by a retinue of smaller Victorias, all wearing gold helmets like the armed warrior Britannia. Locke asked us to imagine what it meant to cross the seas in a small boat such as this as we simultaneously considered the British imperial history of sending statues of leaders across the length and breadth of the empire (as the Romans did), from Brisbane to Belfast to Bangalore. Locke's work never feels accusatory or angry but rather asks everyone to question history and search for ways in which we can all change for the better.

Locke was awarded an OBE in 2023; Yinka Shonibare CBE RA has incorporated his honour into his name. This makes Locke an Officer of the Order of the British Empire, with its motto 'For God and the Empire', and Shonibare a Commander of the Order of the British Empire. What does this mean for these artists whose cultural heritage is tied up with colonialism? Both were born in Britain but spent their childhoods in the countries of their parents' birth (Guyana and Nigeria, both former British colonies). These honorific titles can seem offensive today, but Locke and Shonibare believe in change from the inside. As Shonibare said: 'Even though I make work about power, the so-called establishment, I was made a Member of the British Empire [in 2004; he became CBE in 2019].' He thought about refusing the honour, as the British Caribbean poet Benjamin Zephaniah had done, but ultimately he felt it was more interesting to accept. 'I think it's better to make an impact from within rather than from without.'[6] Accepting these titles helps address the meaning of 'empire', to recalibrate it to place all those who once lived within it on an equal footing rather than emphasising the historical sense of empire as something predatory, a place of subjugation for all those who lived in colonised countries.

Artists such as John Akomfrah, Isaac Julien (born 1960) and Alberta Whittle (born 1980) make films and installations that tackle the complexity of colonial history and the Afro-Caribbean diaspora, from the slave trade to migration and what V.S. Naipaul called the 'enigma of arrival'.[7] The Singh Twins (born 1966) look at the legacy of the British empire in India in works such as *Casualty of War: A Portrait*

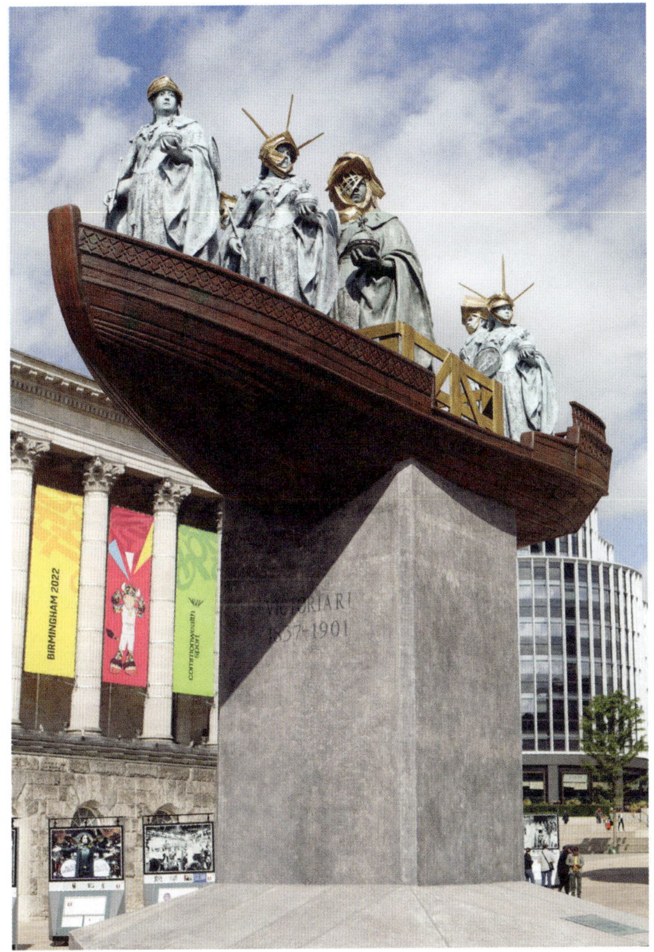

Hew Locke, *Foreign Exchange*, steel, glass fibre, wood, resin and acrylic surrounding
Thomas Brock's 1901 statue of Queen Victoria in Victoria Square, Birmingham, 2022

of Maharaja Duleep Singh (2013), the last ruler of the Sikh empire
who was deposed by the British in 1849.

Mohammed Sami (born 1984), Joy Gerrard (born 1971) and Steve
McQueen (born 1969) work through more recent histories such as
prisoner abuse at Abu Ghraib in Iraq, protest marches and the Grenfell
Tower fire. Art can help us reconsider the past from new viewpoints
and increasingly artists are drawn to socio-historical and geopolitical
subjects. As Cornelia Parker has said, 'This is the time we all need
to politically engage. We need art more than ever because it's like a
digestive system, a way of processing.'[8]

EXTINCTION BECKONS

Art helps us locate ourselves within the present, too. In our climate emergency British artists such as Heather Ackroyd & Dan Harvey (both born 1959) and Rachel Whiteread have responded to the changing conditions in the Arctic, bringing a heightened awareness of the damage we are doing to our planet. The Irish photographer Richard Mosse (born 1980) says that 'climate change is such a complex subject – any artist will struggle to find a way to represent something that's beyond human perception'.[9] He highlights environmental concerns in his aerial photographs and films by using infrared cameras to turn vegetation cerise. In *Intensive Cattle Feedlot, Rondônia* (2020) this makes visible that whole areas of land have been cleared of almost all trees to rear beef cattle; in *Samuel Dam, Rondônia* (2021) a copse of trees on a vast empty plain glows like a cancer cell under a microscope.

Standing in a vast subterranean gallery watching his immersive multi-screen film *Broken Spectre* (2018–22) about the deforestation

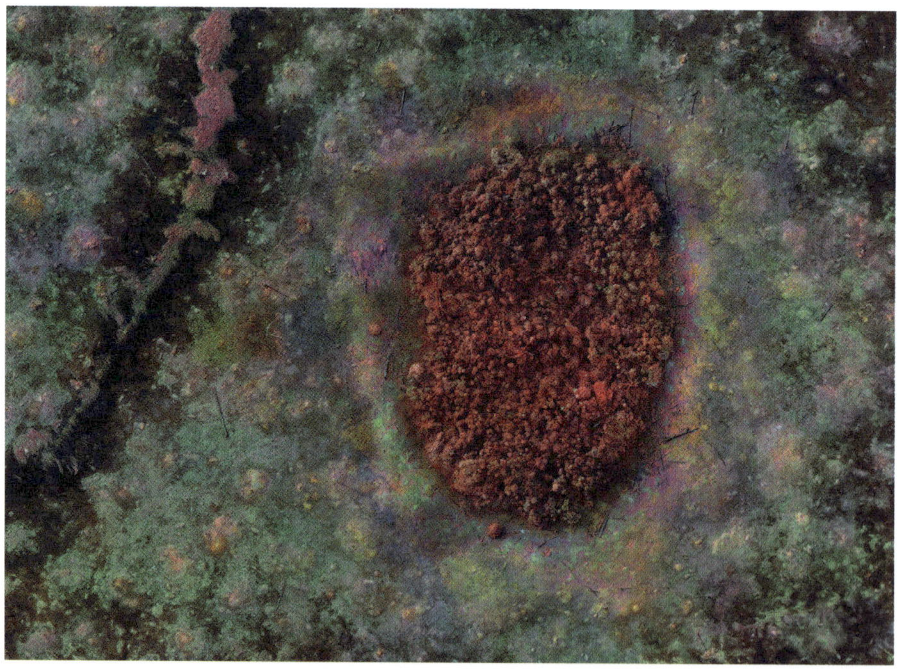

Richard Mosse, *Samuel Dam, Rondônia*, archival pigment print, 2021

of the Amazon, I felt a deep emotional connection to the beauty of the world he showcases and simultaneously a vertiginous horror at humankind's destruction of it. This is the contemporary sublime, a shudder down your spine as flame-red grass sways in the breeze, ice-blue water snakes along the valley and trees are felled to a soundtrack that crackles with purposefully lit forest fires.[10]

Noémie Goudal (born 1984) also draws on earth's changing climate for her photographic installations, but in works such as *Inhale Exhale* (2021) she travels back in time to imagine earth's climate 300 million years ago. Using palaeoclimatology she explores how changeable our world has been. In visualising deep time she reveals the slippage of our momentary reality as reproductions of the tropical landscape are lowered into a slow-moving river. Each panel is submerged, then reappears, as if the water level itself is changing, reminding us that the earth and its climate will always be in flux. Her films and photographs present complex ideas with clarity and purpose, and – as with Mosse's work – I find myself still reflecting on their content days and months after viewing them.

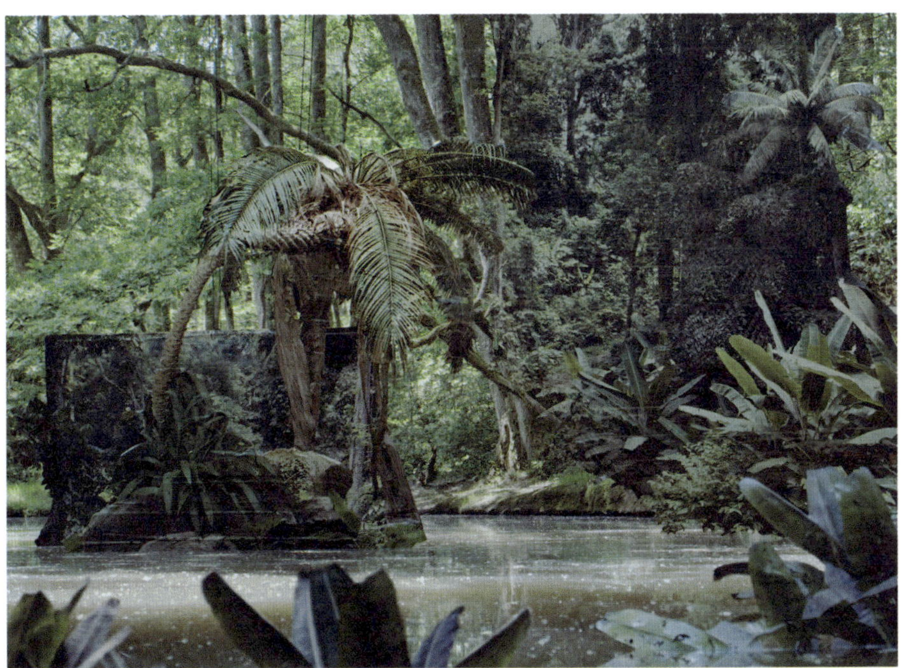

Still from Noemie Goudal's *Inhale Exhale*, single-channel HD video, 2021

STRENGTH IN NUMBERS

In 2021 the Turner Prize was awarded to Array Collective, a group of eleven artist-activists working together in Northern Ireland who tackle current political and social issues head-on. *The Druthaib's Ball* (2021) features photographs and films shown within a small *síbín* (unlicensed bar). A headless man lounges next to a tray of chips, wearing a tie made of bank notes. A pineapple ice bucket wears an eye mask that reads 'laissez-fair'. A small needlepoint above the bar reads 'The rich get richer, the poor get prison'. You can pull up a chair and imagine drinking a glass of hooch as you watch the films playing on the far wall or study the protest banners draped across the ceiling. *The Druthaib's Ball* offers a multi-faceted view of the *síbín*'s history as somewhere hidden from authority but simultaneously known to the local community. It is a form of resistance, a joint two fingers to authority.

An artists' group was guaranteed to win the Turner Prize in 2021 as only collectives made it onto the shortlist. This was a conscious decision by the judges, partially based on Covid and how artists necessarily had to explore options beyond the (closed) gallery. It also highlights a rising trend of artists banding together and creating work without a single authorial voice. Each of the shortlisted collectives worked directly with specific local communities and many used activism to engage with audiences. Does this mean that art is leaving the gallery for the streets again? Or that the era of the alpha artist is behind us? Probably not, but it does open up new possibilities about what art can be as it engages with diverse audiences away from traditional settings.

This idea of working together, of harnessing collective energy to create art, is paralleled by the renewed interest in local traditions such as the Padstow 'Obby 'Oss, the straw bear of Whittlesea or the flaming tar barrels of Ottery St Mary, all meticulously captured in paint by folklore specialist Ben Edge. There's something increasingly urgent, instinctive perhaps, about pulling together on a local level when the world is increasingly virtual. This may explain the rise in the making of art from a position embedded within specific communities, art that serves a purpose beyond the commercial. As artists confront this new virtual age and eye up the opportunities and threats posed by artificial intelligence

(AI), art may become increasingly experiential again, relying on visitors and their own unique emotive responses to complete each work.

WELCOME TO THE TECHNOCENE

In this, the final section of the final chapter of *The Art Isles*, we have reached the edge of the abyss. Looking over, we can see only darkness, a void as absolute as Anish Kapoor's matt-black infinities. We have reached the edge of the future, the boundary of lived experience. But wait, what's this? It looks like a pull cord for a light. Are we curious, foolish or brave enough to pull on it? We are.

The abyss lights up with future possibilities, as if electric eels are snapping through the depths. This is what it feels like as we contemplate the future of art in the digital age, as machine learning becomes an integral part of our lives. Want to show how your sculpture will look in a yet-to-be-built gallery space? AI can model that for you. Want to conflate time and space and cause Old Master paintings to glitch and dissolve? Open-access software can distort any image in the blink of an eye. Fancy a trip to the British Museum in London but you live in Orkney or Anglesey? The Sandbox metaverse[11] can offer that to you, 24/7. Want to hang art on the walls of your metaverse store? NFTs are the answer.

Artists have been working in this virtual field for a few decades now, although until recently digital art was considered something of an outlier, as if the use of technology somehow overwhelmed artistic integrity. In reality the early pioneers embraced the new opportunities offered by computing rather like Julia Margaret Cameron harnessed the early possibilities of the camera. The technologies of mass communication have been growing for centuries – the telegraph was invented in the British Isles and launched in 1844, the telephone arrived in 1877, the radio in 1896. The Computer Arts Society was founded in London and *Cybernetic Serendipity* opened at the ICA in 1968; the following year the V&A purchased its first computer-generated images. With the rise of the personal computer in the 1970s, the fax in the 1980s and the internet and mobile phones in the 1990s, artists working in the British Isles became part of a global communication network (when we still called the internet the World Wide Web).

Images proliferated like never before. The cultural theorist Walter Benjamin wrote about art in the era of mass reproduction as early as

1936, and in 1967 the philosopher Guy Debord felt compelled to write that 'all that once was directly lived has become mere representation'.[12] But with the invention of the iPhone in 2007 the sharing of images reached unprecedented heights. They proliferated in a decontextualised, ahistorical way – a snapshot of a Rembrandt portrait could be sent along with a photo of a family member standing next to an Ice Age mummy in a museum. Everything was drawn into the present, into the 'now' of daily life.

Dehistoricised image proliferation runs hand in hand with a reimagining of time. The pre-industrial cyclical sense of time had long been lost, but digital time was different from the bright lights of industrial time we were used to, a linear but artificially controlled time that allowed factories to stay open after the sun set. With digital time, bank holidays, religious holidays and maintenance closures were discarded. The internet never slept, never took a lunch break, was never sick. In the 1980s Hockney explored the shifts of light and gesture over time in his photocollages such as *The Crossword Puzzle, Minneapolis, January 1983*, but by the 2000s thinking about time in this way had become redundant. Time became dislocated. As the art historian Jonathan Crary has noted, the past began to be erased 'as part of the fantasmatic construction of the present'.[13] Past, present and future were conflated and became an ouroboros, a continuous loop of presentness. And now we are on the cusp of quantum time, where every outcome to every question will be simultaneously possible.

Today the smartphone in our pocket contains more knowledge than the lost library of Alexandria where Ptolemy wrote his *Geography*. As a species we produce more data in forty-eight hours than it took civilisation to produce from the dawn of time to 2003. Gordon Cheung (born 1975), whose multimedia work uses new technologies to critique capitalism, sees the internet and mobile phones as responsible for 'reconfiguring our perceptions of time and space into a state of constant flux'.[14] So what happens when artists step into the digital world today? To date we have considered art made from a wide range of materials and ideas, but what happens when artists use technologies such as ChatGPT, Midjourney and DeepDream? Will artists end up bypassing the bricks-and-mortar gallery altogether and showing in the metaverse (a virtual online world)?

Cheung's multimedia paintings and sculptures span both the material and digital worlds. His trademark use of the stock listings from the

Financial Times with their relentless rain of numbers rising and falling creates a backdrop for his futuristic landscapes and complex still lifes such as *Three Kingdoms (Chengdu)* (2024). Using 3D printing and AI-designed elements, he builds up the surface to be both painting and sculpture, something handmade yet also technologically imagined, a work that refuses to be pinned down or categorised. His paintings offer us a line of sight from the nineteenth-century sublime of John Martin to the science fiction of Philip K. Dick and the dystopias of J.G. Ballard, and on towards the bespoke future of avatars and digital worlds where the hyperreal (an imagined, preferred fiction of 'reality') becomes a substitute for everyday life.

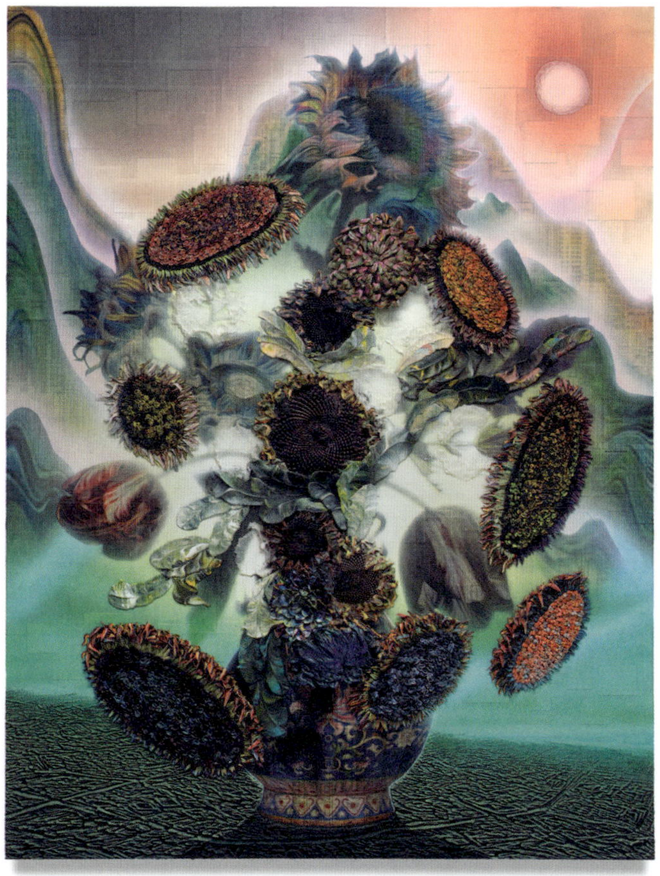

Gordon Cheung, *Three Kingdoms (Chengdu)*,
Financial Times newspaper, archival inkjet, acrylic and sand on linen, 2024

Well into his eighties Hockney embraced the latest technology, creating drawings on his iPad and immersive experiences such as *Bigger & Closer (not smaller & further away)* (2023). The YBA Mat Collishaw (born 1966) created a series of NFTs for his 2023 exhibition at Kew Gardens in London. NFTs or non-fungible tokens are a form of digital fingerprint, an encrypted and unique piece of computer code using blockchain technology that allows for digital ownership. For *Heterosis* (2023) Collishaw created a series of digital 'seeds'. If you collected two or more 'seeds' you were able to breed your own digital flowers, combining and recombining your blooms to create new and unexpected hybrids (mine was a leopard-print waterlily in iridescent turquoise). Kew has long been associated with collecting new species, many of which were recorded by Mary Delany in the eighteenth century (Chapter 9) and Marianne North in the nineteenth century (Chapter 11). Collishaw asked questions of the institution and the nature of collecting by introducing the possibility of infinite digital hybridity.

Artists such as Anna Ridler (born 1985) and Nye Thompson (born 1966) work with the large datasets used as training tools for AI. These vast collections of words and images allow AI to learn how to recognise that something is, for example, a sculpture rather than a person

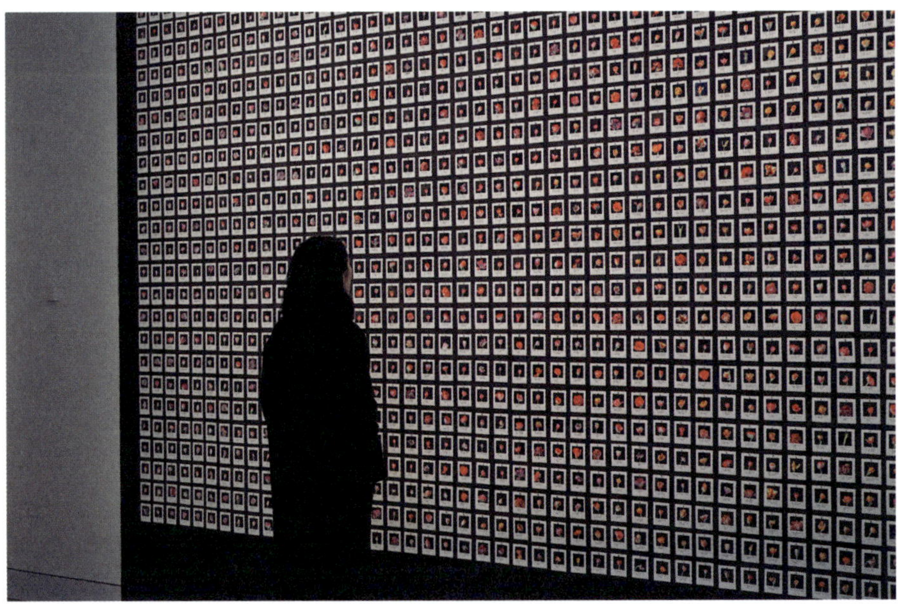

Anna Ridler, *Myriad (Tulips)*, C-type digital prints with handwritten annotations, magnetic paint and magnets, 2018

or a tree trunk. In 2018 Ridler took 10,000 photographs of tulips for *Myriad (Tulips)*, creating a dataset for AI that revealed the human bias inherent in all such training models. Should the selection include striped tulips? Should a particular bloom be catalogued as orange or red? How many tulips is enough?

All these artists see AI as a tool, much like a paintbrush or a camera, something that can be used to make art but that doesn't contribute as an active participant. Mat Dryhurst (born 1984) and his collaborator, the American artist Holly Herndon (born 1980), believe AI is destined to have a different relationship with artists. For their ambitious 2024 exhibition *The Call* at the Serpentine Gallery in London they worked with fifteen different choirs from across the British Isles, recording each group singing hymnals that could be collated into a dataset to train AI on choral harmony. They see AI as a 'creative instrument' and want to demystify its learning processes.[15] The exhibition followed the process of recording the original choirs to the development of computer-generated choral harmonies. It even offered you a chance to interact with the AI model. You had to enter one gallery alone and the space felt intimidating, like standing in a luxurious funeral parlour or private chapel, its walls made of pink drapes and an altarpiece of ascending figures at one end. In the middle was a microphone into which you could sing and harmonise with AI and (enhanced by the room's design) it felt as if you were interacting with a spiritual being.

The artistic director of the Serpentine Gallery, Hans Ulrich Obrist, believes AI will change art at a fundamental level. He believes that instead of presenting discrete works of art completed in a studio, the use of AI will allow works to be open-ended and ever-changing. It is arguable that 1970s performance art – and experiential pieces such as *Longplayer* (1999–ongoing) by Jem Finer (born 1955) – already accomplished this, but AI certainly opens up future possibilities for artistic production on a mind-blowing scale when it is used as part of an artist's creative practice and even beyond it. (Ai-Da, 'the world's first ultra-realistic humanoid robot artist', was breathed into life by the gallerist Aidan Meller in 2019 and uses AI to create works of art. 'Her' portrait of Alan Turing sold at Sotheby's for £774,000 in October 2024, with Meller and his team – not Ai-Da – pocketing the proceeds.[16])

Whatever your view of future technologies and their impact on art, it is safe to say that we are in the Technocene, a term used to indicate how technology and life are now irrevocably intertwined. Imagine when William Caxton imported the first printing press to the British Isles in the 1470s. Before that date, all books had to be handwritten. The printing press ushered in a revolution in communication, for good (rising literacy) and bad (religious conflict). The digital age and the emergence of AI seem to suggest a similarly cataclysmic shift. Our concept of time and history is rapidly changing and our understanding of intelligence and what makes us human is being questioned. AI cannot yet show empathy or original creativity, both of which underpin the production of art. But will this change?

Marcus du Sautoy argued in *The Creativity Code* that 'a Rembrandt portrait seems to capture so much more than just what the sitter looks like. How can a machine ever hope to replace or even to compete with Mozart, Shakespeare or Rembrandt?'[17] Despite his assertion, a recent poll of artists suggested that 77 per cent felt their work and practice was threatened by AI.[18] And there are many whose forecast is even gloomier, as the technologist James Bridle explained in *Ways of Being*:

> The ways in which the development of these supposedly intelligent tools might harm, efface and ultimately supplant us has become the subject of a wide field of study, involving computer scientists, programmers and technology firms, as well as theorists and philosophers of machine intelligence itself.[19]

Perhaps this rapidly changing landscape (metascape?) will allow for a greater acceptance of hybridity than the recent rise in populist political parties leads us to believe. Surely in an overheating world with rising artificial intelligence, the cultural differences that potentially divide us are far smaller than the unique qualities that make us all human. Like Collishaw's flowers we are all hybrids, always in a process of change, our unique experiences of the world shaping our views, moulding our beliefs. This is what Grayson Perry described as the accretions of life in the opening chapter. Cheung agrees:

> We are all constantly shaped by external forces, whether through conscious engagement or subtle indoctrination, caught in the ongoing process of becoming. We are woven into the fabric of multiple histories, cultures, and technologies, all of which reflect the fluidity of existence, where nothing remains fixed.[20]

It is these accretions, these hybridities, that make us unique. And it is this that makes us human and allows art to happen. As Cheung says, 'Art is a human endeavour, a mark of humanity that transmits through time and history. As long as artists adapt to changes, they will remain relevant.'[21]

ACKNOWLEDGEMENTS

THIS BOOK IS dedicated to all the volunteers who enable hundreds of Britain and Ireland's best-loved art destinations to remain open. As I toured the British Isles I was struck by how many places have to rely on the goodwill of thousands of people who give their time, energy, enthusiasm and expertise for free. Thank you to all those who took time to tell me their stories and share their love of art with me. Thanks to Sheila at Castle Howard, Jennifer at St Serf's church in Dunning, Jan at Coventry's Holy Trinity church, Nigel at Arundel Castle, Nancy at the Burrell Collection, the volunteers at Pitzhanger Manor, the Watts Gallery – Artists' Village, the Uffington White Horse, Petworth House, Burghley House, Ewelme church, Kettle's Yard, Sandram Memorial Chapel, the Pitt Rivers Museum and many, many others. Particular thanks to Stuart Plant at Middleton church in North Yorkshire, who provided me with research on Viking crosses, and Robert Richards, who did the same for the *Pricke of Conscience* stained-glass window in All Saints North Street in York.

Others went out of their way to offer me tours of buildings and sites not open to the public, including Sister Gemma and Sister Laura at Ince Blundell Hall in Liverpool, James 'Jim' Irvine in an ancient field full of hidden Roman tesserae, Rob Lowe at Brangwyn Hall and Pippa Hardman at Cathole Cave in the Gower (and the team at Natural Resources Wales who made this possible: Michele Johnston, Ed Tucker and Nick Edwards). My thanks also to my two tour guides for the murals of Northern Ireland, Gleann Doherty in Derry and Patrick in Belfast.

Curators, specialists, researchers and archivists were incredibly generous with their time and patience as I asked to see particular works from the stores or made repeat visits to exhibitions and collections. A massive thank you to George Nash for his guidance on Ice Age art, Chrissie Partheni and Anne Fahy at National Museums Liverpool for information on Henry Blundell's Grand Tour collection of classical sculpture, Sue Brunning at the British Museum for helping me navigate religion at Sutton Hoo and Sian Iles, curator of medieval archaeology at the National Museum of Wales. Martin Myrone and Jenny Gaschke of the British Art Network offered new routes through well-trodden territories. Riann Coulter, curator and manager of the F.E. McWilliam Gallery, curators Anna Liesching and Anne Stewart at the Ulster Museum in Belfast, Brendan Rooney at the National Gallery of Ireland and Nuria Carballeira at IMMA all offered me valuable insights into the complex history of Irish art.

My thanks also to the team at the Joseph Wright Study Room at Derby Museum and Art Gallery, Vivienne Roberts at the College of Psychic Studies, Jo Baring, director of the Ingram Collection of Modern British Art, Rhydian Davies at the National Library of Wales, Mark Pomeroy, Lois Oliver and Adam Waterton at the Royal Academy of Arts, Andrew Lewis at Arundel Castle, John S. Thomas of University of Leicester Archaeology Services, Andrew Nairne at Kettle's Yard, Lucy Peter, Suzanne Casey and Amy Parris at the Royal Collection Trust, Rob Airey of the Wilhelmina Barns-Graham Trust, Mark Hedges and the team at *Country Life* and all those who helped me at the numerous galleries and museums I visited. Also thanks to Beth Banks, Holly Black, Erica Bolton, Fiona Bradley, Dennis Chang, Paddy Duffy, Neil Evans, Mark Harris, Marcus Jack, Katie Jenkins, Kate Jesson, Tracy Jones, Gemma Lewis, Monse Pis Marcos, Lorna McBride, David Neal, Stephen Snoddy, Chris Wardle and Alison Wright.

I criss-crossed the British Isles researching this book and I couldn't have done it without the support of my incredible family and a strong network of friends, many of whom joined me for one or more research trips. Huge thanks to Michael Bird, Sian Chamberlain (remember the bats?), Helen Daly, Georgiana Head (top chauffeur), Barnaby Hopson, Felicity Mara, Ian 'Doggz' Massey, Carol Ripley, Emma Tait, Marion Taylor, Mary Turner (ace detective), Sinead Woodhouse (whose cousins led me astray in Dublin), the Mullins, Ayres and Dodd families and in particular Paul, Malachy and Saskia.

When it came to writing *The Art Isles* my thanks first and foremost go to the artists who answered my questions about mapping and identity, postcolonialism, feminism and the future of art. I am fortunate to have worked with many incredible artists but special thanks to Grayson Perry for allowing me to use his print *Map of Nowhere* on the cover and Sutapa Biswas, Gordon Cheung, Michael Craig-Martin, Dorothy Cross, Layla Curtis, Jeremy Deller, Ben Edge, Noémie Goudal, Lubaina Himid, Sin Wai Kin, Hew Locke, Catherine McWilliams, Richard Mosse, Con Mulholland, Rosalind Nashashibi, Chris Ofili, Hetain Patel, Abigail Reynolds, Liz Rideal, Anna Ridler, Yinka Shonibare CBE RA, Alison Wilding and Rachel Whiteread. My thanks also to my Instagram community who helped me out when I was puzzled, particularly @medievalart62, @the_epigrapher and @mike.farthing.

Editing a book of this scope is always going to be a challenge because of its extreme range. I thank wholeheartedly my essential expert readers on Ireland's history and the deep time of geology, John O'Beirne Ranelagh and Pamela Raine. Both subjects required a nuanced use of specialist language and I was comforted (and corrected) by their expertise. Any subsequent errors are my own. Yale's rigorous academic pedigree means this book was also read by two anonymous peer reviewers and I thank them for their guidance and support.

I couldn't have worked with a better team to bring this book to print. Led by the indefatigable Heather McCallum, Yale University Press has an expert team of commissioning editors, copy editors, proofreaders and picture researchers. My thanks to my brilliant commissioning editor Sophie Neve, and to the hugely capable Susannah Stone, Daphne Fordham-Smith, Leonie Kellman, Anna Morrison, Martin Brown, Robert Davies and Sara Magness who smoothly ushered this book through production, and to Lizzie Curtin, Charlotte Stafford and Emily Richardson at Yale and my agent Georgina Capel and her team for their enthusiasm and support in its promotion.

Final thanks go to you, for picking up *The Art Isles* and making it to the end. I do hope you will venture to see some of the paintings, sculptures and art installations I have touched upon – the British Isles teems with cultural history and it has been my privilege to introduce you to some of the very best examples that remain in existence today.

Notes

1. What's in a Name? An Introduction

1. John Playfair, *Biographical Account of John Hutton* (Edinburgh, 1805), p. 35.
2. I use 'British Isles' to indicate the 6,000 or so islands in the geographic region, and 'Britain' to mean the British mainland and – during times of empire – Britain's colonial territories. Following the partition of Ireland in 1922, I use 'United Kingdom of Great Britain and Northern Ireland' (shortened to 'UK'), paired with 'Ireland' to indicate the twenty-six counties that comprise Ireland today. England passed legislation to unite with Wales in 1536, and with Scotland in 1707. When 'Britain' is referred to before these dates it is for ease of navigation. It is used to indicate the landmass and cultural events witnessed across this shared terrain, and not as a political statement.
3. Ptolemy's *Prima Europe Tabula*, printed by Johann Reger, 1486, 35 × 50 centimetres, hand-coloured printed map, fol. 152, National Library of Wales, Aberystwyth.
4. Layla Curtis, interview with Charlotte Mullins, 5 December 2023.
5. Grayson Perry, interview with Charlotte Mullins, 9 June 2023.
6. Charlotte Mullins, 'Sex, Drags and Pottery Roll', *Country Life*, 19 July 2023, pp. 112–17 (p. 115).
7. Mullins, 'Sex, Drags and Pottery Roll', p. 115.
8. Robert Winder, *Bloody Foreigners: The Story of Immigration to Britain* (London: Abacus, 2013), p. 8.
9. Catherine Hall and Sonya Rose, 'Introduction', in Catherine Hall and Sonya Rose, eds, *At Home with the Empire: Metropolitan Culture and the Imperial World* (Cambridge: Cambridge University Press, 2009), pp. 1–31 (p. 4).
10. Sathnam Sanghera, *Empireland: How Imperialism Has Shaped Modern Britain* (London: Viking, 2021), p. 69.
11. David Olusoga's tweet is cited in Sanghera, *Empireland*, p. 69.

2. Life Before History

1. George Nash et al., 'A Discovery of Possible Upper Paleolithic Parietal Art in Cathole Cave, Gower Peninsula, South Wales', *Proceedings of the*

University of Bristol Spelaeological Society 25:3 (2012), pp. 327–36, and George Nash, 'Further Possible Discoveries of Engravings within Cathole Cave, Gower, Swansea', *Proc. Univ. Bristol Spelaeol. Soc.* 26:3 (2015), pp. 1–10.

2. The word 'artist' only came into widespread use in English in the sixteenth century and its meaning continues to change over time. For clarity I have chosen to use 'artist' to refer to all makers of what we today consider to be art.

3. George Eogan and Elizabeth Shee Twohig, eds, *The Megalithic Art of the Passage Tombs at Knowth, County Meath* (Dublin: Royal Irish Academy, 2022), p. 312.

3. Immigration or Attack?

1. Alice Roberts, *The Celts: Search for a Civilization* (London: Quercus, 2015), p. 30.

2. Julius Caesar, *The Gallic Wars*, 6:14, in Miranda Aldhouse-Green, *The Celtic Myths: A Guide to the Ancient Gods and Legends* (London: Thames & Hudson, 2015), p. 38.

3. H. Michell, 'The Edict of Diocletian: A Study of Price Fixing in the Roman Empire', *Canadian Journal of Economics and Political Science* 13:1 (1947), pp. 1–12 (p. 6).

4. Bede, *The Ecclesiastical History of the English People*, ed. Judith McClure and Roger Collins (Oxford: Oxford University Press, 2008), p. 98.

4. Christianity as Creative Impulse

1. See Mary Wellesley, *Hidden Hands: The Lives of Manuscripts and their Makers* (London: riverrun, 2021), p. 166.

2. Gerald of Wales (Giraldus Cambresis), *The History and Topography of Ireland*, trans. John J. O'Meara (London: Penguin, 1982), p. 84.

3. See Neil Price, *The Children of Ash & Elm: A History of the Vikings* (London: Penguin, 2020), p. 282.

4. See Price, *The Children of Ash & Elm*, p. 281.

5. Simeon of Durham, 'History of the Kings of England', cited in Joseph Stevenson, ed., *The Church Historians of England*, vol. 3 (London: Seeleys, 1855), p. 457.

6. See Price, *The Children of Ash & Elm*, p. 273.

7. Seamus Heaney, 'Viking Dublin: Trial Pieces', in Heaney, *Selected Poems 1965–75* (London: Faber & Faber, 1980), pp. 107–10.

5. To Be a Pilgrim

1. Cambridge: Corpus Christi College, MS 189, fol. 68v. See also *William Thorne's Chronicle of Saint Augustine's Abbey Canterbury*, trans. A.H. Davis (Oxford: Blackwell, 1934), p. 100.

2. Bede, *The Ecclesiastical History of the English People*, ed. Judith McClure and Roger Collins (Oxford: Oxford World's Classics, 2008), p. 245.
3. See Diana Webb, *Pilgrims and Pilgrimage in the Medieval West* (London: I.B. Tauris, 1999), p. 125.
4. Neil MacGregor, *Living with the Gods* (London: Penguin, 2018), p. 203.
5. This is based on people working six days a week, fifty weeks a year. See https://www.nationalarchives.gov.uk/currency-converter, accessed 27.04.24.

6. APOCALYPSE NOW: THE ANNIHILATION OF HISTORY

1. Quoted in David Starkey, ed., *Henry VIII: A European Court in England* (London: National Maritime Museum, 1991), p. 12.
2. Max Porter, *Lanny* (London: Faber & Faber, 2019), p. 9.

7. FOR QUEEN (AND KING) AND COUNTRY

1. Edmond Howes, quoted in Christina J. Faraday, *Tudor Liveliness: Vivid Art in Post-Reformation England* (London: Paul Mellon Centre for Studies in British Art, 2023), p. 145.
2. See Neil Oliver, *A History of Scotland* (London: BBC Books, 2009), pp. 239–40.
3. Letter to Peiresc, 9 August 1629, translated in Ruth S. Magurn, *The Letters of Peter Paul Rubens* (Cambridge, MA: Harvard University Press, 1955), p. 322. Buckingham had made many enemies through his close relationship with the king and he was assassinated in 1628.

8. THE UNSPEAKABLE PRICE OF THE GRAND TOUR

1. See Tabitha Barber, ed., *Mary Beale: Portrait of a Seventeenth-Century Painter, Her Family and Her Studio* (London: Geffrye Museum, 1999), p. 30.
2. Bainbrigg Buckeridge, 'Essay towards an English School of Painters', in Roger de Piles et al., *The Art of Painting: And the Lives of Painters* (London: J. Nutt, 1706), p. 403.
3. Adam Eaker, *Van Dyck and the Making of English Portraiture* (London: Paul Mellon Centre for Studies in British Art, 2022), p. 19.
4. Richard Lassels, *The Voyage of Italy, or a Compleat Journey through Italy* (Paris: Vincent du Moutier, 1670).
5. See Marianna D'Ezio, 'The Advantages of "Demi-Naturalization": Mutual Perceptions of Britain and Italy in Hester Lynch Piozzi's *Observations and Reflections Made in the Course of a Journey through France, Italy and Germany*', *Journal for Eighteenth-Century Studies* 33:2 (2010), pp. 165–80 (p. 169).

6. See D'Ezio, 'The Advantages of "Demi-Naturalization"', p. 172.

7. See James Stourton and Charles Sebag-Montefiore, *The British as Art Collectors: From the Tudors to the Present* (London: Scala, 2012), p. 137.

8. See Victoria Avery and Jake Subryan Richards, *Black Atlantic: Power People Resistance* (Cambridge: Fitzwilliam Museum, 2023), p. 119.

9. Numbers vary wildly in different eighteenth-century sources; see Winder, *Bloody Foreigners*, p. 129. In 1768 the abolitionist lawyer Granville Sharp suggested there were as many as 20,000 Black servants in London alone; see Gretchen Gerzina, *Black England: A Forgotten Georgian History*, revised edition (London: John Murray, 2022), pp. 5–6.

10. See Gerzina, *Black England*, p. 7.

11. See Avery and Richards, *Black Atlantic*, p. 113.

12. See David Olusoga, *Black and British: A Forgotten History* (London: Macmillan, 2016), p. 94.

13. Peter Orlando Hutchinson, ed., *The Diary and Letters of His Excellency Thomas Hutchinson, Esq.* (London: Sampson Low, Marston, Searle & Rivington, 1886), vol. 2, pp. 276–7.

14. See Olusoga, *Black and British*, p. 137.

9. AGE OF 'ENLIGHTENMENT'?

1. See James Delbourgo, *Collecting the World: The Life and Curiosity of Hans Sloane* (London: Penguin, 2017), p. xxi.

2. Lucy Bamford and Jonathan Wallis, *Joseph Wright of Derby* (Derby: Derby Museums, 2017), p. 18.

3. Bamford and Wallis, *Joseph Wright of Derby*, p. 26.

4. See Tabitha Barber, ed., *Now You See Us: Women Artists in Britain 1520–1920* (London: Tate Publishing, 2024), p. 97.

5. Advert in the *Morning Herald*, 18 January 1787, p. 1, quoted in Geoff Quilley and John Bonehill, eds, *William Hodges 1744–1797: The Art of Exploration* (London: National Maritime Museum, 2004), p. 139.

6. Edward Said, *Culture and Imperialism* (London: Vintage, 1993), pp. xxiii–xxiv.

7. John Stedman, *Narrative, of a Five Years' Expedition, against the Revolted Negroes of Surinam, in Guiana* (London: J. Johnson and J. Edwards, 1796).

8. Winder, *Bloody Foreigners*, p. 129.

10. RADICAL LANDSCAPES

1. Royal Society minutes of the meeting of 23 January 1689, quoted in Alasdair Kennedy, 'In Search of the "True Prospect": Making and Knowing the Giant's Causeway as a Field Site in the Seventeenth Century', *British Journal for the History of Science* 41:1 (2008), pp. 19–41 (at pp. 21–2).

2. Lady Llanover, ed., *The Autobiography and Correspondence of Mary Granville, Mrs Delany* (London: 1861), vol. 3, p. 521.

3. William Gilpin, *An Essay on Prints: Containing Remarks on the Principles of Picturesque Beauty* (London: J. Robson, 1768), p. xii.

4. William Gilpin, *Three Essays: on Picturesque Beauty; on Picturesque Travel; and on Sketching Landscape* (London: R. Blamire, 1792), pp. 67–8.

5. William Combe, *The Tour of Dr Syntax: In Search of the Picturesque*, engravings by Thomas Rowlandson (1809; second edition, London: R. Ackermann's Repository of the Arts, 1812), canto 1; original emphasis.

6. Edmund Burke, *A Philosophical Enquiry into the Origin of Our Ideas of the Sublime and Beautiful* (1757; repr. London: N. Hailes, 1824), p. 54.

7. Ephraim Hardcastle (William Henry Pyne), *Wine and Walnuts, or After Dinner Chit-Chat* (London, 1823), vol. 1, pp. 281–304 (p. 286).

8. See Ann Bermingham, 'Technologies of Illusion: De Loutherbourg's Eidophusikon in Eighteenth-Century London', *Art History*, 39:2 (2016), pp. 376–99 (p. 382).

9. https://www.scottishpoetrylibrary.org.uk/poem/my-heart-leaps-up/, accessed 26.08.24.

10. Jonathan Crary, *Techniques of the Observer: On Vision and Modernity in the Nineteenth Century* (Cambridge, MA: MIT Press, 1990; repr. 1992), p. 5.

11. *Examiner*, June 1812, pp. 413–14, quoted in Martin Myrone, ed., *John Martin: Apocalypse* (London: Tate Publishing, 2011), p. 68.

12. See Martin Myrone, ed., *John Martin: Apocalypse* (London: Tate Publishing, 2011), p. 9.

13. Allan Cunningham, *The Life of Sir David Wilkie, with His Journals, Tours, and Critical Remarks on Works of Art; and a Selection of His Correspondence* (London: Murray, 1843), vol. 1, p. 58.

14. See Frédéric Ogée, ' "A New and Unforeseen Creation": Turner, English Landscape, and the Anthropo(s)cene', in Charlotte Gould and Sophie Mesplède, eds, *British Art and the Environment: Changes, Challenges, and Responses since the Industrial Revolution* (London: Routledge, 2022), pp. 166–81 (p. 176).

15. *Art Journal*, 1 October 1855, p. 285, quoted in Jennifer Green-Lewis, *Framing the Victorians: Photography and the Culture of Realism* (Ithaca, NY: Cornell University Press, 1996), p. 109.

16. John Ruskin, *Modern Painters* (London: George Allen, 1906), vol. 1 (first published anonymously in 1843), p. 448.

17. W.M. Thackeray, 'Important from the Seat of War! Letters from the East, by Our Own Bashi-Bozouk', *Punch*, 24 June 1854, quoted in Richard Pearson, *W.M. Thackeray and the Mediated Text: Writing for Periodicals in the Mid-Nineteenth Century* (Aldershot: Ashgate, 2000), p. 168.

18. W.M. Thackeray, *Notes on a Journey from Cornhill to Grand Cairo* (1845; repr. Wokingham: Dodo Press, 2011), p. 50.

19. Thackeray, *Notes on a Journey from Cornhill to Grand Cairo*, p. 43.
20. See Nicholas Tromans, *Richard Dadd: The Artist and the Asylum* (London: Tate Publishing, 2011), p. 53.

11. Women's Work

1. Sarah Biffin, letter to Daniel Lysons, 25 March 1810, quoted in Emma Rutherford and Ellie Smith, eds, *'Without Hands': The Art of Sarah Biffin* (London: Philip Mould and Company, 2022), p. 23.
2. Quoted in Barber, ed., *Now You See Us*, p. 113.
3. Quoted in Michelle Payne, *Marianne North: A Very Intrepid Painter* (London: Royal Botanic Gardens Kew, 2023), p. 89.
4. See Jennifer Higgie, *The Other Side: A Journey into Women, Art and the Spirit World* (London: Weidenfeld & Nicolson, 2023), p. 64.
5. https://www.poetryfoundation.org/poems/146804/in-an-artist39s-studio, accessed 10.10.2022.
6. See Elizabeth Prettejohn, *The Art of the Pre-Raphaelites* (London: Tate Publishing, 2000), p. 80.
7. See *William and Evelyn De Morgan* (Barnsley: De Morgan Foundation, 2016), p. 19.
8. Quoted in Lachlan Goudie, *The Story of Scottish Art* (London: Thames & Hudson, 2020), p. 252.
9. See Ysanne Holt, 'Cockburnspath to Kirkcudbright: Travelling East to West', in Laura Newton, ed., *Painting at the Edge: British Coastal Art Colonies 1880–1930* (Bristol: Sansome & Company, 2005), pp. 134–58 (p. 135).
10. Stanhope Forbes, 'Cornwall from a Painter's Point of View', 1900 lecture, quoted in Alison Bevan, 'Newlyn: "A Sort of English Concarneau"', in Newton, ed., *Painting at the Edge*, pp. 26–45 (p. 33).
11. See Julian Treuherz, *Victorian Painting* (London: Thames & Hudson, 1993), pp. 131–2.
12. See Charlotte Mullins, *A Little History of Art* (London: Yale University Press, 2022), pp. 209–10.

12. War's Rapid Rattle

1. *Blast*, no. 2, https://monoskop.org/Blast, accessed 09.09.24.
2. *Blast*, no. 2, https://monoskop.org/Blast, accessed 09.09.24.
3. Wilfred Owen, 'Anthem for Doomed Youth', in Jon Stallworthy, ed., *The Poems of Wilfred Owen* (London: Hogarth Press, 1985), p. 76.
4. Quoted in Barber, ed., *Now You See Us*, p. 186.
5. See *Scottish National War Memorial: Official Guide* (Norwich: Jarrold, n.d.), p. 4.
6. Roger Fry, 'Negro Art', in *Vision and Design* (1920; repr. Oxford: Oxford University Press, 1981), pp. 70–3 (at pp. 71–2).
7. Ronald Moody, 'Discovering Art: A Sculptor', broadcast on *Calling the West Indies*, BBC Overseas Service, 1946, transcript in Ego Ahaiwe

Sowinski, *Ronald Moody: Sculpting Life*, ed. Eleanor Clayton (London: Thames & Hudson, 2024), pp. 82–7 (p. 84).

8. Henry Moore, 'Primitive Art', *Listener*, 24 April 1941, p. 598, quoted in Frances Spalding, *The Real and the Romantic: English Art between Two World Wars* (London: Thames & Hudson, 2022), p. 195.

9. Barbara Hepworth, artist statement, in Herbert Read, ed., *Unit 1: The Modern Movement in English Architecture, Painting and Sculpture* (London: Cassell, 1934), p. 19.

10. Gwen John in a letter to Ursula Tyrwhitt, 6 June 1917, quoted in Alicia Foster, *Gwen John: Art and Life in London and Paris* (London: Thames & Hudson, 2023), p. 57.

11. Celia Paul, *Letters to Gwen John* (London: Jonathan Cape, 2022), p. 1.

12. Paul, *Letters to Gwen John*, p. 2.

13. Virginia Woolf, *A Room of One's Own and Three Guineas* (Oxford: Oxford University Press, 2008), p. 116.

13. THE SEARCH FOR SELF

1. Riann Coulter and Fintan O'Toole, 'Decoration: Mainie Jellett', in Fintan O'Toole, ed., *Modern Ireland in 100 Artworks* (Dublin: Royal Irish Academy, 2016), pp. 22–24 (p. 22) and Catherine Marshall and Yvonne Scott, eds, *Irish Art 1920–2020: Perspectives on Change* (Dublin: Royal Irish Academy, 2022), p. 38.

2. This process involved translating initial geometric shapes by moving them up, down and side to side before tilting or rotating them. See Catherine Marshall and Yvonne Scott, eds, *Irish Art 1920–2020: Perspectives on Change* (Dublin: Royal Irish Academy, 2022), p. 38.

3. Mainie Jellett, notes on her first lesson with Albert Gleizes, in Marshall and Scott, eds, *Irish Art 1920–2020*, p. 38.

4. See Diana Douhami, *Gluck: Her Biography* (London: Quercus, 2013), p. 5.

5. See David Boyd Haycock, 'Tendencies to Irrationality: Surrealism in Britain', in *British Surrealism* (London: Dulwich Picture Gallery, 2020), pp. 12–25 (p. 15).

6. Reviews in the *Daily Mail*, *Daily Telegraph* and *Spectator* quoted in Boyd Haycock, 'Tendencies to Irrationality', p. 18.

7. Eileen Agar, *A Look at My Life* (London: Methuen, 1988), p. 121.

8. Quoted in Joanna Moorhead, *Surreal Spaces: The Life and Art of Leonora Carrington* (London: Thames & Hudson, 2023), p. 76.

9. Quoted in Susan L. Aberth, *Leonora Carrington: Surrealism, Alchemy and Art* (London: Lund Humphries, 2010), p. 12.

14. RUINATION AND REBIRTH

1. Lee Miller, 'Through the Alsace Campaign', British *Vogue*, April 1945, pp. 50–53, 80, 83–84, 86, 90.

2. Lee Miller, 'Hitleriana', British *Vogue*, July 1945, pp. 36–37, 72–74.

3. Lee Miller, 'Germany – The War That Is Won', British *Vogue*, June 1945, pp. 40–44, 84, 86, 89.

4. Gerald Barry to Ian Cox, 26 April 1949, quoted in F.M. Leventhal, ' "A Tonic to the Nation": The Festival of Britain, 1951', *Albion* 27:3 (1995), pp. 445–53 (p. 450).

5. Herbert Read, *New Aspects of British Sculpture* (1952), quoted in *Geometry of Fear: Works from the Arts Council Collection*, pamphlet, Hayward Touring Exhibition, 2007, p. 2.

6. Aubrey Williams: 'In those days it was the mother country, you know; I felt I was privileged to be in Britain and doing my art in the mother country.' Quoted in Kwesi Owusu, ed., *Black British Culture and Society: A Text Reader* (London: Routledge, 2000), p. 474. See also Olusoga, *Black and British*, p. 495.

7. Quoted in Winder, *Bloody Foreigners*, p. 333.

8. Sam Selvon, *The Lonely Londoners* (1956; repr. London: Penguin, 2006), p. 21.

9. See Alex Farquharson and David A. Bailey, eds, *Life between Islands: Caribbean-British Art 1950s–Now* (London: Tate, 2021), p. 82. See also Olusoga, *Black and British*, p. 509.

10. Quoted in Michael Bird, *This Is Tomorrow: Twentieth-Century Britain and Its Artists* (London: Thames & Hudson, 2022), p. 289.

11. Francis Newton Souza, *Words and Lines* (London: Villiers, 1959), p. 7.

12. This was inscribed in Urdu on his 1962 painting *One to Nine and One to Seven*.

15. ART'S EXPANDED FIELD

1. Quoted in Laura Freeman, *Ways of Life: Jim Ede and the Kettle's Yard Artists* (London: Jonathan Cape, 2023), p. 232.

2. Barbara Hepworth, 'Approach to Sculpture', *The Studio*, October 1946, pp. 97–101 (p. 98).

3. See Michael Bird, *The St Ives Artists: A Biography of Place and Time* (London: Lund Humphries, 2016), p. 117.

4. Peter Lanyon, letter to Paul Feiler, 1952, quoted in Andrew Lanyon, *Peter Lanyon 1918–1964* (Penzance: Andrew Lanyon, 1990), p. 125.

5. Jacquetta Hawkes, *A Land* (London: Cresset Press, 1951), p. 1.

6. Patrick Heron, 'Art Is Autonomous', *The Twentieth Century*, September 1955, repr. in *Painter as Critic: Patrick Heron Selected Writings*, ed. Mel Gooding (London: Tate Gallery, 1998), pp. 93–9 (p. 95).

7. https://www.michaelcraigmartin.co.uk/artworks/11-an-oak-tree/, accessed 07.10.24.

8. See Andrew Wilson, ed., *Conceptual Art in Britain 1964–1979* (London: Tate Publishing, 2016), p. 39.

16. STAND UP AND BE COUNTED

1. Rosalind Delmar, 'Women and Work: A Document on the Division of Labour and Industry', *Spare Rib* 40 (1975), pp. 32–3, repr. in Rozsika Parker and Griselda Pollock, *Framing Feminism: Art and the Women's Movement 1970–1985* (London: HarperCollins, 1987), pp. 201–2.

2. Germaine Greer, *The Female Eunuch* (1971; repr. London: HarperCollins, 1993), p. 14.

3. Greer, *The Female Eunuch*, p. 13.

4. See Jo Spence, *Work (Part I)* and *Work (Part II)* (London: SPACE and Studio Voltaire, 2012), at https://hymancollection.org/bodies-of-work/jo-spence-the-history-lesson-self-as-image-also-known-as-remodelling-photo-history-1982-83/, accessed 08.10.24.

5. Lubaina Himid discussing *Framing Feminism* with Griselda Pollock, ICA, London, 21.01.1988, https://blogs.bl.uk/sound-and-vision/2020/08/recording-of-the-week-.html, accessed 08.10.24.

6. Boyce and Johnson were born in Britain. Himid was born in Zanzibar but raised in Britain. Ryan was born in Montserrat, a British Overseas Territory, and was also raised in Britain. Niati is an Algerian artist who moved to Britain as a student.

7. The term 'Afro-Asian' was used by Rasheed Araeen in *The Other Story* exhibition (1989) but many find this collective grouping of people from disparate regions problematic.

8. Lubaina Himid, *The Thin Black Line* (London: ICA, 1985), n.p.

9. Sutapa Biswas, 'Artist's Statement 1987', in *Sutapa Biswas* (London: Institute of International Visual Arts, 2004), p. 20.

10. Stuart Hall, 'Thinking the Diaspora: Home-Thoughts from Abroad' (1999), quoted in Farquharson and Bailey, eds, *Life between Islands*, p. 11.

11. See Jean Fisher, 'The Other Story and the Past Imperfect', *Tate Papers* 12 (2009), https://www.tate.org.uk/research/tate-papers/12/the-other-story-and-the-past-imperfect, accessed 08.10.24.

12. See Hammad Nasar, 'Like a Fever: Navigating the Afterlife of *The Other Story*', *Field Notes* 4 (2015), https://aaa.org.hk/en/like-a-fever/like-a-fever/notes-from-the-field-navigating-the-afterlife-of-the-other-story, accessed 08.10.24.

13. See Rianna Jade Parker, *A Brief History of Black British Art* (London: Tate Publishing, 2021), p. 82.

14. Kim Lim, letter to Andrew Dempsey, 9 June 1988, in the Rasheed Araeen Archives, quoted in Nasar, 'Like a Fever'.

15. Many of the murals discussed are included in the Murals of Northern Ireland digital archive at https://ccdl.claremont.edu/digital/collection/mni, accessed 11.10.24.

16. Shaws Road, Belfast (1981). See Bill Rolston, *Politics and Painting: Murals and Conflict in Northern Ireland* (Rutherford, NJ: Fairleigh Dickinson University Press, 1991), p. 85.

17. Murals of Northern Ireland digital archive, ref. mni00393.
18. Chamberlain Street, Derry (1985), in Rolston, *Politics and Painting*, p. 97.
19. Seamus Heaney, 'Whatever You Say, Say Nothing', originally published in *North* (1975), reprinted in Seamus Heaney, *Opened Ground: Poems 1966–1996* (London: Faber & Faber, 1998), pp. 131–3.
20. GFA is the Good Friday Agreement of 1998. In 2023 the twenty-fifth anniversary (GFA 25) was commemorated.
21. Heaney, 'Whatever You Say, Say Nothing', p. 132.

17. COOL BRITANNIA?

1. Douglas Crimp, 'The End of Painting', *October* 16 (1981), pp. 69–86 (p. 75).
2. See for example Richard Shone, 'A New Spirit in Painting at the Royal Academy', *Burlington Magazine* 123:936 (1981), pp. 182–3, 185 (p. 185).
3. *A New Spirit in Painting* (London: Royal Academy of Arts, 1981), pp. 14–15.
4. *A New Spirit in Painting*, p. 16.
5. For example, the New Glasgow Boys never made it onto the Turner Prize shortlist. They were searingly honest realist painters who graduated from Glasgow School of Art in the 1980s and included Steven Campbell, Peter Howson, Adrian Wiszniewski and Ken Currie.
6. Michael Craig-Martin quoted in Richard Shone, 'From "Freeze" to *House*: 1988–94', in *Sensation: Young British Artists from the Saatchi Collection* (London: Thames & Hudson/Royal Academy of Arts, 1997), pp. 12–25 (p. 18).
7. Gillian Wearing, *Signs that say what you want them to say not signs that say what someone else wants you to say* (1992–3).
8. Quoted in Charlotte Mullins, *Rachel Whiteread* (London: Tate Publishing, 2017), p. 54.
9. There were no Black women artists included. There were three Black men artists: Chris Ofili, Yinka Shonibare and Alain Miller.
10. Relative newcomers Jupiter Artland in West Lothian and Tremenheere Sculpture Gardens in Penzance, Cornwall, opened in 2009 and 2012 respectively.
11. Rudyard Kipling articulated this in his colonial poem 'We and They' from 1926: 'Father, Mother, and Me, / Sister and Auntie say, / All the people like us are "We", / And every one else is "They"'. Cited in Carl Bridge and Kent Fedorowich, *The British World: Diaspora, Culture and Identity* (London: Frank Cass, 2003), p. 1.
12. Homi K. Bhabha, *The Location of Culture* (London: Routledge, 1994), p. 19.
13. 'Yinka Shonibare CBE RA in Conversation with Charlotte Mullins', in *Ritual Ecstasy of the Modern* (London: Cristea Roberts Gallery, 2023), pp. 6–18 (p. 7).
14. 'Yinka Shonibare CBE RA in Conversation with Charlotte Mullins', p. 7.

15. Yinka Shonibare, interview with Charlotte Mullins, 23 June 2023 (unpublished transcript).
16. 'Yinka Shonibare CBE RA in Conversation with Charlotte Mullins', p. 7.
17. The central library of the University of Mosul is one of the lost libraries inscribed on the porcelain walls of *Library in Exile*, along with the ancient library of Alexandria. See https://www.britishmuseum.org/exhibitions/edmund-de-waal-library-exile, accessed 16.10.24, and https://www.theguardian.com/books/2022/feb/25/a-symbol-of-new-beginning-mosuls-university-library-reopens, accessed 27.10.24. Abigail Reynolds's film *Lost Libraries* (2018) similarly considers these erasures from history. Her film and book are based on her five-month journey along the historic Silk Road, looking for traces of these lost centres of knowledge. See Abigail Reynolds, *Lost Libraries* (Berlin: Hatje Cantz, 2017).
18. Rosalind Nashashibi, statement, 15 October 2023, https://lux.org.uk/event/electrical-gaza-rosalind-nashashibi, accessed 16.10.2024.
19. When the Israel–Hamas conflict erupted on 7 October 2023, Nashashibi published a statement relating to *Electrical Gaza*. See https://lux.org.uk/event/electrical-gaza-rosalind-nashashibi/, accessed 15.10.24.
20. Two performances of *Mathroo Basha* were staged at the Barbican Centre in London on 11–12 October 2024, as part of Dance Umbrella.
21. Hetain Patel, 'Q&A', *Tate Magazine*, Spring 2023, pp. 19–20 (p. 20).
22. Sin Wai Kin and Tai Shani, 'Altar Egos', *Elephant* 47 (2022), pp. 86–101 (p. 97).

18. THE FUTURE NOW

1. See Noni Stacey, *Leave to Remain: A Snapshot of Brexit* (London: Lund Humphries, 2023), pp. 88–9 and cover.
2. Hannah Rose Woods, *Rule, Nostalgia: A Backwards History of Britain* (London: W.H. Allen, 2022), p. 35.
3. David Olusoga, 'The History of British Slave Ownership Has Been Buried: Now Its Scale Can Be Revealed', *Observer*, 12 July 2015, https://www.theguardian.com/world/2015/jul/12/british-history-slavery-buried-scale-revealed, accessed 21.01.25.
4. See Gareth Harris, *Censored Art Today* (London: Lund Humphries/Sotheby's Institute of Art, 2022), p. 76.
5. Jonathan Heaf, 'Windrush Memorial Artist: "Marc Quinn's Jen Reid Statue Colonised the Colston Plinth and Hijacked the BLM Movement. It's a Con"', *GQ*, 20 July 2020, https://www.gq-magazine.co.uk/culture/article/marc-quinns-jen-reid-statue-thomas-j-price, accessed 21.01.25.
6. 'Anthony Downey and Yinka Shonibare', *Bomb* 93 (2005), pp. 24–31 (p. 29).
7. See Johanne Løgstrup, *The Contemporary Condition 14: Co-existence of Times – A Conversation with John Akomfrah* (Berlin: Sternberg Press, 2020), pp. 24–5.
8. Cornelia Parker, exhibition text for Room 8: Politics, at her solo exhibition *Cornelia Parker*, Tate Britain, London, 19 May–16 October 2022.

9. Hans Ulrich Obrist, 'Interview with Richard Mosse', *FACT* 4 (2022), pp. 104–35 (p. 123).

10. *Broken Spectre* is a collaboration between Mosse, cinematographer Trevor Tweeten and composer Ben Frost.

11. https://www.sandbox.game/en/experiences/The%20British%20Museum%20Experience/bff3cdfc-f704-4d88-97c6-33975c51a43d/page/, accessed 31.05.2025.

12. Guy Debord, *The Society of the Spectacle* (1967), quoted in Michael Horsham, *Hello Human: A History of Visual Communication* (London: Thames & Hudson, 2022), p. 188.

13. Jonathan Crary, *24/7: Late Capitalism and the Ends of Sleep* (London: Verso, 2014), p. 45.

14. Instagram message exchange between Gordon Cheung and Charlotte Mullins, 20–2 October 2024.

15. Holly Herndon and Mat Dryhurst, *The Call*, exhibition pamphlet (London: Serpentine, 2024), p. 2.

16. Meller loves an art pun – Ai-Da's name is a conflation of mathematician Ada Lovelace, AI and Aida-n's own name rolled into one. https://www.ai-darobot.com/, accessed 23.10.24. See also Horsham, *Hello Human*, p. 209, and Carlie Porterfield, 'Painting by the AI Robot Ai-Da Sells for More Than $1m at Sotheby's', *Art Newspaper*, 8 November 2024, https://www.theartnewspaper.com/2024/11/08/ai-da-robot-painting-sells-one-million-sothebys, accessed 21.01.25.

17. Marcus du Sautoy, *The Creativity Code: How AI Is Learning to Write, Paint and Think* (London: 4th Estate, 2019), pp. 2–3.

18. See Victoria Ivanova, Eva Jäger, Alasdair Milne and Gardy Zhexi Zhang, *Future Art Ecosystems: Art x Public AI* (London: Serpentine Gallery, 2024), p. 126.

19. James Bridle, *Ways of Being: Animals, Plants, Machines: The Search for a Planetary Intelligence* (London: Penguin, 2023), p. 6.

20. Instagram message exchange between Gordon Cheung and Charlotte Mullins, 20–2 October 2024.

21. Interview with Gordon Cheung, posted 4 September 2024, https://www.dacs.org.uk/news-events/interview-with-artist-gordon-cheung-on-art-and-technology, accessed 22.10.24.

FURTHER READING

GENERAL TITLES FOR FURTHER READING

There are many intersections between these discrete areas of history (such as Black history and imperial history), but I hope the subdivisions offer a useful way of approaching the wide range of material covered. These are all titles that I referred to while writing various chapters of *The Art Isles*.

NATIONAL HISTORY

Peter Ackroyd, *Civil War* (London: Pan Books, 2014)

Jeremy Black, *A Short History of Britain*, second edition (London: Bloomsbury, 2015)

Barry Cunliffe, *Bretons & Britons: The Fight for Identity* (Oxford: Oxford University Press, 2021)

Brian Feeney, *A Short History of the Troubles* (Dublin: O'Brien Press, 2004)

Charlotte Higgins, *Under Another Sky: Journeys in Roman Britain* (London: Vintage Books, 2014)

John O'Beirne Ranelagh, *A Short History of Ireland* (Cambridge: Cambridge University Press, 1999)

Neil Oliver, *A History of Ancient Britain* (London: Weidenfeld & Nicolson, 2012)

Neil Oliver, *A History of Scotland* (London: BBC Books, 2009)

Susan Owens, *Imagining England's Past: Inspiration, Enchantment, Obsession* (London: Thames & Hudson, 2023)

Chris Stringer, *Homo Britannicus: The Incredible Story of Human Life in Britain* (London: Penguin, 2006)

Robert Winder, *Bloody Foreigners: The Story of Immigration to Britain* (London: Abacus, 2013)

Hannah Rose Woods, *Rule, Nostalgia: A Backwards History of Britain* (London: W.H. Allen, 2022)

NATIONAL ART HISTORY

Patricia Allerston, ed., *Scottish Art in 100 Works* (Edinburgh: National Galleries of Scotland, 2023)

Bruce Arnold, *A Concise History of Irish Art* (New York: Oxford University Press, 1977)

Fionna Barber, *Art in Ireland since 1910* (London: Reaktion Books, 2013)

Tabitha Barber, ed., *Now You See Us: Women Artists in Britain 1520–1920* (London: Tate Publishing, 2024)

David Bindman, general ed., *The History of British Art*, three vols (New Haven, CT: Yale Center for British Art, 2008): vol. 1 600–1600; vol. 2 1600–1870; vol. 3 1870–2008

Stephen Ellcock and Mat Osman, *England on Fire: A Visual Journey through Albion's Psychic Landscape* (London: Watkins Media, 2022)

James Fenton, *School of Genius: A History of the Royal Academy of Arts* (London: Royal Academy of Arts, 2006)

Lachlan Goudie, *The Story of Scottish Art* (London: Thames & Hudson, 2020)

Charlotte Gould and Sophie Mesplède, eds, *British Art and the Environment: Changes, Challenges, and Responses since the Industrial Revolution* (London: Routledge, 2022)

Murdo Macdonald, *Scottish Art* (London: Thames & Hudson, 2021)

Catherine Marshall and Yvonne Scott, eds, *Irish Art 1920–2020: Perspectives on Change* (Dublin: Royal Irish Academy, 2022)

Charlotte Mullins, *A Little History of Art* (London: Yale University Press, 2022)

Fintan O'Toole, ed., *Modern Ireland in 100 Artworks* (Dublin: Royal Irish Academy, 2016)

Susan Owens, *Spirit of Place: Artists, Writers & the British Landscape* (London: Thames & Hudson, 2020)

Eric Rowan, ed., *Art in Wales 2000 BC–AD 1850* (Cardiff: University of Wales Press, 1978)

Jennifer Scott, *The Royal Portrait: Image and Impact* (London: Royal Collection, 2010)

James Stourton and Charles Sebag-Montefiore, *The British as Art Collectors: From the Tudors to the Present* (London: Scala Publishers, 2012)

IMPERIAL HISTORY

Carl Bridge and Kent Fedorowich, *The British World: Diaspora, Culture and Identity* (London: Frank Cass, 2003)

Antoinette Burton, ed., *Politics and Empire in Victorian Britain: A Reader* (New York: Palgrave, 2001)

Rosie Dias and Kate Smith, *British Women and Cultural Practices of Empire, 1770–1940* (London: Bloomsbury, 2019)

Catherine Hall and Sonya Rose, eds, *At Home with the Empire: Metropolitan Culture and the Imperial World* (Cambridge: Cambridge University Press, 2009)

John M. MacKenzie, *A Cultural History of the British Empire* (London: Yale University Press, 2022)

Thomas Pakenham, *The Scramble for Africa* (London: Abacus, 1991)

Alice Procter, *The Whole Picture: The Colonial Story of the Art in Our Museums and Why We Need to Talk about It* (London: Cassell, 2020)

Edward W. Said, *Culture and Imperialism* (London: Vintage, 1993)

Sathnam Sanghera, *Empireland: How Imperialism Has Shaped Modern Britain* (London: Viking, 2021)

BLACK HISTORY

Victoria Avery and Jake Subryan Richards, *Black Atlantic: Power People Resistance* (Cambridge: Fitzwilliam Museum, 2023)

Paul Gilroy, *The Black Atlantic: Modernity and Double Consciousness* (1993; repr. London: Verso, 2022)

Stuart Hall, *The Fateful Triangle: Race, Ethnicity, Nation* (Cambridge, MA: Harvard University Press, 2017)

Afua Hirsch, *BRIT(ish): On Race, Identity and Belonging* (London: Vintage, 2018)

David Olusoga, *Black and British: A Forgotten History* (London: Macmillan, 2016)

Olivette Otele, *African Europeans: An Untold Story* (London: Hurst & Company, 2020)

Kwesi Owusu, ed., *Black British Culture and Society: A Text Reader* (London: Routledge, 2000)

HELPFUL WEBSITES

Most museums and galleries have useful websites, and many have a substantial part of their holdings accessible online. See also:

https://artuk.org The Art UK database of art in public collections

https://collections.britishart.yale.edu/catalog Yale Center for British Art in New Haven, Connecticut

http://www.gothicivories.courtauld.ac.uk A global database for Gothic ivories run by the Courtauld Institute of Art in London

https://www.megalithic.co.uk A useful guide to the UK and Ireland's megalithic tombs and sites

http://www.megalithicireland.com A guide to Ireland's megalithic tombs and sites

I used websites for the latest census information (www.cso.ie; www.scotland census.gov.uk; www.nisra.gov.uk; www.ons.gov.uk) and for converting historical currency into a contemporary equivalent (https://www.nationalarchives.gov.uk/currency-converter). The history of the royal family can be researched at www.royal.uk and the history of Parliament at www.parliament.uk.

CHAPTER-SPECIFIC FURTHER READING AND RESOURCES

Because this bibliography is already unwieldy, I have not listed the many excellent guidebooks I used from the churches, chapels, ancient burial grounds, museums and galleries I visited. Mostly they can only be acquired at the venue and often no author is named, but they were nevertheless a vital resource. I have also not listed individual artist monographs or exhibition catalogues unless they were vital to the development of a chapter.

1. WHAT'S IN A NAME? AN INTRODUCTION

James R. Akerman and Robert W. Karrow Jr, eds, *Maps: Finding Our Place in the World* (Chicago: University of Chicago Press, 2007)

Jerry Brotton, *A History of the World in Twelve Maps* (London: Penguin, 2012)

Denis Cosgrove, *Apollo's Eye: A Cartographic Genealogy of the Earth in the Western Imagination* (Baltimore, MD: Johns Hopkins University Press, 2003)

Helen Gordon, *Notes from Deep Time* (London: Profile, 2021)

Paul Lyle, *The Abyss of Time: A Study in Geological Time and Earth's History* (Edinburgh: Dunedin Academic Press, 2016)

Tim Marshall, *The Power of Geography* (London: Elliott & Thompson, 2021)

Doreen Massey, 'Places and Their Pasts, History Workshop Journal' 39 (1995), pp.182–92

Doreen Massey, *Space, Place and Gender* (Cambridge: Polity Press, 1994)

2. LIFE BEFORE HISTORY

Andy Burnham, *The Old Stones: A Field Guide to the Megalithic Sites of Britain and Ireland* (London: Watkins Media, 2018)

Andrew Cochrane and Andrew Meirion Jones, eds, *Visualising the Neolithic: Abstraction, Figuration, Performance, Representation* (Oxford: Oxbow Books, 2012)

Jill Cook, *Ice Age Art: The Arrival of the Modern Mind* (London: British Museum Press, 2013)

George Eogan and Elizabeth Shee Twohig, eds, *The Megalithic Art of the Passage Tombs at Knowth, County Meath* (Dublin: Royal Irish Academy, 2022)

Duncan Garrow and Neil Wilkin, *The World of Stonehenge* (London: British Museum Press, 2022)

David Lewis-Williams, *The Mind in the Cave* (London: Thames & Hudson, 2002)

George Nash, 'Further Possible Discoveries of Engravings within Cathole Cave, Gower, Swansea', *Proceedings of the University of Bristol Spelaeological Society* 26:3 (2015), pp. 1–10

George Nash et al., 'A Discovery of Possible Upper Paleolithic Parietal Art in Cathole Cave, Gower Peninsula, South Wales', *Proceedings of the University of Bristol Spelaeological Society* 25:3 (2012), pp. 327–36

Mary-Ann Ochota, *Secret Britain: Unearthing Our Mysterious Past* (London: Frances Lincoln, 2020)

Paul Pettitt, Paul Bahn and Sergio Ripoll, eds, *Palaeolithic Cave Art at Creswell Crags in European Context* (Oxford: Oxford University Press, 2007)
Mike Pitts, *Digging Up Britain: A New History in Ten Extraordinary Discoveries* (London: Thames & Hudson, 2019)
www.creswell-crags.org.uk/virtual-tour

3. IMMIGRATION OR ATTACK?

Miranda Aldhouse-Green, *The Celtic Myths: A Guide to the Ancient Gods and Legends* (London: Thames & Hudson, 2015)
Barbican Research Associates, *The Staffordshire Hoard: An Anglo-Saxon Treasure*, online dataset, https://doi.org/10.5284/1041576
Bede, *The Ecclesiastical History of the English People* (c.731, repr. Oxford: Oxford University Press, 2008)
Stephen R. Cosh with David S. Neal, 'The Rutland Achilles and Hector Mosaic', *ARA News* 47 (2002), pp. 10–13
Jas Elsner, *The Art of the Roman Empire*, second edition (Oxford: Oxford University Press, 2018)
Chris Fern, Tania Dickinson and Leslie Webster, *The Staffordshire Hoard: An Anglo-Saxon Treasure* (London: Society of Antiquaries, 2019)
A.P. Fitzpatrick, 'The Finds from La Tène in the British Museum: La Tène, un site, un mythe 6', *Antiquaries Journal* 98 (2018), pp. 43–80
James Graham-Campbell, *Viking Art* (London: Thames & Hudson, 2013)
Richard Hobbs and Ralph Jackson, *Roman Britain* (London: British Museum Press, 2010)
Venceslas Kruta, *Celtic Art,* trans. Keith and Angela Bradford (London: Phaidon, 2015)
Kevin Leahy, Roger Bland, Della Hooke, Alex Jones and Elisabeth Okasha, 'The Staffordshire (Ogley Hay) Hoard: Recovery of a Treasure', *Antiquity* 85 (2011), pp. 202–20
Legion: Life in the Roman Army (London: British Museum Press, 2024)
Ruth and Vincent Megaw, *Celtic Art: From Its Beginnings to the Book of Kells* (London: Thames & Hudson, 1989)
H. Michell, 'The Edict of Diocletian: A Study of Price Fixing in the Roman Empire', *Canadian Journal of Economics and Political Science* 13:1 (1947), pp. 1–12
D.S. Neal and S.R. Cosh, *Roman Mosaics of Britain*, vol. 1, *Northern Britain, Incorporating the Midlands and East Anglia* (London: Society of Antiquaries, 2002)
Graham Robb, *The Ancient Paths: Discovering the Lost Map of Celtic Europe* (London: Picador, 2013)
Alice Roberts, *The Celts: Search for a Civilization* (London: Quercus, 2015)
John Thomas, Jennifer Browning and Jane Masséglia, 'When Troy Came to Rutland', *ARGO*, Autumn/Winter 2022, pp. 11–13
Leslie Webster, *Anglo-Saxon Art* (London: British Museum Press, 2012)
https://sashamaps.net/images/roman_roads_britain_150.png

4. CHRISTIANITY AS CREATIVE IMPULSE

Michelle P. Brown, *The Lindisfarne Gospels and the Early Medieval World* (London: British Library, 2011)

David H. Caldwell, Mark A. Hall and Caroline M. Wilkinson, *The Lewis Chessmen Unmasked* (Edinburgh: NMS Enterprises Ltd, 2010)

Gordon Ewart, Dennis Gallagher and Anna Ritchie, 'The Dupplin Cross: Recent Investigations', *Proceedings of the Society of Antiquities in Scotland* 137 (2007), pp. 319–36

Jill Harden, *The Picts* (Edinburgh: Historic Scotland, 2022)

George Henderson and Isabel Henderson, *The Art of the Picts: Sculpture and Metalwork in Early Medieval Scotland* (London: Thames & Hudson, 2004)

Colum Hourihane, ed., *Insular & Anglo-Saxon Art and Thought in the Early Medieval Period* (University Park, PA: Penn State University Press, 2011)

Eleanor Jackson, *The Lindisfarne Gospels: Art, History & Inspiration* (London: British Library, 2022)

Lloyd Laing, 'How Late Were Pictish Symbols Employed?', *Proceedings of the Society of Antiquaries of Scotland* 130 (2000), pp. 637–50

Julian Luxford, 'The Relics of Thomas Becket in England', *Journal of the British Archaeological Association* 173:1 (2020), pp. 124–42

Bernard Meehan, *The Book of Kells* (London: Thames & Hudson, 2018)

Gordon Noble, Martin Goldberg and Derek Hamilton, 'The Development of the Pictish Symbol System: Inscribing Identity beyond the Edges of Empire', *Antiquity* 92:365 (2018), pp. 1329–48

Neil Price, *The Children of Ash & Elm: A History of the Vikings* (London: Penguin, 2020)

M. Redknap, N. Edwards, S. Youngs, A. Lane and J. Knight, eds, *Pattern and Purpose in Insular Art* (Oxford: Oxbow Books, 2001)

Roger Stalley, 'Iona, the Vikings and the Making of the Book of Kells', *History Ireland* 21:3 (2013), pp. 14–17

Matthew Townend, *Viking Age Yorkshire* (Pickering: Blackthorn Press, 2014)

Mary Wellesley, *Hidden Hands: The Lives of Manuscripts and Their Makers* (London: riverrun, 2021)

Gareth Williams, Peter Pentz and Matthias Wemhoff, eds, *Vikings: Life and Legend* (London: British Museum Press, 2014)

https://digitalcollections.tcd.ie/concern/works/hm50tr726?locale=en (The Book of Kells)

5. TO BE A PILGRIM

Sally Badham and Sophie Oosterwijk, *Monumental Industry: The Production of Tomb Monuments in England and Wales in the Long Fourteenth Century* (Donington: Shaun Tyas, 2010)

Andrew Bridgeford, *1066: The Hidden History in the Bayeux Tapestry* (New York: Walker & Co., 2005)

John Butler, *The Quest for Becket's Bones: The Mystery of the Relics of St Thomas Becket of Canterbury* (New Haven, CT: Yale University Press, 1995)

Elizabeth Carson Pastan and Stephen D. White, 'Problematizing Patronage: Odo of Bayeux and the Bayeux Tapestry', in Martin K. Foys, Karen Eileen Overbey and Dan Terkla, eds, *The Bayeux Tapestry: New Interpretations* (Woodbridge: Boydell Press, 2009), pp. 1–24

Geoffrey Chaucer, *The Canterbury Tales*, trans. Nevill Coghill (London: Penguin, 1977)

Francis Cheetham, *English Medieval Alabasters* (Woodbridge: Boydell Press, 2005)

Enamels of Limoges 1100–1350 (New York: Metropolitan Museum of Art, 1996)

Colum Hourihane, ed., *From Minor to Major: The Minor Arts in Medieval Art History* (University Park, PA: Penn State University Press, 2012)

Neil MacGregor, 'To Be a Pilgrim', in MacGregor, *Living with the Gods* (London: Penguin, 2018), pp. 200–16

Zuleika Murat, ed., *English Alabaster Carvings and Their Cultural Contexts* (Woodbridge: Boydell Press, 2019)

David Musgrove and Michael Lewis, *The Story of the Bayeux Tapestry: Unravelling the Norman Conquest* (London: Thames & Hudson, 2021)

Christopher Norton, 'Viewing the Bayeux Tapestry, Now and Then', *Journal of the British Archaeological Association* 172:1 (2019), pp. 52–89

Stella Rubenstein, 'Some Limoges Reliquaries of the Late Twelfth Century', *Arts & Decoration* 7:6 (1917), pp. 304–6, 322

Brian Spencer, *Pilgrim Souvenirs and Secular Badges: Medieval Finds from Excavations in London* (London: Stationery Office, 1998)

Diana Webb, *Pilgrimage in Medieval England* (London: Hambleton and London, 2000)

Diana Webb, *Pilgrims and Pilgrimage in the Medieval West* (London: I.B. Tauris, 1999)

Kim Woods, *Cut in Alabaster: A Material of Sculpture and Its European Traditions 1330–1530* (London: Harvey Miller, 2018)

https://www.chichestercathedral.org.uk/visiting/cathedral-plan/delve-deeper-chichester-reliefs

https://www.peterborough-cathedral.org.uk/history.aspx

https://www.westminster-abbey.org

6. APOCALYPSE NOW: THE ANNIHILATION OF HISTORY

Eamon Duffy, *The Stripping of the Altars: Traditional Religion in England, 1400–1580* (London: Yale University Press, 1992)

Ben Edge, *Folklore Rising* (London: Watkins Media, 2024)

Susan Foister, *Holbein in England* (London: Tate Publishing, 2006)

Barbara Freitag, *Sheela-na-Gigs: Unravelling an Enigma* (London: Routledge, 2004)

Dillian Gordon, 'A Possible French Source for the Left Wing of the Wilton Diptych', *Burlington Magazine* 157:1353 (2015), pp. 821–6

Dillian Gordon et al., *The Wilton Diptych* (London: National Gallery, 2015)

Susan L. Green, *Tree of Jesse Iconography in Northern Europe in the Fifteenth and Sixteenth Centuries* (London: Routledge, 2019)

Kate Heard, *Holbein at the Tudor Court* (London: Royal Collection, 2023)

Susan E. James, *The Feminine Dynamic in English Art 1485–1603: Women as Consumers, Patrons and Painters* (Farnham: Ashgate, 2009)

Miranda Kaufmann, *Black Tudors: The Untold Story* (London: Oneworld, 2017)

Ashby Kinch, *Imago Mortis: Mediating Images of Death in Late Medieval Culture* (Leiden: Brill, 2013)

Nina Lyon, *Uprooted: On the Trail of the Green Man* (London: Faber & Faber, 2016)

Richard Marks, *Stained Glass in England during the Middle Ages* (London: Routledge, 1993)

Mavis E. Mate, *Women in Medieval English Society* (Cambridge: Cambridge University Press, 1999)

John Phillips, *The Reformation of Images: Destruction of Art in England, 1535–1660* (Berkeley: University of California Press, 1973)

Georgia Rhoades, 'Decoding the Sheela-na-gig', *Feminist Formations* 22:2 (2010), pp. 167–94

David Starkey, ed., *Henry VIII: A European Court in England* (London: National Maritime Museum, 1991)

7. FOR QUEEN (AND KING) AND COUNTRY

David Arnold, *The Age of Discovery: 1400–1600*, second edition (London: Routledge, 2002)

Tarnya Cooper, *Elizabeth I and Her People* (London: National Portrait Gallery, 2013)

David Esterly, *Grinling Gibbons and the Art of Carving* (London: V&A Publications, 1998)

Christina J. Faraday, *Tudor Liveliness: Vivid Art in Post-Reformation England* (London: Paul Mellon Centre for Studies in British Art, 2023)

Karen Hearn, *Rubens and Britain* (London: Tate Publishing, 2011)

James R. Jewitt, 'Eliza Fortuna: Reconsidering the Ditchley Portrait of Elizabeth I', *Burlington Magazine* 156:1334 (2014), pp. 293–8

Victoria Leatham, Jon Culverhouse and Eric Till, *Burghley: England's Greatest Elizabethan House* (Peterborough: Jarrold, 2022)

Gregory Martin, *Rubens in London: Art and Diplomacy* (London: Harvey Miller, 2011)

Kim Sloan, *A New World: England's First View of America* (London: British Museum Press, 2007)

Letizia Treves, *Artemisia* (London: National Gallery, 2020)

Christopher White, *Anthony van Dyck and the Art of Portraiture* (London: Modern Art Press, 2021)

https://www.rmg.co.uk/stories/topics/why-are-there-three-versions-armada-portrait

8. The unspeakable price of the Grand Tour

Tabitha Barber, ed., *Mary Beale: Portrait of a Seventeenth-Century Painter, Her Family and Her Studio* (London: Geffrye Museum, 1999)

Elizabeth Bartman, *The Ince Blundell Collection of Classical Sculpture*, vol. 3, *The Ideal Sculpture* (Liverpool: National Museums & Galleries on Merseyside, 2017). See also Jane Fejfer and Edmund Southworth, vol. 1, part 1: *The Female Portraits* (Liverpool: National Museums & Galleries on Merseyside, 1991) and Jane Fejfer, vol. 1, part 2: *The Male Portraits* (Liverpool: National Museums & Galleries on Merseyside, 1997)

Adam Eaker, *Van Dyck and the Making of English Portraiture* (London: Paul Mellon Centre for Studies in British Art, 2022)

Entangled Pasts, 1768–Now: Art, Colonialism and Change (London: Royal Academy of Arts, 2024)

Bernadette Fort and Angela Rosenthal, eds, *The Other Hogarth: Aesthetics of Difference* (Princeton, NJ: Princeton University Press, 2001)

Gretchen Gerzina, *Black England: A Forgotten Georgian History*, revised edition (London: John Murray, 2022)

Christopher Hussey, 'Ince Blundell Hall, Lancashire – I', *Country Life* 123:3195 (1958), pp. 756–9. See also Part II, *Country Life* 123:3196 (1958), pp. 816–19, and Part III, *Country Life* 123:3197 (1958), pp. 876–9

Catharine Macleod and Julia Marciari Alexander, *Painted Ladies: Women at the Court of Charles II* (London: National Portrait Gallery, 2001)

Alison Smith, David Blayney Brown and Carol Jacobi, eds, *Artists and Empire: Facing Britain's Imperial Past* (London: Tate Publishing, 2016)

https://philipmould.com/news/364-interracial-double-portraits-portrait-of-dido-belle-and-lady-elizabeth-murray/

https://www.scone-palace.co.uk/dido-belle

9. Age of 'Enlightenment'?

Lucy Bamford and Jonathan Wallis, *Joseph Wright of Derby* (Derby: Derby Museums, 2017)

Stephanie Barczewski, *Country Houses and the British Empire 1700–1930* (Manchester: Manchester University Press, 2014)

Timothy Barringer, Geoff Quilley and Douglas Fordham, *Art and the British Empire* (Manchester: Manchester University Press, 2007)

James Delbourgo, *Collecting the World: The Life and Curiosity of Hans Sloane* (London: Penguin, 2017)

Renate Dohmen, ed., *Empire and Art: British India* (Manchester: Manchester University Press, 2017)

Olaudah Equiano, *The Interesting Narrative of the Life of Olaudah Equiano, or Gustavus Vassa, The African, Written by Himself* (London, 1789)

Jocelyn Hackforth-Jones, *Between Worlds: Voyagers to Britain 1700–1850* (London: National Portrait Gallery, 2007)

T.J. Mitchell, *Landscape and Power*, second edition (Chicago: University of Chicago Press, 2002)

Geoff Quilley and John Bonehill, eds, *William Hodges 1744–1797: The Art of Exploration* (London: National Maritime Museum, 2004)

Nick Robins, *The Corporation that Changed the World: How the East India Company Shaped the Modern Multinational* (London: Pluto Press, 2012)

Charles Saumarez Smith, *The Company of Artists: The Origins of the Royal Academy of Arts in London* (London: Modern Art Press, 2012)

Robert W. Uphaus, 'The Ideology of Reynolds's Discourses on Art', *Eighteenth-Century Studies* 12:1 (1978), pp. 59–73

https://web.prm.ox.ac.uk/cookvoyages/index.php/en/index.html

10. RADICAL LANDSCAPES

Ann Bermingham, *Landscape and Ideology: The English Rustic Tradition 1740–1860* (London: Thames & Hudson, 1987)

Ann Bermingham, 'Technologies of Illusion: De Loutherbourg's Eidophusikon in Eighteenth-Century London', *Art History* 39:2 (2016), pp. 376–99

Edmund Burke, *A Philosophical Enquiry into the Origin of Our Ideas of the Sublime and Beautiful* (London: R. & J. Dodsley, 1757)

Jonathan Crary, *Techniques of the Observer: On Vision and Modernity in the Nineteenth Century* (Cambridge, MA: MIT Press, 1992)

Corinne Fowler, *Green Unpleasant Land: Creative Responses to Rural England's Colonial Connections* (Leeds: Peepal Tree, 2020)

Reverend William Gilpin, *Observations on the River Wye, and Several Parts of South Wales, etc., Relative Chiefly to Picturesque Beauty* (1782; repr. London: R. Blamire, 1789)

Jennifer Green-Lewis, *Framing the Victorians: Photography and the Culture of Realism* (Ithaca, NY: Cornell University Press, 1996)

Jocelyn Hackforth-Jones and Mary Roberts, *Edges of Empire: Orientalism and Visual Culture* (Oxford: Blackwell, 2005)

Alasdair Kennedy, 'In Search of the True Prospect: Making and Knowing the Giant's Causeway as a Field Site in the Seventeenth Century', *British Journal for the History of Science* 41:1 (2008), pp. 19–41

Anna Liesching, 'The Giant's Causeway: A Layered Site of Exchange', in Linda Schädler, ed., *Daniela Keiser: Blue Links, Cyanotypes* (Zürich: Graphische Sammlung ETH, 2022)

Saree Makdisi, *Romantic Imperialism: Universal Empire and the Culture of Modernity* (Cambridge: Cambridge University Press, 1998)

Simon Morley, ed., *The Sublime* (London: Whitechapel Gallery, 2010)

Charlotte Mullins, *The World on a Plate: The Impact of Photography on Travel Imagery and its Dissemination in Britain 1839–1888*, PhD thesis (University of Sussex, 2013), pp. 61–83

Martin Myrone, ed., *John Martin: Apocalypse* (London: Tate Publishing, 2011)

Nobleness & Grandeur: Forging Historical Landscape in Britain 1760–1850, exh. pamph., Yale Center for British Art, 2005

Darren Pih and Laura Bruni, eds, *Radical Landscapes: Art, Identity and Activism* (London: Tate Publishing, 2022)

Charles Read, *The Great Famine in Ireland and Britain's Financial Crisis* (Woodbridge: Boydell Press, 2022)

William S. Rodner, *J.M.W. Turner: Romantic Painter of the Industrial Revolution* (Berkeley: University of California Press, 1997)

Patricia Smyth, 'Virtual Environments in the Nineteenth Century: The Spectacle of Old London', *European Journal of English Studies* 27:2 (2023), pp. 228–57

Nicholas Tromans, ed., *The Lure of the East: British Orientalist Painting* (London: Tate Publishing, 2008)

https://www.bgs.ac.uk/discovering-geology/maps-and-resources/office-geology/the-giants-causeway-and-causeway-coast

https://royalsociety.org/blog/2021/02/standing-on-the-boulders-of-giants

11. WOMEN'S WORK

Stephen Calloway and Lynn Federle Orr, eds, *The Cult of Beauty: The Aesthetic Movement 1860–1900* (London: V&A Publishing, 2011)

Oliver Fairclough, ed., *Things of Beauty: What Two Sisters Did for Wales* (Cardiff: National Museum Wales, 2018)

Anna Gruetzner Robins, 'Degas and Sickert: Notes on Their Friendship', *Burlington Magazine* 130:1020 (1988), pp. 19, 210–11, 225–9

Jennifer Higgie, *The Other Side: A Journey into Women, Art and the Spirit World* (London: Weidenfeld & Nicolson, 2023)

Laura Newton, ed., *Painting at the Edge: British Coastal Art Colonies 1880–1930* (Bristol: Sansome & Company, 2005)

Lois Oliver, 'Berthe Morisot and England', in Marianne Mathieu, ed., *Berthe Morisot: Shaping Impressionism* (London: Dulwich Picture Gallery, 2023), pp. 42–59

Michelle Payne, *Marianne North: A Very Intrepid Painter* (London: Royal Botanic Gardens Kew, 2023)

Elizabeth Prettejohn, *The Art of the Pre-Raphaelites* (London: Tate Publishing, 2000)

Julian Treuherz, *Victorian Painting* (London: Thames & Hudson, 1993)

Mike Weaver, *British Photography in the Nineteenth Century* (Cambridge: Cambridge University Press, 1989)

Arlene Young, *From Spinster to Career Woman: Middle-Class Women and Work in Victorian England* (Montreal: McGill-Queen's University Press, 2019)

12. WAR'S RAPID RATTLE

Amanda Bradley and Howard Watson, eds, *Stanley Spencer: Heaven in a Hell of War* (Chichester: Pallant House Gallery, 2014)

Eleanor Clayton, *Barbara Hepworth: Art and Life* (London: Thames & Hudson, 2021)

Richard Cork, *Wild Thing: Epstein, Gaudier-Brzeska, Gill* (London: Royal Academy of Arts, 2009)

Penelope Curtis, *Sculpture 1900–1945* (Oxford: Oxford University Press, 1999)

Penelope Curtis, ed., *Sculpture in 20th-Century Britain*, vol. 1 (Leeds: Henry Moore Institute, 2003)

Alicia Foster, *Gwen John: Art and Life in London and Paris* (London: Thames & Hudson, 2023)

James Fox, *British Art and the First World War 1914–1924* (Cambridge: Cambridge University Press, 2015)

Roger Fry, *Vision and Design* (1920; repr. London: Oxford University Press, 1981)

Dan Hicks, *The Brutish Museums: The Benin Bronzes, Colonial Violence and Cultural Restitution* (London: Pluto Press, 2020)

Hettie Judah, *Acts of Creation: On Art and Motherhood* (London: Thames & Hudson, 2024)

Jenny Macleod, 'By Scottish Hands, with Scottish Money, on Scottish Soil: The Scottish National War Memorial and National Identity', *Journal of British Studies* 49:1 (2010), pp. 73–96

Barnaby Phillips, *Loot: Britain and the Benin Bronzes* (London: Oneworld Publications, 2021)

Frances Spalding, *The Real and the Romantic: English Art between Two World Wars* (London: Thames & Hudson, 2022)

Hermione Waterfield and J.C.H. King, *Provenance: Twelve Collectors of Ethnographic Art in England 1760–1990* (Paris: Somogy Éditions d'Art, 2006)

Virginia Woolf, *A Room of One's Own and Three Guineas* (Oxford: Oxford University Press, 2008)

13. THE SEARCH FOR SELF

Jo Baring, ed., *Revisiting Modern British Art* (London: Lund Humphries, 2022)

David Boyd Haycock, 'Tendencies to Irrationality: Surrealism in Britain', in *British Surrealism* (London: Dulwich Picture Gallery, 2020), pp. 12–25

British Surrealism (London: Dulwich Picture Gallery, 2020)

David Burke, *The Lawn Road Flats: Spies, Writers and Artists* (Woodbridge: Boydell Press, 2014)

Eleanor Clayton, ed., *Lee Miller and Surrealism in Britain* (London: Lund Humphries, 2018)

Amy Hale, *Genius of the Fern Loved Gully: The Supersensual Life of Ithell Colquhoun, Artist and Occultist* (Cambridge, MA: MIT Press, 2020)

Caroline Maclean, *Circles & Squares: The Lives & Art of the Hampstead Modernists* (London: Bloomsbury, 2020)

Jennifer Mundy, ed., *Surrealism: Desire Unbound* (London: Tate Publishing, 2001)

Laura Smith, 'Eileen Agar: Angel of Anarchy', in *Eileen Agar: Angel of Anarchy* (London: Whitechapel Art Gallery, 2021), pp. 8–19
https://www.thepinknews.com/2022/02/10/uk-lesbian-ban-lgbt-history/

14. RUINATION AND REBIRTH

Jane Alison, ed., *Postwar Modern: New Art in Britain 1945–1965* (London: Barbican, 2022)

Michael Bird, *This Is Tomorrow: Twentieth-Century Britain and Its Artists* (London: Thames & Hudson, 2022)

Eddie Chambers, *Black Artists in British Art: A History since the 1950s* (London: I.B. Tauris, 2014)

Alex Farquharson and David A. Bailey, eds, *Life between Islands: Caribbean-British Art 1950s–Now* (London: Tate Publishing, 2021)

Denise Ferran, *F.E. McWilliam at Banbridge* (Banbridge: F.E. McWilliam Gallery, 2008)

Brian Foss, *War Paint: Art, War, State and Identity in Britain 1939–1945* (London: Yale University Press, 2007)

Margaret Garlake, *New Art New World: British Art in Postwar Society* (London: Yale University Press, 1998)

Alistair Hicks, *The School of London: The Resurgence of Contemporary Painting* (Oxford: Phaidon, 1989)

Róisín Kennedy, 'Art for the Public: William Scott and F.E. McWilliam at Altnagelvin', *Irish Arts Review Yearbook* 18 (2022), pp. 55–61

F.M. Leventhal, 'A Tonic to the Nation: The Festival of Britain, 1951', *Albion* 27:3 (1995), pp. 445–53

Antony Penrose, *The Lives of Lee Miller* (London: Thames & Hudson, 2021)

Paula M. Salvio, 'Uncanny Exposures: A Study of the Wartime Photojournalism of Lee Miller', *Curriculum Inquiry* 39:4 (2009), pp. 521–36

15. ART'S EXPANDED FIELD

Michael Bird, *The St Ives Artists: A Biography of Place and Time* (London: Lund Humphries, 2016)

Michael Bird, *Studio Voices: Art and Life in 20th-Century Britain* (London: Lund Humphries, 2018)

Conceptual Art in Britain 1964–1979 (London: Tate Publishing, 2016)

Keven Concannon, 'Yoko Ono's *Cut Piece*: From Text to Performance and Back Again', *A Journal of Performance and Art* 30:3 (2008), pp. 81–93

Paul Denison et al., *Modern Art and St Ives: International Exchanges 1915–65* (London: Tate Publishing, 2014)

Laura Freeman, *Ways of Life: Jim Ede and the Kettle's Yard Artists* (London: Jonathan Cape, 2023)

Martin Gayford, *Modernists & Mavericks: Bacon, Freud, Hockney and the London Painters* (London: Thames & Hudson, 2018)

Margaret Garlake, *Artists Making Landscapes in Post-War Britain* (London: Modern Art Press, 2021)

Rosalind Krauss, 'Sculpture in the Expanded Field', *October* 8 (April 1979), pp. 31–44

Anne Massey, 'The Independent Group: Towards a Redefinition', *Burlington Magazine* 129:1009 (1987), pp. 232–42

Ian Massey, *Queer St Ives and Other Stories* (London: Ridinghouse, 2022)

Hammad Nasar, 'Artistic Britishness? Questions of Nationality', in Jo Baring, ed., *Revisiting Modern British Art* (London: Lund Humphries, 2022), pp. 131–42 https://www.michaelcraigmartin.co.uk/artworks/11-an-oak-tree/

16. STAND UP AND BE COUNTED

Tony Crowley, 'The Art of Memory: The Murals of Northern Ireland and the Management of History', *Field Day Review* 7 (2011), pp. 22–49

Adrienne Dengerink Chaplin et al., *Art, Conflict and Remembering: The Murals of the Bogside Artists* (Coventry: Coventry Cathedral, 2017)

Jean Fisher, 'The Other Story and the Past Imperfect', *Tate Papers* 12 (2009), https://www.tate.org.uk/research/tate-papers/12/the-other-story-and-the-past-imperfect

Gregory Goalwin, 'The Art of War: Instability, Insecurity, and Ideological Imagery in Northern Ireland's Political Murals 1979–1998', *International Journal of Politics, Culture and Society* 26:3 (2013), pp. 189–215

Germaine Greer, *The Female Eunuch* (1971; repr. London: HarperCollins, 1993)

Liam Kelly, 'Language, Memory and Conflict: Acts of Interrogation', in Mark Dorrian and Gillian Rose, eds, *Deterritorialisations . . . Revisioning: Landscapes and Politics* (London: Black Dog Publishing, 2003), pp. 309–20

Debbie Lisle, 'Local Symbols, Global Networks: Rereading the Murals of Belfast', *Alternatives: Global, Local, Political* 31:1 (2006), pp. 27–52

Catherine Marshall, 'Visualising Irish History: Conflicting Utopias', in Catherine Marshall and Yvonne Scott, eds, *Irish Art 1920–2020: Perspectives on Change* (Dublin: Royal Irish Academy, 2022), pp. 70–101

Kim Mawhinney, *Troubles Art from the Ulster Museum Collection* (Belfast: National Museums NI, 2023)

Charlotte Mullins, *A Little Feminist History of Art* (London: Tate Publishing, 2019)

Hammad Nasar, 'Like a Fever: Navigating the Afterlife of The Other Story', *Field Notes* 4 (2015), https://aaa.org.hk/en/like-a-fever/like-a-fever/notes-from-the-field-navigating-the-afterlife-of-the-other-story

Rianna Jade Parker, *A Brief History of Black British Art* (London: Tate Publishing, 2021)

Rozsika Parker and Griselda Pollock, *Framing Feminism: Art and the Women's Movement 1970–1985* (London: HarperCollins, 1987)

Rozsika Parker and Griselda Pollock, *Old Mistresses: Women, Art and Ideology* (1981; repr. London: I.B. Tauris, 2013)
Griselda Pollock, 'How the Political World Crashes in on My Personal Everyday', *Afterall* 43 (2017), pp. 18–29
Hilary Robinson, ed., *Feminism – Art – Theory: An Anthology 1968–2014*, second edition (Chichester: John Wiley & Sons, 2015)
Bill Rolston, *Politics and Painting: Murals and Conflict in Northern Ireland* (Rutherford, NJ: Fairleigh Dickinson University Press, 1991)
Anne Walmsley, *The Caribbean Artists Movement 1966–72: A Literary and Cultural History* (London: New Beacon Books, 1992)
https://ccdl.claremont.edu/digital/collection/mni (murals of Northern Ireland digital archive)
https://lubainahimid.com/portfolio/the-thin-black-line/

17. COOL BRITANNIA?

Nick Baker, 'Expanding the Field: How the New Sculpture Put British Art on the Map in the 1980s', *British Art Studies* 3, https://dx.doi.org/10.17658/issn.2058-5462/issue-03/nbaker
Homi K. Bhabha, *The Location of Culture* (London: Routledge, 1994)
Blast to Freeze: British Art in the 20th Century (Wolfsburg: Kunstmuseum Wolfsburg, 2002)
Michael Bracewell, *The Nineties: When Surface Was Depth* (London: Flamingo, 2002)
Louisa Buck, *Moving Targets: A User's Guide to British Art Now* (London: Tate Publishing, 1997)
Penelope Curtis and Keith Wilson, *Modern British Sculpture* (London: Royal Academy of Arts, 2011)
Sarah Kent, *Shark Infested Waters: The Saatchi Collection of British Art in the 90s* (London: Zwemmer, 1994)
Mixing It Up: Painting Today (London: Hayward Publishing, 2021)
A New Spirit in Painting (London: Royal Academy of Arts, 1981)
Sensation: Young British Artists from the Saatchi Collection (London: Thames & Hudson / Royal Academy of Arts, 1997)
Spellbound (London: Hayward Gallery, 1996)
Julian Stallabrass, *High Art Lite: The Rise and Fall of Young British Art*, revised and expanded edition (London: Verso, 2006)
'Yinka Shonibare CBE RA in Conversation with Charlotte Mullins', in *Ritual Ecstasy of the Modern* (London: Cristea Roberts Gallery, 2023), pp. 6–18
https://www.tate.org.uk/art/turner-prize

18. THE FUTURE NOW

'Anthony Downey and Yinka Shonibare', *Bomb* 93 (2005), pp. 24–31
Pita Arreola, Corinna Gardner and Melanie Lenz, *Digital Art: 1960s–Now* (London: Thames & Hudson, 2024)

Ray Barnett, 'Displaying the Statue of Edward Colston at M Shed, Bristol: A Case Study', *Sculpture Journal* 31:3 (2022), pp. 367–73

James Bridle, *Ways of Being: Animals, Plants, Machines: The Search for a Planetary Intelligence* (London: Penguin, 2023)

Eddie Chambers, 'The Beauty of an Empty Plinth', *Art Journal* 81:2 (2022), pp. 5–6

Mat Collishaw, *Petrichor* (London: Kew Gardens, 2023)

Jonathan Crary, *24/7: Late Capitalism and the Ends of Sleep* (London: Verso, 2014)

Yuval Noah Harari, *Homo Deus: A Brief History of Tomorrow* (London: Harvill Secker, 2016)

Yuval Noah Harari, *Nexus: A Brief History of Information Networks from the Stone Age to AI* (London: Fern Press, 2024)

Gareth Harris, *Censored Art Today* (London: Lund Humphries / Sotheby's Institute of Art, 2022)

Michael Hatt, 'Counter-Ceremonial: Contemporary Artists and Queen Victoria Monuments', *19: Interdisciplinary Studies in the Long Nineteenth Century* 23 (2022), https://doi.org/10.16995/ntn.4732

Michael Horsham, *Hello Human: A History of Visual Communication* (London: Thames & Hudson, 2022)

Christina Horvath and Richard S. White, *Breaking the Dead Silence: Engaging with the Legacies of Empire and Slave-Ownership in Bath and Bristol's Memoryscapes* (Liverpool: Liverpool University Press, 2024)

Victoria Ivanova, Eva Jäger, Alasdair Milne and Gardy Zhexi Zhang, *Future Art Ecosystems: Art x Public AI* (London: Serpentine Gallery, 2024)

Johanne Løgstrup, *The Contemporary Condition 14: Co-Existence of Times – A Conversation with John Akomfrah* (Berlin: Sternberg Press, 2020)

Mike Nelson: Extinction Beckons (London: Hayward Gallery, 2023)

Julie Milne, 'The Abyss That Abides', in Martin Myrone, ed., *John Martin: Apocalypse* (London: Tate Publishing, 2011), pp. 53–9

Madhumita Murgia, *Code Dependent: Living in the Shadow of AI* (London: Picador, 2024)

Hans Ulrich Obrist, 'Interview with Richard Mosse', *FACT Magazine* 4 (2022), pp. 104–35

Nadim Samman, *Poetics of Encryption: Art and the Technocene* (Berlin: Hatje Cantz, 2023)

Marcus du Sautoy, *The Creativity Code: How AI Is Learning to Write, Paint and Think* (London: 4th Estate, 2019)

Noni Stacey, *Leave to Remain: A Snapshot of Brexit* (London: Lund Humphries, 2023)

Mustafa Suleyman, *The Coming Wave: AI, Power and the 21st Century's Greatest Dilemma* (London: Bodley Head, 2023)

https://www.ai-darobot.com/

https://www.frieze.com/article/ai-technologies-roundtable-239?utm_source=FRIEZE&utm_campaign=a51b8b5adc-newsletter-can-machine-

creativity-truly-exist&utm_medium=email&utm_term=0_f0ebe20dcf-a51b8b5adc-208701626
https://gordoncheungartist.wixsite.com/gordon/nft-tulip-maniac
https://metaversol.com/future-art-galleries-art-sales-metaverse/
https://www.sandbox.game/en/blog/what-is-the-metaverse-a-guide-to-the-future-of-the-web/3362
https://uk.icom.museum/the-british-museum-will-enter-the-metaverse-via-the-sandbox/

ILLUSTRATIONS

INDEX

Illustrations are shown by a page reference in *italics*.